SELECTED POETRY AND PROSE OF DANIEL DEFOE

Edited By
MICHAEL F. SHUGRUE
New York University

HOLT, RINEHART AND WINSTON
New York · Chicago · San Francisco · Atlanta
Dallas · Toronto · Montreal · London

RINEHART EDITIONS
General Editor
WAYNE C. BOOTH

Printed in the United States of America

1 2 3 4 5 6 7 8 9

CONTENTS

INTRODUCTION

What Did Defoe Write?

Most readers know Daniel Defoe as the author of *Robinson Crusoe,* frequently adapted for children and for the movies, and of *Moll Flanders,* first noticed behind a prurient cover on the newsstands and later read in college. If Defoe had written nothing else, these works of fiction would assure his place in English literature. In fact, however, they represent only one part of the work of one phase of a long and incredibly productive career. Had he not written these two works, which continue to draw the principal attention of critics in the twentieth century, he would still be considered a major figure in eighteenth-century English literature and in the study of the political, social, and cultural history of the Augustan Age. As Louis Kronenberger has noted, "Defoe saw London, saw England, with a width matched by no other writer of his day. He alone was really in the midst of life, and if Swift's dark pages are the greatest art, Defoe's are the greatest document of the age." [1] His *Review,* his immensely popular *True-Born Englishman, The Shortest-Way With The Dissenters, A Journal Of The Plague Year, Col. Jacque,* and the fascinating *Tour Thro' The Whole Island Of Great Britain* assure his literary reputation. But these titles, too, represent only a small portion of the known works of this indefatigable writer. John Robert Moore, the leading twentieth-century student of Defoe, estimates that Defoe published 547 separate works, including large portions of 27 periodicals.[2]

This collection includes selections from Defoe's known works that have not been easily accessible in this century, but which, in their own day, attracted wide attention, and, in ours, still evoke interest. These poems, projects, newspaper articles, and criminal biographies suggest the range of Defoe's activities and outline his principal in-

[1] Louis Kronenberger, *Kings and Desperate Men* (New York, 1959, orig. publ. 1942), 118.
[2] John Robert Moore, *A Checklist of the Writings of Daniel Defoe* (Bloomington, 1960).

terests. One hopes they will give the reader pleasure and contribute to his understanding and appreciation of Defoe's major novels.

How much Defoe actually wrote during his lifetime will probably never be known. Most of the works attributed to him are unsigned. He himself used at least three pseudonyms: Alexander Goldsmith, Claude Guilot, and Andrew Moreton, Esq. The secretive nature of much of his work for the government after 1704 not only prevented him from claiming most of his writing, but led him deliberately to conceal his authorship and even to deny having written some works which are certainly his. In his *Appeal To Honour And Justice* (1715) Defoe himself complained that many tracts had been falsely attributed to him: "My Name has been hackney'd about the Street by the Hawkers, and about the Coffee-Houses by the Politicians, at such a rate, as no Patience could bear. One Man will swear to the Style; another to this or that Expression; another to the Way of Printing; and all so positive, that it is no purpose to oppose it." As early as 1753, a cautious biographer, writing about Defoe, observed, "It is impossible to arrive at the knowledge of half the tracts and pamphlets which were written by this laborious man, as his name is not prefixed, and many of them being temporary, have perished like all other productions of that kind, when the subjects upon which they were written are forgot."[3] Despite these obstacles, the list of approximately 100 works proposed by George Chalmers in 1790 had grown to 254 by 1869 and to more than 385 by 1913.[4]

One can, however, learn much about the extent of Defoe's writings in four ways. Some works are actually signed "Daniel Defoe." Perhaps the best known of this small group of publications is the *Appeal To Honour And Justice,* his most impressive autobiographical piece, but there are such others as *An Answer to the L[or]D H[aver]Sham's Speech. By Daniel D'Foe* (1705) and *Daniel Defoe's Hymn for the Thanksgiving* (1706). Within this group of

---

[3] *The Lives of the Poets of Great Britain and Ireland* (London, 1753), IV, 323.

[4] George Chalmers, *The Life of Daniel De Foe* (London, 1790), 440; William Lee, *Daniel Defoe: His Life, and Recently Discovered Writings: Extending from 1716 to 1729* (London, 1869), I, xxv; William P. Trent, "Defoe—The Newspaper and the Novel," *Cambridge History of English Literature,* ed. A. W. Ward and A. R. Waller (Cambridge, 1913), IX, 446–482.

signed works, one can also include such publications as *An Essay Upon Projects* (1697), his first full-length book, and *The Compleat Art of Painting* (1720), his attempt to rival John Dryden in the art of translation, both of which are signed with the initials *D.F.*[5]

In individual works, in his letters, and in *A True Collection Of The Writings Of The Author Of The True Born Englishman* (1703), which contained his portrait, Defoe also confirmed his authorship of certain poems, tracts, and pamphlets. In the *Appeal* he noted that he "gave birth to a Trifle which I never could hope should have met with so general an Acceptation as it did, I mean, *The True-Born Englishman,*" and also admitted, "I wrote Two Pamphlets, one entituled *What if the* Pretender *should come?* The other, *Reasons against the Succession of the House of Hanover*" (1713). On 7 July 1704 he confessed to Robert Harley that he was "Something Impatient to have it from your Self, that I had Explain'd the Review to your Satisfaction and That in Reading it you have been Pleas'd to Note the Caution I mention'd." [6] The very fact that *The Mock-Mourners "By the Author of the True-born Englishman"* is included in the *True Collection* establishes its place in the canon.

His critics identified Defoe as the author of certain titles. At the direction of the Earl of Nottingham, whom Defoe later castigated as "Don Dismal," the *London Gazette* (14 January 1703) advertised a reward of £50 for "Daniel De Foe *alias* de Fooe," "charged with writing a scandalous and seditious pamphlet entitled The Shortest Way with the Dissenters." *The Scribler's Doom* (1703) informed its London audience later in the year that "the chiefest Tophick now" is *"Du Foo's* being Pillor'd according to his late Sentence, for being the Author of a late scurrilous Pamphlet, entituled, *The Shortest Way with the Dissenters.*" An angry James Clark, in *A Just Reprimand to Daniel De Foe: In a Letter to a Gentleman in South Britain,* began, "Sir, I Doubt not, but by this time, you have seen Mr. *De Foe's History of the Union;* wherein

[5] John Robert Moore, in *Daniel Defoe: Citizen of the Modern World* (Chicago, 1958), points out that Defoe and his contemporaries spelled his name in various ways throughout his lifetime (8). Hereafter cited as *Defoe.*

[6] George H. Healey, ed. *The Letters of Daniel Defoe* (Oxford, 1955), 26. Hereafter cited as *Letters.*

he represents me to the World in Black enough Colours. . . ." Even in 1719, Charles Gildon attacked Defoe in *The Life and Strange Surprizing Adventures of Mr. D----- De F--, . . . In a Dialogue between Him, Robinson Crusoe, and his Man Friday,* and in so doing helped establish the Defoe canon.

Most difficult, however, are attributions which must be based on circumstantial and internal evidence. William Lee believed that "Long and critical study of a great author may result in so full an aquaintance, that his writings will be recognized by the student in a moment, as the voice of a familiar friend." [7] William P. Trent, too, felt that it was possible to discover Defoe's works by using "a variety of tests based upon . . . his favorite ideas, his anecdotes, and a number of other special features." [8] Although scholars have tried to analyze Defoe's style carefully enough to be able to "recognize" his hand in an unsigned pamphlet, no one has yet "proved" Defoe's authorship of many titles tentatively accepted in the Defoe canon.

Perhaps the most spectacular step in the growth of the Defoe canon was taken by William Lee in 1869 with the publication of *Daniel Defoe: His Life, and Recently Discovered Writings.* "The Key to this discovery" of new Defoe materials, Lee wrote, "consists of certain Letters, in his own handwriting, found in 1864, in the State Paper Office, directly naming several political Journals upon which he was engaged during some years after his supposed retirement" to Stoke Newington in 1715 after a stroke. [9] In one of these six letters, Defoe wrote to Charles De la Faye, an undersecretary of state, on 26 April 1718, "I Introduced my Self in the Disguise of a Translator of the Forreign News to be So farr Concernd in This Weekly Paper of *Mists,* as to be able to keep it within the Circle of a Secret Mannagement, also, prevent the Mischievous Part of it, and yet Neither Mist or any of those Concernd with him have the least Guess or Suspicion By whose Direction I do it. . . . by this Mannagemt The Weekly Journall and Dormers Letter as Also the Mercurious Politicus, which is in the Same Nature of Mannagemt as The journall, Will be allwayes kept

[7] Lee, I, v–vi.
[8] "Bibliographical Notes on Defoe III," *Nation* (29 August 1907), 181.
[9] Lee, I, v.

(mistakes Excepted) To Pass as Tory Papers, and yet be Dissabled and Ennervated, So as to do no Mischief or give any Offence to the Govermt." [10] On the basis of his studies, Lee attributed to Defoe dozens of works published between 1716 and 1731, including the articles from *Applebee's Original Weekly Journal* and the two criminal lives which are included in this collection. Fortunately, an excellent case can be made from circumstantial evidence to show Defoe's hand in these works.

Applebee's Journal was radically reorganized in July 1720. [11] On 16 July an elaborate masthead was adopted and "The Muses Gazette," a weekly feature of the journal since March, was replaced by an introductory essay or "Letter Introductory." Foreign communiqués were gathered under the general heading of FOREIGN AFFAIRS and analyzed for Applebee's readers by someone who understood the complicated European political scene, was able not only to translate but to interpret foreign dispatches, and could present his material in lively prose. The author of the letter introductory demonstrated a vitality that had never before been characteristic of the journal. Whoever took charge on 16 July and remained the principal author until 27 August 1726 sketched characters and scenes skillfully and demonstrated great interest in the bankruptcy laws, the plague which threatened England from 1720–1722, crime and criminals, and the political situation in England. He maintained a cautious journal which avoided libel and sought to entertain and inform Applebee's growing public. Could Defoe have been that author?

During 1720 Defoe was threatened with prosecution for libel for articles appearing in *Mist's Journal*. Nathaniel Mist had tried to convince the government that Defoe was responsible for the libelous passages in the journal in January, but Defoe, writing again to De la Faye on 7 June 1720, denied his guilt: "I am Very Well assur'd I had no Concern in the Paragraph in question, and he can not Lay it justly to my Charge unless he had my Coppie to produce." [12] Thanks to De la Faye's good offices, Defoe escaped prosecution,

---

[10] *Letters,* 453.
[11] See "*Applebee's Original Weekly Journal, Newberry Library Bulletin,* I, 4 (March 1964), 108–121.
[12] *Letters,* 461.

but Defoe, feuding with Mist and facing prison for perhaps the eighth time in his life, might well have changed employers at about this time and continued his efforts to moderate criticism of the government by attaching himself to another of the leading weekly journals. The circumstances would be right for an agent of the ministry to temper Applebee's political opinions (Applebee had been in Custody for "Treasonable Practices" late in 1715 and was reported in trouble with the government again in March 1718), a person who knew politics, had wide-ranging interests, and could give broad and thorough interpretations of international news as Defoe admitted he had done for Mist and for others. Did Defoe take over the direction of *Applebee's Journal* in July 1720?

Because no letter by Defoe exists between 1720 and 1728, one must rely on circumstantial evidence. If one examines Defoe's known works during these years and the columns of *Applebee's Journal*, he learns that the resurgence of plague in southern France between 1719 and 1722 attracted Defoe's interest (*Due Preparations For The Plague* and *A Journal Of The Plague Year* were both published early in 1722) as it did Applebee's author. Late in 1721 Applebee's author examined the mortality bills, which recorded the deaths during the London plague of 1665. On 18 November 1721, he promised, "How this was in the Time of the late Plague; and how it will be, if another should come, I shall take the liberty to tell you more at large hereafter." And indeed, Defoe's books on the plague, both using the bills of mortality, appeared within four months. One notes further that both Defoe and Applebee's author supported the transportation of convicted felons to Virginia (*Col. Jacque*, published 20 December 1722; *Applebee's Journal*, 26 January 1723). One finds Applebee's author showing such an intimate knowledge of Defoe's works that he can make an amusing play on words with the title *The Shortest Way With The Dissenters* on 17 February 1722, almost twenty years after the publication of the pamphlet. Applebee's author replied heatedly to the sniping criticism of *Robinson Crusoe* in the *London Journal* on 18 September and again on 20 November 1725. He knows that Defoe was not committed to jail (12 August 1721) and defends Defoe's son, Benjamin Norton Defoe (26 August 1721). As such circumstantial evidence mounts, Defoe's association with *Applebee's Journal* becomes increasingly apparent. And it follows, upon close examina-

tion of parallel texts, that the author of the *Journal* and of the
two criminal lives must be the same. We can safely attribute these
titles to Daniel Defoe.

One must be wary, however, of several pamphlets and poems
which are included in the canon primarily because they carry *"By
the author of the True-Born Englishman"* on their title page. I
have regretfully omitted a delightful satire entitled *Good Advice
to the Ladies* (1702) because its inclusion rests on that phrase,
despite Defoe's denial of authorship in the *Little Review*, No. 5
(20 June 1705) and the fact that the poem does not appear in
Defoe's *True Collection*. Establishing an accurate Defoe canon is
still the greatest scholarly problem in Defoe scholarship, a problem
which Professor Moore's thoughtful and illuminating *Checklist of
the Writings of Daniel Defoe* makes it possible to approach.

What Did Defoe Write About?

The importance of economics in the works of Defoe has often
been overestimated. The analysis of Robinson Crusoe's "book-
keeping conscience"; the reminder that "Robinson Crusoe, like
Defoe's other main characters, Moll Flanders, Roxana, Colonel
Jacque, and Captain Singleton, is an embodiment of economic in-
dividualism";[13] the observation that Defoe was a man for whom
"a bill of lading was a poem," [14] an author who "In his later economic writings . . . synthesized . . . ideas into a harmonious economic system";[15] the judgment that "It is going too far to say of
Defoe that he knew the price of everything and the value of nothing; but it is going, certainly, in the right direction," [16] all contribute to the mistaken notion that Defoe wrote only—or mostly

[13] Ian Watt, *The Rise of the Novel* (Berkeley and Los Angeles, 1965,
   orig. publ. 1957), 63.
[14] Samuel H. Monk, ed., "Introduction" to *Col. Jacque* (Oxford, 1965),
   xviii.
[15] Maximillian E. Novak, *Economics and the Fiction of Daniel Defoe*
   (Berkeley and Los Angeles, 1962), 11.
[16] Kronenberger, 144.

—about economics. As valuable as these insights about the importance of economics to Defoe have been, as much as they help the
reader understand many of Defoe's works and his age, they mask
the greater range of his interests and depict the man as too much
the middle-class merchant pamphleteer.

A healthy reappraisal of such major novels as *Robinson Crusoe*
has recently helped balance the view of Defoe's artistic achievements. Both J. Paul Hunter and G. A. Starr note that *Robinson
Crusoe* is "ultimately about man's spiritual development." [17] Professor Hunter aptly observes "that the traditional approaches have
not suggested the full range and complexity of what happens in
Robinson Crusoe, nor have they defined adequately the artistic
techniques which Defoe develops from Puritan thought patterns
and a rich subliterary art" (xi). Dorothy Van Ghent's discussion of
Moll Flanders illuminates best Defoe's conscious artistry, his ability
to do more than present economic ideas in a fictional narrative,
and his significance for the twentieth-century reader: "In understanding his creature without the slightest divarication from her
movements and her thoughts, he gave to Moll the immense and
seminal reality of an Earth Mother, progenetrix of the wasteland,
sower of our harvests of technological skills, bombs, gadgets, and
the platitudes and stereotypes and absurdities of a morality suitable
to a wasteland world." [18] Her observations rescue Defoe from the
oblivion of mere historical significance and establish his critical
relevance to the twentieth century. Defoe wrote about subjects of
consuming importance to him and to his age, subjects frequently
similar to those that occupy modern society. For the threat of
plague, about which he wrote over a period of twenty years, one
can substitute fear of atomic war, the devastation of Hiroshima and
Nagasaki, and the measures taken by world powers to control an
ominous force which could destroy human life on our planet.

When a light "Distemper" reached England in 1712, Defoe
warned the citizens of London to prepare for plague: "That you
may learn a little better how to behave yourselves, when such a

[17] J. Paul Hunter, *The Reluctant Pilgrim* (Baltimore, 1966), xiii; see
G. A. Starr, *Defoe and Spiritual Autobiography* (Princeton, 1965),
viii.
[18] Dorothy Van Ghent, "On *Moll Flanders*," *The English Novel: Form
and Function* (New York, 1961, orig. publ. 1953), 43.

terrible Stroke shall reach you, I shall, in my next, give you a little
Sketch or Draft of the dreadful Havock the last Plague made in
this City" (*Review*, 23 August 1712). On 26 August he continued,
"I need not tell the Reader here, that at the Time . . . the City
was so thin of Inhabitants, that one might walk from *Aldgate* to
Ludgate, and not meet, or see, 100 People; . . . That above 70000
were dead at that Time of the Plague, and in their Graves, . . . ;
That Grass grew in the Streets, in the Markets, and on the Exchange; and nothing but Death and Horror was to be seen in every
place." It is estimated that 70,000 persons died at Hiroshima; some
300,000 died of plague in Austria alone in 1711.[19]

When plague decimated southern France between 1719 and
1722, killing an estimated 100,000 persons, Defoe worried as every
Englishman did that the scourge would soon reach England. When
the government put into effect a quarantine in February 1721 "for
the better preventing the Plague being brought from foreign Ports,"
burned ships and cargoes from infected ports in June, and gave
George I sweeping powers in February 1722 to issue proclamations
effectually forbidding contacts with infected places, Defoe defended
the policies of the ministry in *Applebee's Journal* by describing
"dismal Accounts from France," including on 20 May 1721 an account of a "Rabble of the People . . . made desperate by their
Diseases, and quite raging by their Hunger" who were beaten and
shot into submission when they tried to break through lines of
troops which had sealed off the area. Even as the threat diminished
and public interest lagged in 1722, Defoe, long fascinated by the
subject, completed and published *Due Preparations For The Plague*
and *A Journal Of The Plague Year*, the latter accepted as a factual
account of the plague of 1665 for more than a hundred years after
its publication. Not only had Defoe written more about plague than
anyone else during this crisis, but a hundred years later he was the
most frequently cited authority on the subject. Neither of these
works can be called a mere economic tract; too late to provide real
support for the government's quarantine policies, neither can be
dismissed as a political tract. *The Journal Of The Plague Year*,
particularly, emerges as an outstanding example of Defoe's uncanny
ability to mesh fact with invention. The work stands with Camus's

[19] Charles F. Mullett, *The Bubonic Plague and England* (Lexington, Ky.,
1956), 262.

La Peste (1948) as a classic statement of man's struggle to meet the crises of civilization. Based on historical records, it also stands with John Hersey's *Hiroshima* (1946) as an absorbing piece of journalism.

Defoe lived in a political age. Born in 1660, the year of the Restoration of Charles II to the English throne, he reached maturity at a time when Parliamentary attempts were being made to exclude James, Duke of York, from the succession, and even participated briefly in the abortive rebellion of the Duke of Monmouth in 1685. Although James II became king in 1685, his Roman Catholicism and arbitrary policies had alienated both Parliament and people within three years. Defoe welcomed the "Glorious or Bloodless Revolution" of 1688–1689, which brought James II's daughter Mary and her husband, William of Orange, to the throne. While James's son, the "Old Pretender," plotted at the court of Louis XIV, Mary's sister Anne became Queen in 1702 upon the death of William III. By the Act of Settlement of 1701, the crown was next to be settled upon the Electress Sophia of Hanover, a granddaughter of James I, and upon her descendants. Despite uprisings by Jacobites in 1707 and 1715, George I acceded in 1714 to begin the long reign of the Hanoverians. From the struggles to maintain a stable succession emerged the labels Whig and Tory in the 1680s, Non-Juror and Jacobite in the 1690s. The period also saw renewed hatred and fear of Roman Catholicism and a continuation of hostilities with France.

Although Defoe and his fellow Englishmen took party politics seriously, Whig and Tory are difficult terms to define precisely. Defoe served a "Whig" King—William, a "Tory" Queen—Anne, and two more "Whig" Kings—George I and George II. He was a civil servant under the Tory Robert Harley and the Whig Sidney Godolphin between 1704 and 1714. Charles B. Realey oversimplifies the distinctions between political parties during much of Defoe's lifetime by defining a Whig as "one who called himself a Whig," and a Tory as "one who chose to designate himself as such," but argues convincingly, ". . . the more clearly the distinctions are drawn and the more orderly the principles are made to appear in our histories, the less value they have in helping us to arrive at an accurate estimate of the party situation in the early eighteenth century. . . . Each party was subdivided into a number of groups, and each of the groups constituted almost a party in itself." He points out further "the difficulty, almost the impossibility, of distinguishing between Moderate or Hanoverian Tories and Moderate Whigs, especially Whigs out of office." [20] If one accepts the difficulty of drawing firm party lines in the period, he can more easily understand James Sutherland's observation that "Defoe, in fact, proceeded in his political life as if he were a permanent civil servant, and at the same time allowed himself the privilege of taking sides." [21]

In international affairs, England and Holland were allied against France in a long struggle to maintain a balance of power in Europe. The Treaty of Ryswick (1697), which ended the Nine Years War, proved only a brief respite before the Grand Alliance (England, Holland, and the Holy Roman Emperor) declared war in 1702 to prevent the French from occupying the throne of Spain. The War of the Spanish Succession, which continued until the Peace of Utrecht (1713), established England as a world power. These wars involved not only territorial rights on the continent, but control of the rich colonial empires which brought gold and goods to the European powers. Defoe, as one would expect, consistently supported England's efforts to contain the ambition of Louis XIV.

Defoe's support of the Revolution of 1688–1689 and of William III are pervasive themes in his writing. When John Tutchin satirized William III in 1700 in *The Foreigners,* Defoe defended William in *The True-Born Englishman,* which sold more than 80,000 copies, a phenomenal record for the period, and established Defoe as one of the most popular poets of the early eighteenth century. Even after William's death in 1702, Defoe published the embarrassingly loyal *Mock-Mourners,* which went through seven editions within a year. In the introduction to the ninth and later editions of *The True-Born Englishman,* Defoe wrote, "[W]hen I see the Town full of Lampoons and Invectives against Dutchmen, Only because they are Foreigners, and the King Reproached and Insulted by Insolent Pedants, and Ballad-making Poets, for employing Foreigners, and for being a Foreigner himself, I confess my self moved by it to re-

[20] Charles B. Realey, *The Early Opposition to Sir Robert Walpole 1720–1727* (Philadelphia, 1931), 37–39.
[21] James Sutherland, *Defoe* (Philadelphia and New York, 1938), 178.

mind our Nation of their own Original." And in *The Consolidator* (1705), his fanciful, imaginative, political voyage to the moon, he described the death of William: *"the Grief* of the usage he had receiv'd, the unkind Treatment he had met with from those very People that brought him thither, had *sunk so* deep upon his Spirits, that he could never recover it; but being very weak in Body and Mind, and join'd to a slight hurt he receiv'd by a fall from his Horse, *he dyed,* to the unspeakable grief of all his Subjects that wish'd him well" (202). In the *Review,* in the *Appeal To Honour And Justice,* and elsewhere, Defoe showed his continued loyalty to the memory of William III.

How early in life Defoe knew William III and how well are matters of conjecture. Although Defoe states in the *Appeal* that *The True-Born Englishman* (1701) "was the Occasion of my being known to his Majesty," Professor Moore postulates that he may have known William as early as 1689 and may have served as an adviser to the King throughout the 1690s *(Defoe,* 70). Even if the details of their acquaintanceship are uncertain, Defoe's admiration for William III remains clear.

Defoe's support of the Revolution of 1688–1689 stemmed not just from loyalty to an individual nor from the political opportunism of which he was so often accused, but from a belief that the power of government was ultimately vested in Parliament and not in a king who ruled arbitrarily or by divine right, a belief which the Revolution and the Declaration of Rights of 1689 guaranteed. As he wrote in *The True-Born Englishman,*

> Where Tyrants once commence, the Kings do cease;
> For arbitrary Power's so strange a thing,
> It makes the Tyrant, and unmakes the King. . . .
>   Kings, when they descend to Tyranny,
> Dissolve the Bond, and leave the Subject free.
> The Government's ungirt when Justice dies,
> And Constitutions are Non-Entities.

Defoe opposed the claims of James II and the Pretender, noting in the *Appeal* that "nothing in the World has been more my Aversion than the Society of *Jacobites."* Both in *The True-Born Englishman* and in *The Consolidator* he outlined the steps which led to the Revolution, showing in both cases that James II's attempts at personal rule had justified the settlement on William and Mary.

When Defoe later supported Queen Anne in *The Mock-Mourners* (1702) and George I in the *Appeal* (1715), he was not engaging in mere political maneuvering or scheming to gain patronage. Opposed to political extremism, he served the government for more than twenty years, surviving from one ministry to another because of the value of his services to those in power. He himself justified his long government service in the *Appeal*: ". . . it was not material to me what ministers Her Majesty was pleas'd to employ, my Duty was to go along with every ministry, . . . to submit to all lawful Commands, and to enter into no Service which was not justifiable by the Laws." That he liked intrigue and involvement in political battles is beyond question. That his praise of a monarch or minister could be effusive, as in the "Britannia" sections of *The True-Born Englishman* and *The Mock-Mourners,* is also apparent. That he could prevaricate when necessary to maintain his usefulness as a government agent, even that he rather coldheartedly withdrew support from Robert Harley in 1715 after Harley's ties with the Jacobites became known, is equally clear. He cannot, however, be dismissed as a political opportunist or political hack, a "Vicar of Bray" willing to espouse any party or cause in order to save his position.

The political event in which he was most deeply involved was the union of Scotland and England, finally accomplished by the Act of Union (1707). He had served Robert Harley in Scotland during 1706–1707 as pamphleteer and intelligence agent to help bring the Union about and his *Review* became the principal journalistic vehicle for arguments supporting the Union. He showed his continuing interest in the Union in 1709 with the publication of *The History Of The Union Of Great Britain.*

In his journals and pamphlets Defoe discussed the peace settlements of his time: Ryswick (1697), the Partition Treaties (1698 and 1700), and Utrecht (1713). While he urged support for the policies of the ministry, he argued vigorously that England must not give in to French demands, even though it must be willing to trade with France. He defended the expansion of English trade and the need for a balance of power in Europe. Although the details of these pacts and treaties are dim in history, Defoe examined them in the *Review* and elsewhere with insight, a command of a great store of facts, and often with passionate conviction. His economics, as Professor Novak has shown, were not advanced, even for his day,[22] but his support of mercantilist principles, colonization, and England's right to trade and obligation to establish a strong colonial empire runs consistently through his writings.

The religious controversies of his lifetime, intricately meshed with the political situation, have much in common with the civil rights movement of today. Since the time of Henry VIII's break with Rome, Roman Catholics had been viewed with suspicion and hostility in England. When Charles II returned to England in 1660, a long struggle began to establish the political rights of those dissenting from the Church of England. Although Roman Catholics were not to achieve their political rights until the nineteenth century, Protestant Dissenters obtained limited social and political rights in Defoe's lifetime. The Test Act of 1673, which required communion in the Church of England as a qualification for public office, was ostensibly passed to check the growing power of Roman Catholics, but it remained a barrier to the employment of Protestant Dissenters as well. In practice, however, one could hold office if he took communion even occasionally in the Anglican Church. This practice of Occasional Conformity became one of the most hotly debated religious and political issues of Defoe's lifetime. Although the Toleration Act of 1689 ended the notion of a state church to which all Englishmen belonged, it did not resolve the issue of Occasional Conformity.

Queen Anne's resolution to support "the interests and religion of the Church of England" sparked new attempts to prohibit Occasional Conformity in 1702. When a bill to prevent Occasional Conformity was passed by the House of Commons and sent to the House of Lords, Defoe began the most crucial religious battle of his life by publishing *The Shortest Way With The Dissenters* on 1 December. Ironically urging the liquidation of Dissenters, Defoe imitated the extremism of Henry Sacheverell's famous Oxford Sermon and outraged both Dissenters and Anglicans. Defoe was indicted for seditious libel in February, apprehended in May, tried

[22] Novak, 31.

in July, and sentenced to stand in the pillory on 29, 30, and 31 July.
Even after the humiliation of the pillory, he was returned to Newgate Prison, where he remained until about 1 November when
Robert Harley released him to work for the ministry. If Defoe
suffered severely for his irony, he had at least the satisfaction of
knowing that his *Shortest Way* had helped defeat the Occasional
Conformity Bill. Not until 1711 was a bill prohibiting Occasional
Conformity finally passed by Parliament and that was, fortunately,
repealed in 1719. Defoe, a Presbyterian Dissenter, opposed Occasional Conformity on the grounds that it compromised one's religious beliefs, but he recognized and defended the right and
obligation of Dissenters to participate in government, especially in
the light of his estimate that two of the approximately five million
persons in England were Dissenters from the Church of England.
Professor Moore estimates that Defoe was imprisoned at least
seven times during his lifetime for libel or for debt.[23] In his *Tour
Thro' The Whole Island Of Great Britain* (1724–1727) Defoe
surveyed the prisons of London, listing twenty-two "Public Gaols,"
five night prisons or "Round-Houses" (The Chink among them),
and 144 "Tolerated Prisons," including "One hundred and nineteen
Spunging Houses" for debtors. Of these "Spunging Houses" he
wrote, "All these private Houses of Confinement, are pretended to
be like little Purgatories, between Prison and Liberty, Places of Advantage for the keeping Prisoners at their own Request, till they
can get Friends to deliver them, and so avoid going into publick
Prisons; tho' in some of them, the Extortion is such, and the Accommodation so bad, that Men choose to be carried away directly"
(II, 155). Although all prisons were, in legal theory, royal,
many were in the possession of private persons and under no effec-
tive supervision from the Crown. These prisons were farmed out
to wardens who appointed jailers and extorted what they could
from prisoners. Rarely used for convicted felons, the prisons served
for the detention of felons before trial and mostly for debtors, who
could be confined for the smallest of sums until the debt was paid
—even for a lifetime.

Defoe's knowledge of prison life, of the criminals whose adventures he reported weekly in *Applebee's Journal* between 1720 and

[23] *Defoe*, 47.

1726, whose biographies he wrote for John Applebee, and whose lives inspired such fictional characters as Moll Flanders and Col. Jacque, came from first-hand experience. Defoe's intimate knowledge of the horrors of imprisonment in the eighteenth century explains, in part, his interest in the plight of the debtor.

Bankrupt himself in 1692 for insuring ships in wartime and overextending his credit, he avoided imprisonment for debt by agreeing to pay his creditors most of the £17,000 he owed, but he wrote movingly of the plight of debtors at the hands of dishonest creditors and their fellow debtors in *An Essay Upon Projects* (1697). Bankrupt again after the failure of his brick and tile factory in 1703, Defoe took advantage of a new law in 1706 to settle with his creditors and avoid imprisonment. Even at the time of his death in 1731, he was hiding from creditors, avoiding the certain imprisonment that faced a debtor who could neither settle his debts nor obtain a warrant against arrest. It is estimated that by 1716 as many as 60,000 debtors, some for the most trifling amounts, were imprisoned in England and Wales. An investigation of the Fleet Prison in 1727 unearthed the appalling conditions which Defoe was trying to expose—a greed so desperate that jailers would sooner shackle and beat a prisoner than forego their bribes, a filth and stench almost beyond the imagination even of the eighteenth century.

In *An Essay Upon Projects* Defoe deplored "the Destruction of the Debtor": "The Severities to the Debtor are unreasonable, and, if I may so say, a little inhuman; for [the law] not only strips him of all in a moment, but renders him for ever incapable of helping himself, or relieving his Family by future Industry," and proposed "A Court of Enquiries" with "Power to Hear, Try, and Determine Causes as to Proof of Debts, and Disputes in Accounts between Debtor and Creditor, without Appeal." He returned to the subject of bankruptcy often in the *Review* and in *Applebee's Journal* for social as well as economic reasons. On 11 February 1710, he worried in the *Review* because "We take the Bed from the Man, and the Man from his Bed—We strip his miserable Family, and turn his Wife and Children naked into the Streets to starve." With this background, one understands why Moll Flanders prays so fervently, *"Give me not Poverty lest I steal."*

The years from 1720 to 1726 mark the period of Defoe's greatest interest in felons and pirates. Not only did he produce fictional acounts of Moll Flanders, pickpocket, thief, and prostitute, and Col. Jacque, the juvenile delinquent who becomes an English gentleman, but he wrote weekly accounts of the crimes, trials, and executions of criminals for *Applebee's Journal* and pamphlet lives of notorious criminals such as John Sheppard and Jonathan Wild.[24]

Sheppard, executed at the age of twenty-three in November 1724, earned the attention given him by the London press through his four spectacular escapes from prison. He inspired biographies, poems, etchings, and even a harlequinade: *Harlequin Shepard* at Drury Lane on 28 November 1724.

During the years that Defoe worked for him, John Applebee had an arrangement with the Ordinary or Chaplain of Newgate to pay for information from prisoners which could be incorporated into criminal lives and sold even during executions at Tyburn. Defoe probably interviewed prisoners, attended their trials, and then wrote popular biographies to be sold to a growing audience for sixpence or a shilling. Defoe may have written an early account of Sheppard's career as a housebreaker called *A Narrative Of All the Robberies, Escapes, & Of John Sheppard*, which went through eight editions between 15 August 1724 and the end of December; he was certainly at work on a more complete life in October when Sheppard escaped from the "Castle," the most secure cell in Newgate Prison. Defoe quickly finished *The History Of the remarkable Life of John Sheppard* and published it on 19 October, replacing the account of Sheppard's dying speech and execution with which he had expected to complete the life with a hurried filler of five pages of bad puns. When Sheppard was recaptured on 31 October, retried on 7 November, and executed on 16 November, his adventures were reported by Defoe in the columns of *Applebee's Journal*. More interesting than the journalistic accounts, however, are the amusing letters and poems in the journal purporting to be from Sheppard himself, from ladies who loved him to distraction, and from fellow criminals, including Betty Blewskin—"Catch me if you can."

Jonathan Wild captured the spotlight in 1725. Wild, who had organized perhaps the first crime syndicate in England, was en-

[24] See Christopher Hibbert, *The Road to Tyburn* (London, 1957) and William R. Irwin, *The Making of Jonathan Wild* (New York, 1941).

snared in 1725 through a special provision in an act passed "For the farther preventing Robberies, Burglaries, and other Felonies, and for the more effectual Transportation of Felons." Designed to trap Wild, the provision made it a felony to take a reward under the pretence of restoring stolen goods to an owner without prosecuting the thieves. Wild's ingenious pattern of operation was well known in London. The victim of a theft might recover what had been stolen or lost by bribing Jonathan Wild; the thief who failed to cooperate with Wild risked transportation or execution. Defoe, who had reported Wild's trial and execution in *Applebee's Journal,* published *The True and Genuine Account of The Life and Actions Of the Late Jonathan Wild* on 8 June 1725; by the 10th it had reached a second edition; by the 12th, a third.

Defoe's knowledge of criminal life and his intimate acquaintance with prisons and bankrupts help explain the vitality of his criminal lives and the accuracy of the details with which they abound. The necessary haste of composition and printing shows in the repetitiousness of some of the material, in the padding used to fill out pages, and in the carelessness in fact and typesetting which one associates with these biographies. In the life of Wild, Defoe dramatized Wild's activities as London's great "fence" in a splendid encounter between a lady of quality who had lost a gold watch and Wild, dressed in his brightly colored "Callimancoe" gown, but the same life contains the stilted prose which Defoe sometimes borrowed from such official accounts as *The Whole Proceedings upon the King's Commission of Oyer and Terminer and Gaol Delivery for the City of London and County of Middlesex.* However subliterary these accounts may finally be, they exhibit a breathless immediacy characteristic of the best of Defoe's journalism and they carry the modern reader into the violent world of the eighteenth century, a world quite unlike the polished and elegant society depicted in Alexander Pope's *Rape of the Lock.*

Defoe's works reflect intimately the issues and topics which excited his age. When he outlines a plan for training English musicians at Christ's Hospital in the *Augusta Triumphans* (1728), he reflects not only the great popularity of Italian opera in England, but the controversy over Charity-Schools in English life, one fanned by Bernard Mandeville in *The Fable of the Bees. With An Essay on Charity and Charity-Schools* (1723) and then taken up by William

Barnes in *Charity and Charity Schools Defended* (1724), William
Hendley in *A Defense of the Charity Schools* (1724), Isaac Watt
in *An Essay towards the Encouragement of Charity Schools* (1728),
and many others. Defoe was the most contemporary of writers,
whether he was discussing politics, religion, international affairs,
crime, economics, the plague, or the arts. His gift was to make
these issues seem alive even to a modern reader.

Whether or not Defoe deserves to be called "the first English
novelist" for his accomplishments in *Robinson Crusoe, Moll Flanders, Col. Jacque,* and *A Journal Of The Plague Year* matters very
little. His clear, strong, idiomatic English prose captures a reader's
attention as completely as his common sense, his enthusiasm, his
passion for facts, and his ability to weave fact and imagination into
a convincing whole. His achievements in polemic poetry and prose,
his forthright and energetic discussions of the controversial issues of
his day, his genuine sympathy with people harmed by the social
organization of England, and his skill in bringing the Augustan
world to life secure his place in English literature.

The Text

The text for this edition is an almost literal reproduction of the
first edition of each work and of the original sheets of the newspapers and journals collated against at least one other first edition
or set of sheets. The copy text in almost every case is from the extensive Defoe collection in the University of Illinois Library. The
text does not include those substantive variants from editions published later in Defoe's lifetime which would be appropriate for a
scholarly edition. Defoe blunted his attacks on John Tutchin and
Sir Charles Duncombe in later editions of *The True-Born Englishman,* but I have chosen to reprint the complete text of the first
edition because it exhibits best the vigor and the love of controversy which characterize much of Defoe's work.

Obvious printing errors, such as inverted letters, have been silently corrected, and missing letters and words indicated within
brackets, but the spelling, capitalization, italics, and pointing of the

original texts have been maintained rather than modernized. The original text will, I hope, provide the reader with an opportunity to savor and to examine the linguistic qualities of eighteenth-century English. Past participles such as "crope" for "crept" were still in use; spelling and contractions had not yet been standardized. The pointing will seem unusually erratic at first. The colon often served Defoe as a period; many of his sentences race breathlessly along through a series of commas and semicolons. Nouns and important words in the text are usually, but not consistently, capitalized or italicized. At times the curious, inconsistent spellings and erratic pointing reflect mere haste on the part of Defoe or of his printer; more frequently they mirror the English of Defoe's day. To deprive the reader of the charm of Defoe's language would be to remove some of the pleasure to be obtained from reading these selections.

I should like to acknowledge the special assistance of Benjamin Boyce (Duke University), John Hurt Fisher (New York University), William McBurney (University of Illinois), and Barbara Packer (New York University) and of John Alden (Boston Public Library), Robert Allen and Marian Harman (University of Illinois Library), Theodore Grieder (New York University Library), and Anthony Warren (New York Public Library). I am grateful to the University of Illinois Library and to the Beinecke Rare Book and Manuscript Library, Yale University, for permission to reproduce the title pages of the Defoe works included in this collection.

CHRONOLOGY

I gratefully acknowledge my debt to Professor John Robert Moore, whose detailed chronology of the life and works of Defoe in *Daniel Defoe: Citizen of the Modern World* and *A Checklist of the Writings of Daniel Defoe* has been my indispensable source.

1660   Born in London

c. 1682 Sets up as a wholesale merchant, dealing in hosiery and later in wine, tobacco, marine insurance, tiles, and bricks.

1684   Marries Mary Tuffley, who brings him a dowry of £3,700.

1685   Participates briefly in Monmouth's Rebellion.

1692   Bankrupt for £17,000.

1697   *An Essay Upon Projects.*

1701   *The True-Born Englishman.*

1702   *The Mock-Mourners.*
        The Shortest-Way With The Dissenters.

1703   Arrested and imprisoned for *The Shortest-Way.*
        Stands in the pillory on 29, 30, and 31 July.
        Released from Newgate Prison in early November through the influence of Robert Harley.

1704   Begins a lifelong career as government agent and pamphleteer.
        Review (1704–1713).

1705   *The Consolidator.*

1713   Arrested both for libel and for debt.

1715   *An Appeal To Honour And Justice.*

1719   *The Life And Strange Surprizing Adventures of Robinson Crusoe.*

1720   *Applebee's Original Weekly Journal* (1720–1726).
        Memoirs of a Cavalier.
        The Life, Adventures, And Pyracies, Of The Famous Captain Singleton.

1722   *The Fortunes And Misfortunes Of The Famous Moll Flanders.*
        Due Preparations For The Plague.
        A Journal Of The Plague Year.

SELECTED BIBLIOGRAPHY

BOULTON, JAMES T. *Daniel Defoe.* New York, 1965.

DEFOE, DANIEL. *The Shakespeare Head Edition of the Novels and Selected Writings of Daniel Defoe.* 14 vols. Oxford, 1927–1928.

HEALEY, GEORGE H., ed. *The Letters of Daniel Defoe.* Oxford, 1955.

HUNTER, J. PAUL. *The Reluctant Pilgrim.* Baltimore, 1966.

LEE, WILLIAM. *Daniel Defoe: His Life, and Recently Discovered Writings Extending From 1716 to 1729.* 3 vols. London, 1869.

MOORE, JOHN ROBERT. *Daniel Defoe: Citizen of the Modern World.* Chicago, 1958.

―――. *A Checklist of the Writings of Daniel Defoe.* Indiana University Humanities Series, Number 47. Bloomington, 1960.

NOVAK, MAXIMILLIAN E. *Defoe and the Nature of Man.* Oxford, 1963.

―――. *Economics and the Fiction of Daniel Defoe.* Berkeley and Los Angeles, 1962.

PAYNE, WILLIAM L. *The Best of Defoe's Review.* New York, 1951.

SECORD, ARTHUR W. *A Review of the Affairs of France.* Facsimile Text Society. 22 vols. New York, 1938.

―――. *Studies in the Narrative Method of Daniel Defoe.* Urbana, 1924.

STARR, G. A. *Defoe and Spiritual Autobiography.* Princeton, 1965.

SUTHERLAND, JAMES. *Defoe.* Philadelphia and New York, 1938, 1950.

SELECTED POETRY AND PROSE OF DANIEL DEFOE

AN
ESSAY
UPON
Projects.

LONDON:

Printed by *R. R.* for *Tho. Cockerill,* at
the Corner of *Warwick-Lane,* near
Pater-noster-Row. MDCXCVII.

AN
ESSAY
UPON
PROJECTS

LONDON:

Printed by R. R. for Tho. Cockerill, at the Corner of
Warwick-Lane, near Pater-noster-Row. MDCXCVII.

In his first long work, published in 1697, Defoe introduces
topics that reappear throughout his works. The present selections are taken from pages 19–35, 178–227, and 282–304 of
the first edition.

THE HISTORY OF PROJECTS

WHEN I speak of Writing a *History of Projects*, I do not
mean either of the Introduction of, or Continuing necessary
Inventions, or the Improvement of Arts and Sciences before
known; but a short Account of Projects, and Projecting, as the
Word is allow'd in the general Acceptation at this present
time, and I need not go far back for the Original of the Practice.

Invention of Arts with Engines and Handycraft Instruments
for their Improvement, requires a Chronology as far back as

the Eldest Son of *Adam,* and has to this day afforded some new Discovery in every Age.

The Building of the Ark by *Noah,* so far as you will allow it a human Work, was the first Project I read of; and no question seem'd so ridiculous to the Graver Heads of that Wise, tho' Wicked Age, that poor *Noah* was sufficiently banter'd for it; and had he not been set on work by a very peculiar Direction from Heaven, the Good old Man would certainly have been laugh'd out of it, as a most senseless ridiculous Project.

The Building of *Babel* was a Right Project; for indeed the true definition of a Project, according to Modern Acceptation, is, as is said before, a vast Undertaking, too big to be manag'd, and therefore likely enough to come to nothing; and yet as great as they are, 'tis certainly true of 'em all, even as the Projectors propose; that according to the old tale, If so many Eggs are hatch'd, there will be so many Chickens, and those Chickens may lay so many Eggs more, and those Eggs produce so many Chickens more, and so on. Thus 'twas most certainly true, That if the People of the Old World cou'd have Built a House up to Heaven, they shou'd never be Drown'd again on Earth, and they only had forgot to Measure the Heighth, *that is,* as in other Projects, it only Miscarri'd, or else 'twou'd have Succeeded.

And yet when all's done, that very Building, and the incredible Heighth it was carri'd, is a Demonstration of the vast Knowledge of that Infant-Age of the World, who had no advantage of the Experiments or Inventions of any before themselves.

> *Thus when Our Fathers touch'd with Guilt,*
> *That* Huge Stupendious Stair-Case *Built;*
> *We Mock indeed the fruitless Enterprize,*
> *For fruitless Actions seldom pass for Wise;*
> *But were the* Mighty Ruins *left, they'd show,*
> *To what Degree that Untaught Age did Know.*

I believe a very diverting Account might be given of this, but I shall not attempt it. Some are apt to say with *Solomon, No new thing happens under the Sun, but what is, has been;* yet I make no question but some considerable Discovery has been made in these latter Ages, and Inventions of Human Original produc'd, which the World was ever without before, either in whole, or in part; and I refer only to two Cardinal Points, the use of the Load-stone at Sea, and the use of Gunpowder and Guns; both which, as to the Inventing-part, I believe the World owes as absolutely to those particular Ages, as it does the Working in Brass and Iron to *Tubal Cain,* or the Inventing of Musick to *Jubal his Brother.*[1] As to Engines and Instruments for Handycraft-Men, this Age, I dare say, can show such as never were so much as thought of, much less imitated before; for I do not call that a real Invention which has something before done like it, I account that more properly an improvement. For Handycraft Instruments, I know none owes more to true genuine Contrivance, without borrowing from any former use, than a Mechanick Engine contriv'd in our time, call'd, *A Knitting Frame,* which built with admirable Symetry, works really with a very happy Success, and may be observ'd by the Curious to have a more than ordinary Composition; for which I refer to the Engine it self, to be seen in every Stocking-Weaver's Garret.

I shall trace the Original of the Projecting Humour that now reigns, no farther back than the Year 1680. dating its Birth as a Monster then, tho' by times it had indeed something of life in the time of the late Civil War. I allow, no Age has been altogether without something of this nature; and some very happy Projects are left to us as a taste of their Success; as the Water-houses for supplying of the City of *London* with Water; and since that, the *New-River,* both very Considerable Undertakings, and Perfect Projects, adventur'd on the risque of Success. In the Reign of King *Charles* the First, infinite Projects were set on foot for Raising Money without a Parliament; Oppressing by Monopolies, and Privy Seals; but these are ex-

cluded our Scheme, as Irregularities; for thus the *French* are
as fruitful in Projects as we; and these are rather Stratagems
than Projects. After the Fire of *London*, the Contrivance of an
Engine to Quench Fires, was a Project the Author was said to
get well by, and we have found to be very useful. But about
the Year 1680. began the Art and Mystery of Projecting to
creep into the World. Prince *Rupert*, Uncle to King *Charles*
the Second, gave great Encouragement to that part of it that
respects Engines, and Mechanical Motions; and Bishop *Wilkins*
added as much of the Theory to it, as writing a Book could do:[2]
The Prince has left us a Metal call'd by his Name; and the
first Project upon that was, as I remember, Casting of Guns of
that Metal, and boring them; done both by a peculiar Method
of his own, and which died with him, to the great loss of the
Undertaker, who to that purpose had, with no small Charge,
erected a Water-Mill at *Hackney-Marsh*, known by the name
of the *Temple-Mill:* Which Mill very happily perform'd all
parts of the Work; and I have seen of those Guns on board
the Royal *Charles*, a First-rate Ship, being of a Reddish Colour,
different either from Brass or Copper. I have heard some
Reasons of State assign'd, why that Project was not permitted
to go forward; but I omit them, because I have no good Authority for it: After this, we saw a Floating Machine, to be
wrought with Horses for the Towing of Great Ships both
against Wind and Tide; and another for the raising of Ballast
which, as unperforming Engines, had the honour of being
Made, Expos'd, Tri'd, and laid by, before the Prince died.

If thus we introduce it into the World under the Conduct
of that Prince; when he died, 'twas left a hopeless Brat, and
had hardly any Hand to own it, till the Wreck-Voyage before-
noted, perform'd so happily by Captain *Phips*, afterwards Sir
William; whose strange Performance set a great many Heads
on work to contrive something for themselves; he was immediately follow'd by my Lord *Mordant*, Sir *John Narborough*,[3]
and others from several Parts, whose Success made 'em soon
weary of the Work.

The Project of the *Penny-Post*, so well known, and still practis'd, I cannot omit; nor the Contriver Mr. *Dockwra*, who has had the honour to have the Injury done him in that Affair, repair'd in some measure by the publick Justice of the Parliament.[4] And the Experiment proving it to be a Noble and Useful Design, the Author must be remembered, where-ever mention is made of that Affair, to his very great Reputation.

'Twas no question a great hardship for a man to be Master of so fine a Thought, that had *both* the *Essential Ends of a Project* in it, *Publick Good*, and *Private Advantage;* and that the Publick shou'd reap the benefit, and the Author be left out; the Injustice of which, no doubt, discourag'd many a Good Design: But since an Alteration in Publick Circumstances has recover'd the lost Attribute of Justice, the like is not to be fear'd. And Mr. *Dockwra* has had the satisfaction to see the former Injury disown'd, and an honourable Return made even by them who did not the Injury, in bare respect to his Ingenuity.

A while before this, several People, under the Patronage of some great Persons, had engag'd in Planting of Foreign Collonies; as *William Pen*, the Lord *Shaftsbury*, Dr. *Cox*,[5] and others, in *Pensilvania*, *Carolina*, *East* and *West Jersey*, and the like places; which I do not call Projects, because 'twas only prosecuting what had been formerly begun: But here began the forming of publick Joint-Stocks, which, together with the *East-India*, *African*, and *Hudson's-Bay* Companies,[6] before establish'd, begot a New Trade, which we call by a new Name, *Stock-Jobbing*, which was at first only the simple Occasional Transferring of Interest and Shares from one to another, as Persons alienated their Estates; but by the Industry of the Exchange-Brokers, who got the business into their hands, it became a Trade; and one perhaps manag'd with the greatest Intriegue, Artifice, and Trick, that ever any thing that appear'd with a face of Honesty could be handl'd with; for while the Brokers held the Box, they made the whole *Exchange* the Gamesters, and rais'd and lower'd the Prices of Stocks as they pleas'd; and always had both Buyers and Sellers who stood ready innocently to commit their Money to the mercy of their Mercenary Tongues. This Upstart of a Trade having tasted the sweetness of Success which generally attends a *Novel Proposal,* introduces the Illigitimate wandring Object I speak of, as a proper Engine to find Work for the Brokers. Thus Stock-Jobbing nurs'd Projecting, and Projecting in return has very diligently pimp'd for its Foster-parent, till both are arriv'd to be Publick Grievances; and indeed are now almost grown scandalous.

OF PROJECTORS

MAN is the worst of all God's Creatures to shift for himself; no other Animal is ever starv'd to death; Nature without, has provided them both Food and Cloaths; and Nature within, has plac'd an Instinct that never fails to direct them to proper means for a supply; but Man must either *Work or Starve, Slave or Dye;* he has indeed Reason given him to direct him, and few who follow the Dictates of that Reason come to such unhappy Exigencies; but when by the Errors of a Man's Youth he has reduc'd himself to such a degree of Distress, as to be absolutely without Three things, *Money, Friends,* and *Health,* he Dies in a Ditch, or in some worse place, *an Hospital.*

Ten thousand ways there are to bring a Man to this, and but very few to bring him out again.

Death is the universal Deliverer, and therefore some who want Courage to bear what they see before 'em, *Hang themselves for fear;* for certainly Self-destruction is the effect of Cowardice in the highest extream.

Others break the Bounds of Laws to satisfy that general Law of Nature, and turn open Thieves, House-breakers, Highwaymen, Clippers, Coiners, &c. till they run the length of the Gallows, and get a Deliverance the nearest way at St. *Tyburn.*

Others being masters of more Cunning than their Neighbours, turn their Thoughts to Private Methods of Trick and

Cheat, a Modern way of Thieving, every jot as Criminal, and in some degree worse than the other, by which honest men are gull'd with fair pretences to part from their Money, and then left to take their Course with the Author, who sculks behind the curtain of a Protection, or in the *Mint* or *Friars,* and bids defiance as well to Honesty as the Law.[7]

Others yet urg'd by the same necessity, turn their thoughts to Honest Invention, founded upon the Platform of Ingenuity and Integrity.

These two last sorts are those we call *Projectors;* and as there was always *more Geese than Swans,* the number of the latter are very inconsiderable in comparison of the former; and as the greater number denominates the less, the just Contempt we have of the former sort, bespatters the other, who like Cuckolds bear the reproach of other Peoples Crimes.

A meer Projector then is a Contemptible thing, driven by his own desperate Fortune to such a Streight, that he must be deliver'd by a Miracle, or Starve; and when he has beat his Brains for some such Miracle in vain, he finds no remedy but to paint up some Bauble or other, *as Players make Puppets talk big,* to show like a strange thing, and then cry it up for a New Invention, gets a Patent for it, divides it into Shares, and *they must be Sold;* ways and means are not wanting to Swell the new Whim to a vast Magnitude; Thousands, and Hundreds of thousands are the least of his discourse, and sometimes Millions; till the Ambition of some honest Coxcomb is wheedl'd to part with his Money for it, and then

——*Nascitur ridiculus mus.*[8]

the Adventurer is left to carry on the Project, and the Projector laughs at him. The *Diver* shall walk at the bottom of the *Thames;* the *Saltpeter-Maker* shall Build *Tom T[ur]ds*[9] Pond into Houses; the Engineers Build Models and Windmills to draw Water, till Funds are rais'd to carry it on, by Men who have more Money than Brains, and then *good night Patent and Invention;* the Projector has done his business, and is gone.

But the Honest Projector is he, who having by fair and plain principles of Sense, Honesty, and Ingenuity, brought any Contrivance to a suitable Perfection, makes out what he pretends to, picks no body's pocket, puts his Project in Execution, and contents himself with the real Produce, as the profit of his Invention.

OF FOOLS

OF all Persons who are Objects of our Charity, none move my Compassion, like those whom it has pleas'd God to leave in a full state of Health and Strength, but depriv'd of Reason to act for themselves. And it is, in my opinion, one of the greatest Scandals upon the *Understanding* of others, to mock at those who want *it.* Upon this account I think the Hospital we call *Bedlam,*[10] to be a Noble Foundation; a visible Instance of the sense our Ancestors had of the greatest Unhappiness which can befal Human Kind: Since as the Soul in Man distinguishes him from a Brute, so where the Soul is dead (for so it is as to acting) *no Brute so much a Beast as a Man.* But since *never to have* it, and to have *lost* it, are synonimous in the Effect, I wonder how it came to pass, that in the Settlement of that Hospital they made no Provision for Persons born without the use of their Reason, such as we call *Fools,* or, more properly, *Naturals.*

We use such in *England* with the last Contempt, which I think is a strange Error, since tho' they are useless to the Commonwealth, they are only so by God's direct Providence, and no previous Fault.

I think 'twould very well become this Wise Age to take care of such: And perhaps they are a particular Rent-Charge on the *Great Family of Mankind;* left by the Maker of us all; like a Younger Brother, who tho' the Estate be given from him, yet his Father expected the Heir should take some care of him.

If I were to be ask'd, Who ought in particular to be charg'd with this Work? I would answer in general, Those who have a Portion of Understanding extraordinary: Not that I would lay a Tax upon any man's Brains, *or discourage Wit, by appointing Wise Men to maintain Fools:* But some Tribute is due to God's Goodness for bestowing extraordinary Gifts; and who can it be better paid to, than such as suffer for want of the same Bounty?

For the providing therefore some Subsistence for such, that Natural Defects may not be expos'd:

It is Propos'd,

That a *Fool-House* be Erected, either by Publick Authority, or by the City, or by an Act of Parliament; into which, all that are *Naturals,* or born Fools, without Respect or Distinction, should be admitted and maintain'd.

For the Maintenance of this, a small stated Contribution, settl'd by the Authority of an Act of Parliament, without any Damage to the Persons paying the same, might be very easily rais'd, by a Tax upon Learning, to be paid by the Authors of Books.

Every Book that shall be Printed in Folio, *from* 40 *sheets and upwards, to pay at the Licensing, (for the whole Impression.)*	5 *l.*
Under 40 *sheets,*	40 *s.*
Every Quarto,	20 *s.*
Every Octavo *of* 10 *sheets and upward,*	20 *s.*
Every Octavo *under* 10 *sheets, and every Bound Book in* 12ˢ.	10 *s.*
Every stitch'd Pamphlet,	2 *s.*
Reprinted Copies the same Rates.	

This Tax to be paid into the Chamber of *London* for the space of Twenty Years, would without question raise a Fund sufficient to Build and Purchase a Settlement for this House.

I suppose this little Tax being to be rais'd at so few places as the Printing-Presses, or the Licensers of Books, and consequently the Charge but very small in gathering, might bring in about 1500 *l. per Annum,* for the term of Twenty Years, which would perform the Work to the degree following.

The House should be Plain and Decent, (for I don't think the Ostentation of Buildings necessary or suitable to Works of Charity); and be built somewhere out of Town, for the sake of the Air.

The Building to cost about 1000 *l.* or if the Revenue exceed, to cost 2000 *l.* at most, and the Salaries mean in proportion.

In the House,

A Steward,	30 *l. per Ann.*
A Purveyor,	20
A Cook,	20
A Butler,	20
Six Women to assist the Cook, and clean the House, 4 *l.* each,	24
Six Nurses to Tend the People, 3 *l.* each,	18
A Chaplain,	20
	152
A Hundred Alms-People, at 8 *l. per Ann.* Dyet, &c.	800
	952 *l. per Ann.*

The Table for the Officers, and Contingencies, and Cloaths for the Alms-People, and Firing, put together,   500 *l. per Ann.*

An Auditor of the Accounts, a Committee of the Governors, and Two Clerks.

Here I suppose 1500 Pounds *per Ann.* Revenue, to be settl'd upon the House, which 'tis very probable might be rais'd from the Tax aforesaid. But since an Act of Parliament is necessary to be had for the Collecting this Duty, *and that Taxes for keeping of Fools would be difficultly obtain'd, while they are so much wanted for Wise Men;* I would propose to raise the Money by voluntary Charity, which wou'd be a Work would leave more Honour to the Undertakers, than Feasts and great Shows, which our Publick Bodies too much diminish their Stocks with.

But to pass all suppositious ways, which are easily thought of, but hardly procur'd; I propose to maintain Fools out of our own Folly: And whereas a great deal of Money has been thrown about in Lotteries, the following Proposal would very easily perfect our Work.

A *Charity-Lottery.*

That a Lottery be set up by the Authority of the Lord-Mayor and Court of Aldermen, for a Hundred thousand Tickets, at Twenty Shillings each, to be drawn by the known Way and Method of drawing Lotteries, as the Million-Lottery was drawn;[11] in which no Allowance to be made to any body; but the Fortunate to receive the full Sum of One hundred thousand Pounds put in, without Discount; and yet this double Advantage to follow:

(1.) That an immediate Sum of One hundred thousand Pounds shall be rais'd and paid into the *Exchequer* for the Publick Use.

(2.) A Sum of above Twenty thousand Pounds be gain'd, to be put into the hands of known Trustees, to be laid out in a Charity for the Maintenance of the Poor.

That as soon as the Money shall be come in, it shall be paid into the *Exchequer,* either on some good Fund, if any suitable, or on the Credit of *Exchequer;* and that when the Lottery is drawn, the Fortunate to receive Tallies or Bills from the *Exchequer* for their Money, payable at Four Years.

The *Exchequer* receives this Money, and gives out Tallies

according to the Prizes, when 'tis drawn, all payable at Four
Years; and the Interest of this Money for Four Years is struck
in Tallies proportion'd to the time, and given to the Trustees;
which is the Profit I propose for the Work.

Thus the Fortunate have an immediate Title to their Prizes,
at Four Years, without Interest; and the Hospital will have
also an immediate Title to 6000 *l. per Ann.* for Four Years,
which is the Interest at 6 *per Cent. per Ann.*

If any should object against the Time of staying for their
Prizes, it should be answer'd thus, That whoever did not like
to stay the Time for the Money, upon discounting Four Years
Interest at 8 *per Cent.* should have their Money down.

I think this Specimen will inform any body what might be
done by Lotteries, were they not hackney'd about in Private
Hands, who by Fraud and Ill Management put them out of
Repute, and so neither gain themselves, nor suffer any useful
handsome Design to succeed.

'Twould be needless, I suppose, to mention, That such a
Proposal as this ought to be set on foot by Publick Approbation,
and by Men of known Integrity and Estates, that there may
be no room left for a suspicion of private advantage.

If this or any equivalent Proposal succeeded to raise the
Money, I would have the House establish'd as aforesaid, with
larger or smaller Revenues, as necessity oblig'd; then the Persons to be receiv'd should be without distinction or respect,
but principally such as were really Poor and Friendless; and
any that were kept already by any Parish-Collection, the said
Parish should allow Forty Shillings Yearly towards their Maintenance; which no Parish would refuse that subsisted them
wholly before.

I make no question but that if such an Hospital was erected
within a Mile or two of the City, one great Circumstance
would happen, (*viz.*) That the common sort of people, who
are very much addicted to rambling in the Fields, would make
this House the customary Walk, to divert themselves with the

Objects to be seen there, and to make what they call Sport with the Calamity of others; as is now shamefully allow'd in *Bedlam*.

To prevent this, and that the condition of such, which deserves Pity, not Contempt, might not be the more expos'd by this Charity, it should be order'd, That the Steward of the House be in Commission of the Peace within the Precincts of the House only, and authoriz'd to punish by limited Fines, or otherwise, any person that shall offer any Abuse to the poor Alms-people, or shall offer to make Sport at their Condition.

If any person at Reading of this, shou'd be so impertinent as to ask, To what purpose I wou'd appoint a Chaplain in an Hospital of *Fools?* I could answer him very well, by saying, For the use of the other Persons, Officers and Attendants in the House.

But besides that, Pray, *Why not a Chaplain for Fools, as well as for Knaves,* since both, tho' in a different manner, are uncapable of reaping any benefit by Religion, unless by some invisible Influence they are made docible; and since the same Secret Power can restore these to their Reason, as must make the other Sensible; Pray, Why not a Chaplain? Ideots indeed were denied the Communion in the Primitive Churches, but I never read they were not to be pray'd for, or were not admitted to hear.

If we allow any Religion, and a Divine Supreme Power, whose Influence works invisibly on the hearts of men (*as he must be worse than the people we talk of, who denies it*), we must allow at the same time, *that Power* can restore the Reasoning-Faculty to an Ideot; and 'tis our part to use the proper means of supplicating Heaven to that end, leaving the disposing-part to the Issue of unalterable Providence.

The Wisdom of Providence has not left us without Examples of some of the most stupid Natural Ideots in the world, who have been restor'd to their Reason, or as one would think, had Reason infus'd after a long Life of *Ideotism;* Perhaps, among other wise ends, to confute that sordid Supposition, That Ideots have no Souls.

OF BANKRUPTS

THis Chapter has some Right to stand next to that of Fools; for besides the common acceptation of late, which makes *every Unfortunate Man a Fool*, I think no man so much made a Fool of as a *Bankrupt*.

If I may be allow'd so much liberty with our Laws, which are generally good, and above all things are temper'd with Mercy, Lenity, and Freedom, This has something in it of Barbarity; it gives a loose to the Malice and Revenge of the Creditor, as well as a Power to right himself, while it leaves the Debtor no way to show himself honest: It contrives all the ways possible to drive the Debtor to despair, and encourages no new Industry, for it makes him perfectly uncapable of any thing but *starving*.

This Law, especially as it is now frequently executed, tends wholly to the Destruction of the Debtor, and yet very little to the Advantage of the Creditor.[12]

(1.) The Severities to the Debtor are unreasonable, and, if I may so say, a little inhuman; for it not only strips him of all in a moment, but renders him for ever incapable of helping himself, or relieving his Family by future Industry. If he 'scapes from Prison, which is hardly done too, if he has nothing left, he must starve, or live on Charity; if he goes to work, no man dare pay him his Wages, but he shall pay it again to the Creditors; if he has any private Stock left for a Subsistence, he can put it no where; every man is bound to be a Thief, and take it from him: If he trusts it in the hands of a Friend, he must receive it again as a great Courtesy, for that Friend is liable to account for it. I have known a poor man prosecuted by a Statute to that degree, that all he had left was a little Money, which he knew not where to hide; at last, that he might not starve, he gives it to his Brother, who had enter-tain'd him; the Brother, after he had his Money, quarrels with him to get him out of his House; and when he desires him to let him have the Money lent him, gives him this for Answer, *I cannot pay you safely, for there is a Statute against you;* which run the poor man to such Extremities, that he destroy'd himself. Nothing is more frequent, than for men who are reduc'd by Miscarriage in Trade, to Compound and Set up again, and get good Estates; but a *Statute,* as we call it, for ever shuts up all doors to the Debtor's Recovery; as if Breaking were a Crime so Capital, that he ought to be cast out of Hu-man Society, and expos'd to Extremities worse than Death. And, which will further expose the fruitless Severity of this Law, 'tis easy to make it appear, That all this Cruelty to the Debtor is so far (generally speaking) from advantaging the Creditors, that it destroys the Estate, consumes it in extrava-gant Charges, and unless the Debtor be consenting, seldom makes any considerable Dividends. And I am bold to say, There is no Advantage made by the prosecuting of a Statute with Severity, but what might be doubly made by Methods more merciful. And tho' I am not to prescribe to the Legisla-tors of the Nation, yet by way of Essay I take leave to give my Opinion and my Experience in the Methods, Consequences, and Remedies of this Law.

All people know, who remember any thing of the Times when that Law was made, that the Evil it was pointed at, was grown very rank, and Breaking to defraud Creditors so much a Trade, that the Parliament had good reason to set up a Fury to deal with it; and I am far from reflecting on the Makers of that Law, who, no question, saw 'twas necessary at that time: But as Laws, tho' in themselves good, are more or less so, as they are more or less seasonable, squar'd, and adapted to the Circumstances and Time of the Evil they are made against; so 'twere worth while (with Submission) for the same Authority to examine:

(1.) Whether the Length of Time since that Act was made, has not given opportunity to Debtors,

1. To evade the Force of the Act by Ways and Shifts to avoid the Power of it, and secure their Estates out of the reach of it?

2. To turn the Point of it against those whom it was made to relieve? Since we see frequently now, that Bankrupts desire Statutes, and procure them to be taken out against themselves.

(2.) Whether the Extremities of this Law are not often carried on beyond the true Intent and Meaning of the Act it self, by Persons, who besides being Creditors, are also Malicious, and gratify their private Revenge, by prosecuting the Offender, to the Ruin of his Family.

If these Two Points are to be prov'd, then I am sure 'twill follow, That this Act is now a Publick Grievance to the Nation; and I doubt not but will be one time or other repeal'd by the same Wise Authority which made it.

(1.) Time and Experience has furnish'd the Debtors with Ways and Means to evade the Force of this Statute, and to secure their Estate against the reach of it; which renders it often insignificant, and consequently, the Knave, against whom the Law was particularly bent, gets off; while he only who fails of mere Necessity, and whose honest Principle will not permit him to practice those Methods, is expos'd to the Fury of this Act: And as things are now order'd, nothing is more easy, than for a man to order his Estate so, that a Statute shall have no power over it, or at least but a little.

If the Bankrupt be a Merchant, no Statute can reach his Effects beyond the Seas; so that he has nothing to secure but his Books, and away he goes into the *Friars.* If a Shopkeeper, he has more difficulty; but that is made easy, for there are Men (and Carts) to be had, *whose Trade it is,* and who in One Night shall remove the greatest Warehouse of Goods, or Cellar of Wines in the Town, and carry them off into those Nurseries of Rogues, the *Mint* and *Friars;* and our Constables and Watch, who are the allow'd Magistrates of the Night, and who shall stop a poor little lurking Thief, that it may be has stole a bundle of old Cloaths, worth 5 *s.* shall let them all pass without any disturbance, and see a hundred honest men robb'd of their Estates before their faces, to the Eternal Infamy of the Justice of the Nation.

And were a man but to hear the Discourse among the Inhabitants of those Dens of Thieves, when they first swarm about a New Comer, to comfort him; for they are not all harden'd to a like degree at once.————— *Well,* says the first, *Come, don't be concern'd, you have got a good Parcel of Goods away, I promise you; you need not value all the World. Ah! wou'd I had done so,* says another, *I'de a laugh'd at all my Creditors. Ay,* says the young Proficient in the harden'd Trade, *but my Creditors! Damn the Creditors,* says a Third, *Why, there's such a one and such a one, they have Creditors too, and they won't agree with them, and here they live like Gentlemen, and care not a farthing for them. Offer your Creditors Half a Crown in the Pound, and pay it them in Old Debts, and if they won't take it, let them alone, they'll come after you, never fear it. O! But a Statute,* says he again. *O! But the Devil,* cries the Minter. *Why, 'tis the Statutes we live by,* say they: *Why, if 'twere not for Statutes, Creditors would comply, and Debtors wou'd compound, and We Honest Fellows here of the Mint wou'd be starv'd. Prithee, What need you care for a Statute? A Thousand Statutes can't reach you here.* This is the *Language of the Countrey,* and the New Comer soon learns to speak it; (for I think I may say, without wronging any man, I have known many a man go in among them Honest, that is, without Ill Design, but I never knew one come away so again.) ————— Then comes a Graver Sort among this Black Crew, (for here, as in Hell, are Fiends of Degrees, and different Magnitude), and he falls into Discourse with the New Comer, and gives him more solid Advice. *Look you, Sir, I am concern'd to see you melancholly, I am in your Cir-*

cumstance too, and if you'll accept of it, I'le give you the best Advice I can; and so begins the Grave Discourse.

The man is in too much trouble, not to want Counsel, so he thanks him, and he goes on: *Send a Summons to Your Creditors, and offer them what you can propose in the Pound* (always reserving a good Stock to begin the World again), *which if they will take, you are a Freeman, and better than you were before; if they won't take it, you know the worst of it, you are on the better side of the hedge with them: If they will not take it, but will proceed to a Statute, you have nothing to do, but to oppose Force with Force; for the Laws of Nature tell you, you must not starve; and a Statute is so barbarous, so unjust, so malicious a way of proceeding against a man, that I do not think any Debtor oblig'd to consider any thing but his own Preservation, when once they go on with that.* ———— *For why,* says the old studi'd Wretch, *should the Creditors spend your Estate in the Commission, and then demand the Debt of you too? Do you owe any thing to the Commission of the Statute?* (No, says he); *Why then,* says he, *I warrant their Charges will come to* 200 l. *out of your Estate, and they must have* 10 s. *a day for starving you and your Family. I cannot see why any man should think I am bound in Conscience to pay the Extravagance of other men. If my Creditors spend* 500 l. *in getting in my Estate by a Statute, which I offer'd to surrender without it, I'le reckon that* 500 l. *paid them, let them take it among them; for Equity is due to a Bankrupt as well as to any man; and if the Laws do not give it us, we must take it.*

This is too rational Discourse not to please him, and he proceeds by this Advice; the Creditors cannot agree, but take out a Statute; and the man that offer'd at first, it may be, 10 *s.* in the Pound, is kept in that cursed place till he has spent it all, and can offer nothing, and then gets away beyond Sea, or after a long Consumption gets off by an Act of Relief to poor Debtors, and all the Charges of the Statute falls among the Creditors. Thus I knew a Statute taken out against a Shopkeeper in the Countrey, and a considerable Parcel of Goods too seiz'd, and yet the Creditors, what with Charges, and two or three Suits at Law, lost their whole Debts, and 8 *s. per* Pound Contribution-Money for Charges; and the poor Debtor, like a man under the Surgeon's hand, died in the Operation.

(2.) Another Evil that Time and Experience has brought to light from this Act, is, when the Debtor himself shall confederate with some particular Creditor to take out a Statute; and this is a Master-piece of *Plot* and Intriegue: For perhaps some Creditor honestly receiv'd in the way of Trade a large Sum of Money of the Debtor for Goods sold him when he was *sui juris;*[13] and he by consent shall own himself a Bankrupt before that time, and the Statute shall reach back to bring in an Honest Man's Estate, to help pay a Rogue's Debt. Or a man shall go and borrow a Sum of Money upon a Parcel of Goods, and lay them to Pledge; he keeps the Money, and the Statute shall fetch away the Goods to help forward the Composition. These are Tricks I can give too good an account of, having more than once suffer'd by the Experiment. I could give a Scheme of more ways, but I think 'tis needless to prove the Necessity of laying aside that Law, which is pernicious to both Debtor and Creditor, and chiefly hurtful to the Honest Man who it was made to preserve.

The next Enquiry is, Whether the Extremities of this Law are not often carried on beyond the true Intent and Meaning of the Act it self, for Malicious and Private Ends, to gratify Passion and Revenge?

I remember the Answer a Person gave me, who had taken out Statutes against several Persons, and some his near Relations, who had fail'd in his Debt; and when I was one time dissuading him from prosecuting a man who ow'd me Money as well as him, I us'd this Argument with him; *You know th man has nothing left to pay. That's true,* says he, *I know that well enough. To what purpose then,* said I, *will you prosecute him? Why, Revenge is sweet,* said he. —————— Now a man that will prosecute a Debtor, not as a Debtor, but by way of Revenge, such a man is, I think, not intentionally within the benefit of our Law.

In order to state the Case right, there are four Sorts of People to be consider'd in this Discourse; and the true Case is how to distinguish them.

(1.) There is the Honest Debtor, who fails by visible Necessity, Losses, Sickness, Decay of Trade, or the like.

(2.) The Knavish, Designing, or Idle, Extravagant Debtor, who fails because either he has run out his Estate in Excesses, or on purpose to cheat and abuse his Creditors.

(3.) There is the moderate Creditor, who seeks but his own, but will omit no lawful Means to gain it, and yet will hear reasonable and just Arguments and Proposals.

(4.) There is the Rigorous Severe Creditor, that values not whether the Debtor be Honest Man or Knave, Able, or Unable; but will have his Debt, *whether it be to be had or no;* without Mercy, without Compassion, full of Ill Language, Passion, and Revenge.

How to make a Law to suit to all these, is the Case: *That a necessary Favour might be shown to the first,* in Pity and Compassion to the Unfortunate, in Commiseration of Casualty and Poverty, which no man is exempt from the danger of. *That a due Rigor and Restraint be laid upon the second,* that Villany and Knavery might not be encourag'd by a Law. *That a due Care be taken of the third,* that mens Estates may, as far as can be, secur'd to them. *And due Limits set to the last,* that no man may have an unlimited Power over his Fellow-Subjects, to the Ruin of both Life and Estate.

All which I humbly conceive might be brought to pass by the following Method; to which I give the Title of

A Court of Enquiries.

This Court should consist of a select Number of Persons, to be chosen Yearly out of the several Wards of the City, by the Lord-Mayor and Court of Aldermen; and out of the several

Inns of Court, by the Lord Chancellor, or Lord Keeper, for the time being, and to consist of,

A *President,*⎫
A *Secretary,*⎬ *To be chosen by the rest, and nam'd every*
A *Treasurer,*⎭ *year also.*

A Judge of Causes for the Proof of Debts.

Fifty two Citizens, out of every Ward two; of which number to be Twelve Merchants.

Two Lawyers (Baristers at least) out of each of the Inns of Court.

That a Commission of Enquiry into Bankrupts Estates be given to these, confirm'd, and settl'd by Act of Parliament, with Power to Hear, Try, and Determine Causes as to Proof of Debts, and Disputes in Accounts between Debtor and Creditor, without Appeal.

The Office for this Court to be at *Guildhall,* where Clerks shou'd be always attending, and a *Quorum* of the Commissioners to sit *de Die in Diem,*[14] from Three to Six a Clock in the Afternoon.

To this Court every man who finds himself press'd by his Affairs, so that he cannot carry on his Business, shall apply himself as follows:

He shall go to the Secretary's Office, and give in his Name, with this short Petition:

To the Honourable the President and Commissioners of His
  Majesty's Court of Enquiries. The humble Petition of *A.B.*
  of the Parish of ⸺ in the ⸺⸺ [,] Haberdasher.
Sheweth,

THat your Petitioner being unable to carry on his Business, by reason of great Losses and Decay of Trade, and being ready and willing to make a full and entire Discovery of his whole Estate, and to deliver up the same to your Honours upon Oath, as the Law directs for the satisfaction of his Creditors, and having to that purpose entred his Name into the Books of your Office on the   of this Instant:

Your Petitioner humbly prays the Protection of this Honourable Court.

And shall ever Pray, &c.

The Secretary is to lay this Petition before the Commissioners, who shall sign it of course; and the Petitioner shall have an Officer sent home with him immediately, who shall take Possession of his House and Goods, and an exact Inventory of every thing therein shall be taken at his Entrance by other Officers also, appointed by the Court; according to which Inventory the first Officer and the Bankrupt also shall be accountable.

This Officer shall supersede even the Sheriff in Possession, excepting by an Extent for the King; only with this Provision;

That if the Sheriff be in Possession by Warrant on Judgment, obtain'd by due Course of Law, and without Fraud or Deceit, and *bona fide,* in Possession before the Debtor entred his Name in the Office, in such case the Plaintiff to have a double Dividend allotted to his Debt; for it was the fault of the Debtor to let Execution come upon his Goods before he sought for Protection; but this not to be allow'd upon Judgment confess'd.

If the Sheriff be in Possession by *fieri facias*[15] for Debt immediately due to the King, the Officer however shall quit his Possession to the Commissioners, and they shall see the King's Debt fully satisfied, before any Division be made to the Creditors.

The Officers in this case to take no Fee from the Bankrupt, nor to use any indecent or uncivil Behaviour to the Family (which is a most notorious Abuse now permitted to the Sheriffs Officers), whose Fees I have known, on small Executions, *on pretence of Civility,* amount to as much as the Debt, and yet behave themselves with unsufferable Insolence all the while.

This Officer being in Possession, the Goods may be remov'd, or not remov'd, the Shop shut up, or not shut up, as the Bankrupt upon his Reasons given to the Commissioners may desire.

The Inventory being taken, the Bankrupt shall have Fourteen Days time, and more if desir'd, upon showing good Reasons to the Commissioners, to settle his Books, and draw up his Accounts; and then shall deliver up all his Books, together with a full and true Account of his whole Estate, Real and Personal; to which Account he shall make Oath, and afterwards to any particular of it, if the Commissioners require.

After this Account given in, the Commissioners shall have Power to examine upon Oath all his Servants, or any other Person; and if it appears that he has conceal'd any thing, in breach of his Oath, to Punish him, as is hereafter specified.

Upon a fair and just Surrender of all his Estate and Effects, *bona fide*, according to the true Intent and Meaning of the Act, the Commissioners shall return to him in Money, or such of his Goods as he shall chuse, at a value by a just Appraisement, 5 *l. per Cent*. of all the Estate he surrender'd to him, together with a full and free Discharge from all his Creditors.

The Remainder of the Estate of the Debtor to be fairly and equally divided among the Creditors, who are to apply themselves to the Commissioners. The Commissioners to make a necessary Enquiry into the Nature and Circumstances of the Debts demanded, that no pretended Debt be claim'd for the private Account of the Debtor: In order to which Enquiry, they shall administer the following Oath to the Creditor, for the Proof of the Debt.

I A.B. DO SOLEMNLY SWEAR AND ATTEST, THAT THE ACCOUNT HERETO ANNEX'D IS TRUE AND RIGHT, AND EVERY ARTICLE THEREIN RIGHTLY AND TRULY STATED AND CHARG'D IN THE NAMES OF THE PERSONS TO WHOM THEY BELONG: AND THAT THERE IS NO PERSON OR NAME NAM'D, CONCEAL'D, OR ALTER'D IN THE SAID ACCOUNT BY ME, OR BY MY KNOWLEDGE, ORDER, OR CONSENT: AND THAT THE SAID —————— DOES REALLY AND bona fide OWE AND STAND INDEBTED TO ME FOR MY OWN PROPER ACCOUNT, THE FULL SUM OF ——— MENTION'D IN

THE SAID ACCOUNT, AND THAT FOR A FAIR AND
JUST VALUE MADE GOOD TO HIM, AS BY THE SAID
ACCOUNT EXPRESS'D; AND ALSO THAT I HAVE NOT
MADE OR KNOWN OF ANY PRIVATE CONTRACT,
PROMISE, OR AGREEMENT BETWEEN HIM THE SAID
——————— (OR ANY BODY FOR HIM) AND ME, OR
ANY PERSON WHATSOEVER.

So help me God.

Upon this Oath, and no Circumstances to render the Person
suspected, the Creditor shall have an unquestion'd Right to his
Dividend, which shall be made without the Delays and
Charges that attend the Commissions of Bankrupts. For,

(1.) The Goods of the Debtor shall upon the first meeting of
the Creditors, be either sold in Parcels, as they shall agree, or
divided among them in due proportion to their Debts.

(2.) What Debts are standing out, the Debtors shall receive
Summons's from the Commissioners, to pay by a certain time
limited; and in the mean time the Secretary is to transmit Accounts to the Persons owing it, appointing them a reasonable
time to consent or disprove the Account.

And every Six Months a just Dividend shall be made among
the Creditors of the Money receiv'd: And so if the Effects lye
abroad, Authentick Procurations shall be sign'd by the Bankrupt to the Commissioners, who thereupon correspond with
the Persons abroad, in whose hands such Effects are, who are
to remit the same as the Commissioners order; the Dividend
to be made, as before, every Six Months, or oftner, if the Court
see cause.

If any man thinks the Bankrupt has so much favour by
these Articles, that those who can dispense with an Oath have
an opportunity to cheat their Creditors, and that hereby too
much Encouragement is given to men to turn Bankrupt; let
them consider the Easiness of the Discovery, the Difficulty of a
Concealment, and the Penalty on the Offender.

(1.) I would have a Reward of 30 *per Cent.* be provided to

be paid to any person who should make discovery of any part of the Bankrupt's Estate conceal'd by him; which would make Discoveries easy and frequent.

(2.) Any person who should claim any Debt among the Creditors, for the account of the Bankrupt, or his Wife or Children, or with design to relieve them out of it, other or more than is, *bona fide,* due to him for Value receiv'd and to be made out; or any person who shall receive in Trust, or by Deed of Gift, any part of the Goods or other Estate of the Bankrupt, with design to preserve them for the use of the said Bankrupt, or his Wife or Children, or with design to conceal them from the Creditors, shall forfeit for every such Act 500 *l.* and have his Name publish'd as a Cheat, and a Person not fit to be credited by any man. This would make it very difficult for the Bankrupt to conceal any thing.

(3.) The Bankrupt having given his Name, and put the Officer into Possession, shall not remove out of the House any of his Books; but during the Fourteen days time which he shall have to settle the Accounts, shall every night deliver the Books into the hands of the Officer; and the Commissioners shall have liberty, if they please, to take the Books the first day, and cause Duplicates to be made, and then to give them back to the Bankrupt to settle the Accounts.

(4.) If it shall appear that the Bankrupt has given in a false Account, has conceal'd any part of his Goods or Debts, in breach of his Oath, he shall be set in the Pillory at his own door, and be imprison'd during Life, without Bail.

(5.) To prevent the Bankrupt concealing any Debts abroad, it should be enacted, That the Name of the Bankrupt being entred at the Office, where every man might search *gratis,* should be Publication enough; and that after such entry, no Discharge from the Bankrupt shou'd be allow'd in Account to any man, but whoever wou'd adventure to pay any Money to the said Bankrupt or his Order, shou'd be still Debtor to the Estate, and pay it again to the Commissioners.

And whereas Wiser Heads than mine must be employ'd to

compose this Law, if ever it be made, they will have time to consider of more ways to secure the Estate for the Creditors, and, if possible, to tye the hands of the Bankrupt yet faster.

This Law, if ever such a Happiness shou'd arise to this Kingdom, would be a present Remedy for a multitude of Evils which now we feel, and which are a sensible detriment to the Trade of this Nation.

(1.) With submission, I question not but it wou'd prevent a great number of Bankrupts, which now fall by divers Causes: For,

1. It wou'd effectually remove all crafty design'd Breakings, by which many Honest Men are ruin'd. And

2. Of course 'twou'd prevent the Fall of those Tradesmen who are forc'd to break by the Knavery of such.

(2.) It wou'd effectually suppress all those Sanctuaries and Refuges of Thieves, the *Mint, Friars, Savoy, Rules,* and the like; and that these two ways;

1. Honest Men wou'd have no need of it, here being a more Safe, Easy, and more Honourable Way to get out of Trouble.

2. Knaves shou'd have no Protection from those Places, and the Act be fortified against those Places by the following Clauses, which I have on purpose reserv'd to this Head.

Since the Provision this Court of Enquiries makes for the ease and deliverance of every Debtor who is honest, is so considerable, 'tis most certain that no man, but he who has a design to Cheat his Creditors, will refuse to accept of the Favour; and therefore it shou'd be Enacted,

That if any man who is a Tradesman or Merchant shall break or fail, or shut up Shop, or leave off Trade, and shall not either pay or secure to his Creditors their full and whole Debts, Twenty Shillings in the Pound, without Abatement or Deduction; or shall convey away their Books or Goods, in order to bring their Creditors to any Composition; or shall not apply to this Office as aforesaid, shall be guilty of Felony, and upon Conviction of the same, shall suffer as a Felon, without Benefit of Clergy.

And if any such person shall take Sanctuary either in the *Mint, Friars,* or other pretended Priviledge-Place, or shall convey thither any of their Goods as aforesaid, to secure them from their Creditors, upon Complaint thereof made to any of his Majesty's Justices of the Peace, they shall immediately grant Warrants to the Constables, *&c.* to search for the said Persons and Goods, who shall be aided and assisted by the Train'd-Bands, if need be, without any Charge to the Creditors, to search for and discover the said Persons and Goods; and whoever were aiding in the carrying in the said Goods, or whoever knowingly receiv'd either the Goods or the Person, shou'd be also guilty of Felony.

For as the Indigent Debtor is a branch of the Commonwealth, which deserves its Care, so the wilful Bankrupt is one of the *worst sort of Thieves.* And it seems a little unequal, that a poor Fellow, who for mere Want steals from his Neighbour some Trifle, shall be sent out of the Kingdom, *and sometimes out of the World;* while a sort of people who defye Justice, and violently resist the Law, shall be suffer'd to carry mens Estates away before their faces, and no Officers to be found who dare execute the Law upon them.

Any man wou'd be concern'd to hear with what Scandal and Reproach Foreigners do speak of the Impotence of our Constitution in this Point: That in a Civiliz'd Government, as ours is, the strangest Contempt of Authority is shown, that can be instanc'd in the world.

I may be a little the warmer on this Head, on account that I have been a larger Sufferer by such means than ordinary: But I appeal to all the world as to the Equity of the Case; What the difference is between having my House broken up in the Night to be robb'd, and a man coming in good Credit, and with a Proffer of Ready Money in the middle of the Day, and buying 500 *l.* of Goods, and carry them directly from my Warehouse into the *Mint,* and the next day laugh at me, and bid me defiance; yet this I have seen done: I think 'tis the justest thing in the world, that the last shou'd be esteem'd the greater Thief, and deserves most to be hang'd.

I have seen a Creditor come with his Wife and Children, and beg of the Debtor only to let him have part of his own Goods again, which he had bought, knowing and designing to break: I have seen him with Tears and Intreaties petition for his own, or but some of it, and be taunted and swore at, and denied by a sawcy insolent Bankrupt: That the poor man has been wholly ruin'd by the Cheat. 'Tis by the Villany of such, many an Honest man is undone, Families starv'd and sent a begging, and yet no Punishment prescrib'd by our Laws for it.

By the aforesaid *Commission of Enquiry,* all this might be most effectually prevented, an Honest, Indigent Tradesman preserv'd, Knavery detected, and punish'd; *Mints, Friars,* and Privilege-Places suppress'd, and without doubt a great number of Insolencies avoided and prevented; of which many more Particulars might be insisted upon, but I think these may be sufficient to lead any body into the Thought; and for the Method, I leave it to the wise Heads of the Nation, who know better than I how to state the Law to the Circumstances of the Crime.

AN ACADEMY FOR WOMEN

I Have often thought of it as one of the most barbarous Customs in the world, considering us as a Civiliz'd and a Christian Countrey, that we deny the advantages of Learning to Women. We reproach the Sex every day with Folly and Impertinence, while I am confident, had they the advantages of Education equal to us, they wou'd be guilty of less than our selves.

One wou'd wonder indeed how it shou'd happen that Women are conversible at all, since they are only beholding to Natural Parts for all their Knowledge. Their Youth is spent to teach them to Stitch and Sow, or make Bawbles: They are taught to Read indeed, and perhaps to Write their Names, or so; and that is the heighth of a Woman's Education. And I wou'd but ask any who slight the Sex for their Understanding, What is a Man (a Gentleman, I mean) good for, that is taught no more?

I need not give Instances, or examine the Character of a Gentleman with a good Estate, and of a good Family, and with tolerable Parts, and examine what Figure he makes for want of Education.

The Soul is plac'd in the Body like a rough Diamond, and must be polish'd, or the Lustre of it will never appear: And 'tis manifest, that as the Rational Soul distinguishes us from Brutes, so Education carries on the distinction, and makes some less brutish than others: This is too evident to need any demonstration. But why then shou'd Women be deni'd the benefit of Instruction? If Knowledge and Understanding had been useless additions to the Sex, God Almighty wou'd never have given them Capacities; for he made nothing needless: Besides, I wou'd ask such, What they can see in Ignorance, that they shou'd think it a necessary Ornament to a Woman? Or how much worse is a Wise Woman than a Fool? Or what has the Woman done to forfeit the Privilege of being taught? Does she plague us with her Pride and Impertinence? Why did we not let her learn, that she might have had more Wit? Shall we upbraid Women with Folly, when 'tis only the Error of this inhuman Custom, that hindred them being made wiser?

The Capacities of Women are suppos'd to be greater, and their Senses quicker than those of the Men; and what they might be capable of being bred to, is plain from some Instances of Female-Wit, which this Age is not without; which upbraids us with Injustice, and looks as if we deni'd Women the advantages of Education, for fear they shou'd *vye* with the Men in their Improvements.

To remove this Objection, and that Women might have at least a needful Opportunity of Education in all sorts of Useful Learning, I propose the Draught of an Academy for that purpose.

I know 'tis dangerous to make Publick Appearances of the Sex; they are not either to be *confin'd* or *expos'd;* the first will disagree with their Inclinations, and the last with their Reputations; and therefore it is somewhat difficult; and I doubt a Method propos'd by an Ingenious Lady, in a little Book, call'd, *Advice to the Ladies,* would be found impracticable.[16] For, saving my Respect to the Sex, the Levity, which perhaps is a little peculiar to them, at least in their Youth, will not bear the Restraint; and I am satisfi'd, nothing but the heighth of Bigotry can keep up a Nunnery: Women are extravagantly desirous of going to Heaven, and will punish their *Pretty Bodies* to get thither; but nothing else will do it; and even in that case sometimes it falls out that *Nature will prevail.*

When I talk therefore of an Academy for Women, I mean both the Model, the Teaching, and the Government; different from what is propos'd by that Ingenious Lady, for whose Proposal I have a very great Esteem, and also a great Opinion of her Wit; different too from all sorts of Religious Confinement, and above all, from *Vows of Celibacy.*

Wherefore the Academy I propose should differ but little from Publick Schools, wherein such Ladies as were willing to study, shou'd have all the advantages of Learning suitable to their Genius.

But since some Severities of Discipline more than ordinary wou'd be absolutely necessary to preserve the Reputation of the House, that Persons of Quality and Fortune might not be afraid to venture their Children thither, I shall venture to make a small Scheme by way of Essay.

The House I wou'd have built in a Form by it self, as well as in a Place by it self.

The Building shou'd be of Three plain Fronts, without any Jettings, or Bearing-Work, that the Eye might at a Glance see from one Coin to the other; the Gardens wall'd in the same Triangular Figure, with a large Moat, and but one Entrance.

When thus every part of the Situation was contriv'd as well as might be for discovery, and to render *Intrieguing* dangerous, I wou'd have no Guards, no Eyes, no Spies set over the Ladies, but shall expect them to be try'd by the Principles of Honour and strict Virtue.

And if I am ask'd, *Why?* I must ask Pardon of my own Sex for giving this reason for it:

I am so much in Charity with Women, and so well acquainted with Men, that 'tis my opinion, There needs no other Care to prevent Intrieguing, than to keep the men effectually away: For tho' *Inclination,* which we prettily call *Love,* does sometimes move a little too visibly in the Sex, and Frailty often follows; yet I think verily, *Custom,* which we miscall *Modesty,* has so far the Ascendant over the Sex, that *Solicitation* always goes before it.

> *Custom with Women 'stead of Virtue rules;*
> *It leads the Wisest, and commands the Fools:*
> *For this alone, when Inclinations reign,*
> *Tho' Virtue's fled, will Acts of Vice restrain.*
> *Only by Custom 'tis that Virtue lives,*
> *And Love requires to be ask'd, before it gives.*
> *For that which we call* Modesty, *is* Pride:
> *They scorn to ask, and hate to be deni'd.*
> *'Tis Custom thus prevails upon their Want;*
> *They'll never beg, what askt they eas'ly grant.*
> *And when the needless Ceremony's over,*
> *Themselves the Weakness of the Sex discover.*
> *If then Desires are strong, and Nature free,*
> *Keep from her Men, and Opportunity.*
> *Else 'twill be vain to curb her by Restraint;*
> *But keep the Question off, you keep the Saint.*

In short, let a Woman have never such a Coming-Principle, she will let you ask before she complies, at least if she be a Woman of any Honour.

Upon this ground I am persuaded such Measures might be taken, that the Ladies might have all the Freedom in the world within their Walls, and yet no Intrieguing, no Indecencies, nor Scandalous Affairs happen; and in order to this, the following Customs and Laws shou'd be observ'd in the Colleges; of which I wou'd propose One at least in every County in *England,* and about Ten for the City of *London.*

After the Regulation of the Form of the Building as before;

(1.) All the Ladies who enter into the House, shou'd set their Hands to the Orders of the House, to signify their Consent to submit to them.

(2.) As no Woman shou'd be receiv'd, but who declar'd her self willing, and that it was the Act of her Choice to enter her self, so no Person shou'd be confin'd to continue there a moment longer than the same voluntary Choice inclin'd her.

(3.) The Charges of the House being to be paid by the Ladies, every one that entred shou'd have only this Incumbrance, That she shou'd pay for the whole Year, tho' her mind shou'd change as to her continuance.

(4.) An Act of Parliament shou'd make it Felony without Clergy, for any man to enter by Force or Fraud into the House, or to solicit any Woman, *tho' it were to Marry,* while she was in the House. And this Law wou'd by no means be severe; because any Woman who was willing to receive the Addresses of a Man, might discharge her self of the House when she pleas'd; and on the contrary, any Woman who had occasion, might discharge her self of the Impertinent Addresses of any Person she had an Aversion to, by entring into the House.

In this House,

The Persons who Enter, shou'd be taught all sorts of Breeding suitable to both their Genius and their Quality; and in particular, *Musick* and *Dancing,* which it wou'd be cruelty to bar the Sex of, because they are their Darlings: But besides this, they shou'd be taught Languages, as particularly *French* and

Italian; and I wou'd venture the Injury of giving a Woman more Tongues than one.

They shou'd, as a particular Study, be taught all the Graces of Speech, and all the necessary Air of Conversation; which our common Education is so defective in, that I need not expose it: They shou'd be brought to read Books, and especially History, and so to read as to make them understand the world, and be able to know and judge of things when they hear of them.

To such whose Genius wou'd lead them to it, I wou'd deny no sort of Learning; but the chief thing in general is to cultivate the Understandings of the Sex, that they may be capable of all sorts of Conversation; that their Parts and Judgments being improv'd, they may be as Profitable in their Conversation as they are Pleasant.

Women, in my observation, have little or no difference in them, but as they are, or are not distinguish'd by Education. Tempers indeed may in some degree influence them, but the main distinguishing part is their Breeding.

The whole Sex are generally Quick and Sharp: I believe I may be allow'd to say generally so; for you rarely see them lumpish and heavy when they are Children, as Boys will often be. If a Woman be well-bred, and taught the proper Management of her Natural Wit, she proves generally very sensible and retentive: And without partiality, a Woman of Sense and Manners is the Finest and most Delicate Part of God's Creation; the Glory of her Maker, and the great Instance of his singular regard to Man, his Darling Creature, to whom he gave the best Gift either God could bestow, or man receive: And 'tis the sordid'st Piece of Folly and Ingratitude in the world, to withhold from the Sex the due Lustre which the advantages of Education gives to the Natural Beauty of their Minds.

A Woman well Bred and well Taught, furnish'd with the additional Accomplishments of Knowledge and Behaviour, *is a Creature without comparison;* her Society is the Emblem of sublimer Enjoyments; her Person is Angelick, and her Conversation heavenly; she is all Softness and Sweetness, Peace, Love, Wit, and Delight: She is every way suitable to the sublimest Wish; and the man that has such a one to his Portion, has nothing to do but to rejoice in her, and be thankful.

On the other hand, Suppose her to be the *very same* Woman, and rob her of the Benefit of Education, and it follows thus;

If her Temper be Good, want of Education makes her Soft and Easy.

Her Wit, for want of Teaching, makes her Impertinent and Talkative.

Her Knowledge, for want of Judgment and Experience, makes her Fanciful and Whimsical.

If her Temper be Bad, want of Breeding makes her worse, and she grows Haughty, Insolent, and Loud.

If she be Passionate, want of Manners makes her Termagant, and a Scold, *which is much at one with Lunatick.*

If she be Proud, want of Discretion (which still is Breeding) makes her Conceited, Fantastick, and Ridiculous.

And from these she degenerates to be Turbulent, Clamorous, Noisy, Nasty, *and the Devil.*

Methinks Mankind for their own sakes, since say what we will of the Women, we all think fit one time or other to be concern'd with 'em, shou'd take some care to breed them up to be *suitable* and *serviceable,* if they expected no such thing as *Delight* from 'em. Bless us! What Care do we take to Breed up a good Horse, and to Break him well! and what a Value do we put upon him when it is done, and all because he shou'd be fit for our use! and why not a Woman? Since all her Ornaments and Beauty, without suitable Behaviour, is a Cheat in Nature, like the false Tradesman, who puts the best of his Goods uppermost, that the Buyer may think the rest are of the same Goodness.

Beauty of the Body, which is the Womens Glory, seems to be now unequally bestow'd, and Nature, or rather Providence, to lye under some Scandal about it, as if 'twas given a Woman for a Snare to Men, and so make a kind of a *She-Devil* of her:

Because they say Exquisite Beauty is *rarely* given with Wit; *more rarely* with Goodness of Temper, and *never at all* with Modesty. And some, pretending to justify the Equity of such a Distribution, will tell us 'tis the Effect of the Justice of Providence in dividing particular Excellencies among all his Creatures, *share and share alike, as it were,* that all might for something or other be acceptable to one another, else some wou'd be despis'd.

I think both these Notions false; and yet the last, which has the shew of Respect to Providence, is the worst; for it supposes Providence to be Indigent and Empty; as if it had not wherewith to furnish all the Creatures it had made, but was fain to be parcimonious in its Gifts, and distribute them by *piecemeal,* for fear of being exhausted.

If I may venture my Opinion against an almost universal Notion, I wou'd say, Most men mistake the Proceedings of Providence in this case, and all the world at this day are mistaken in their Practice about it. And because the Assertion is very bold, I desire to explain my self.

That Almighty First Cause which made us all, is certainly the Fountain of Excellence, as it is of Being, and by an Invisible Influence could have diffused Equal Qualities and Perfections to all the Creatures it has made, as the Sun does its Light, without the least Ebb or Diminution to himself; and has given indeed to every individual sufficient to the Figure his Providence had design'd him in the world.

I believe it might be defended, if I should say, That I do suppose God has given to all Mankind equal Gifts and Capacities, in that he has given them all *Souls* equally capable; and that the whole difference in Mankind proceeds either from Accidental Difference in the Make of their Bodies, or from the *foolish Difference* of Education.

1. *From Accidental Difference in Bodies.* I wou'd avoid discoursing here of the Philosophical Position of the Soul in the Body: But if it be true as Philosophers do affirm, That the Understanding and Memory is dilated or contracted accord-

ing to the accidental Dimensions of the Organ through which
'tis convey'd; then tho' God has given a Soul as capable to me
as another, yet if I have any Natural Defect in those Parts of
the Body by which the Souls shou'd act, I may have the same
Soul infus'd as another man, and yet he be a Wise Man, and
I a very Fool. *For example,* If a Child naturally have a Defect
in the Organ of Hearing, so that he cou'd never distinguish
any Sound, that Child shall never be able to speak or read, tho'
it have a Soul capable of all the Accomplishments in the
world. The Brain is the Centre of the Souls actings, where all
the distinguishing Faculties of it reside; and 'tis observable, A
man who has a narrow contracted Head, in which there is not
room for the due and necessary Operations of Nature by the
Brain, is never a man of very great Judgment; and that Proverb, *A Great Head and Little Wit,* is not meant by Nature, but
is a Reproof upon Sloth; as if one shou'd, by way of wonder,
say, *Fye, fye, you that have a Great Head, have but Little
Wit, that's strange! that must certainly be your own fault.*
From this Notion I do believe there is a great matter in the
Breed of Men and Women; not that Wise Men shall always get
Wise Children; but I believe Strong and Healthy Bodies have
the Wisest Children; and Sickly Weakly Bodies affect the Wits
as well as the Bodies of their Children. We are easily persuaded to believe this in the Breed of Horses, Cocks, Dogs,
and other Creatures; and I believe 'tis as visible in Men.

But to come closer to the business; the great distinguishing
difference which is seen in the world between Men and
Women, is in their Education; and this is manifested by com-
paring it with the difference between one Man or Woman,
and another.

And herein it is that I take upon me to make such a bold
Assertion, That all the World are mistaken in their Practice
about Women: For I cannot think that God Almighty ever
made them so delicate, so glorious Creatures, and furnish'd
them with such Charms, so Agreeable and so Delightful to
Mankind, with Souls capable of the same Accomplishments

with Men, and all to be only Stewards of our Houses, *Cooks and Slaves.*

Not that I am for exalting the Female Government in the least: But, in short, *I wou'd have Men take Women for Companions, and Educate them to be fit for it.* A Woman of Sense and Breeding will scorn as much to encroach upon the Prerogative of the Man, as a Man of Sense will scorn to oppress the *Weakness* of the Woman. But if the Womens Souls were refin'd and improv'd by Teaching, that word wou'd be lost; to say, *The Weakness of the Sex,* as to Judgment, wou'd be Nonsense; for Ignorance and Folly wou'd be no more to be found among Women than Men. I remember a Passage which I heard from a very Fine Woman, she had Wit and Capacity enough, and Extraordinary Shape and Face, and a Great Fortune, but had been cloyster'd up all her time, and for fear of being stoll'n had not had the liberty of being taught the common necessary knowledge of Womens Affairs; and when she came to converse in the world, her Natural Wit made her so sensible of the want of Education, that she gave this short Reflection on her self:

I am asham'd to talk with my very Maids, says she, *for I don't know when they do right or wrong: I had more need go to School, than be Married.*

I need not enlarge on the Loss the Defect of Education is to the Sex, nor argue the Benefit of the contrary Practice; 'tis a thing will be more easily granted than remedied: This Chapter is but an Essay at the thing, and I refer the Practice to those Happy Days, if ever they shall be, when men shall be wise enough to mend it.

THE

True-Born *Englishman.*

A

S A T Y R.

Statuimus Pacem, & Securitatem, & Concordiam Judicium & Justitiam inter Anglos *&* Normannos, Francos *&* Britones, Walliæ, *&* Cornubiæ, Pictos *&* Scotos, Albaniæ, *similiter inter* Francos *&* Insulanos *Provincias, & Patrias, quæ pertinent ad Coronam nostram, & inter omnes nobis Subjectos, firmiter & inviolabiliter observari.*
Charta Regis Willielmi Conquisitoris de Pacis Publica, *Cap.* I.

Printed in the Year MDCC.

THE
TRUE-BORN
ENGLISHMAN.
A
SATYR.

Statuimus Pacem, & Securitatem, & Concordiam Judicium & Justitiam inter *Anglos & Normannos, Francos & Britones, Walliae, & Cornubiae, Pictos & Scotos, Albaniae,* similiter inter Francos & Insulanos Provincias, & Patrias, quae pertinent ad Coronam nostrum, & inter omnes nobis Subjectos, firmiter & inviolabiliter observari.
Charta Regis Willielmi Conquisitoris de Pacis Publica, Cap. I.[1]

Printed in the Year MDCC.

The title is taken from *Richard II*, I, iii, 309. Defoe's reply to John Tutchin's attack on William III in *The Foreigners* (1700) became his most famous poem. The poem was published in January 1701 and sold, Defoe estimated, more than 80,000 copies. The ninth edition and those following omitted the attack on Tutchin as Shamwig and blunted the attack on Sir Charles Duncombe.

The Preface

THE End of Satyr is Reformation: And the Author, tho he doubts the Work of Conversion is at a general Stop, has put his Hand to the Plow.

I expect a Storm of Ill Language from the Fury of the Town, and especially from those whose English *Talent it is to Rail: And without being taken for a Conjurer, I may venture to foretell, That I shall be Cavil'd at about my* Mean Stile, Rough Verse, *and* Incorrect Language; *Things I might indeed have taken more Care in. But the Book is Printed; and tho I see some Faults, 'tis too late to mend them. And this is all I think needful to say to them.*

Possibly somebody may take me for a Dutchman; *in which they are mistaken: But I am one that would be glad to see* Englishmen *behave themselves better to Strangers, and to Governors also; that one might not be reproach'd in Foreign Countries, for belonging to a* Nation that wants Manners.

I assure you, Gentlemen, *Strangers use us better abroad; and we can give no reason but our Ill Nature for the contrary here.*

Methinks an Englishman, *who is so proud of being call'd* A Goodfellow, *shou'd be civil: And it cannot be denied but we are in many Cases, and particularly to Strangers, the Churlishest People alive.*

As to Vices, who can dispute our Intemperance, *while an* Honest Drunken Fellow *is a Character in a man's Praise? All our Reformations are Banters, and will be so, till our Magistrates and Gentry Reform themselves by way of Example; then, and not till then, they may be expected to punish others without* blushing.

As to our Ingratitude, *I desire to be understood of that particular People, who pretending to be Protestants, have all along endeavour'd to reduce the Liberties and Religion of this Nation into the Hands of King* James *and his Popish Powers:*

Together with such who enjoy the Peace and Protection of the present Government, and yet abuse and affront the King who procur'd it, and openly profess their Uneasiness under him: These, by whatever Names or Titles they are dignified or distinguish'd, are the People aim'd at: Nor do I disown, but that it is so much the Temper of an Englishman to abuse his Benefactor, that I could be glad to see it rectified.

They who think I have been guilty of any Error, in exposing the Crimes of my own Countrymen to themselves, may among many honest Instances of the like nature, find the same thing in Mr. Cowly, in his Imitation of the second Olympick Ode of Pindar: [2] *His Words are these;*

> But in this Thankless World, the Givers
> Are envi'd even by th' Receivers:
> 'Tis now the Cheap and Frugal Fashion,
> Rather to hide than pay an Obligation.
> Nay, 'tis much worse than so;
> It now an *Artifice* doth grow,
> *Wrongs* and *Outrages* to do,
> Lest men should think we *Owe*.

The Introduction

SPeak, *Satyr;* for there's none can tell like thee,
Whether 'tis Folly, Pride, or Knavery,
That makes this discontented Land appear
Less happy now in Times of Peace, than War:[3]
Why Civil Feuds disturb the Nation more
Than all our Bloody Wars have done before.
    Fools out of Favour grudge at Knaves in Place,
And men are always honest in Disgrace:
The Court-Preferments make men Knaves in course:
But they which wou'd be in them wou'd be worse.
'Tis not at Foreigners that we repine,

Wou'd Foreigners their Perquisites resign:
The Grand Contention's plainly to be seen,
To get some men put out, and some put in.
For this our S[enato]rs make long Harangues,
And florid M[embe]rs whet their polish'd Tongues.
Statesmen are always sick of one Disease;
And a good Pension gives them present Ease.
That's the Specifick makes them all content
With any King, and any Government.
Good Patriots at Court-Abuses rail,
And all the Nation's Grievances bewail:
But when the *Sov'reign Balsam*'s once appli'd,
The Zealot never fails to change his Side.
And when he must the *Golden Key*⁴ resign,
The *Railing Spirit* comes about again.
   Who shall this Bubbl'd Nation disabuse,
While they their own Felicities refuse?
Who at the Wars have made such mighty Pother,
And now are falling out with one another:
With needless Fears the Jealous Nation fill,
And always have been sav'd against their Will:
Who Fifty Millions *Sterling* have disburs'd,
To be with Peace and too much Plenty curs'd.
Who their Old Monarch eagerly undo,
And yet uneasily obey the New.
Search, *Satyr*, search, a deep Incision make;
The Poyson's strong, the Antidote's too weak.
'Tis pointed Truth must manage this Dispute,
And down-right English *Englishmen* confute.
   Whet thy just Anger at the Nation's Pride;
And with keen Phrase repel the Vicious Tide.
To *Englishmen* their own beginnings show,
And ask them why they slight their Neighbours so.
Go back to Elder Times, and Ages past,
And Nations into long Oblivion cast;
To Old *Britannia*'s Youthful Days retire,

And there for *True-Born Englishmen* enquire.
Britannia freely will disown the Name,
And hardly knows her self from whence they came:
Wonders that They of all men shou'd pretend
To *Birth* and *Blood*, and for a Name contend.
Go back to Causes where our Follies dwell,
And fetch the dark Original from Hell:
Speak, *Satyr*, for there's none like thee can tell.

THE *TRUE-BORN ENGLISHMAN*

PART I

*WHereever God erects a House of Prayer,
The Devil always builds a Chappel there:
And 'twill be found upon Examination,
The latter has the largest Congregation:
For ever since he first debauch'd the Mind,
He made a perfect Conquest of Mankind.
With Uniformity of Service, he
Reigns with a general Aristocracy.
No Nonconforming Sects disturb his Reign,
For of his Yoak there's very few complain.
He knows the Genius and the Inclination,
And matches proper Sins for ev'ry Nation.
He needs no Standing-Army Government;
He always rules us by our own Consent:
His Laws are easy, and his gentle Sway
Makes it exceeding pleasant to obey.
The List of his Viceregents and Commanders,
Outdoes your *Caesars*, or your *Alexanders*.
They never fail of his Infernal Aid,
And he's as certain ne're to be betray'd.

---

* An *English* Proverb, *Where God has a Church, the Devil has a Chappel*.[5]

Through all the World they spread his vast Command,
And Death's Eternal Empire's maintain'd.
They rule so politickly and so well,
As if they were L[ords] J[ustices] of Hell.
Duly divided to debauch Mankind,
And plant Infernal Dictates in his Mind.
   Pride, the First Peer, and President of Hell,
To his share *Spain,* the largest Province, fell.
The subtile Prince thought fittest to bestow
On these the Golden Mines of *Mexico;*
With all the Silver Mountains of *Peru;*
Wealth which would in wise hands the World undo:
Because he knew their Genius was such;
Too Lazy and too Haughty to be Rich.
So proud a People, so above their Fate,
That if reduc'd to beg, they'll beg in State.
Lavish of Money, to be counted Brave,
And Proudly starve, because they scorn to save.
Never was Nation in the World before,
So very Rich, and yet so very Poor.
   Lust chose the Torrid Zone of *Italy,*
Where Blood ferments in Rapes and Sodomy:
Where swelling Veins o'reflow with living Streams,
With Heat impregnate from *Vesuvian* Flames:
Whose flowing Sulphur forms Infernal Lakes,
And human Body of the Soil partakes.
There Nature ever burns with hot Desires,
Fann'd with Luxuriant Air from Subterranean Fires:
Here undisturb'd in Floods of scalding Lust,
Th' Infernal King reigns with Infernal Gust.
   Drunk'ness, the Darling Favourite of Hell,
Chose *Germany* to rule; and rules so well,
No Subjects more obsequiously obey,
None please so well, or are so pleas'd as they.
The cunning Artist manages so well,
He lets them Bow to Heav'n, and Drink to Hell.

If but to Wine and him they Homage pay,
He cares not to what Deity they Pray,
What God they worship most, or in what way.
Whether by *Luther, Calvin,* or by *Rome,*
They sail for Heav'n, by Wine he steers them home.

Ungovern'd Passion settled first in *France,*
Where Mankind lives in haste, and thrives by Chance.
A *Dancing Nation,* Fickle and Untrue:
Have oft undone themselves, and others too:
Prompt the Infernal Dictates to obey,
And in Hell's Favour none more great than they.

The *Pagan* World he blindly leads away,
And Personally rules with Arbitrary Sway:
The Mask thrown off, *Plain Devil* his Title stands;
And what elsewhere he Tempts, he there Commands.
There with full Gust th' Ambition of his Mind
Governs, as he of old in Heav'n design'd.
Worshipp'd as God, his *Painim*[6] *Altars* smoke,
Embru'd with Blood of those that him Invoke.

The rest by Deputies he rules as well,
And plants the distant Colonies of Hell.
By them his secret Power he maintains,
And binds the World in his Infernal Chains.

By Zeal the *Irish;* and the *Rush* by Folly:
Fury the *Dane:* The *Swede* by Melancholly:
By stupid Ignorance, the *Muscovite:*
The *Chinese* by a *Child of Hell,* call'd Wit:
Wealth makes the *Persian* too Effeminate:
And Poverty the *Tartars* Desperate:
The *Turks* and *Moors* by *Mah'met* he subdues:
And God has giv'n him leave to rule the Jews:
Rage rules the *Portuguese;* and Fraud the *Scotch:*
Revenge the *Pole;* and Avarice the *Dutch.*

Satyr be kind, and draw a silent Veil,
Thy *Native England's* Vices to conceal:

Or if that Task's impossible to do,
At least be just, and show her Virtues too;
Too Great the first, Alas! the last too Few.

   England unknown as yet, unpeopled lay;
Happy, had she remain'd so to this day,
And not to ev'ry Nation been a Prey.
Her Open Harbours, and her Fertile Plains,
The Merchants Glory these, and those the Swains,
To ev'ry Barbarous Nation have betray'd her,
Who conquer her as oft as they Invade her.
So Beauty guarded but by Innocence,
That ruins her which should be her Defence.

   Ingratitude, a Devil of *Black Renown,*
Possess'd her very early for his own.
An Ugly, Surly, Sullen, Selfish Spirit,
Who Satan's worst Perfections does inherit:
Second to him in Malice and in Force,
All *Devil without,* and all within him *Worse.*

   He made her First-born Race to be so rude,
And suffer'd her to be so oft subdu'd:
By sev'ral Crowds of Wandring Thieves o're-run,
Often unpeopl'd, and as oft undone.
While ev'ry Nation that her Pow'rs reduc'd,
Their Languages and Manners introduc'd.
From whose mixt Relicks our compounded Breed,
By Spurious Generation does succeed;
Making a Race uncertain and unev'n,
Deriv'd from all the Nations under Heav'n.

   The *Romans* first with *Julius Caesar* came,
Including all the Nations of that Name,
Gauls, Greeks, and *Lombards;* and by Computation,
Auxiliaries or Slaves of ev'ry Nation.
With *Hengist, Saxons; Danes* with *Sueno* came,
In search of Plunder, not in search of Fame.
Scots, Picts, and *Irish* from th' Hibernian Shore:

And Conqu'ring *William* brought the *Normans* o're.
  All these their Barb'rous Offspring left behind,
The Dregs of Armies, they of all Mankind;
Blended with *Britains* who before were here,
Of whom the *Welsh* ha' blest the Character.
  From this Amphibious Ill-born Mob began
That vain ill-natur'd thing, an Englishman.
The Customs, Sirnames, Languages, and Manners,
Of all these Nations are their own Explainers:
Whose Relicks are so lasting and so strong,
They ha' left a *Shiboleth* upon our Tongue;
By which with easy search you may distinguish
Your *Roman-Saxon-Danish-Norman* English.
  The great Invading *Norman** let us know
What Conquerors in After-Times might do.
To ev'ry *Musqueteer*** he brought to Town,
He gave the Lands which never were his own.
When first the *English* Crown he did obtain,
He did not send his *Dutchmen* home again.
No Reassumptions in his Reign were known,
D'avenant[7] might there ha' let his Book alone.
No Parliament his Army cou'd disband;
He rais'd no Money, for he paid in Land.
He gave his Legions their Eternal Station,
And made them all Freeholders of the Nation.
He canton'd out the Country to his Men,
And ev'ry Soldier was a Denizen.
The Rascals thus enrich'd, he call'd them *Lords,*
To please their Upstart Pride with new-made Words;
And *Doomsday-Book* his Tyranny records.
  And here begins the Ancient Pedigree
That so exalts our Poor Nobility:
'Tis that from some *French* Trooper they derive,
Who with the *Norman* Bastard did arrive:

* W^m *the Conq.*
** *Or Archer.*

The Trophies of the Families appear;
Some show the Sword, the Bow, and some the Spear,
Which their Great Ancestor, *forsooth*, did wear.

These in the Heralds Register remain,
Their Noble Mean Extraction to explain.
Yet who the Hero was, no man can tell,
Whether a Drummer or a Colonel:
The silent Record blushes to reveal
Their Undescended Dark Original.
     But grant the best, How came the Change to pass;
A *True-Born Englishman* of *Norman* Race?
A *Turkish* Horse can show more History,
To prove his Well-descended Family.
Conquest, as by the *Moderns 'tis exprest,
May give a Title to the Lands possest:
But that the Longest Sword shou'd be so Civil,
To make a *Frenchman English,* that's the Devil.
     These are the Heroes that despise the *Dutch,*
And rail at new-come Foreigners so much;
Forgetting that themselves are all deriv'd
From the most Scoundrel Race that ever liv'd.
A horrid Medly of Thieves and Drones,
Who ransack'd Kingdoms, and dispeopl'd Towns.
The *Pict* and Painted *Britain,* Treach'rous *Scot,*
By Hunger, Theft, and Rapine, hither brought.
Norwegian Pirates, Buccaneering *Danes,*
Whose Red-hair'd Offspring ev'ry where remains.
Who join'd with *Norman-French,* compound the Breed
From whence your *True-Born Englishman* proceed.
     And lest by Length of Time it be pretended,
The Climate may this Modern Breed ha' mended,
Wise Providence, to keep us where we are,
Mixes us daily with exceeding Care:
We have been *Europe*'s Sink, *the Jakes* where she

* *Dr.* Sherl. *De Facto.*[8]

Voids all her Offal Out-cast Progeny.
From our Fifth *Henry*'s time, the Strolling Bands
Of banish'd Fugitives from Neighb'ring Lands,
Have here a certain Sanctuary found:
The Eternal Refuge of the Vagabond.
Where in but half a common Age of Time,
Borr'wing new Blood and Manners from the Clime,
Proudly they learn all Mankind to contemn,
And all their Race are *True-Born Englishmen.*

    Dutch, Walloons, Flemings, Irishmen, and *Scots,*
Vaudois and *Valtolins,* and *Hugonots,*
In good Queen *Bess*'s Charitable Reign,
Suppli'd us with Three hundred thousand Men.
Religion, *God we thank thee,* sent them hither,
Priests, Protestants, the Devil and all together:
Of all Professions, and of ev'ry Trade,
All that were persecuted or afraid;
Whether for Debt or other Crimes they fled,
David at *Hackelah* was still their Head.

    The Offspring of this Miscellaneous Crowd,
Had not their new Plantations long enjoy'd,
But they grew *Englishmen,* and rais'd their Votes
At Foreign Shoals of *Interloping Scots.*
The *Royal Branch from Pict-land did succeed,
With Troops of *Scots* and Scabs from *North-by-Tweed.*
The Seven first Years of his Pacifick Reign,
Made him and half his Nation *Englishmen.*
Scots from the *Northern* Frozen Banks of *Tay,*
With Packs and Plods came *Whigging* all away:
Thick as the Locusts which in *Egypt* swarm'd,
With Pride and hungry Hopes compleatly arm'd:
With Native Truth, Diseases, and No Money,
Plunder'd our *Canaan* of the Milk and Honey.
Here they grew quickly Lords and Gentlemen,
And all their Race are *True-Born Englishmen.*

* K[ing]. J[ames]. I.

   The Civil Wars, the common Purgative,
Which always use to make the Nation thrive,
Made way for all that strolling Congregation,
Which throng'd in Pious *Ch[arle]s*'s Restoration.   K. *C*. II.
The *Royal Refugeé* our Breed restores,
With *Foreign Courtiers*, and with *Foreign Whores:*
And carefully repeopled us again,
Throughout his Lazy, Long, Lascivious Reign,
With such a blest and True-born *English* Fry,
As much Illustrates our Nobility.
A Gratitude which will so black appear,
As future Ages must abhor to hear:
When they look back on all that Crimson Flood,
Which stream'd in *Lindsey*'s, and *Caernarvon*'s Blood:
Bold *Strafford, Cambridge, Chapel, Lucas, Lisle*,[9]
Who crown'd in Death his Father's Fun'ral Pile.
The Loss of whom, in order to supply
With True-Born *English* Nobility,
Six Bastard Dukes survive his Luscious Reign,
The Labours of Italian *C[astlemai]n,*
French P[ortsmout]h, Tabby S[co]t, and *Cambrian*.[10]
Besides the Num'rous Bright and Virgin Throng,
Whose Female Glories shade them from my Song.
   This Offspring, if one Age they multiply,
May half the House with *English* Peers supply:
There with true *English* Pride they contemn
S[chomber]g and P[ortlan]d, new-made Noblemen.[11]
   French Cooks, *Scotch* Pedlars, and *Italian* Whores,
Were all made Lords, or Lords Progenitors.
Beggars and Bastards by his new Creation,
Much multipli'd the Peerage of the Nation;
Who will be all, e're one short Age runs o're,
As True-Born Lords as those we had before.
   Then to recruit the Commons he prepares,
And heal the latent Breaches of the Wars:
The Pious Purpose better to advance,

H'invites the banish'd Protestants of *France:*
Hither for God's sake and their own they fled,
Some for Religion came, and some for Bread:
Two hundred thousand Pair of Wooden Shooes,
Who, God be thank'd, had nothing left to lose;
To Heaven's great Praise did for Religion fly,
To make us starve our Poor in Charity.
In ev'ry Port they plant their fruitful Train,
To get a Race of *True-Born Englishmen:*
Whose Children will, when riper Years they see,
Be as Ill-natur'd and as Proud as we:
Call themselves *English,* Foreigners despise,
Be surly like us all, and just as wise.

 Thus from a Mixture of all Kinds began,
That Het'rogeneous Thing, *An Englishman:*
In eager Rapes, and furious Lust begot,
Betwixt a Painted *Britton* and a *Scot:*
Whose gend'ring Offspring quickly learnt to bow,
And yoke their Heifers to the *Roman* Plough:
From whence a Mongrel half-bred Race there came,
With neither Name nor Nation, Speech or Fame.
In whose hot Veins new Mixtures quickly ran,
Infus'd betwixt a *Saxon* and a *Dane.*
While their Rank Daughters, to their Parents just,
Receiv'd all Nations with Promiscuous Lust.
This Nauseous Brood directly did contain
The well-extracted Blood of *Englishmen.*

 Which Medley canton'd in a Heptarchy,
A Rhapsody of Nations to supply,
Among themselves maintain'd eternal Wars,
And still the Ladies lov'd the Conquerors.

 The *Western* Angles all the rest subdu'd;
A bloody Nation, barbarous and rude:
Who by the Tenure of the Sword possest
One Part of *Britain,* and subdu'd the rest.
And as great things denominate the small,

The Conqu'ring Part gave Title to the Whole.
The *Scot, Pict, Britain, Roman, Dane* submit,
And with the *English-Saxon* all unite:
And these the Mixture have so close pursu'd,
The very Name and Memory's subdu'd:
No *Roman* now, no *Britain* does remain;
Wales strove to separate, but strove in vain:
The silent Nations undistinguish'd fall,
And *Englishman's* the common Name for all.
Fate jumbl'd them together, *God knows how;*
Whate're they were, they're *True-Born English* now.

 The Wonder which remains is at our Pride,
To value that which all wise men deride.
For *Englishmen* to boast of Generation,
Cancels their Knowledge, and lampoons the Nation.
A *True-Born Englishman's* a Contradiction,
In Speech an Irony, in Fact a Fiction.
A Banter made to be a Test of Fools,
Which those that use it justly ridicules.
A Metaphor invented to express
A man *a-kin* to all the Universe.

 For as the *Scots,* as Learned Men ha' said,
Throughout the World their Wandring Seed ha' spread;
So open-handed *England,* 'tis believ'd,
Has all the Gleanings of the World receiv'd.
Some think of *England* 'twas our Saviour meant,
The Gospel should to all the World be sent:
Since when the blessed Sound did hither reach,
They to all Nations might be said to Preach.

 'Tis well that Virtue gives Nobility,
Else God knows where we had our Gentry;
Since scarce one Family is left alive,
Which does not from some Foreigner derive.
Of Sixty thousand *English* Gentlemen,
Whose Names and Arms in Registers remain,
We challenge all our Heralds to declare

Ten Families which *English-Saxon* are.
   France justly boasts the Ancient Noble Line
Of *Bourbon, Mommorency,* and *Lorrain.*
The *Germans* too their House of *Austria* show,
And *Holland* their Invincible *Nassau.*
Lines which in Heraldry were Ancient grown,
Before the Name of *Englishman* was known.
Even *Scotland* too her Elder Glory shows,
Her *Gourdons, Hamiltons,* and her *Monroes;*
Douglas, Mackays, and *Grahams,* Names well known,
Long before Ancient *England* knew her own.
   But *England,* Modern to the last degree, ⎫
Borrows or makes her own Nobility,   ⎬
And yet she boldly boasts of Pedigree: ⎭
Repines that Foreigners are put upon her,
And talks of her Antiquity and Honour:
Her S[ackvi]lls, S[avi]ls, C[eci]ls, De[la] M[ee]rs, ⎫
M[ohu]ns and M[ontag]ues, D[ura]s and V[ee]rs, ⎬
Not one have *English* Names, yet all are *English* Peers. ⎭
Your H[oublo]ns, P[api]llons, and L[ethu]liers, ⎫
Pass now for True-Born *English* Knights and Squires, ⎬
And make good Senate-Members, or Lord-Mayors. ⎭
Wealth, howsoever, got in *England* makes
Lords of Mechanicks, Gentlemen of Rakes.
Antiquity and Birth are needless here;
'Tis Impudence and Money makes a P[ee]r.
   Innumerable City-Knights we know,
From *Blewcoat Hospitals* and *Bridewell* flow.[12]
Draymen and Porters fill the City Chair,
And Footboys Magisterial Purple wear.
Fate has but very small Distinction set
Betwixt the *Counter* and the Coronet.
Tarpaulin Lords, Pages of high Renown,
Rise up by Poor Mens Valour, not their own.
Great Families of yesterday we show,
And Lords, whose Parents were *the Lord knows who.*

PART II

THE Breed's describ'd: Now, *Satyr,* if you can,
Their Temper show, for *Manners make the Man.*
Fierce as the *Britain,* as the *Roman* Brave;
And less inclin'd to Conquer than to Save:
Eager to fight, and lavish of their Blood;
And equally of *Fear and Forecast* void.
The *Pict* has made 'em Sowre, the *Dane* Morose;
False from the *Scot,* and from the *Norman* worse.
What Honesty they have, the *Saxon* gave them,
And That, now they grow old, begins to leave them.
The Climate makes them Terrible and Bold;
And *English* Beef their Courage does uphold:
No Danger can their Daring Spirit pall,
Always provided that their Belly's full.
   In close Intriegues their Faculty's but weak,
For gen'rally whate're they know, they speak:
And often their own Councils undermine
By their Infirmity, and not design.
From whence the Learned say it does proceed,
That *English* Treasons never can succeed:
For they're so open-hearted, you may know
Their own most secret Thoughts, and others too.
   The Lab'ring Poor, in spight of Double Pay,
Are Sawcy, Mutinous, and Beggarly:
So lavish of their Money and their Time,
That want of Forecast is the Nation's Crime.
Good Drunken Company is their Delight;
And what they get by Day, they spend by Night.
Dull Thinking seldom does their Heads engage,
But Drink their Youth away, and hurry on Old Age.
Empty of all good Husbandry and Sense;
And void of Manners most, when void of Pence.
Their strong Aversion to Behaviour's such,

They always talk too little, or too much.
So dull, they never take the pains to think;
And seldom are good-natur'd, *but in Drink*.
  In *English* Ale their dear Enjoyment lies,
For which they'll starve themselves and Families.
  An *Englishman* will fairly drink as much
As will maintain Two Families of *Dutch:*
Subjecting all their Labours to the Pots;
The greatest Artists are the greatest Sots.
  The Country Poor do by Example live;
The Gentry Lead them, and the Clergy drive:
What may we not from such Examples hope?
The Landlord is their God, the Priest their Pope.
A Drunken Clergy, and a Swearing Bench,
Has giv'n the Reformation such a Drench,
As wise men think there is some cause to doubt,
Will purge Good Manners and Religion out.
  Nor do the Poor alone their Liquor prize,
The Sages join in this great Sacrifice.
The Learned Men who study *Aristotle,*
Correct him with an Explanation-Bottle;
Praise *Epicurus* rather than *Lysander,*
And *Aristippus more than *Alexander*.
The Doctors too their *Galen* here resign,
And gen'rally prescribe *Specifick Wine*.
The Graduates Study's grown an easier Task,
While for the *Urinal* they toss the *Flask*.
The Surgeons Art grows plainer ev'ry Hour,
And Wine's the Balm which into Wounds they pour.
  Poets long since *Parnassus* have forsaken,
And say the Ancient Bards were all mistaken.
Apollo's lately abdicate and fled,
And good King *Bacchus* reigneth in his stead:
He does the Chaos of the Head refine,

* The Drunkards Name for Canary.[13]

And Atom-Thoughts jump into Words by Wine:
The Inspiration's of a finer Nature;
As Wine must needs excel *Parnassus* Water.
  Statesmen their weighty Politicks refine,
And Soldiers raise their Courages by Wine.
Caecilia[14] gives her Choristers their Choice,
And lets them all drink Wine to clear the Voice.
  Some think the Clergy first found out the way,
And Wine's the only Spirit by which they Pray.
But others less prophane than so, agree,
It clears the Lungs, and helps the Memory:
And therefore all of them Divinely think,
Instead of Study, 'tis as well to drink.
  And here I wou'd be very glad to know,
Whether our *Asgilites*[15] may drink or no.
Th' Enlight'ning Fumes of Wine would certainly
Assist them much *when they begin to fly:*
Or if a Fiery Chariot shou'd appear,
Inflam'd by Wine, they'd ha' the less to fear.
  Even the gods themselves, as Mortals say,
Were they on Earth, wou'd be as drunk as they:
Nectar would be no more Celestial Drink,
They'd all take Wine, to teach them how to Think.
But *English* Drunkards, gods and men outdo,
Drink their Estates away, and Senses too.
Colon's in Debt, and if his Friends should fail
To help him out, must dye at last in Gaol:
His *Wealthy Uncle* sent a Hundred Nobles,
To pay his Trifles off, and rid him of his Troubles:
But *Colon*, like a *True-Born Englishman*,
Drank all the Money out in bright Champaign;
And *Colon* does in Custody remain.
Drunk'ness has been the Darling of the Realm,
E're since a Drunken Pilot had the Helm.
  In their Religion they are so unev'n,

That each man goes *his own By-way to Heav'n.*
Tenacious of Mistakes to that degree,
That ev'ry man pursues it sep'rately,
And fancies none can find the Way but he:
So shy of one another they are grown,
As if they strove to get to Heav'n alone.
Rigid and Zealous, Positive and Grave,
And ev'ry Grace, but Charity, they have:
This makes them so Ill-natur'd and Uncivil,
That all men think an *Englishman* the Devil.
  Surly to Strangers, Froward to their Friend;
Submit to Love with a reluctant Mind;
Resolv'd to be ungrateful and unkind.
If by Necessity reduc'd to ask,
The Giver has the difficultest Task:
For what's bestow'd they awkwardly receive,
And always Take less freely than they Give.
The Obligation is their highest Grief;
And never love, where they accept Relief.
So sullen in their Sorrows, that 'tis known,
They'll rather dye than their Afflictions own:
And if reliev'd, it is too often true,
That they'll abuse their Benefactors too:
For in Distress their Haughty Stomach's such,
They hate to see themselves oblig'd too much.
Seldom contented, often in the wrong;
Hard to be pleas'd at all, and never long.
  If your Mistakes their ill Opinion gain,
No Merit can their Favour reobtain:
And if they're not Vindictive in their Fury,
'Tis their unconstant Temper does secure ye:
Their Brain's so cool, their Passion seldom burns;
For all's condens'd before the Flame returns:
The Fermentation's of so weak a Matter,
The Humid damps the Fume, and runs it all to Water.
So tho the Inclination may be strong,

They're pleas'd by Fits, and never angry long.
   Then if Good Nature shows some slender proof,
They never think they have Reward enough:
But like our *Modern Quakers* of the Town,
Expect your Manners, and return you none.
   Friendship, th' abstracted Union of the Mind,
Which all men seek, but very few can find:
Of all the Nations in the Universe,
None talk on't more, or understand it less:
For if it does their Property annoy,
Their Property their Friendship will destroy.
   As you discourse them, you shall hear them tell
All things in which they think they do excel:
No Panegyrick needs their Praise record;
An Englishman *ne're wants his own good word.*
His first Discourses gen'rally appear
Prologu'd with his own wondrous Character:
When, to illustrate his own good Name,
He never fails his Neighbour to defame:
And yet he really designs no wrong;
His Malice goes no further than his Tongue.
But pleas'd to Tattle, he delights to Rail,
To satisfy the Lech'ry of a Tale.
His own dear Praises close the ample Speech,
Tells you how Wise he is; *that is, how Rich:*
For Wealth is Wisdom; he that's Rich is wise;
And all men Learned Poverty despise.
His Generosity comes next, and then
Concludes that he's a *True-Born Englishman;*
And they, 'tis known, are Generous and Free,
Forgetting, and Forgiving Injury:
Which may be true, thus rightly understood,
Forgiving Ill Turns, and Forgetting Good.
   Chearful in Labour when they've undertook it;
But out of Humour, when they're out of Pocket.
But if their Belly and their Pocket's full,

They may be Phlegmatick, but never Dull:
And if a Bottle does their Brains refine,
It makes their Wit as sparkling as their Wine.
    As for the general Vices which we find
They're guilty of in common with Mankind,
Satyr, forbear, and silently endure;
We must conceal the Crimes we cannot cure.
Nor shall my Verse the brighter Sex defame;
For *English* Beauty will preserve her Name.
Beyond dispute, Agreeable and Fair;
And Modester than other Nations are:
For where the Vice prevails, the great Temptation
Is want of Money, more than Inclination.
In general, this only is allow'd,
They're something Noisy, and a little Proud.
    An *Englishman* is gentlest in Command;
Obedience is a Stranger in the Land:
Hardly subjected to the Magistrate;
For Englishmen *do all Subjection hate.*
Humblest when Rich, but peevish when they're Poor;
And think whate're they have, they merit more.
Shamwhig[16] pretends t' ha' serv'd the Government,
But baulk't of due Reward, turns Malecontent.
For English *Christians always have regard*
To future Recompences of Reward.
His forfeit Liberty they did restore,
And gave him Bread, which he had not before.
But *True-Born English Shamwhig* lets them know,
His Merit must not lye neglected so.
As Proud as Poor, his Masters he'll defy;
And writes a *Piteous* *Satyr upon *Honesty.*
Some think the Poem had been pretty good,
If he the Subject had but understood.
He got Five hundred Pence by this, and more,
As sure as he had ne're a Groat before.

* Satyr in Praise of Folly and Knavery.

In Bus'ness next some Friends of his employ'd him;
And there he prov'd that Fame had not bely'd him:
His Benefactors quickly he abus'd,
And falsly to the Government accus'd:
But they, defended by their Innocence,
Ruin'd the Traytor in their own Defence.

Thus kick'd about from Pillars unto Posts,
He whets his Pen against the Lord of Hosts:
Burlesques his God and King in Paltry Rhimes:
Against the *Dutch* turns Champion for the Times;
And Huffs the King, upon that very score,
On which he Panegyrick't him before.

Unhappy *England,* hast thou none but such,
To plead thy Scoundrel Cause against the Dutch?
This moves their Scorn, and not their Indignation;
He that Lampoons the Dutch, *Burlesques the Nation.*

The meanest *English* Plowman studies Law,
And keeps thereby the Magistrates in Awe:
Will boldly tell them what they ought to do,
And sometimes punish their Omissions too.

Their Liberty and Property's so dear,
They scorn their Laws or Governors to fear:
So bugbear'd with the Name of Slavery,
They can't submit to their own Liberty.
Restraint from Ill is Freedom to the Wise;
But Englishmen *do all Restraint despise.*
Slaves to the Liquor, Drudges to the Pots,
The Mob are Statesmen, and their Statesmen Sots.

Their Governors they count such dangerous things,
That 'tis their custom to affront their kings:
So jealous of the Power their Kings possess'd,
They suffer neither Power nor Kings to rest.
The Bad with Force they eagerly subdue;
The Good with constant Clamours they pursue:
And did King Jesus reign, they'd murmur too.
A discontented Nation, and by far

Harder to rule in Times of Peace than War:
Easily set together by the Ears,
And full of causeless Jealousies and Fears:
Apt to revolt, and willing to rebel,
And never are contented when they're well.
No Government cou'd ever please them long,
Cou'd tye their Hands, or rectify their Tongue.
In this to Ancient Israel *well compar'd,*[17]
Eternal Murmurs are among them heard.
    It was but lately that they were opprest,
Their Rights invaded, and their Laws supprest:
When nicely tender of their Liberty,
Lord! what a Noise they made of Slavery.
In daily Tumults show'd their Discontent;
Lampoon'd their King, and mock'd his Government.
And if in Arms they did not first appear,
'Twas wont of Force, and not for want of Fear.
In humbler Tone than *English* us'd to do,
At Foreign Hands for Foreign Aid they sue.
    William *the Great Successor of* Nassau,
Their Prayers heard, and their Oppressions saw:
He saw and sav'd them: God and Him they prais'd;
To This their Thanks, to That their Trophies rais'd.
But glutted with their own Felicities,
They soon their New Deliverer despise;
Say all their Prayers back, their Joy disown,
Unsing their Thanks, and pull their Trophies down:
Their Harps of Praise are on the Willows hung;
For Englishmen *are ne're contented long.*
    The Rev'rend Clergy too! and who'd ha' thought ⎤
That they who had such Non-Resistance taught, ⎬
Should e're to Arms against their Prince be brought? ⎦
Who up to Heav'n did Regal Pow'r advance;
Subjecting *English* Laws to Modes of *France.*
Twisting Religion so with Loyalty,
As one cou'd never live, and t'other dye.

And yet no sooner did their Prince design
Their Glebes and Perquisites to undermine,
But all their Passive Doctrines laid aside;
The Clergy their own Principles deny'd:
Unpreach'd their Non-Resisting Cant, and pray'd
To Heav'n for Help, and to the *Dutch* for Aid.
The Church chim'd all her Doctrines back again,
And Pulpit-Champions did the Cause maintain;
Flew in the face of all their former Zeal,
And Non-Resistance did at once repeal.

The *Rabbies* say it would be too prolix, ⎤
To tye Religion up to Politicks: ⎬
The Church's Safety is Suprema Lex.   ⎦
And so by a new Figure of their own,
Do all their former Doctrines disown.
As Laws *Post Facto* in the Parliament,
In urgent Cases have obtain'd Assent;
But are as dangerous Precednts laid by;
Made lawful only by Necessity.

The Rev'rend Fathers then in Arms appear,
And Men of God became the Men of War.
The Nation, *fir'd by them,* to Arms apply;
Assault their Antichristian Monarchy;
To their due Channel all our Laws restore,
And made things what they shou'd ha' been before.
But when they came to Fill the Vacant Throne,
And the *Pale Priests* look'd back on what they had done;
How *English* Liberty began to thrive,
And Church-of-*England* Loyalty out-live:
How all their Persecuting Days were done,
And their Deliv'rer plac'd upon the Throne:
The Priests, *as Priests are wont to do,* turn'd Tail;
They're Englishmen, and *Nature will prevail.*
Now they deplore the Ruins they ha' made,
And Murmur for the Master they Betray'd.
Excuse those Crimes they cou'd not make him mend;

And suffer for the Cause they can't defend.
Pretend they'd not ha' carry'd things so high;
And Proto-Martyrs make for Popery.
    Had the Prince done as they design'd the thing,
Ha' set the Clergy up to rule the King;
Taken *a Donative* for coming hither,
And so ha' left their King and them together,
We had say they been now a happy Nation.
No doubt we had seen a Blessed Reformation:
For Wise Men say 't's as dangerous a thing,
A *Ruling Priesthood, as a Priest-rid King.*
And of all Plagues with which Mankind are curst,
Ecclesiastick Tyranny's the worst.
    If all our former Grievances were feign'd,
King *James* has been abus'd, and we trepann'd;
Bugbear'd with Popery and Power Despotick,
Tyrannick Government, and Leagues Exotick:
The Revolution's a Phanatick Plot,
W[illiam] a Tyrant, S[underland] a Sot:[18]
A Factious Army and a Poyson'd Nation,
Unjustly forc'd King *James's* Abdication.
    But if he did the Subjects Rights invade,
Then he was punish'd only, not betray'd:
And punishing of Kings in no such Crime,
But Englishmen *ha' done it many a time.*
    When Kings the Sword of Justice first lay down,
They are no Kings, though they possess the Crown.
Titles are Shadows, Crowns are empty things,
The Good of Subjects is the End of Kings;
To guide in War, and to protect in Peace:
Where Tyrants once commence, the Kings do cease:
For Arbitrary Power's so strange a thing,
It makes the *Tyrant,* and unmakes the *King.*
If Kings by Foreign Priests and Armies reign,
And lawless Power against their Oaths maintain, }
Then Subjects must ha' reason to complain.

If Oaths must bind us when our Kings do ill;
To call in Foreign Aid is to rebel.
By Force to circumscribe our Lawful Prince,
Is wilful Treason in the largest sense:
And they who once rebel, most certainly
Their God, and King, and former Oaths defy.
If we allow no Male-Administration
Could cancel the Allegiance of the Nation;
Let all our Learned *Sons of Levi* try,
This Eccles'astick Riddle to unty:
How they could make a Step to Call the Prince,
And yet pretend to Oaths and Innocence.
   By th' first Address they made beyond the Seas,
They're perjur'd in the most intense Degrees;
And without Scruple for the time to come,
May swear to all the Kings in *Christendom.*
And truly did our Kings consider all,
They'd never let the Clergy swear at all:
Their Politick Allegiance they'd refuse;
For Whores and Priests do never want excuse.
   But if the *Mutual Contract* was dissolv'd,
The Doubt's explain'd, the Difficulty solv'd:
That Kings, when they descend to Tyranny,
Dissolve the Bond, and leave the Subject free.
The Government's ungirt when Justice dies,
And Constitutions are Non-Entities.
The Nation's all a Mob, there's no such thing
As Lords or Commons, Parliament or King.
A great promiscuous Crowd the Hydra lies,
Till Laws revive, and mutual Contract ties:
A Chaos free to chuse for their own share,
What Case of Government they please to wear:
If to a King they do the Reins commit,
All men are bound in Conscience to submit:
But then that King must by his Oath assent
To *Postulata's*[19] of the Government;

Which if he breaks, he cuts off the Entail,
And Power retreats to its Original.
   This Doctrine has the Sanction of Assent,
From Nature's Universal Parliament.
The Voice of Nations, and the Course of Things,
Allow that Laws superior are to Kings.
None but Delinquents would have Justice cease,
Knaves rail at Laws, as Soldiers rail at Peace:
For Justice is the End of Government,
As Reason is the Test of Argument.
   No man was ever yet so void of Sense,
As to debate the Right of Self-Defence;
A Principle so grafted in the Mind,
With Nature born, and does like Nature bind:
Twisted with Reason, and with Nature too;
As neither one nor t'other can undo.
   Nor can this Right be less when National;
Reason which governs one, should govern all.
Whate're the Dialect of Courts may tell,
He that his Right demands, can ne're rebel.
Which Right, if 'tis by Governors deny'd,
May be procur'd by Force, or Foreign Aid.
For *Tyranny's* a Nation's Term for Grief;
As Folks cry *Fire*, to hasten in Relief.
And when the hated word is heard about,
All men shou'd come to help the People out.
   Thus *England* groan'd, *Britannia's* Voice was heard;
And Great *Nassau* to rescue her, appear'd:
Call'd by the Universal Voice of Fate;
God and the Peoples Legal Magistrate.
Ye Heav'ns regard! Almighty *Jove* look down,
And view thy Injur'd Monarch on the Throne.
On their Ungrateful Heads due Vengeance take,
Who sought his Aid, and then his part forsake.
Witness, ye Powers! it was Our Call alone,
Which now our Pride makes us asham'd to own.

Britannia's Troubles fetch'd him from afar,
To court the dreadful Casualties of War:
But where Requital never can be made,
Acknowledgement's a Tribute seldom paid.
   He dwelt in Bright *Maria*'s[20] Circling Arms,
Defended by the Magick of her Charms,
From Foreign Fears, and from Domestick Harms.
Ambition found no Fuel for her Fire,
He had what God cou'd give, or Man desire.
Till *Pity* rowz'd him from his soft Repose,
His Life to unseen Hazards to expose:
Till *Pity* mov'd him in our Cause t' appear;
Pity! *that Word which now we hate to hear.*
But *English* Gratitude is always such,
To hate the Hand which does oblige too much.
   Britannia's Cries gave Birth to his Intent,
And hardly gain'd his unforeseen Assent:
His boding Thoughts foretold him he should find
The People Fickle, Selfish, and Unkind.
Which Thought did to his Royal Heart appear
More dreadful than the Dangers of the War:
For nothing grates a Generous Mind so soon,
As base Returns for hearty Service done.
   Satyr be silent, awfully prepare
Britannia's Song, and *William*'s Praise to hear.
Stand by, and let her chearfully rehearse
Her Grateful Vows in her Immortal Verse.
Loud Fame's Eternal Trumpet let her sound;
Listen ye distant Poles, and endless Round.
May the strong Blast the welcome News convey
As far as Sound can reach, or Spirit fly.
To *Neighb'ring Worlds*, if such there be, relate
Our Hero's Fame, for theirs to imitate.
To distant Worlds of Spirits let her rehearse:
For Spirits without the helps of Voice converse.
May Angels hear the gladsome News on high,

Mixt with their everlasting Symphony.
And Hell it self stand in suspence to know
Whether it be the Fatal Blast, or no.

BRITANNIA

The Fame of Virtue 'tis for which I sound,
And Heroes with Immortal Triumphs crown'd.
Fame built on solid Virtue swifter flies,
Than Morning Light can spread my Eastern *Skies.*
The gath'ring Air returns the doubling Sound,
And lowd repeating Thunders force it round:
Ecchoes return from Caverns of the Deep:
Old Chaos dreams on't in Eternal Sleep.
Time hands it forward to its latest Urn,
From whence it never, never shall return,
Nothing is heard so far, or lasts so long;
'Tis heard by ev'ry Ear, and spoke by ev'ry Tongue.
  My Hero, with the Sails of Honour furl'd,
Rises like the Great Genius of the World.
By Fate and Fame wisely prepar'd to be
The Soul of War, and Life of Victory.
He spreads the Wings of Virtue on the Throne,
And ev'ry Wind of Glory fans them on.
Immortal Trophies dwell upon his Brow,
Fresh as the Garlands he has worn but now.
  By different Steps the high Ascent he gains,
And differently that high Ascent maintains.
Princes for Pride and Lust of Rule make War,
And struggle for the Name of Conqueror.
Some fight for Fame, and some for Victory.
He Fights to Save, and Conquers to set Free.
  Then seek no Phrase his Titles to conceal,
And hide with Words what Actions must reveal.
No Parallel from Hebrew Stories take,
Of God-like Kings my Similies to make:

No borrow'd Names conceal my living Theam;
But Names and Things directly I proclaim.
'Tis honest Merit does his Glory raise;
Whom that exalts, let no man fear to praise.
Of such a Subject no man need be shy;
Virtue's above the Reach of Flattery.
He needs no Character but his own Fame,
Nor any flattering Titles, but his Name.
    William*'s the Name that's spoke by ev'ry Tongue:*
William*'s the Darling Subject of my* Song.
Listen ye Virgins to the Charming Sound,
And in Eternal Dances hand it round:
Your early Offerings to this Altar bring;
Make him at once a Lover and a King.
May he submit to none but to your Arms;
Nor ever be subdu'd, but by your Charms.
May your soft Thoughts for him be all sublime;
And ev'ry tender Vow be made for him.
May he be first in ev'ry Morning-Thought,
And Heav'n ne're hear a Pray'r where he's left out.
May ev'ry Omen, ev'ry boding Dream,
Be Fortunate *by mentioning his Name.*
May this one Charm Infernal Powers affright,
And guard you from the Terrors of the Night.
May ev'ry chearful Glass as it goes down
To William*'s Health,* be Cordials to your own.
Let ev'ry Song be Chorust with his Name.
And Musick pay her Tribute to his Fame.
Let ev'ry Poet tune his Artful Verse,
And in Immortal Strains his Deeds rehearse.
And may Apollo *never more inspire*
The Disobedient Bard with his Seraphick Fire.
May all my Sons their grateful Homage pay;
His Praises sing, and for his Safety pray.
    Satyr return to our Unthankful Isle,
Secur'd by Heav'n's Regard, and *William's* Toil.

To both Ungrateful, and to both Untrue;
Rebels to God, and to Good Nature too.
　If e're this Nation be distress'd again,
To whomsoe're they cry, they'll cry in vain.
To Heav'n they cannot have the face to look;
Or if they should, it would but Heav'n provoke.
To hope for Help from Man would be too much;
Mankind would always tell 'em of the Dutch:
How they came here our Freedoms to maintain,
Were *Paid,* and *Curs'd,* and *Hurry'd home again.*
How by their Aid we first dissolv'd our Fears,
And then our Helpers damn'd for Foreigners.
'Tis not our *English* Temper to do better;
For *Englishmen* think ev'ry man their Debtor.
　'Tis worth observing, that we ne're complain'd
Of Foreigners, nor of the Wealth they gain'd,
Till all their Services were at an End.
Wise men affirm it is the *English* way,
Never to Grumble till they come to Pay;
And then they always think their Temper's such,
The Work too little, and the Pay too much.
　As frighted Patients, when they want a Cure,
Bid any Price, and any Pain endure:
But when the Doctor's Remedies appear,
The Cure's too Easy, and the Price too Dear.
　Great *Portland* ne're was banter'd, when he strove
For Us his Master's kindest Thoughts to move.
We ne're lampoon'd his Conduct, when employ'd
King *James's* Secret Councils to divide:
Then we caress'd him as the only Man,
Which could the Doubtful Oracle explain:
The only *Hushai* able to repell
The Dark Designs of *our Achitophel.*
Compar'd his Master's Courage to his Sense;
The Ablest Statesman, and the Bravest Prince.
On his wise Conduct we depended much,

And lik'd him ne're the worse for being Dutch.
Nor was he valued more than he deserv'd;
Freely he ventur'd, faithfully he serv'd.
In all King *William*'s Dangers he has shar'd;
In *England*'s Quarrels always he appear'd:
The *Revolution* first, and then the *Boyne*;[21]
In Both his Counsels and his Conduct shine.
His Martial Valour *Flanders* will confess;
And *France Regrets* his Managing the Peace.
Faithful to *England*'s Interests and her King:
The greatest Reason of our Murmuring.
Ten Years in *English* Service he appear'd,
And gain'd his Master's and the World's Regard:
But 'tis not England's *Custom to Reward.*
The Wars are over, *England* needs him not;
Now he's a *Dutchman,* and *the Lord knows what.*
   Schonbergh, the Ablest Soldier of his Age,
With *Great Nassau* did in our Cause engage:
Both join'd for *England*'s Rescue and Defence;
The Greatest Captain, and the Greatest Prince.
With what Applause his Stories did we tell?
Stories which *Europe*'s Volumes largely swell.
We counted him an Army in our Aid:
Where he commanded, no man was afraid.
His Actions with a constant Conquest shine,
From *Villa-Vitiosa* to the *Rhine.*[22]
France, Flanders, Germany, his Fame confess;
And all the World was fond of him, but Us.
Our Turn first serv'd, we grudg'd him the Command.
Witness the Grateful Temper of the Land.
We blame the K[ing] that he relies too much
On Strangers, *Germans, Hugonots,* and *Dutch;*
And seldom does his great Affairs of State
To *English* Counsellors communicate.
The Fact might very well be answer'd thus;
He has so often been betray'd by us,

He must have been a Madman to rely
On *English* G[odolphi]ns Fidelity.[23]
For laying other Arguments aside,
This Thought might mortify our *English* Pride,
That Foreigners have faithfully obey'd him,
And none but *Englishmen* have e're betray'd him.
They have our Ships and Merchants bought and sold,
And barter'd *English* Blood for Foreign Gold.
First to the *French* they sold our *Turky*-Fleet,
And Injur'd *Talmarsh* next at *Camaret*.[24]
The King himself is shelter'd from their Snares,
Not by his Merit, but the Crown he wears.
Experience tells us 'tis the *English* way,
Their Benefactors always to betray.

 And lest Examples should be too remote,⎤
A Modern Magistrate of Famous Note,[25] ⎬
Shall give you his own History by Rote. ⎦
I'll make it out, deny it he that can,
His Worship is a True-born *Englishman,*
In all the Latitude that Empty Word
By Modern Acceptation's understood.
The Parish-Books his Great Descent record,
And now he hopes e're long to be a Lord.
And truly as things go, it wou'd be pity
But such as he bore Office in the City:
While Robb'ry for Burnt-Offering he brings,
And gives to God what he has stole from Kings:
Great Monuments of Charity he raises,
And good St. Magnus *whistles out his Praises.*
To City-Gaols he grants a Jubilee,
And hires Huzza's from his own Mobile.[26]

 Lately he wore the Golden Chain and Gown,
With which Equipt he thus harangu'd the Town.
 Sir C[harle]s D[uncom]b'*s Fine Speech, &c.*
 WIth Clouted Iron Shooes and Sheepskin Breeches,
More Rags than Manners, and more Dirt than Riches:

From driving Cows and Calves to *Layton*-Market,
While of my Greatness there appear'd no Spark yet,
Behold I come, to let you see the Pride
With which Exalted Beggars always ride.
   Born to the Needful Labours of the Plow,
The Cart-Whip grac't me as the Chain does now.
Nature and Fate in doubt what course to take,
Whether I shou'd a Lord or Plough-Boy make;
Kindly at last resolv'd they wou'd promote me,
And first *a Knave*, and then *a Knight* they vote me.
What Fate appointed, Nature did prepare,
And furnish'd me with an exceeding Care.
To fit me for what they design'd to have me;
And ev'ry Gift *but Honesty* they gave me.
   And thus Equipt, to this Proud Town I came,
In quest of Bread, and not in quest of Fame.
Blind to my future Fate, an humble Boy,
Free from the *Guilt and Glory* I enjoy.
The Hopes which my Ambition entertain'd,
Were in the Name of *Foot-Boy* all contain'd.
The Greatest Heights from Small Beginnings rise;
The Gods were Great on Earth, before they reach'd the Skies.
   B[ack]well, the Generous Temper of whose Mind,
Was always to be bountiful inclin'd:
Whether by his Ill Fate or Fancy led,
First took me up, and furnish'd me with Bread.
The little Services he put me to,
Seem'd Labours rather than were truly so.
But always my Advancement he design'd;
For 'twas his very Nature to be kind.
Large was his Soul, his Temper ever Free;
The best of Masters and of Men to me.
And I who was before decreed by Fate,
To be made Infamous as well as Great,
With an obsequious Diligence obey'd him,
Till trusted with his All, and then betray'd him.

All his past Kindnesses I trampled on,
Ruin'd his Fortunes to erect my own.
So Vipers in the Bosom bred, begin
To hiss at that Hand first which took them in.
With eager Treach'ry I his Fall pursu'd,
And my first Trophies were *Ingratitude*.

Ingratitude's the worst of Human Guilt,
The basest Action Mankind can commit;
Which like the Sin against the Holy Ghost,
Has least of Honour, and of Guilt the most.
Distinguish'd from all other Crimes by this,
That 'tis a Crime which no man will confess.
That Sin alone, which shou'd not be forgiv'n
On Earth, altho perhaps it may in Heav'n.

Thus my first Benefactor I o'rethrew;
And how shou'd I be to a second true?
The Publick Trust came next into my Care,
And I to use them scurvily prepare:
My Needy Sov'reign Lord I play'd upon,
And Lent him many a Thousand of his own;
For which, great Int'rests I took care to charge,
And so my Ill-got Wealth became so large.[27]

My Predecessor *Judas* was a Fool,
Fitter to ha' been whipt, and sent to School,
Then Sell a Saviour: Had I been at hand,
His Master had not been so cheap Trepann'd;
I wou'd ha' made the eager *Jews* ha' found,
For Thirty Pieces, Thirty thousand Pound.

My Cousin *Ziba*, of Immortal Fame,
(Ziba *and I shall never want a Name:*)
First-born of Treason, nobly did advance
His Master's Fall, for his Inheritance.
By whose keen Arts old *David* first began
To break his Sacred Oath to *Jonathan:*
The Good Old King, 'tis thought, was very loth
To break his Word, and therefore broke his Oath.

Ziba's a Traytor of some Quality,
Yet *Ziba* might ha' been inform'd by me:
Had I been there, he ne're had been content
With half th' Estate, nor half the Government.
  In our late Revolution 'twas thought strange,
That I of all mankind shou'd like the Change:
But they who wonder'd at it, never knew,
That in it I did my Old Game pursue:
Nor had they heard of Twenty thousand Pound,
Which ne're was lost, yet never cou'd be found.
  Thus all things in their turn to Sale I bring,
God and my Master first, and then the King:
Till by successful Villanies made bold,
I thought to turn the Nation into Gold;
And so to Forg[er]y my Hand I bent,   ⎫
Not doubting I could gull the Government;   ⎬
But there was ruffe'ed by the Parliament.   ⎭
And if I 'scap'd th' Unhappy Tree to climb,
'Twas want of Law, and not for want of Crime.
  But my *Old Friend,* who printed in my Face
A needful Competence of *English* Brass,
Having more business yet for me to do,
And loth to lose his Trusty Servant so,
Manag'd the matter with such Art and Skill,
As sav'd his Hero, and threw out the B[il]l.
  And now I'm grac'd with unexpected Honours,
For which I'll certainly abuse the Donors:
Knighted, and made a Tribune of the People,
Whose Laws and Properties I'm like to keep well:
The *Custos Rotulorum*[28] of the City,
And Captain of the Guards of their *Banditti.*
Surrounded by my Catchpoles, I declare
Against the Needy Debtor open War.
I hang poor Thieves for stealing of your Pelf,
And suffer none to rob you, buy my self.

* *the Devil.*

The King commanded me to help Reform ye,[29]
And how I'll do't, Miss ——— shall inform ye.
I keep the best Seraglio in the Nation,
And hope in time to bring it into Fashion.
No *Brimstone-Whore* need fear the Lash from me,
That part I'll leave to Brother *Jeffery*.[30]
Or Gallants need not go abroad to *Rome*,
I'll keep a Whoring Jubilee at home.
Whoring's the Darling of my Inclination;
A'n't I a Magistrate for Reformation?
For this my Praise is sung by ev'ry Bard,
For which *Bridewell* wou'd be a just Reward.
In Print my Panegyricks fill the Street,
And hir'd Gaol-birds their Huzza's repeat.
Some Charities contriv'd to make a show,
Have taught the Needy Rabble to do so:
Whose empty Noise is a Mechanick Fame,
Since for Sir *Belzebub* they'd do the same.

The Conclusion

THen let us boast of Ancestors no more,
Or Deeds of Heroes done in days of Yore,
In latent Records of the Ages past,
Behind the Rear of Time, in long Oblivion plac'd.
For if our Virtues must in Lines descend,
The Merit with the Families would end:
And Intermixtures would most fatal grow;
For Vice would be Hereditary too;
The Tainted Blood wou'd of necessity,
Involuntary Wickedness convey.
Vice, like Ill Nature, for an Age or two,
May seem a Generation to pursue;
But Virtue seldom does regard the Breed;
Fools do the Wise, and Wise Men Fools succeed.
What is't to us, what Ancestors we had?

If Good, what better? or what worse, if Bad?
Examples are for Imitation set,
Yet all men follow Virtue with Regret.
    Cou'd but our Ancestors retrieve their Fate,
And see their Offspring thus degenerate;
How we contend for Birth and Names unknown,
And build on their past Actions, not our own;
They'd cancel Records, and their Tombs deface,
And openly disown the vile degenerate Race:
For Fame of Families is all a Cheat,
'Tis Personal Virtue only makes us great.

THE
𝕸𝖔𝖈𝖐 𝕸𝖔𝖚𝖗𝖓𝖊𝖗𝖘.
A
SATYR,
By way of
ELEGY
ON
King *WILLIAM*.

By the Author of
The True-born Englishman.

London, Printed 1702.

THE
MOCK MOURNERS.
A
SATYR,
By way of
ELEGY
ON
KING *WILLIAM.*

By the *Author of* The True-born *Englishman*

London, *Printed 1702.*

Defoe's admiration for William III is nowhere more clearly seen than in this poem, published about May 1702. After going through seven editions, it appeared in Defoe's collected works in 1703.

TO THE QUEEN

MADAM,

Your Majesty has so often declar'd Your just Concern for the Nations Loss, and Your Value for the Memory of the late King: You have so publickly approv'd his Conduct, so visibly mov'd in the same Steps, and pursu'd the wise Measures of this Your Glorious Ancestor, *that it cannot be thought displeasing to Your Majesty, to reprehend those who make a Mock at the Sorrow of Your Majesty and Three Nations.*

Your Majesty was the first who told us he cou'd not be sufficiently lamented. *May those who are not of the same Mind find no Favour with Your Majesty, nor their Maker, till they repent that Sin against his Merit, and the Voice of their Native Country.*

Here are no Reflections upon Your Majesties Household, or Council, or Courts of Justice, or either House of Parliament, and consequently no Offence against Your Royal Proclamation.[1] 'Twou'd be an Affront to Your Majesty to imagine there were any under all those Heads of Your Government cou'd deserve the Reproof of the following Satyr.

Your Majesty has an entire Possession of the Hearts of Your People, but their Affection is still the deeper rooted by that generous Sorrow you have express'd for the Loss of him to whom they owe the full Possession of their Liberty under Your Government.

How they can be faithful Subjects to Your Majesty that were not true Friends to such a King, is a Mystery out of humane Understanding, since the Happiness we enjoy by Your Government proceeds from his defending us against those who wou'd not have had Your Majesty to Reign over us.

'Twou'd be a Crime against Your Majesty, which deserv'd no Pardon to suggest you shou'd be offended at that part of the Satyr which points at our Immoralities: Your Majesties Example, as well as Command, has encourag'd us all to declare War against Vice, and there we are sure of Your Royal Protection.

For the rest, if an extraordinary Concern for the Glorious Memory of the late King, has led the Author into any Excesses, he begs Your Majesty wou'd place it to the Account of that just Passion *every honest Man retains for his extraordinary Merit;* believing that no Man can have an Indifferency for the

Memory of King William, *and at the same time have any*
Desire for the Welfare of his Native Country.

While Your Majesty pursues the true Interest of England,
the Protestant Religion, and the Welfare of Europe, *as he did,*
you will have the same Enemies that he had, the same to op-
pose You abroad, and reproach You at home; but You will
thereby engage all Your honest Subjects to adhere the firmer
to their Duty, all your Protestant Neighbours to depend upon
Your Protection, and God shall Crown Your Majesty and these
Nations with His Special Favour and Benediction.

Amen.

A SATYR, &c

SUCH has been this Ill-Natur'd Nations Fate,
Always to see their Friends and Foes too late;
By Native Pride, and want of Temper led,
Never to value Merit till 'tis Dead:
And then Immortal Monuments they raise,
And Damn their Former Follies by their Praise,
With just Reproaches Rail at their own Vice,
And Mourn for those they did before despise
So they who *Moses* Government defied,
Sincerely sorrow'd for him when he Died.

And so when *Brittain's* Genius fainting lay,
Summon'd by Death, which Monarchs must obey:
Trembling, and Soul-less half the Nation stood,
Upraided by their own Ingratitude.

They, who with true born Honesty before,
Grudg'd him the Trophies he so justly wore,
Were, with his Fate, more than himself dismay'd,
Not for their King, but for themselves afraid.
He had their Rights and Liberties restor'd,
In Battle purchas'd, and by Peace secur'd:
And they with *English* Gratitude began,
To feel the Favour and despise the Man.

But when they saw that his Protection ceas'd,
And Death had their Deliverer possest;
How Thunder struck they stood! What cries they rais'd!
They look't like Men Distracted and Amaz'd:
Their Terror did their Conscious Guilt explain,
And wish't their injur'd Prince Alive again.
They Dream't of Halters, Gibbets and of Jails,
French Armies, Popery and Prince of *Wales*,[2]
Descents, Invasions, Uproars in the State,
Mobs, Irish Massacres, and God knows what:
Imaginary Enemies appear'd,
And all they knew they Merited, they Fear'd.
    'Tis strange that Pride and Envy should prevail,
To make Men's Sence as well as Vertue fail:
That where they must depend they should abuse,
And slight the Man they were afraid to loose.
    But *William* had not Govern'd Fourteen Year,
To be an unconcern'd Spectator here:
His Works like Providence were all Compleat,
Which made a Harmony we Wonder'd at.
The Legislative Power he set Free,
And led them step by step to Liberty,
'Twas not his Fault if they cou'd not Agree.
Impartial Justice He Protected so,
The Laws did in their Native Channels flow,
From whence our sure Establishment begun,
And *William* laid the first Foundation Stone:
On which the stately Fabrick soon appear'd,
How cou'd they sink when such a Pilot steer'd?
He taught them due defences to prepare,
And make their future Peace their present care:
By him directed, Wisely they Decreed,
What Lines shou'd be expell'd, and what succeed;
That now he's Dead, there's nothing to be done,
But to take up the Scepter he laid down.
    The Circle of this Order is so round,

So Regular as nothing can confound:
In Truth and Justice all the Lines commence,
And Reason is the vast circumference:
William's the moving Centre of the whole,
'T had else a Body been without a Soul.
Fenc'd with just Laws, impregnable it stands,
And will for ever last in *Honest Hands*,
For Truth and Justice are the Immortal Springs,
Give Life to Constitutions and to Kings:
In either case, if one of these decay,
These can no more Command than those obey:
Right is the only Fountain of Command,
The Rock on which Authority must stand.
And if executive Power steps awry,
On either hand it splits on Tyranny:
Oppression is a plague on Mankind sent,
To infect the Vitals of a Government.
Convulsions follow, and such Vapours rise,
The Constitution Suffocates and Dies:
Law is the Grand specific to restore,
And unobstructed, never fails to Cure,
All other Remedies compar'd to that,
Are Tampering and Quacking with the State.
  The Constitution's like a vast Machine,[3]
That's full of curious Workmanship within:
Where tho' the parts unwieldy may appear,
It may be put in Motion with a Hair.
The Wheels are Officers and Magistrates,
By which the whole contrivance operates:
Laws are the Weights and Springs which make it move,
Wound up by Kings as Managers above;
And if they'r screw'd too high or down too low,
The movement goes too fast or else too slow.
The Legislators are the Engineers,
Who when 'tis out of Order make Repairs:

The People are the Owners, 'twas for them,
The first Inventor drew the Ancient Scheme.
'Tis for their Benefit it works, and they
The Charges of maintaining it defray:
And if their Governours unfaithful prove,
They, Engineers or Managers remove,
Unkind Contention sometimes there appears,
Between the Managers and Engineers,
Such strife is always to the Owners wrong,
And once it made the work stand still too long.
Till *William* came and loos'd the Fatal Chain,
And set the Engineers to work again:
And having made the wondrous thing compleat,
To *Anne's* unerring hand he left the Helm of State.
    Anne like *Elisha* when just *William* went,
Receiv'd the Mantle of his Government:
And by Divine Concession does inherit,
A Double Portion of his Ruling Spirit.
The Dying Hero loaded with Renown,   ⎫
Gave her the Nations Blessing with the Crown, ⎬
From God, the People, and the Laws her own. ⎭
Told her that he had Orders from on High,
To lay aside the Government and Dye:
What he had Fought for, gave her up in Peace,
And chear'd her Royal Heart with Prospects of Success.
While he, who Death in all its Shapes had seen,
With full Composure quiet and serene,
Passive and undisorder'd at his Fate,
Quitted the English Throne without Regret.
No Conscious Guilt disturb'd his Royal Breast,
Calm as the Regions of Eternal Rest:
Before his Life went out, his Heaven came in,
For all was bright without and clear within.
The blest Rewards did to his sight appear,
The Passage easie, and the prospect near:

His parting Eye the gladsom Regions spied,
Just so, before his Dear Maria *Dyed.*
   His High concern for *England* he express't,
England, the Darling of his Royal Breast:
The Transports of his parting Soul he spent,
Her dis-united Parties to Lament.
His Wishes then supplied his want of Power,
And Pray'd for them, for whom he Fought before.
   Speak Envy, if you can, inform us what
Cou'd this unthankful Nation Murmur at?
But Discontent was always our Disease,
For *English-men* what Government can please.
We always had our Sons of *Belial* here,
Who knew no God nor Government to Fear:
No Wonder these dislik'd his Gentle sway, ⎫
Unwilling Homage to his Scepter Pay,   ⎬
And only did for want of Power, Obey.   ⎭
   Some soft excuse for them we might contrive,
Had he not been the Gentlest Prince Alive:
Had he not born with an exalted Mind,
All that was disobliging and unkind.
Peaceful and Tender Thoughts his Mind possess't,
And High Superior Love conceal'd the rest:
Our Discontents wou'd oft his Pity move,
But all his Anger was supprest by Love.
That Heaven-born Passion had subdu'd his Soul,
Possess't the greatest part, and Rul'd the whole:
This made him strive his People to possess,
Which he had done, had he oblig'd 'em less.
He knew that Titles are but empty things,
And Hearts of Subjects are the strength of Kings:
Justice and Kindness were his constant care,
He scorn'd to Govern Mankind by their Fear.
   Their Universal Love he strove to Gain,
'Twas hard that we should make him strive in vain:
That he should here our English Humours find,

And we, that he had sav'd, shou'd be unkind.
By all endearing stratagems he strove,
To draw us by the secret springs of Love:
And when he could not Cure our Discontent,
It always was below him to Resent.

Nature was never seen in such excess,
All Fury when Abroad, at Home all Peace:
In War all Fire and Blood, in Peace enclin'd,
To all that's Sweet, and Gentle, Soft and Kind,
Ingratitude for this, must needs Commence,
In want of Honesty, or want of Sence.

When King's to Luxury and Ease Resign'd,
Their Native Countries just defence declin'd;
This High pretending Nation us'd to plead,
What they'd perform had they a King to lead.
What Wondrous Actions had by them been done,
When they had Martial Monarchs to lead on?
And if their Prince would but with *France* make War,
What Troops of English Heroes wou'd appear?

William the bottom of their Courage found,
False like themselves, meer emptiness and sound:
For call'd by Fate to Fight for *Christendom,*
They sent their King abroad, and stay'd at Home;
Wisely declin'd the hazards of the War,
To Nourish Faction and Disorders here.
Wrapt in Luxurious plenty they Debauch,
And load their Active Monarch with Reproach:
Backward in Deeds, but of their Censures free,
And slight the Actions which they dare not see.
At Home they bravely teach him to Command,
And Judge of what they are afraid to mend:
Against the hand that saves them they exclaim,
And Curse the strangers, tho' they Fight for them.
Tho' some who wou'd excuse the matter say,
They did not grudge their Service, but their Pay:
Where are the Royal bands that now advance,

To spread his dreadful Banners into *France*.
Britannia's Noble Sons her Interest fly,
And Foreign Heroes must their place supply;
Much for the Fame of our Nobility.
Posterity will be asham'd to hear,
Great *Britain's* Monarch did in Arms appear,
And scarce an English Nobleman was there.
Our Ancestors had never Conquer'd *France*,
For Kingdoms seldom are subdu'd by Chance:
Had *Talbott*, *Vere* and *Montacute* with-held,[4]
The Glory, for the danger of the Field.
Had English Honesty been kept alive,
The Ancient English Glory would survive
But Gallantry and Courage will decline,
Where Pride and all Confederate Vices joyn.
Had we kept up the Fame of former Years,
Landen had been as Famous as *Poictiers*;[5]
Ormond and *Essex* had not Fought alone,[6]
The only English Lords our Verse can own:
The only Peers of whom the World can say,
That they for Honour Fought, and not for Pay.
   A Regimented *Few* we had indeed,
Who serv'd for neither Pride nor Fame, but Bread:
Some Bully L[ord]s, *Protection P[eer]s*, and some
Went out, because they dare not stay at Home.
Loaded with Noxious Vices they appear,
A Scandal to the Nation and the War:
Heroes in Midnight scuffles with the Watch,
And Lewd enough an Army to Debauch.
Flesh't with cold Murthers and from Justice fled,
Pursu'd by Blood, in Drunken Quarrels shed:
In vain they strive with Bravery to appear,
For where there's Guilt, there always will be Fear.
These are the Pillars of the English Fame,
Such Peers as History must blush to Name.
   When future Records to the World relate,

Marsaglia's Field and Gallant *Schomberg*'s Fate:
W[*ürttemberg*] *was Captive made,* it was severe,[7]
Fate took the *Honest Man,* and left the *Peer.*
The World owes Fame for Ages long before,
To the Great stile of W[*ürttemberg*] which he bore:
But when we come the branches to compare,
'Tis a *Hero* Ancestor, a *Bully* Heir:
The Vertues the Posterity forsake,
And all their Gallant Blood is dwindl'd to a *Rake.*
More might be said, but *Satyr* stay thy Rhimes,
And mix not his misfortune with his Crimes;
We need not Rake the Ashes of the Dead,
There's living Characters enough to Read.
   How cou'd this Nation ever think of Peace?
Or how look up to Heaven for Success?
While lawless Vice in Fleets and Camps appear'd,
And Oaths were louder than their Cannon heard:
No wonder English *Israel* has been said,
Before the French *Philistines* Fleet t'ha' fled.
While T[*orrington*] *Embrac'd with Whores* appear'd,
And Vice it self the Royal Navy Steer'd.[8]
   William oppos'd their Crimes with steady hand,
By his Example First, and then Command,
Prompted the Laws their Vices to suppress,
For which no doubt the Guilty Lov'd him less.
   Ye Sons of Envy Railers at the Times,
Be bold like English-Men and own your Crimes:
For shame put on no Black, but let us see
Your Habits always, and your Tongues agree.
Envy ne'r Blushes: Let it not be said,
You Hate him Living and you Mourn him Dead:
No Sorrow show where you no Love possess,
There are no Hypocrites in Wickedness.
Great Bonfires make, and tell the World y'are glad
Y'hav[e] lost the greatest Blessing e're you had:
So Mad-Men sing in Nakedness and Chains,

For when the Sense is gone, the Song remains.
So Thankless *Israel*, when they were set free,
Reproach't the Author of their Liberty:
And wish'd themselves in *Egypt* back again;
What pity 'twas they wisht, or wisht in vain?
   Stop, Satyr, let *Britannia* now relate
Her *William*'s Character, and her own Fate;
Let her to him a grateful Trophy raise,
She best can sigh his Loss that sung his Praise.

BRITANNIA

Of all my Sons by Tyranny bereft,
A Widow desolate and Childless left,
By Violence and Injury opprest,
To Heaven I cast my Eyes, and sigh'd the rest.
I need but sigh, for I was always heard,
And *William* on my welcome Shores appear'd.
With Wings of speed to rescue me he came,
And all my Sorrows vanisht into Flame.
New Joys sprung up, new Triumphs now abound,
And all my Virgin Daughters hear the sound:
Eternal Dances move upon my Plains,
And youthful Blood springs in my ancient Veins.
With open Arms I yielded my Embrace,
And *William* saw the Beauties of my Face.
He had before the knowledge of my Charms,
For he had my *Maria* in his Arms.
While he remain'd, I gave eternal Spring,
Made him my Son, my Darling, and my King;
While all the wondring World my Choice approve,
Congratulate his Fate, and justifie my Love.
   Of *British* Blood in *Belgian* Plains he liv'd,
My only Foreign Off-spring that surviv'd.
Batavian Climates nourisht him a while,
Too great a Genius for so damp a Soil:

And freely then surrendred him to me,
For wise Men freely will the Fates obey.
Yet in my *William* they had equal Share,
And he defended them with equal Care.
They were the early Trophies of his Sword,
His Infant Hand their Liberty restor'd.
His Nurse, that Belgick Lion, roar'd for Aid,
And planted early Lawrels on his Head.
His easie Victories amaz'd Mankind;
We wonder'd what the dreadful Youth design'd.
Fearless he Fought his Country to set Free,
And with his Sword Cut out their Liberty.
The Journals of his Actions always seem'd
So wonderful, as if the World had dream'd:
So swift, so full of Terror he went on,
He was a Conqueror before a Man.
    The *Bourbon* Sword, tho' it was brighter far,
Yet drawn for Conquest, and oppressive War,
Had all the Triumphs of the World Engrost,
But quickly all those Triumphs to him lost.
Justice to *William* early Trophies brought;
William *for Truth and Justice always fought;*
    He was the very Mystery of War,
He gain'd by't when he was not Conqueror.
And if his Enemies a Battle won,
He might be beaten, they wou'd be undone.
Antaeus like from every fall he rose,
Strengthen'd with double Vigor to oppose;
Those Actions Mankind judg'd Unfortunate,
Serv'd but as secret Steps to make him Great.
Then let them boast their Glory at *Landen*, ⎫
In vain th' Embattl'd Squadrons crowded in, ⎬
Their's was the Victory, the Conquest mine. ⎭
    Of all the Heroes, Ages past adore,
Back to the first Great Man, and long before;
Tho' Virtue has sometimes with Valour join'd,

The Barren World no Parallel can find.

   If back to *Israel's* Tents I shou'd retire,
And of the *Hebrew* Heroes there enquire,
I find no Hand did *Judah's* Scepter wear,
Comes up to *William's* Modern Character.
Namure's Gygantick Towers he o'erthrew;
David did less when he *Goliah* slew.[9]
Here's no Uriah's for Adult'ry slain,
Nor Oaths forgot to faithful *Jonathan*.
And if to *Jesse's* Grandson we ha' recourse,
William his Wisdom had without his Whores.

   Joshua might still ha' staid on *Jordan's* Shore,
Must he, as *William* did the *Boyne,* pass o'er.
Almighty Power was forc'd to interpose,
And frighted both the Water and his Foes:
But had my *William* been to pass that Stream,
God needed not to part the Waves for him.
Not Forty Thousand *Canaanites* cou'd stand,
In spight of Waves or *Canaanites* he'd land:
Such Streams ne'er stemm'd his Tide of Victory;
No, not the Stream; no, nor the Enemy.

   His Bombs and Cannon wou'd ha' made the Wall,
Without the Help of Jewish Rams-Horns, fall.
When his dear *Israel* from their Foes had fled,
Because of stoln Spoils by *Achan* hid:
He'd never, like *Joshua,* on the Ground ha' laid,
He'd certainly ha' fought as well as pray'd.

   The Sun would rather ha' been thought to stay,
Amaz'd to see how soon he had won the Day,
Than to give time the Canaanites to slay.

   The greatest Captains of the Ages past,
Debauch'd their Fame with Cruelty at last:
William did only Tyrants subdue;
These conquer'd Kings, and then the People too:
The Subjects reap'd no Profit for their Pains,
And only chang'd their Masters, not their Chains;

Their Victories did for themselves appear,
And made their Peace as dreadful as the War:
But *William* fought Oppression to destroy,
That Mankind might in Peace the World enjoy.
   The *Pompeys, Caesars, Scripio's, Alexanders,*
Who croud the World with Fame, were great Commanders:
These too brought Blood and Ruin with their Arms,
But *William* always fought on other Terms:
Terror indeed might in his Front appear,
But Peace and Plenty follow'd in his Rear:
And if Oppression forc'd him to contend,
Calmness was all his Temper, Peace his End:
He was the only Man we e'er saw fit
To regulate the World, or conquer it.
Who can his Skill in Government Gainsay,
He that can *England*'s brittle Scepter sway,
Where Parties too much rule, and Kings obey?
He always reign'd by Gentleness and Love,
An Emblem of the Government above.
   Vote me not Childless then in Christendom,
I yet have Sons in my suspended Womb;
And 'till just Fate such due Provision makes,
A Daughter my Protection undertakes.
Crowns know no Sexes, and my Government
To either Kind admits a just Descent.
Queens have to me been always fortunate,
E'er since my *English Phoenix* rul'd the State;[10]
Who made my People rich, my Country great.
Satyr be just, and when we lash their Crimes,
Mingle some Tears for *William* with our Rhimes.
Tho' Baseness and Ingratitude appear,
Thank Heaven that we ha' weeping Millions here:
Then speak our hearty Sorrows if you can,
Superior Grief in feeling Words explain:
Accents that wound, and all the Senses numb,
And while they speak may strike the Hearer dumb:

Such Grief never was for King before,
And such as never, never shall be more.
  See how Authority comes weeping on,
And view the Queen lamenting on his Throne.
With Just Regret she takes the Sword of State,
Not by her Choice directed, but his Fate;
Accepts the sad Necessity with Tears,
And mournfully for Government prepares.
The Peoples Acclamations she receives
With sadn'd Joy, and a Content that grieves.
  View next the sad Assemblies that appear,
To tell their Grief for Him, and Joy for Her.
The first confounds the last with such Excess,
They hardly can their noble Thoughts express.
The illustrious Troop address her to condole,
And speak such Grief as wound her to the Soul:
They lodge their Sorrows in the Royal Breast;
The Harbour where the Nation looks for Rest.
  Next these, the Representatives arise,
With all the Nations Sorrow in their Eyes.
The Epithets they righteously apply ⎫
To the Restorer of their Liberty,   ⎬
Are Tokens of their Sence and Honesty. ⎭
For as a Body we were always true,
But 'tis our Parties that our Peace undo.
Who can like them the Peoples Grief express?
They shew her all the Tokens of Excess:
O'erwhelm'd with Sorrow, and supprest with Care,
They place the Nation's Refuge now in her:
Nothing but her Succession cou'd abate
The Nation's Sorrow for their Monarch's Fate:
And nothing but his Fate cou'd their true Joy
For her Succession lessen or destroy.
  The Civil Sword to her, as Heaven saw fit,
With general Satisfaction they commit:
How can it in a Hand like hers miscarry?

But who shall for us weild the Military?
Who shall the jarring Generals unite;
First teach them to agree, and then to fight?
Who shall renew'd Alliances contrive,
And keep the vast Confederacies alive?
Who shall the growing Gallick Force subdue?
'Twas more than all the World, but him, cou'd do.
  Sighs for departed Friends are senseless things,
But 'tis not so when Nations mourn for Kings:
When wounded Kingdoms such a Loss complain,
As Nature never can repair again;
The Tyrant Grief, like Love, obeys no Laws,
But blindly views the Effect, and not the Cause.
  Dark are the Works of Sovereign Providence,
And often clash with our contracted Sence:
But if we might with Heavens Decrees debate,
And of our Maker's Works expostulate,
Why shou'd he form a Mind supreamly great, ⎫
And to his Charge commit the Reins of Fate, ⎬
And at one hasty Blow the World defeat? ⎭
A Blow so sudden, so severe and swift,
We had no time for Supplication left:
As if Almighty Power had been afraid,
Such Prayers wou'd by such Multitudes be made;
Such *Moses*'s wou'd to his Altars go, ⎫
To whom he never did, or wou'd say no; ⎬
He hardly cou'd know how to strike the Blow. ⎭
  For Prayer so much the Sovraign Power commands, ⎫
Ev'n God himself sometimes as conquer'd stands, ⎬
And calls for Quarter at the Wrestler's Hands. ⎭
  How Strenuous then had been the Sacred Strife,
While all the kneeling World had begg'd his Life,
With all that Earnestness of Zeal, and more
Than ever Nation begg'd for King before?
See how the neighbouring Lands his Fame improve,
And by their Sorrows testifie their Love;

Sprinkle his Memory with grateful Tears,
And hand his Glory to succeeding Years.
    With what Contempt will *English* Men appear,
When future Ages read his Character?
They'll never bear to hear in time to come,
How he was lov'd abroad, and scorn'd at home.
The World will scarce believe it cou'd be true,
And Vengeance must such Insolence pursue.
Our Nation will by all Men be abhorr'd,
And *William*'s juster Fame be so restor'd.
    Posterity, when Histories relate
His Glorious Deeds, will ask, *What Giant's that?*
For common Vertues may Mens Fame advance,
But an immoderate Glory turns Romance.
Its real Merit does it self undo,
Men talk it up so high, it can't be true:
So *William*'s Life, encreas'd by doubling Fame,
Will drown his Actions to preserve his Name.
The Annals of his Conduct they'll revise,
As Legends of Impossibilities.
'Twill all a Life of Miracles appear,
Too great for Him to do, or Them to hear.
And if some faithful Writer shou'd set down
With what Uneasiness he wore the Crown;
What thankless Devil had the Land possest;
This will be more prodigious than the rest.
With Indignation 'twill their Minds inspire,
And raise the Glory of his Actions higher.
The Records of their Fathers they'll Deface,
And blush to think they sprung from such a Race.
They'll be asham'd their Ancestors to own,
And strive their Father's Follies to atone.
New Monuments of Gratitude they'll raise,
And Crown his Memory with Thanks and Praise.
    Thou, Satyr, shalt the grateful Few rehearse,
And solve the Nations Credit in thy Verse;

Embalm his Name with Characters of Praise,
His Fame's beyond the Power of Time to rase.
    From him let future Monarchs learn to Rule,
And make his lasting Character their School.
For he who wou'd in time to come be Great,
Has nothing now to do but imitate.
Let dying Parents when they come to bless,
Wish to their Children only his Success.
Here their Instructions very well may end, ⎫
William's Example only recommend,   ⎬
And leave the Youth his History t'attend. ⎭
    But we have here an Ignominious Croud,
That boast their Native Birth and English Blood,
Whose Breasts with Envy and Contention burn,
And now rejoice when all the Nations mourn:
Their awkward Triumphs openly they Sing;
Insult the Ashes of their injur'd King;
Rejoice at the Disasters of his Crown;
And Drink the Horse's Health that threw him down.[11]
    Blush, Satyr, when such Crimes we must reveal,
And draw a silent Curtain to conceal.
Actions so vile shall ne'er debauch our Song;
Let Heaven alone, tho' Justice suffers long.
Her Leaden Wings, and Iron Hands, may show
That she is certain, tho' she may be slow.
His Foreign Birth was made the Fam'd Pretence,
Which gave our Home-Born Englishmen Offence.
But Discontent's the antient English Fashion,
The Universal Blemish of the Nation.
And 'tis a Question, whether God cou'd make
That King whom every Englishman wou'd *like?*
Nor is it any Paradox to say,
William *had more of English Blood than they;*
The *Royal Life* flow'd in his sprightly Veins,
The same that in the *Noble Stock* remains;
The same which now his Glorious Scepter weilds,

To whom Three Nations just Obedience yeilds.
  ANNE, the remaining Glory of our Isle,
Well she becomes the Royal English Stile:
In *William*'s Steps sedately she proceeds,
William's *a Patern to immortal Deeds*.
Preserves his Memory with generous Care; ⎫
Forgetting him is Disobliging her; ⎬
Where shall the murmuring Party then appear! ⎭
Where wou'd the Nation, but for her, ha' found
So safe a Cure for such a sudden Wound?
And cou'd she but as well the Camp supply,
The World the sooner wou'd their grief lay by;
But there the Fatal Breach is made so wide,
That Loss can never, never be—supply'd.
Ye Men of Arms, and English Sons of War,
Now learn from him how you may Fight for her;
Your Grief for him express upon her Foes,
For William *lov'd such Funeral Tears as those*.

  'Tis *William*'s Glorious Scepter which she bears,
Like *William* she for Liberty appears.
She Mounts to Honour by the Steps of Truth,
And his Example Imitates in Both.
'Tis you must make her blooming Fame Increase,
'Tis you must bring her Honour, Wealth and Peace:
And let it once more to the World be seen,
Nothing can make us Greater than a Queen.

THE
SHORTEST-WAY
WITH THE
DISSENTERS:
OR
PROPOSALS
FOR THE
ESTABLISHMENT
OF THE
CHURCH.

Daniel Defoe

LONDON:
Printed in the Year MDCCII.

THE SHORTEST-WAY WITH THE DISSENTERS:

OR

PROPOSALS

For the
ESTABLISHMENT
Of the

CHURCH

LONDON:

Printed in the Year MDCCII

For writing this satire, published 1 December 1702, Defoe stood in the pillory on July 29, 30, and 31 1703, and was confined to Newgate Prison until early November. The pamphlet satirized Dr. Henry Sacheverell's famous Oxford sermon of June 1702, which urged the Church of England to take extreme measures against the Dissenters.

THE SHORTEST-WAY WITH THE DISSENTERS, &c.

SIR *Roger L'Estrange* tells us a Story in his Collection of Fables, of the Cock and the Horses.[1] The Cock was gotten to Roost in the Stable, among the Horses, and there being no Racks, or other Conveniencies for him, it seems, he was forc'd to roost upon the Ground; the Horses jostling about for room, and putting the Cock in danger of his Life, he gives them this grave Advice; *Pray Gentlefolks let us stand still, for fear we should tread upon one another.*

THERE are some People in the World, who now they are *unpearcht*, and reduc'd to an Equality with other People, and under strong and very just Apprehensions of being further treated as they deserve, begin with *Æsop*'s-Cock, to Preach up Peace and Union, and the Christian Duties of Moderation, forgetting, that when they had the Power in their Hands, those Graces were Strangers in their Gates.

It is now near Fourteen Years, that the Glory and Peace of the purest and most flourishing Church in the World has been Ecclips'd, Buffetted, and Disturb'd, by a sort of Men, who God in his Providence has suffer'd to insult over her, and bring her down; these have been the Days of her Humiliation and Tribulation: She has born with an invincible Patience the Reproach of the Wicked, and God has at last heard her Prayers, and deliver'd her from the Oppression of the Stranger.

And now they find their Day is over, their Power gone, and the Throne of this Nation possest by a Royal, *English*, True, and ever Constant Member of, and Friend to the Church of *England*. Now they find that they are in danger of the Church of *England*'s just Resentments; now they cry out *Peace, Union, Forbearance*, and *Charity*, as if the Church had not too long harbour'd her Enemies under her Wing, and nourish'd the viperous Brood, till they hiss and fly in the Face of the Mother that cherish'd them.

No Gentlemen, the Time of Mercy is past, your *Day of Grace is over;* you shou'd have practis'd Peace, and Moderation, and Charity, if you expected any your selves.

We have heard none of this Lesson for Fourteen Years past: We have been huff'd and bully'd with your Act of Tolleration;[2] you have told us that you are the *Church establish'd by Law,* as well as others; have set up your Canting-Synagogues at our Church-Doors, and the Church and her Members have been loaded with Reproaches, with Oaths, Associations, Abjurations, and what not; where has been the Mercy, the Forbearance, the Charity you have shewn to *tender Consciences of the Church of England,* that cou'd not take Oaths *as fast as you made 'em;* that having sworn Allegiance to their lawful and rightful King, cou'd not dispence with that Oath, *their King being still alive,* and swear to your new *Hodge-podge of a Dutch-Government.*[3] These ha' been turn'd out of their Livings, and they and their Families left to starve; their Estates double Tax'd, to carry on a War they had *no Hand in,* and you *got nothing by:* What Account can you give of the Multitudes you have forc'd to comply, against their Consciences, with your new *sophistical Politicks,* who like the new Converts in *France,* Sin because they can't Starve. And now the Tables are turn'd upon you, you *must not be Persecuted, 'tis not a Christian Spirit.*

You have *Butcher'd* one King, *Depos'd* another King, and made a *mock King* of a Third; and yet you cou'd have the Face to expect to be employ'd and trusted by the Fourth; any body that did not know the Temper of your Party, wou'd stand amaz'd at the Impudence, as well as Folly, to think of it.

Your Management of your *Dutch Monarch,* whom you reduc'd to a meer *King of Cl[ub]s,* is enough to give any future Princes such an Idea of your Principles, as to warn them sufficiently from coming into your Clutches; and God be thank'd, the Queen is out of your Hands, knows you, and will have a care of you.

There is no doubt but the supreme Authority of a Nation has in its self a Power, *and a Right to that Power,* to execute the Laws upon any Part of that Nation it governs. The execution of the known Laws of the Land, and that with but a weak and gentle Hand neither, was all that the phanatical Party of this Land have ever call'd Persecution; this they have magnified to a height, that the Sufferings of the *Hugonots* in *France* were not to be compar'd with ———— Now to execute the known Laws of a Nation upon those who transgress them, after having first been voluntarily consenting to the making those Laws, can never be call'd Persecution, but Justice: But Justice is always Violence to the Party offending, for every Man is Innocent in his own Eyes. The first execution of the Laws against Dissenters in *England*, was in the Days of King *James* the First; and what did it amount to, truly, the worst they suffer'd, was at their own request, to let them go to *New-England*, and erect a new Collony, and give them great Privileges, Grants, and suitable Powers, keep them under Protection, and defend them against all Invaders, and receive no Taxes or Revenue from them. This was the cruelty of the Church of *England*, fatal Lenity! 'Twas the ruin of that excellent Prince, King *Charles* the First. Had King *James* sent all the Puritans in *England* away to the *West-Indies*, we had been a national unmix'd Church; the Church of *England* had been kept undivided and entire.

To requite the Lenity of the Father, they take up Arms against the Son; Conquer, Pursue, Take, Imprison, and at last put to Death the anointed of God, and Destroy the very Being and Nature of Government, setting up a sordid Imposter, who had neither Title to Govern, nor Understanding to Manage, but supplied that want with Power, bloody and desperate Councils and Craft, without Conscience.

Had not King *James* the First witheld the full execution of the Laws; had he given them strict Justice, he had clear'd the Nation of them, and the Consequences had been plain; his *Son had never been murther'd by them,* nor the Monarchy overwhelm'd; 'twas *too much Mercy* shewn them, was the ruin of his Posterity, and the ruin of the Nation's Peace.

One would think the Dissenters should not have the Face to believe that we are to be wheedl'd and canted into Peace and Toleration, when they know that they have once requited us with a civil War, and once with an intollerable and unrighteous Persecution for our former Civillity.

Nay, to encourage us to be Easy with them, 'tis apparent, that they never had the Upper-hand of the Church, but they treated her with all the Severity, with all the Reproach and Contempt as was possible: What Peace, and what Mercy did they shew the Loyal Gentry of the Church of *England* in the time of their Triumphant Common-wealth? How did they put all the Gentry of *England* to ransom, whether they were actually in Arms for the King or not, making People compound for their Estates, and starve their Families? How did they treat the Clergy of the Church of *England,* sequester'd the Ministers, devour'd the Patrimony of the Church, and divided the Spoil, by sharing the Church-Lands among their Soldiers, and turning her Clergy out to starve; just such Measure as they have mete, shou'd be measur'd to them again.

Charity and Love is the known Doctrine of the Church of *England,* and 'tis plain she has put it in practice towards the Dissenters, even beyond what they ought, till she has been wanting to her self, and in effect, unkind to her own Sons; particularly, in the too much Lenity of King *James* the First, mentioned before, had he so rooted the Puritans from the Face of the Land, which he had an opportunity early to ha' done, they had not the Power to vex the Church, as since they have done.

IN the Days of King *Charles* the Second, how did the Church reward their bloody Doings with Lenity and Mercy, *except the barbarous Regicides of the pretended Court of Justice;* not a Soul suffer'd for all the Blood in an unnatural War: King *Charles* came in all Mercy and Love, cherish'd them, preferr'd them, employ'd them, witheld the rigour of the Law, and oftentimes, even against the Advice of his Parliament, gave them liberty of Conscience; and how did they requite him with the villainous Contrivance to Depose and Murther him and his Successor at the *Rye-Plot*.[4]

KING *James*, as if Mercy was the inherent Quality of the Family, began his Reign with unusual Favour to them: Nor could their joining with the Duke of *Monmouth* against him, move him to do himself Justice upon them; but that mistaken Prince thought to win them by Gentleness and Love, proclaim'd an universal Liberty to them, and rather discountenanc'd the Church of *England* than them; how they requited him all the World knows.[5]

THE late Reign is too fresh in the Memory of all the World to need a Comment; how under Pretence of joining with the Church in redressing some Grievances, they pusht things to that extremity, in conjunction with some mistaken Gentlemen, as to Depose the late King, as if the Grievance of the Nation cou'd not ha' been redress'd but by the absolute ruin of the Prince: Here's an Instance of their Temper, their Peace, and Charity. To what height they carried themselves during the Reign of a King of their own; how they crope into all Places of Trust and Profit; how they insinuated into the Favour of the King, and were at first preferr'd to the highest Places in the Nation; how they engrost the Ministry, and *above all, how pitifully they Manag'd*, is too plain to need any Remarks.

BUT particularly, their Mercy and Charity, the Spirit of Union, they tell us so much of, has been remarkable in *Scotland*, if any Man wou'd see the Spirit of a Dissenter, let him look into *Scotland;* there they made an entire Conquest of the Church, trampled down the sacred Orders, and supprest the Episcopal Government,[6] with an absolute, and as they suppose, irretrievable Victory, tho', 'tis possible, *they may find themselves mistaken:* Now 'twou'd be a very proper Question to ask their *Impudent Advocate, the Observator,*[7] Pray how much Mercy and Favour did the Members of the Episcopal Church find in *Scotland*, from the *Scotch* Presbyterian-Government; and I shall undertake for the Church of *England*, that the Dissenters shall still receive as much here, tho' they deserve but little.

In a small Treatise of the Sufferings of the Episcopal Clergy in *Scotland*,[8] 'twill appear, what Usage they met with, how they not only lost their Livings, but in several Places, were plunder'd and abus'd in their Persons; the Ministers that cou'd not conform, turn'd out, with numerous Families, and no Maintenance, and hardly Charity enough left to relieve them with a bit of Bread; and the Cruelties of the Party are innumerable, and not to be attempted in this short Piece.

And now to prevent the distant Cloud which they perceiv'd to hang over their Heads from *England;* with a true Presbyterian Policy, they put in for *a union of Nations,* that *England* might unite their Church with the Kirk of *Scotland,* and their Presbyterian Members sit in our House of Commons, and their Assembly of *Scotch* canting Long-Cloaks in our Convocation; what might ha' been, if our Phanatick, Whiggish-States-men had continu'd, God only knows; but we hope we are out of fear of that now.[9]

'Tis alledg'd by some of the Faction, and they began to Bully us with it; that if we won't unite with them, they will not settle the Crown with us again, but when her Majesty dies, will chuse a King for themselves.

If they won't, we must make them, and 'tis not the first time we have let them know that we are able: The Crowns of these Kingdoms have not so far disowned the right of Succession, but they may retrieve it again, and if *Scotland* thinks to come off from a Successive to an Elective State of Government, *England* has not promised not to assist the right Heir, and put them into possession, without any regard to their ridiculous Settlements.

THESE are the Gentlemen, these their ways of treating the Church, both at home and abroad. Now let us examine the Reasons they pretend to give why we shou'd be favourable to them, why we should continue and tollerate them among us.

First, THEY are very Numerous, they say, they are a great
    Part of the Nation, and we cannot suppress them.

To this may be answer'd 1. THEY are not so Numerous as
the Protestants in *France,* and yet the *French* King effectually
clear'd the Nation of them at once,[10] and we don't find he
misses them at home.

But I am not of the Opinion they are so Numerous as is
pretended; their Party is more Numerous than their Persons,
and those mistaken People of the Church, who are misled
and deluded by their wheedling Artifices, to join with them,
make their Party the greater; but those will open their Eyes,
when the Government shall set heartily about the work, and
come off from them, as some Animals, which they say, always
desert a House when 'tis likely to fall.

2dly. The more Numerous, the more Dangerous, and therefore the more need to suppress them; and God has suffer'd
us to bear them as Goads in our sides, for not utterly extin-
guishing them long ago.

3dly. If we are to allow them, only because we cannot
suppress them, then it ought to be tryed whether we can
or no; and I am of Opinion 'tis easy to be done, and cou'd
prescribe Ways and Means, if it were proper, but I doubt
not but the Government will find effectual Methods for the
rooting the Contagion from the Face of this Land.

ANOTHER Argument they use, which is this, That 'tis a
    time of War, and we have need to unite against the
    common Enemy.[11]

WE answer, this common Enemy had been no Enemy, if
they had not made him so; he was quiet in peace, and no
way disturb'd, or encroach'd upon us, and we know no reason
we had to quarrel with him.

But further, We make no question but we are able to deal
with this common Enemy without their help; but why must

we unite with them because of the Enemy, will they go over to the Enemy, if we do not prevent it by a union with them —————— We are very well contented they shou'd; and make no question, we shall be ready to deal with them and the common Enemy too, and better without them than with them.

Besides, if we have a common Enemy, there is the more need to be secure against our private Enemies; if there is one common Enemy, we have the less need to have an Enemy in our Bowels.

'Twas a great Argument some People used against suppressing the Old-Money,[12] that 'twas a time of War, and 'twas too great a Risque for the Nation to run, if we shou'd not master it, we shou'd be undone; and yet the Sequel prov'd the Hazard was not so great, but it might be mastered; and the Success was answerable. The suppressing the Dissenters is not a harder Work, nor a Work of less necessity to the Publick; we can never enjoy a settled uninterrupted Union and Tranquility in this Nation, till the Spirit of Whiggisme, Faction, and Schism is melted down like the Old-Money.

To talk of the Difficulty, is to Frighten our selves with Chimaeras and Notions of a Powerful Party, which are indeed a Party without Power; Difficulties often appear greater at a distance, than when they are search'd into with Judgment, and distinguish'd from the Vapours and Shadows that attend them.

We are not to be frightned with it; this Age is wiser than that, by all our own Experience, *and theire's too,* King *Charles* the First, had early supprest this Party, if he had took more deliberate Measures. In short, 'tis not worth arguing, to talk of their Arms, their *Monmouths,* and *Shaftsburys,* and *Argiles*[13] are gone, their *Dutch-Sanctuary* is at an end, Heaven has made way for their Destruction, and if we do not close with the Divine occasion, we are to blame our selves, and may remember that we had once an opportunity to serve the Church of *England,* by extirpating her implacable Enemies, and having let slip the Minute that Heaven presented, may experimentally Complain, *Post est Occasio Calvo*.[14]

Here are some popular Objections in the way.

> As first, THE Queen has promis'd them, to continue them in their tollerated Liberty; and has told us she will be a religious Observer of her Word.

WHAT her Majesty will do we cannot help, but what, as the Head of the Church, she ought to do, is another Case: Her Majesty has promised to Protect and Defend the Church of *England,* and if she cannot effectually do that without the Destruction of the Dissenters, she must of course dispence with one Promise to comply with another. But to answer *this Cavil more effectually:* Her Majesty did never promise to maintain the Tolleration, to the Destruction of the Church; but it is upon supposition that it may be compatible with the well being and safety of the Church, which she had declar'd she would take especial Care of: Now if these two Interests clash, 'tis plain her Majesties Intentions are to Uphold, Protect, Defend, and Establish the Church, and this we conceive is impossible.

> Perhaps it may be said, THAT the Church is in no immediate danger from the Dissenters, and therefore 'tis time enough: But this is a weak Answer.

For first, IF a Danger be real, the Distance of it is no Argument against, but rather a Spur to quicken us to prevention, lest it be too late hereafter.

And 2dly, Here is the Opportunity, and the only one perhaps that ever the Church had to secure her self, and destroy her Enemies.

The Representatives of the Nation have now an Opportunity, the Time is come which all good Men ha' wish'd for, that the Gentlemen of *England* may serve the Church of *England;*

now they are protected and encouraged by a Church of *England* Queen.

What will ye do for your Sister in the Day that she shall be spoken for.[15]

If ever you will establish the best Christian Church in the World.

If ever you will suppress the Spirit of Enthusiasm.

If ever you will free the Nation from the viperous Brood that have so long suck'd the Blood of their Mother.

If you will leave your Posterity free from Faction and Rebellion, this is the time.

This is the time to pull up this heretical Weed of Sedition, that has so long disturb'd the Peace of our Church, and poisoned the good Corn.

> BUT, says another Hot and Cold Objector, this is renewing Fire and Faggot, reviving the Act *De Heret. Comburendo:*[16] This will be Cruelty in its Nature, and Barbarous to all the World.

I answer, 'TIS Cruelty to kill a Snake or a Toad in cold Blood, but the Poyson of their Nature makes it a Charity to our Neighbours, to destroy those Creatures, not for any personal Injury receiv'd, but for prevention; not for the Evil they have done, but the Evil they may do.

Serpents, Toads, Vipers, &c. are noxious to the Body, and poison the sensative Life; these poyson the Soul, corrupt our Posterity, ensnare our Children, destroy the Vitals of our Happyness, our future Felicity, and contaminate the whole Mass.

Shall any Law be given to such wild Creatures: Some Beasts are for Sport, and the Huntsmen give them advantages of Ground; but some are knock'd on Head by all possible ways of Violence and Surprize.

I do not prescribe Fire and Fagot, but a[s] *Scipio* said of *Carthage, Dilenda est Carthago;*[17] they are to be rooted out of this Nation, if ever we will live in Peace, serve God, or enjoy our own: As for the Manner, I leave it to those Hands who have a right to execute God's Justice on the Nation's and the Church's Enemies.

BUT if we must be frighted from this Justice, under the specious Pretences, and odious Sense of Cruelty, nothing will be effected: 'Twill be more Barbarous and Cruel to our own Children, and dear Posterity, when they shall reproach their Fathers, as we do ours, and tell us, "You had an Opportunity to root out this cursed Race from the World, under the Favour and Protection of a true *English* Queen; and out of your foolish Pity you spared them, because, forsooth, you would not be Cruel, and now our Church is supprest and persecuted, our Religion trampl'd under Foot, our Estates plundered, our Persons imprisoned and dragg'd to Jails, Gibbets, and Scaffolds; your sparing this *Amalakite* Race is our Destruction, your Mercy to them proves Cruelty to your poor Posterity."

HOW just will such Reflections be, when our Posterity shall fall under the merciless Clutches of this uncharitable Generation, when our Church shall be swallow'd up in Schism, Faction, Enthusiasme, and Confusion; when our Government shall be devolv'd upon Foreigners, and our Monarchy dwindled into a Republick.

'Twou'd be more rational for us, if we must spare this Generation, to summon our own to a general Massacre, and as we have brought them into the World Free, send them out so, and not betray them to Destruction by our supine negligence, and then cry *it is Mercy*.

Moses was a merciful meek Man, and yet with what Fury did he run thro' the Camp, and cut the Throats of Three and thirty thousand of his dear *Israelites*,[18] that were fallen into Idolatry; what was the reason? 'twas Mercy to the rest, to make these be Examples, to prevent the Destruction of the whole Army.

How many Millions of future Souls we save from Infection and Delusion, if the present Race of poison'd Spirits were purg'd from the Face of the Land.

'TIS vain to trifle in this matter, the light foolish handling of them by Mulcts, Fines, &c. 'tis their Glory and their Advantage; if the Gallows instead of the Counter, and the Gallies instead of the Fines, were the Reward of going to a Conventicle, to preach or hear, there wou'd not be so many Sufferers, the Spirit of Martyrdom is over; they that will go to Church to be chosen Sheriffs and Mayors, would go to forty Churches rather than be Hang'd.[19]

If one severe Law were made, and punctually executed, that who ever was found at a Conventicle, shou'd be Banished the Nation, and the Preacher be Hang'd, we shou'd soon see an end of the Tale, they wou'd all come to Church; and one Age wou'd make us all One again.

TO talk of 5 s. a Month for not coming to the Sacrament, and 1 s. per Week for not coming to Church, this is such a way of converting People as never was known, this is selling them a Liberty to transgress for so much Money: If it be not a Crime, why don't we give them full Licence? And if it be, no Price ought to compound for the committing it, for that is selling a Liberty to People to sin against God and the Government.

If it be a Crime of the highest Consequence, both against the Peace and Welfare of the Nation, the Glory of God, the Good of the Church, and the Happiness of the Soul, let us rank it among capital Offences, and let it receive a Punishment in proportion to it.

We Hang Men for Trifles, and Banish them for things not worth naming, but an Offence against God and the Church, against the Welfare of the World, and the Dignity of Religion, shall be bought off for 5 s. this is such a shame to a Christian Government, that 'tis with regret I transmit it to Posterity.

IF Men sin against God, affront his Ordinances, rebell against his Church, and disobey the Precepts of their Superiors, let them suffer as such capital Crimes deserve, so will Religion flourish, and this divided Nation be once again united.

And yet the Title of Barbarous and Cruel will soon be taken

off from this Law too. I am not supposing that all the Dissenters in *England* shou'd be Hang'd or Banish'd, but as in cases of Rebellions and Insurrections, if a few of the Ring-leaders suffer, the Multitude are dismist, so a few obstinate People being made Examples there's no doubt but the Severity of the Law would find a stop in the Compliance of the Multitude.

To make the reasonableness of this matter out of question, and more unanswerably plain, let us examine for what it is that this Nation is divided into Parties and Factions, and let us see how they can justify a Separation, or we of the Church of *England* can justify our bearing the Insults and Inconveniences of the Party.

ONE of their leading Pastors,[20] and a Man of as much Learning as most among them, in his Answer to a Pamphlet, entituled, *A[n] Enquiry into the occasional Conformity*, hath these words, P. 27 *Do the Religion of the Church and the Meeting-houses make two Religions? Wherein do they differ? The Substance of the same Religion is common to them both; and the Modes and Accidents are the things in which only they differ.* P. 28 *Thirty nine Articles are given us for the summary of our Religion, Thirty six contain the Substance of it, wherein we agree; Three the additional Appendices, about which we have some differences.*[21]

Now, if as by their own acknowledgement, the Church of *England* is a true Church, and the Differences between them is only a few *Modes and Accidents,* Why shou'd we expect that they will suffer Gallows and Gallies, corporeal Punishment and Banishment for these Trifles; there is no question but they will be wiser; even their own Principles won't bear them out in it, they will certainly comply with the Laws, and with Reason, and tho' at the first, Severity may seem hard, the next Age will feel nothing of it; the Contagion will be rooted out; the Disease being cur'd, there will be no need of the Operation, but if they should venture to transgress, and fall into the Pit, all the World must condemn their Obstinacy, as being without Ground from their own Principles.

Thus the Pretence of Cruelty will be taken off, and the Party actually supprest, and the Disquiets they have so often brought upon the Nation, prevented.

THEIR Numbers, and their Wealth, makes them Haughty, and that is so far from being an Argument to perswade us to forbear them, that 'tis a Warning to us, without any more delay, to reconcile them to the Unity of the Church, or remove them from us.

AT present, Heaven be prais'd, they are not so Formidable as they have been, and 'tis our own fault if ever we suffer them to be so; Providence, and the Church of *England,* seems to join in this particular, that now the Destroyers of the Nations Peace may be overturn'd, and to this end the present Opportunity seems to be put into our Hands.

To this end her present Majesty seems reserv'd to enjoy the Crown, that the Ecclesiastick as well as Civil Rights of the Nation may be restor'd by her Hand.

To this end the Face of Affairs have receiv'd such a Turn in the process of a few Months, as never has been before; the leading Men of the Nation, the universal Cry of the People, the unanimous Request of the Clergy, agree in this, that the Deliverance of our Church is at hand.

For this end has Providence given us such a Parliament, such a Convocation, such a Gentry, and such a Queen as we never had before.

AND what may be the Consequences of a Neglect of such Opportunities? The Succession of the Crown has but a dark Prospect, another *Dutch* Turn may make the Hopes of it ridiculous, and the Practice impossible: Be the House of our future Princes never so well inclin'd, they will be Foreigners; and many Years will be spent in suiting the Genius of Strangers to the Crown, and to the Interests of the Nation; and how many Ages it may be before the *English* Throne be fill'd with so much Zeal and Candour, so much Tenderness, and hearty Affection to the Church, as we see it now cover'd with, who can imagine.

'Tis high time then for the Friends of the Church of *England,* to think of Building up, and Establishing her, in such a manner, that she may be no more Invaded by Foreigners, nor Divided by Factions, Schisms, and Error.

IF this cou'd be done by gentle and easy Methods, I shou'd be glad, but the Wound is coroded, the Vitals begin to mortifie, and nothing but Amputation of Members can compleat the Cure; all the ways of Tenderness and Compassion, all perswasive Arguments have been made use of in vain.

THE Humour of the Dissenters has so encreas'd among the People, that they hold the Church in Defiance, and the House of God is an Abomination among them: Nay, they have brought up their Posterity in such pre-possest Aversions to our Holy Religion, that the ignorant Mob think we are all Idolaters, and Worshippers of *Baal;* and account it a Sin to come within the Walls of our Churches.

The primitive Christians were not more shie of a Heathen-Temple, or of Meat offer'd to Idols, nor the *Jews* of Swine's-Flesh, than some of our Dissenters are of the Church, and the Divine Service solemnized therein.

THIS Obstinancy must be rooted out with the Profession of it, while the Generation are left at liberty daily to affront God Almighty, and Dishonour his Holy Worship, we are wanting in our Duty to God, and our Mother the Church of *England.*

How can we answer it to God, to the Church, and to our Posterity, to leave them entangled with Fanaticisme, Error, and Obstinacy, in the Bowels of the Nation; to leave them an Enemy in their Streets, that in time may involve them in the same Crimes, and endanger the utter Extirpation of Religion in the Nation.

WHAT's the Difference betwixt this, and being subjected to the Power of the Church of *Rome,* from whence we have reform'd? If one be an extreme on one Hand, and one on another, 'tis equally destructive to the Truth, to have Errors settled among us, let them be of what Nature they will.

Both are Enemies of our Church, and of our Peace, and why shou'd it not be as criminal to admit an Enthusiast as a Jesuit? Why shou'd the *Papist* with his Seven Sacraments be worse than the *Quaker* with no Sacraments at all? Why shou'd Religious-houses be more intollerable than Meeting-houses —— *Alas the Church of England!* What with Popery on one Hand, and Schismaticks on the other; how has she been Crucify'd between two Thieves.

Now *let us Crucifie the Thieves.* Let her Foundations be establish'd upon the Destruction of her Enemies: The Doors of Mercy being always open to the returning Part of the deluded People: Let the Obstinate be rul'd with the Rod of Iron.

Let all true Sons of so Holy an Oppressed Mother, exasperated by her Afflictions, harden their Hearts against those who have oppress'd her.

And may God Almighty put it into the Hearts of all the Friends of Truth, to lift up a Standard against Pride and Antichrist, that the Posterity of the Sons of Error may be rooted out from the Face of this Land for ever ——.

THE
CONSOLIDATOR:
—— OR, ——
MEMOIRS
—— OF ——
Sundry Transactions

FROM THE

World in the Moon.

Translated from the Lunar
LANGUAGE,

By the AUTHOR of
The True-born English Man.

LONDON:
Printed, and are to be Sold by *Benj. Bragg*
at the *Blue Ball* in *Ave-mary-lane*, 1705.

THE CONSOLIDATOR:

OR

MEMOIRS

Of

SUNDRY TRANSACTIONS

From the

WORLD in the MOON.

Translated

from the Lunar LANGUAGE,

By the AUTHOR of
THE TRUE-BORN ENGLISH MAN.

LONDON:

Printed, and are to be Sold by Benj. Bragg *at the* Blue Ball *in* Ave-mary-lane, *1705.*

118

Advertised in the *Review,* the *Consolidator* was published on 26 March 1705. Defoe allegorizes the political and personal events of his lifetime in this lengthy discussion of the world in the moon. The present selection is taken from pages 32–55 of the first edition.

As all these noble Acquirements came down with this wonderful Man from the World in the *Moon,* it furnisht me with these useful Observations.[1]

1. That Country must needs be a Place of strange Perfection, in all parts of extraordinary Knowledge.

2. How useful a thing it would be for most sorts of our People, especially Statesmen, P[ries] t-men, Convocation-men, Phylosophers, Physicians, Quacks, Mountebanks, Stock-jobbers, and all the Mob of the Nation's Civil or Ecclesiastical *Bone-setters,* together with some Men of the Law, some of the Sword, and all of the Pen: I say, how useful and improving a thing it must be to them, to take a Journey up to the World in the *Moon;* but above all, how much more beneficial it would be to them that stay'd behind.

3. That it is not to be wonder'd at, why the *Chinese* excell so much all these Parts of the World, since but for that Knowledge which comes down to them from the World in the *Moon,* they would be like other People.

4. No Man need to Wonder at my exceeding desire to go up to the World in the *Moon,* having heard of such extraordinary Knowledge to be obtained there, since in the search of Knowledge and Truth, wiser Men than I have taken as unwarrantable Flights, and gone a great deal higher than the *Moon,* into a strange Abbys of dark *Phaenomena,* which they neither could make other People understand, nor ever rightly understood themselves, witness *Malbranch,* Mr. *Lock, Hobbs,* the Honour-

able *Boyle,* and a great many others, besides Messieurs *Norris, Asgil, Coward,* and the *Tale of a Tub.*[2]

This great Searcher into Nature has, besides all this, left wonderful Discoveries and Experiments behind him; but I was with nothing more exceedingly diverted, than with his various Engines, and curious Contrivances, to go to and from his own Native Country the *Moon.* All our Mechanick Motions of Bishop *Wilkins,* or the artificial Wings of the Learned *Spaniard,*[3] who could have taught God Almighty how to have mended the Creation, are Fools to this Gentleman; and because no Man in *China* has made more Voyages up into the *Moon* than my self, I cannot but give you some Account of the easyness of the Passage, as well as of the Country.

Nor are his wonderful Tellescopes of a mean Quality, by which such plain Discoveries are made, of the Lands and Seas in the *Moon,* and in all the habitable Planets, that one may as plainly see what a Clock it is by one of the Dials in the *Moon,* as if it were no farther off than *Windsor-Castle;* and had he liv'd to finish the Speaking-trumpet which he had contriv'd to convey Sound thither, *Harlequin's Mock-Trumpet*[4] had been a Fool to it; and it had no doubt been an admirable Experiment, to have given us a general Advantage from all their acquir'd Knowledge in those Regions, where no doubt several useful Discoveries are daily made by the Men of Thought for the Improvement of all sorts of humane Understanding, and to have discoursed with them on those things, must have been very pleasant, besides, its being very much to our particular Advantage.

I confess, I have thought it might have been very useful to this Nation, to have brought so wonderful an Invention hither, and I was once very desirous to have set up my rest here, and for the Benefit of my Native Country, have made my self Master of these Engines, that I might in due time have convey'd them to our Royal Society,[5] that once in 40 Years they might have been said to do something for Publick Good; and that the Reputation and Usefulness of the *so so's* might be recovered in *England;* but being told that in the Moon there were many of these Glasses to be had very cheap, and I having declar'd my Resolution of undertaking a Voyage thither, I deferred my Design, and shall defer my treating of them, till I give some Account of my Arrival there.

But above all his Inventions for making this Voyage, I saw none more pleasant or profitable, than a certain Engine formed in the shape of a Chariot,[6] on the Backs of two vast Bodies with extended Wings, which spread about 50 Yards in Breadth, compos'd of Feathers so nicely put together, that no Air could pass; and as the Bodies were made of *Lunar Earth* which would bear the Fire, the Cavities were fill'd with an Ambient Flame, which fed on a certain Spirit deposited in a proper quantity, to last out the Voyage; and this Fire so order'd as to move about such Springs and Wheels as kept the Wings in a most exact and regular Motion, always ascendant; thus the Person being placed in this airy Chariot, drinks a certain dozing Draught, that throws him into a gentle Slumber, and Dreaming all the way, never wakes till he comes to his Journey's end.

Of the Consolidator.

These Engines are call'd in their Country Language, *Dupe-kasses;* and according to the Ancient *Chinese,* or *Tartarian, Apezolanthukanistes;* in *English,* a *Consolidator.*

The Composition of this Engine is very admirable; for, as is before noted, 'tis all made up of Feathers, and the quality of the Feathers, is no less wonderful than their Composition; and therefore, I hope the Reader will bear with the Description for the sake of the Novelty, since I assure him such things as these are not to be seen in every Country.

The number of Feathers are just 513,[7] they are all of a length and breadth exactly, which is absolutely necessary to the *floating Figure,* or else one side or any one part being wide or longer than the rest, it would interrupt the motion of the whole Engine; only there is one extraordinary Feather which, as there is an odd one in the number, is placed in the Center, and is the Handle, or rather Rudder to the whole Machine:[8] This Feather is every way larger than its Fellows, 'tis almost as long and broad again; but above all, its Quill or Head is much larger, and it has *as it were* several small bushing *Feathers* round the bottom of it, which all make but one presiding or superintendent Feather, to guide, regulate, and pilot the whole Body.

Nor are these common Feathers, but they are pickt and cull'd out of all parts of the Lunar Country, by the Command of the Prince; and every Province sends up the best they can find, *or ought to do so at least*, or else they are very much to blame; for the Employment they are put to being of so great use to the Publick, and the Voyage or Flight so exceeding high, it would be very ill done if, when the King sends his Letters about the Nation, to pick him up the best Feathers they can lay their Hands on, they should send weak, decay'd, or half-grown Feathers, and yet sometimes it happens so; and once there was such rotten Feathers collected, whether it was a bad Year for Feathers, or whether the People that gather'd them had a mind to abuse their King; but the Feathers were so bad, the Engine was good for nothing, but broke before it was got half way; and by a double Misfortune, this happen'd to be at an unlucky time, when the King himself had resolv'd on a Voyage, or Flight to the Moon; but being deceiv'd, by the unhappy Miscarriage of the deficient Feathers, he fell down from so great a height, that he struck himself against his own Palace, and beat his Head off.[9]

Nor had the Sons of this Prince much better Success, tho' the first of them was a Prince[10] mightily belov'd by his Subjects; but his Misfortunes chiefly proceeded from his having made use of one of the Engines so very long, that the Feathers were quite worn out, and good for nothing: He used to make a great many Voyages and Flights into the *Moon,* and then would make his Subjects give him great Sums of Money to come down to them again; and yet they were so fond of him,

That they always complyed with him, and would give him every thing he askt, rather than to be without him: *But they grew wiser since.*

At last, this Prince used his Engine so long, it could hold together no longer; and being obliged to write to his Subjects to pick him out some new Feathers, *they did so;* but withall sent him such *strong* Feathers, and so *stiff,* that when he had placed 'em in their proper places, and made a very beautiful Engine, it was *too heavy for him to manage:* He made a great many Essays at it, and had it placed on the top of an old Idol Chappel, dedicated to an old *Bramyn*[11] Saint of those Countries, called, *Phantosteinaschap;* in *Latin, chap. de Saint Stephano;* or in *English,* St. *Stephen's:* [12] Here the Prince try'd all possible Contrivances, and a vast deal of Money it cost him; but the Feathers were *so stiff* they would not work, and *the Fire within* was so choaked and smother'd with its *own Smoak,* for want of due Vent and Circulation, that it *would not burn;* so he was oblig'd to take it down again; and from thence he carried it to his College of *Bramyn* Priests, and set it up in one of their Publick Buildings: There he drew Circles of Ethicks and Politicks, and fell to casting of Figures and Conjuring, but all would not do, *the Feathers* could not be brought to move; and, indeed, I have observ'd, That these Engines are seldom helpt by Art and Contrivance; there is no way with them, but to have the People spoke to, to get *good Feathers;* and they are easily placed, and perform all the several Motions with the greatest Ease and Accuracy imaginable; *but it must be all Nature;* any thing of Force distorts and dislocates them, and the whole Order is spoiled; and if there be but one Feather out of place, or pincht, or stands wrong, *the D[evi]l would not ride in the Chariot.*

The Prince thus finding his Labour in vain, broke the Engine to pieces, and sent his Subjects Word what bad Feathers they had sent him: But the People, who knew it was his own want of Management, and that the Feathers were good enough, only a little stiff at first, and with good Usage would have been brought to be fit for use, took it ill, and never would send him any other as long as he liv'd: However, it had this good effect upon him, That he never made any more Voyages to the *Moon* as long as he reign'd.

His Brother succeeded him;[13] and truly he was resolved upon a Voyage to the *Moon,* as soon as ever he came to the Crown. He had met with some unkind Usgae from the Religious *Lunesses* of his own Country; and he turn'd *Abogratzi-arian,* a zealous fiery Sect something like our *Anti-every-body-arians* in England. 'Tis confest, some of the *Bramyns* of his Country were very false to him, put him upon several Ways of extending his Power over his Subjects, contrary to the Customs of the People, and contrary to his own Interest; and when the People expressed their Dislike of it, he thought to have been supported by those Clergymen; but they failed him, and made good that Old *English* Verse;

That Priests of all Religions are the same.

He took this so hainously, that he conceiv'd a just Hatred against those that had deceiv'd him; and as Resentments seldom keep Rules, unhappily entertain'd Prejudices against all the rest; and not finding it easy to bring all his Designs to pass better, he resolved upon a Voyage to the *Moon.*

Accordingly, he sends a Summons to all his People according to Custom, to collect the usual quantity of Feathers for that purpose; and because he would be sure not be used as his Brother and Father had been, he took care to send certain Cunning-men Express, all over the Country, to bespeak the People's Care, in collecting, picking and culling them out, these were call'd in their Language, *Tsopablesdetoo;* which being Translated may signify in *English, Men of Zeal,* or *Booted Apostles:* Nor was this the only Caution this Prince used; for he took care, as the Feathers were sent up to him, to search and examine them one by one in his own Closet, to see if they were fit for his purpose; but, alas! he found himself in his

Brother's Case exactly; and perceived, That his Subjects were generally disgusted at his former Conduct, about *Abrogratzianism,* and such things, and particularly set in a Flame by some of their Priests, call'd, *Dullobardians,*[14] or *Passive-Obedience-men,* who had lately turn'd their Tale, and their Tail too upon their own Princes; and upon this, he laid aside any more Thoughts of the Engine, but took up a desperate and implacable Resolution, *viz.* to fly up to the Moon without it; in order to [do] this, abundance of his Cunning-men were summon'd together to assist him, strange Engines contriv'd, and Methods propos'd; and a great many came from all Parts, to furnish him with Inventions and equivalent for their Journey; but all were so preposterous and ridiculous, that his Subjects seeing him going on to ruin himself, and by Consequence them too, unanimously took Arms; and if their Prince had not made his Escape into a foreign Country,[15] 'tis thought they would have secur'd him *for a Mad-man.*

And here 'tis observable, That as it is in most such Cases, the mad Councellors of this Prince, when the People begun to gather about him, fled; and every one shifted for themselves; nay, and some of them plunder'd him first of his Jewels and Treasure, and never were heard of since.[16]

From this Prince none of the Kings or Government of that Country have ever seem'd to incline to the hazardous Attempt of the Voyage to the *Moon,* at least not in such a hair-brain'd manner.

However, the Engine has been very accurately Re-built and finish'd; and the People are now oblig'd by a Law, to send up new Feathers every three Years,[17] to prevent the Mischiefs which happen'd by that Prince aforesaid, keeping one Set so long, that it was dangerous to venture with them; and thus the Engine is preserved fit for use.

And yet has not this Engine been without its continual Disasters, and often out of repair; for though the Kings of the Country, as has been Noted, have done riding on the back of it, yet the *restless* Courtiers and Ministers of State have frequently obtained the Management of it, from the too easy Goodness of their Masters, or the Evils of the Times.

To cure this, the Princes frequently chang'd Hands, turn'd one Set of Men out and put another in: But this made things still worse; for it divided the People into Parties and Factions in the State, and still the Strife was, who should ride in this Engine; and no sooner were these *Skaet-Riders*[18] got into it, but they were for *driving all the Nation up to the* Moon: But of this by it self.

Authors differ concerning the Original of these Feathers, and by what most exact Hand they were first appointed to this particular use; and as their Original is hard to be found, so it seems a Difficulty to resolve from what sort of Bird these Feathers are obtained: Some have nam'd one, some another; but the most Learned in those Climates call it by a hard Word, which the Printer having no Letters to express, and being in that place Hieroglyphical, I can translate no better, than by the Name of a *Collective:* This must be a strange Bird without doubt; it has Heads, Claws, Eyes and Teeth innumerable; and if I should go about to describe it to you, the History would be so Romantick, it would spoil the Credit of these more Authentick Relations which are yet behind.

'Tis sufficient, therefore, for the present, only to leave you this short Abridgement of the Story, as follows: This great Monstrous Bird, call'd the *Collective*, is very seldom seen, and indeed never, but upon *Great Revolutions*, and portending terrible Desolations and Destructions to a Country.

But he frequently sheds his Feathers; and they are carefully pickt up, by the *Proprietors* of those Lands where they fall; for *none but those Proprietors may* meddle with them; and they no sooner pick them up but they are sent to Court, where they obtain a new Name, and are called in a Word equally difficult to pronounce as the other, but very like our *English* Word, *Representative;* and being placed in their proper Rows, with the *Great Feather* in the Center, and fitted for use, they lately obtained the Venerable Title of, *The Consolidators;* and the Machine it self, the *Consolidator;* and by that Name the Reader is desir'd for the future to let it be dignified and distinguish'd.

I cannot, however, forbear to descant a little here, on the Dignity and Beauty of these Feathers, being such as are hardly to be seen in any part of the World, but just in these remotest Climates.

And First, Every Feather has various Colours, and according to the Variety of the Weather, are apt to look brighter and clearer, or paler and fainter, as the *Sun* happens to look on them with a stronger or weaker Aspect. The Quill or Head of every Feather is *or ought to be* full of a vigorous Substance, which gives Spirit, and supports the brightness and colour of the Feather; and as this is more or less in quantity, the bright Colour of the Feather is increased, or turns languid and pale.

'Tis true, some of those Quills are exceeding empty and dry; and the Humid being totally exhal'd, those Feathers grow very useless and insignificant in a short time.

Some again are so full of Wind, and puft up with the Vapour of the Climate, that there's not Humid enough to Condence the Steam; and these are so fleet, so light, and so continually fluttering and troublesome, that they greatly serve to disturb and keep the Motion unsteddy.

Others either placed too near the inward concealed Fire, or the Head of the Quill being thin, the Fire causes too great a Fermentation; and the Consequence of this is so fatal, that sometimes it mounts the Engine up too fast, and indangers Precipitation: But 'tis happily observed, That these ill Feathers are but a very few, compar'd to the whole number; at the most, I never heard they were above 134[19] of the whole number: As for the empty ones, they are not very dangerous, but a sort of *Good-for-nothing Feathers,* that will fly when the greatest number of the rest fly, or stand still when they stand still. The fluttering hotheaded Feathers are the most dangerous, and frequently struggle hard to mount the Engine to extravagant heights; but still the greater number of the Feathers being staunch, and well fixt, as well as well furnisht, they always prevail, and check the Disorders the other would bring upon the Motion; so that upon the whole Matter, tho' there has sometimes been oblique Motions, Variations, and sometimes great Wandrings out of the way, which may make the Passage tedious, yet it has always been a certain and safe Voyage; and no Engine was ever known to miscarry or overthrow, but that one mentioned before, and that was very much owing to the precipitate Methods the Prince took in guiding it; and tho' all the fault was laid in the Feathers, *and they were to blame enough,* yet I never heard any Wise Man, but what blam'd his Discretion, and particularly, a certain great Man has wrote three large Tracts of those Affairs, and call'd them, *The History of the Opposition of the Feathers;*[20] wherein, tho' it was expected he would have curst the Engine it self and all the Feathers to the Devil, on the contrary, he lays equal blame on the Prince, who guided the Chariot with so unsteddy a Hand, now as much too slack, as then too hard, turning them this way and that so hastily, that the Feathers could not move in their proper order; and this at last put the Fire in the Center quite out, and so the Engine over-set at once. This Impartiality has done great Justice to the Feathers, and set things in a clearer light: But of this I shall say more, when I come to treat of the *Works of the Learned* in this Lunar World.

This is hinted here only to inform the Reader, That this Engine is the safest Passage that ever was found out; and that saving that one time, it never miscarried; nor if the common Order of things be observed, cannot Miscarry; for the good Feathers are always *Negatives,* when any precipitant Motion is felt, and immediately suppress it by their number; and these *Negative Feathers* are indeed the Travellers safety; the other are always upon the flutter, and upon every occasion *hey for the Moon,* up in the Clouds presently; but these *Negative Feathers* are never for going up, but when there is occasion for it; and from hence these fluttering fermented Feathers were called by the Antients *High-flying Feathers*,[21] and the blustering things seem'd proud of the Name.

But to come to their general Character, the Feathers, speaking of them all together, are generally very Comely, Strong, Large, Beautiful things, their Quills or Heads well fixt, and the Cavities fill'd with a solid substantial Matter, which tho' it is full of Spirit, has a great deal of Temperament, and full of suitable well-dispos'd Powers, to the Operation for which they are design'd.

These placed, as I Noted before, in an extended Form like two great Wings, and operated by that sublime Flame; which being concealed in proper Receptacles, obtains its vent at the Cavities appointed, are supplied from thence with Life and Motion; and as Fire it self, in the Opinion of some Learned Men, is nothing but Motion, and Motion tends to Fire: It can no more be a Wonder, if exalted in the Center of this famous Engine, a whole Nation should be carried up to the world in the *Moon*.

'Tis true, this Engine is frequently assaulted with fierce Winds, and furious Storms, which sometimes drive it a great way out of its way; and indeed, considering the length of the Passage, and the various Regions it goes through, it would be strange if it should meet with no Obstructions: These are oblique Gales, and cannot be said to blow from any of the Thirty-two Points, but Retrograde and Thwart: Some of these are call'd in their Language, *Pensionazima,* which is as much as to say, being Interpreted, a *Court-breeze;* another sort of Wind, which generally blows directly contrary to the *Pensionazima,* is the *Clamorio,* or in *English,* a *Country Gale;* this is generally Tempestuous, full of Gusts and Disgusts, Squauls and sudden Blasts, not without claps of Thunder, and not a little flashing of Heat and Party-fires.

There are a great many other Internal Blasts, which proceed from the Fire within, which sometimes not circulating right, breaks out in little Gusts of Wind and Heat, and is apt to indanger setting Fire to the Feathers, and this is more or less dangerous, according as among which of the Feathers it happens; for some of the Feathers are more apt to take Fire than others, as their Quills or Heads are more or less full of that solid Matter mention'd before.

The Engine suffers frequent Convulsions and Disorders from these several Winds; and which if they chance to overblow very much, hinder the Passage; but the Negative Feathers always apply Temper and Moderation; and this brings all to rights again.

For a Body like this, what can it not do? what cannot such an Extension perform in the Air? And when one thing is tackt to another, and properly *Consolidated* into one mighty *Consolidator,* no question but whoever shall go up to the *Moon,* will find himself so improv'd in this wonderful Experiment, that not a Man ever perform'd that wonderful Flight, but he certainly came back again as wise as he went.

Well, Gentlemen, and what if we are call'd *High-flyers* now, and an Hundred Names of Contempt and Distinction, what is this to the purpose? who would not be a *High-flyer,* to be Tackt and *Consolidated* in an Engine of such sublime Elevation, and which lifts Men, Monarchs, Members, yea, and whole Nations, up into the Clouds; and performs with such wondrous Art, the long expected Experiment of a Voyage to the *Moon?* And thus much for the Description of the *Consolidator.*

The first Voyage I ever made to this Country, was in one of these Engines; and I can safely affirm, I never wak'd all the way; and now having been as often there as most that have us'd that Trade, it may be expected I should give some Account of the Country; for it appears, I can give but little of the Road.

Only this I understand, That when this Engine, by help of these Artificial Wings, has raised it self up to a certain height, the Wings are as useful to keep it from falling into the *Moon,* as they were before to raise it, and keep it from falling back into this Region again.

This may happen from an alteration of Centers, and Gravity having past a certain Line, the Equipoise changes its Tendency, the Magnetick Quality being beyond it, it inclines of Course, and pursues a Center, which it finds in the *Lunar World,* and lands us safe upon the Surface.[22]

A
REVIEW
OF THE
STATE
OF THE
BRITISH NATION.

VOL. VII.

LONDON:

Printed in the Year MDCCXI.

(Price Two Pence.)

A
REVIEW
OF THE
STATE
OF THE
BRITISH NATION

Vol. VII.

LONDON:

Printed in the Year MDCCXI.
(PRICE TWO PENCE)

From 19 February 1704 to 11 June 1713 Defoe's *Review* gives a superb view of life in eighteenth-century England. Defoe writes not only of the Scotch Union and party politics, but of religion, economics, music, theatre, and the manners and mores of his age.

THURSDAY, *MARCH* 31. 1709.

THo the Printing this Paper has been long enough Discourst of, and the Gentlemen who have Encourag'd it in *Scotland* by

their generous Subscription, are not to be supposed Ignorant
of the Design in it; yet it may not be improper to say something
by way of Introduction, at its first appearing in *Scotland*, to
signifie to the Publick what may be expected from the Author,
and what the Author expects from the Age this comes out in.

To begin with the Author, and if he speaks of South *Britain*
singly, truly he expects his Usage shall be, *as it has been,* very
indifferent, according, not only to the Temper of the Times he
lives in, but according to the differing Interests, Parties, Opinions, and Expectations of the People: He has Wrote now five
Volumes of this Work, and this, tho it be the first in *Scotland,*
begins the sixth,—[1] And to tell you a little what Treatment it
has met with in the World, you may take it in a few Words.
—The Enemies of our Peace[2] have tacitly Acknowledg'd its
Efficacy by their Noise, Uneasiness, and violent Treatment
both of the Author and the Work: This he takes for a Testimony of the Wholsomness of his Work, as the Physician does
of the Operation of his Medicine; when the Patient grows
Sick, Vomits, Purges, and Cries out—: He Professes to Point
at, and if possible, to pierce through the Principles of *Jacobi-
tism,* sum'd up in Tyranny and Passive Obedience: To reprove
Vice, Expose our Inclinations to Bondage, our Negligence in
State Politicks, *and indeed in all our Politicks:* In short, to
declare open War with every thing that obstructs the Peace,
Prosperity, Trade and Reformation of *Britain,* and if this makes
some People uneasie, it is a Testimony both of the Occasion,
and of the Efficacy of the Work.

For this Reason he is to be Maltreated, his Morals Examined,
all his Sins, and more Sins than his own Charged upon him in
Publick—. He desires to begin the Reformation he presses to,
as all Reformers should begin, viz. *at himself,* and he freely
Challenges the World, as he has often done, to Charge on him,
humane Frailty excepted, the least Crime that can unqualify
him to Reprove others, he expects to be as the Prophet. *Without Honour in his own Country:* He expects ill Language,
ill Usage, and all sorts of Contempt, from those whose Follies

are too plainly Remark'd in these Papers: And he is fully prepared for all this Usage, to which he gives the World no other Return, than pursuing boldly and impartially the Work he is upon, regarding no Clamour, no Slander, nor any farther concerning himself in the Noise of the World, than to clear up the Truth of every thing he says, and defend it from Calumny and Reproach.

But this is not all, He expects to be Slighted, and often Disregarded, nay to be spoken ill of, even by the People he Serves; and that while he is serving them—; That the very Truths he shall Advance, shall receive some Diminution from the Meanness of the Instrument—. *Thus it was* when the poor blind Man reproved the stupid *Jews,* in their opposing and lessening the Honour of the Miracle wrought by our blessed LORD, in opening his Eyes; *Thou wert altogether Born in Sin, and dost thou Teach us?* And yet all the poor Man said was True, and their Ignorance deserved the greatest Satyr, *viz.* That they should not know whence our Saviour was, *and yet,* says the poor Man, *He has opened mine Eyes.* If this Man were not of GOD, *he could do nothing*—: So, in Answer to these sort of People the Author says, TRUTH is a simple uncompounded Jewel, recommending it self to the Understandings of all rational Creatures, who indeed are no otherwise rational than by being Capable of Judging, Arguing, and Determining of Truth, and Falsehood: TRUTH carries a convincing Efficacy with it, which forces its way into the Souls and Consciences of Men;—*This Truth* receives no Advantage, nor suffers Loss by the Greatness, or Lowness of the Messenger that brings it; Especially when Impartial Judgments weigh it, if therefore the Messenger that brings it does not please you, yet *Good People,* receive the Truth for its own sake, and freely paying Homage to the powerful Influence of Demonstration, Treat the Author of this as you please, he seeks neither Profit nor Applause. . . .

SATURDAY, FEBRUARY 4. 1710.

THis Paper, I hope, shall never want a Word for the Miserable, and the Time to speak it is, when it may do them Good, or never—I saw in a late Vote of the *House* of *Commons*, that the *House* would set a Day apart to consider the Condition of the Bankrupts in this Nation—Indeed, the Case of the miserable Families, that now groan under the Weight of that Case, is such, as well deserves the Consideration of a *House* of *Commons;* and on the other hand is so nice, that nothing but a *House* of *Commons* can apply suitable Remedies to.[3]

There are two Extremes, which have long contended with one another, and for Want of a *Medium*, for which Thousands of Families are made wretched, and never can be either deliver'd for themselves, or restor'd to the Common-Wealth—And nothing but a *House* of *Commons* can steer between these Rocks—These are, the Cruelty of the Creditor, and the Knavery of the Debtor. I shall speak a little of both.

By the Knavery of the Debtor, the Law is evaded, innocent Men abus'd, Trading Men ruin'd, honest Men cheated, and the Bowels and Tenderness of Creditors to their honester Debtors, harden'd and dry'd up—This is, (1.) when Men get Credit in Trade, with wicked Designs to defraud and deceive, and by a civil Artifice rob Mens Houses, get Possession of their Goods, and plunder them of their Estates—Or, (2.) when Men, however casually, they come to fail, yet by Tricks reserve false Accounts and Concealment of their Effects, bring their Creditors to small Compositions, and raise themselves new Fortunes, out of the Havock they have made of other Mens Families— These indeed are the Men that make Creditors cruel, and that provoke the most Merciful to be Inexorable; that cause many an honest Family to perish in Return for their Knavery, *who had really no hand in that Knavery,* and who really in some

Measure merit to be us'd without Mercy, like Men to whom no Favour shou'd be shewn.

To these indeed I am for giving no Quarter, like Beasts of Prey, to whom we give no Law; they ought to be run down with a full Cry by the whole Nation—And let no Man spare them—They are the worst Sort of Thieves—they rob Families, lay Snares for their Neighbours, and devour every one indifferently that comes in their Way—In short, they make Havock of Justice, Honesty, and Conscience; they are a publick Grievance to Property, to Commerce, and to Credit—They ruin Families, that's a personal Injury; they ruin Credit, that's a publick Injury; and they destroy Trade, that's a general Injury —There can be no Plea for such, no honest Man can say a Word for them; Foreign Nations send them to the Gallows, and it is great Pity we do not do so also—.

If there were none of these Bankrupts, there would not be half so many honest Bankrupts—Let any Man show me a Man in Trade that fails, but he can write his Destruction at first, or second-hand, to such Villains as these. How many miserable Families owe their Fall to the Villany of fraudulent Bankrupts? And give me leave to say (with Respect) as my own Opinion only, even the Legislature it self seems under some Obligation to be compassionate to the honest unfortunate Bankrupt, who falls by these Disasters—while they leave the other unhang'd —That Nation that encourages Thieves, ought to make some Provision for those that are robb'd—If Men shipwreck on Sands, or split on Rocks, where no Buoy, or Sea-mark, or Lighthouse is erected to warn them—it would be hard to punish them for Neglect. Indeed it seems to me, that some keen Laws, for the severe Punishment of willful premeditated Bankruptcy, would take away the Occasion of compassionate Laws to the honest necessitous Debtor.

Willful Frauds impoverish Trade it self, and bring Tradesmen in general into Distress—It weakens the giving reasonable Credit to honest Men, and thereby disables them to trade;

and thus many may drop with meer Decay of Trade; but where the Fraud falls, it blows up like a Mine—destroys like an Earthquake—and overturns the most flourishing Families —How many Families date their Misfortunes at this Time from some of our late Capital Bankrupts, who had both more Credit and more Substance, than many eminent Traders that are now flourishing—I may proceed to give you some short Abstracts of the Families, that have been overwhelm'd by the *Pitkins* of this Age—And, I think, it may not be a useless Calculation.

Would the Parliament take this into Consideration—and delivering the honest Debtor, who is willing to strip himself of all he has, and desires not to eat his Creditors Bread, make some Laws so strict, as that no willful fraudulent Bankrupt should escape the severest Punishment, it would be an Honour to the Nation, and be the greatest Blessing to Trade, that has happen'd in our Age—Especially in a Time, when Trade so much wants some extraordinary Help to raise it from the Decay and languishing Distempers, this long War has brought it into.

I shall come to the honest Debtors Case in my next.

TUESDAY, FEBRUARY 7. 1710.

I Enter'd a little last *Review* upon the Subject of Bankrupts, as what the Parliament seems inclin'd to take into Consideration; I nam'd the two fatal Extremes, upon which all the Attempts of Relief in this unhappy Case have hitherto split, *Viz.* The Cruelty of Creditors, and the Knavery of Debtors—I readily acknowledge, the last is very much the Cause of the first, or at least it is very much the Excuse for the first—but it is certainly true, that Anger may be unjust, and ought to be restrain'd, tho' it proceeds from just Grounds.

I began to state the Case of the two Sorts of Bankrupts that make up the Term, *viz.* The willful, fraudulent, designing Bankrupt: And this consists of two Sorts; (1.) Him that breaks on Purpose, with Design to defraud his Creditors; or, (2.) Him, who having been oblig'd by Necessity to break, takes Occasion by Fraud, Reserve, and Concealment, to bring his Creditors to a small Composition, and rebuild his Fortunes out of their just Dues—Of these I say—They merit no Quarter; Compassion is not a Debt to them; they ought, like the less guilty Highway-men, be esteem'd Felons, and dismiss'd Human Society at St. *Tyburn*—No honest Man can say one Word for them, but as *Solomon* says of the Murtherer, *Let him flee to the Pit, let no Man stay him.*

But there is another Kind of Bankrupt in the World, for whom something more may be said; and I'll first give you his Character, and then recommend him to the Mercy of the Parliament; he must be something less than Human, that can wish he should not be pity'd and reliev'd.

He has been a Trader, more or less considerable; either his Ships have been taken, or his House has been burnt, or he has been surpriz'd in his Trade by Goods falling on his Hand, or his Charge increasing, and his Family decaying; He consumes, or Knaves break in his Debt, *the Last the most common,* or by some such Thing unforeseen, &c. so to him inevitable; he is forc'd to break, and he calls his Creditors together.

The Man, honest in Principle, tho' distressed in Circumstances, calls his Creditors together, offers frankly to surrender all he has in the World to them, upon Oath, to pay them as far as it will go. But Mr. *W.* . . . . calls him a thousand Rogues. Mr. . . . . says, He can't be an honest Man that can't pay his Debts—*Tho'* at the same time he could not pay his own, and is convicted *EX ORE SUO,*[4] *for he Broke in three Months after;* and the inexorable Gentlemen refusing the Poor Man's Offer, throw him into Gaol; there he is forc'd to spend the Money, which he would have given them in Payment, for Bread for himself and Children; and when that is gone, he starves, and they are all unpaid.

Or, refusing his just Offer and compleat Surrender, the Man strives for his Liberty by the help of the *Fleet* or *Queen's-*

Bench; is then taken upon an Escape-Warrant, and put to Death by Immuring—that is, he is Imprison'd for Life; a Punishment which some say is not agreeable to the Crime at all—and which I humbly leave to the Consideration of our Representative under these two Suggestions.

1. Whether it be consistent with Humanity or Christianity, to commit a Man to Prison for Life, in Case of Debt, who is willing to give up all he has—or who, if confin'd, must perish there for want of Bread?
2. Whether it be consistent with the Claim of Right, which says, That exorbitant Punishments are illegal.

I shall explain my self further in my next.

SATURDAY, February 11. 1710.[5]

IN the Case of Bankrupts, I suggested two Enquiries in my last, which I humbly recommended to those, in whose Hands the Power of redressing this mighty Grievance remains.

1. Whether it be consistent with Humanity or Christianity, to put Men into Prison in Case of Debt *for Life,* when they are willing to surrender All they have in the World to their Creditors, and when they have not Bread to keep them from starving in their Confinement?
2. Whether such Imprisonment be consistent with the *Claim of Right,* which says, *that Exorbitant Punishments are Illegal?*

I do not say, That the Affirmative of these Things is true— I will not be charg'd with flying in the Face of the Law, *much less of the Law-Makers;* but there have been Laws repeal'd —There have been Acts of Parliament, which the same Parliament that made them have found inconvenient, and have therefore thought fit to rectifie, explain, amend, and repeal—

Inconvenience may appear after a Law is made, which even to Parliaments did not appear before, and our Parliaments always allow'd the Subject humbly to represent those Inconveniencies that may be redress'd; for as no Body of Men in the World are infallible, so the Parliaments of *Britain* make no Pretences to that ridiculous Imagination, nor does it ever displease them to have the World told so.

I describ'd the Debtor I am speaking of in my last, and I shall frequently revive his Character; for I know who I have to do with, and how ready some will be to clamour, as if I were encouraging Men to Frauds, and pleading for a general Lenity to Bankrupts, under whatever Circumstances: If it were in my Power to procure Laws against fraudulent Bankrupts, Clippers and Coyners, Highway-men and House-breakers would find more Mercy from Mankind than these; and if such were under the Sentence of Death, I would reprieve any thing but a Murtherer, before them. They are first the Ruin of honest Men, and then the Preventers of their restoring; like a malicious Murtherer, who first having wounded a Man, prevents his being cur'd—they ruin Men by getting into their Debt, and they prevent their being restor'd, by making the World believe, others break fraudulently as they do.

These are Men of Mischief so many Ways that no honest Man can desire good Terms for them—But 'tis very hard—indeed very hard, that because there are such Villains as these in the World, therefore no Concern, no Compassion, no Mercy should be shown to the Men, who being reduc'd by no visible Fraud of their own, but unhappily are overthrown in the World, and are willing to give up All they are able to make Satisfaction for their Debts—To punish these Men, to prevent their restoring themselves by their Industry, and mingle them with Thieves and Cheats—is an Act beyond the Cruelty of Death; it never was Criminal to be Unhappy. Debt was no where, that ever I read of, punish'd with Death before—No Law of Men ever directed it, and the Law of GOD is directly against it—Nay, the Scripture seems to command Pity and Compassion to such Men—If he has nothing to pay, if he cannot, if it be not in his Power, *Why should you take his Bed from under him?* How can you be so cruel, so inhuman, so barbarous?

But we go farther, We take the Bed from the Man, and the Man from his Bed—We strip his miserable Family, and turn his Wife and Children naked into the Streets to starve; be the Man never so indigent; nay, if he has a Fever upon him, if he be sick in his Bed, we will take him away, carry him to Gaol, lay him on the bare Boards, and if he has not to feed him, he must starve and perish—I wish, the Parliament would command to be laid before them an Account of the Hardships suffer'd the last severe Winter in our Prisons, by poor Insolvents imprison'd by Escape-Warrants, and how many of them have perish'd with Cold and Hunger. I have had some Accounts of these Things, as would make the Heart of any Christian bleed within him—While inexorable Creditors have not been mov'd to show the least Compassion—and have almost grudg'd to see the miserable Corps carry'd out of Prison to the Grave.

The Law is a *Medium* in all other Cases, between the Offender and the Offended; if a Thief rob me, if an Enemy beats me, it is not in my Breast what Punishment he shall have, but the Law decides it, and takes him out of my Hands —And we say to one another, What have you to do with him, he has satisfy'd the Law? And 'tis very just that it should be so, because Man is a furious, passionate Creature, and cannot set Bounds to his Revenge. But here the miserable Debtor (the Offender) is put into the Hands of the Creditor (the Offended), and he has him in his Power; if he pleases, *he may let him go;* if he pleases not, *he must die* in Misery and a Gaol—This really seems contrary to the Nature and Meaning of LAW, and at least gives a single Person the absolute Dominion over his Neighbours Life; a Thing, *English* Liberty, I think, was never subjected to before—This is my second Article. And,

This is the Thing, that I cannot but hope, the Parliament will enquire into, when they shall please to consider the Laws relating to Bankrupts in *England*—Whether it is agreeable to our Constitution, to the Liberty of *English* Men, I do not say *Britains* in this, for in Scotland it is quite otherwise; the only Thing in which they enjoy a Liberty we do not—The Claim of Right says expressly, that Exorbitant Punishments are illegal, and in other Cases a Man is not to be fin'd *ultra Tenementum*,[6] but by the Act of Parliament, which we call vulgarly *the Escape-Warrant Act*,[7] the Man is put into the Mercy of his Creditor, who, if he pleases, condemns him to perpetual Imprisonment; this I call putting him to Death by *Immuring;* for if the Man have it not to pay, *as many really have not,* and if the Creditor have no Compassion, *as really some have not,* it is nothing less—And I cannot but think, would the *House* review this Law, they would be moved to Compassion by the Miseries of those that languish under it—To think of some milder Way to treat the *English* Subject, than sacrifizing them thus to the ungovern'd Rage of one another.

In the *Israelites* Law, the great Original of statuted Justice, the Debtor was to be sold for Satisfaction of the Creditor, and then he had as full Payment as it could be imagin'd, any Man could desire—And then at the End of the Term the Man was free. This had two Pieces of Justice in it.

First, To the Creditor—*Secondly,* To the Debtor.

1. To the Creditor it was a Justice, that when a Debtor had no Goods to satisfie the Creditor, he should work for him a certain Number of Years, in order to pay the Debt—And this was the uttermost Severity that ever GOD Himself allow'd; *Of which by it self.*

2. To the Debtor, that having thus been sold, and having serv'd the Legal Time, the Law suppos'd the Creditor satisfy'd, or at least pacify'd, and the Man was then to have leave to go free, that he might labour then for Himself and Family, or as we call it, That he might try his Fortune in the World again.

How much milder, how much juster, and how much sooner it would be chosen by the miserable Bankrupts now languishing in Gaol, whether on the publick or private Account of

Debt, rather than the present Method of Confinement on this most terrible Escape-Warrant, I shall examine in my next.

SATURDAY, AUGUST 23. 1712.

IT is not unknown to you all, that a light Distemper or Indisposition, has generally touch'd the whole Nation;[8] and I believe few Families, from even her Majesty's Household to the meanest Subjects, have been free from it, and that not only here, but in *France, Holland, Flanders,* and all this part of *Europe.*

I have not said any Thing more to it, than I did from my *Highland* Prophecy,[9] if I had not found all the notices which have been taken of it, and the Thing itself also, turn'd into Ridicule and Banter, by the People of this Age; no less than by three different Companies was I accosted in this manner in one day—*Are you one of the Fools that make such an Out-cry,* said the first to me, *about this little Sickness the People have had among them?* What, *do you not know it is the Dog-days, and faint Weather, and that we have always something they call the New Distemper at this Time of the Year?*

And thus they went on, till they thought they had jested it quite off with me.

I had scarce been a quarter of an Hour gone from those, but I met with another—*What, have you heard the Dog-star bark,* says he, *and has it frighted you into Fits? Prithee DANIEL, What dost ail? What is the matter that you make such ado about a little Summer Sickness, and disorder the People with Melancholly Notions of the Plague? You are much in the wrong, and it may be of ill Consequence; I wonder the Government does not take notice of you for it!*

In the Evening of the same Day, coming into some very grave Company, they were pleas'd to tell me, *I had got the Hyppo;*[10] *And what is the matter with you?* says one, Old enough to have had more Wit; *you have dream't of nothing, I warrant you, but of Graves and Sepulchres this Fortnight—I warrant you, you have bought two or three Bottles of Plague Water to carry into the Country with you—I expected you would not have come Abroad without a Sprig of RUE in your Mouth?* And thus he went on, till at last, as all the Company knows, he grew offensively Prophane.

This added to the Jests of an Eminent Physician,[11] who said publickly some time since, *That if we could but have the Plague here, they should have fine Sport:* These Things, I say, extort one Paper or two more from me upon this Serious Subject.

I do confess, I think it a fitter Text for the Pulpit than the Coffee-House; for *a Sermon* than for *the Review;* and the little notice our Divines have taken of it, is not to me the best Token of that just Concern which I think we should all have about it; I wish those Gentlemen would consider, whether it be worth their notice or no.

I will not say, *nor do I remember, what some affirm,* viz. That we had a shock like this, before the last Dreadful Plague.

I will not undertake to say positively in this Paper, *as my Highland Prophet does in his,* that the Plague shall certainly reach hither next Year; tho' I assuredly expect and believe it, and perhaps on good Grounds too.

But two Things I will recommend to you all to consider, and I think them both very remarkable.

1. That the Plague has now for eight Years past, taken a gradual Course, or kind of Circuit, through a great part of *Europe,* and every Year it has come a Step nearer and nearer to this Nation, and that if it takes but two Steps more in the same manner, it cannot but reach us effectually.

2. That before the great Plague, *Anno* [1] 542.[12] when, in a manner, all the World was Ravaged by the greatest and most dreadful Pestilence that ever was known; there was the like Distemper, or Mortality, among the Cattle, as has

of late Raged in *Italy* and *Germany,* and is now spreading into *Milan* and *France.*

As to the first Observation, *viz.* Of the gradual Approach of the Plague, you may look back to the Year 1704, thereabouts we may say it begun: The *Turkish* Countries of *Bulgaria* and *Walachia,* felt its first Fury, tho' I think that very Year it reach'd as far this Way as *Cassovia* in the *Upper Hungaria.*

I could trace it back to *Constantinople,* and the Towns on the *Black Sea,* where, we are told it Raged before that, but this is Remote.

In 1705, *Upper Poland* was dreadfully Visited, the City of *Crackow* Desolated, and it Raged over the *Southern Poland,* quite up to the *Ukrain,* and the Confines of *Muscovy* and *Tartaria.*

In 1706, It came down the *Vistula,* Attack'd *Warsaw,* and the *Lower Poland,* in a Dreadful manner; they Buryed 16000 People in *Warsaw* only, and the City was almost left empty of People.

In 1707, it came on this Way; *Dantzick* felt the Terrible Visitation, and that to such a degree, as I need not relate, being so fresh in our Memories; I have seen an Account of 51000 People, which, as they said, Perish'd in the City and District of *Dantzick only.*

The next Year, 1708, *Dantzick* not quite free; the Cities of *Riga, Thorn, Elbing, Marienburgh,* and *Koningsburgh,* were Visited, and from thence (*Riga*) it pass'd over into *Sweden.*

Stockholm, and all that part of *Sweden,* suffer'd under it in a lamentable manner all the Year, 1709; and it spread itself in that same Year, and the next, into *Eastergothia* and *Schonen,* where it made like Desolation, *Ann.* 1710; this was a large Step this Way.

In 1711, It came on this side the *Sound,* and seiz'd the City of *Copenhagen* and Isle of *Seeland,* where it Raged with such Fury, that 21500 People Perish'd in the Town, besides those

that died at *Elsenore* and other Parts of the Island; where
many whole Villages were entirely Desolated and not any
People left alive; and the like on the Continent.

This present Year it has made a long stride, and has enter'd
Holstein, spread itself to *Gluckstat* on the *Elb*, and with the
Danish Army, is come over that River into the Duchy of
Bremen, above an Hundred Mile nearer to us than it was
before.

Let any Man tell me, if it makes two such Steps more, how
can we be suppos'd to escape? But that which is more terrible
yet to reflect on than all this, is, that whatever some may tell
us of a like Distemper to ours now forerunning the former
Plague, which we had here in 1665, this is certain, that in all
the Places abovesaid, they were actually Visited with such
a Distemper as this, the very Year before they had the Plague,
only with this difference, that it was more Mortal to them than
this, God be praised, has been with us.

The Learned Cavillers at this Paper, pretend this is an
Unseasonable Discourse, tends to make the People Uneasie,
and discourage Trade; I differ from them in the Thing's being
Unseasonable, and think just the contrary; and that as none but
a stupid Generation, that scoff at every Judgment of Heaven,
and value not their Maker till they feel his Hand, can be so
blind, as not to see the visible Approaches of such a Thing to
us; so nothing, but a dreadful Indifferency in the Event, can
make the Hints I have given, Unseasonable. As to the Discouraging Trade, it is a mean Pretence, and not Concern'd in
the Thing; the Ruin of our Trade is owing to visible Causes of
another kind, and which I shall be more particular in hereafter.

I shall make no Theological Inferences, from this Discourse
of the Plague, I leave that Work to your Ministers, whose
Province it is, and from whom, no question, you will better
accept it—In me, you will call it Canting, and Preaching, and
perhaps mock, rather than improve it to your own Advantage;
but that you may learn a little better how to behave yourselves,

when such a terrible Stroke shall reach you, I shall, in my next, give you a little Sketch or Draft of the dreadful Havock the last Plague made in this City; till then, I conclude with only reminding you of one Thing, *viz.* How thankful we ought all to be, that this general Shock has been so light, that it has been scarce Mortal any where; that Death has only given every one of us something like a jog on the Elbow, or a pull by the Sleeve as he pass'd by, *as it were*, to bid us get ready against next time he comes this Way—A suitable Instruction for which Occasion, you have in the Sacred Text, *Isaiah* [6]. 9. *When the Judgments of God are in the Earth, the Inhabitants of the World will learn Righteousness.*

TUESDAY, AUGUST 26. 1712.

I Promised you in my last, a Sketch or Draft of the dreadful Havock the last Plague made in this very City, and accordingly I here present you with the exact Copy of one of the Bills of Mortality, or Weekly Bills, being for the third Week in *September*, 1665.[13]

I need not tell the Reader here, that at the Time that this Bill was so high, the City was so thin of Inhabitants, that one might walk from *Aldgate* to *Ludgate*, and not meet, or see, 100 People; That the generallity of the People were all fled, at least all such as had any Retreat; That above 70000 were dead at that Time of the Plague, and in their Graves, *Inclusive of this Week;* That Grass grew in the Streets, in the Markets, and on the Exchange; and nothing but Death and Horror was to be seen in every place.

I need not tell you, that even before this Plague begun, the City itself and Suburbs, were nothing near so extended in Building, or so Populous, as they are now, and that by a modest Computation, there are at least 200000 People more in *London* now, than there were then: The Bills of Mortality prove this, which in time of Health that Year, were generally about 250 to 300; whereas now we reckon 400 a very moderate Weekly Bill.

Yet even at this Time see the Desolation made by this. Raging Distemper.

You will also observe, that the Number of other Distempers are strangely Encreas'd at that Time, so that besides those set down to die of the Plague, the Bill for that Week of other Distempers, appears to be 1132; the Reason of which is plain, *viz.* That such Families as could conceal their being Infected, were very Industrious to do it, and so when any died among them, they rather put them down of any other Distemper, to prevent its being known that their Families were touch'd, which was many Ways prejudicial to them—While at the same time none can think, but the unusual Numbers of other Distempers were occasion'd by the Plague, if not really so; I shall make no other Comment on this dreadful Text, but referr you to the following Bill, which was,

From the 12th of *September*, to the 19th. Anno 1665.
Diseases *and* Casualties *this* Week.[14]

Abortive	5	Frighted	3
Aged	43	Gout	1
Ague	2	Grief	3
Apoplexies, and suddenly	2	Griping in the Guts	51
Bleeding	2	Jaundies	5
Burnt in his Bed at St. *Giles Cripplegate*	1	Imposthume	11
		Infants	16
Canker	1	Killed by a Fall from the Bellfrey at *Alhallows* the Great	1
Childbed	42		
Chrisoms	18		
Consumption	134	King's Evil	2
Convulsion	64	Lethargy	1
Cough	2	Palsie	1
Dropsie	33	Plague	7165
Fever	309	Rickets	17
Flox and Small-Pox	5	Rising of the Lights	11

Scowring	5	Teeth	121
Scurvy	2	Thrush	5
Spleen	1	Tympany	1
Spotted-Fever	101	Tissick	11
Stilborn	17	Vomiting	3
Stone and Strangury	3	Wind	3
Stopping of the Stomach	9	Worms	15
Surfeit	49		

Buried   Males ———4095

          Females ——4202 whereof of the Plague, 7165.

          in all——8297

Parishes clear of the Plague   4

Parishes Infected   126

Increased in the Burials this Week   607.

This is a Week of that dreadful Year, of which the Misery and Horror is inexpressible; I shall spend none of your Time in Commenting on so Melancholly a Subject; you may guess a little of it, from two small Articles in the Bill of Mortality abovesaid, and of which 'tis observ'd, some are in every Bill of that Year, viz. Frighted—3. Grief—3. The terrible Appearance of Death in so many dismal Shapes, must needs be very surprizing to many, and that issued in the first Article; and the weighty Sorrows of others, either such as Parents, who lost whole Families of their Children; or Children losing their Parents, and the like, sunk many into the Grave, meerly with the Grief of their Loss.

I think no one can call this terrifying the People; I think the Thing a little too much forgotten among us; but if ye think otherwise, I will terrifie you no longer, this may be sufficient for those that make a Mock of the present Circumstances, to let them see what kind of a Thing a Plague is in this City, and what it may be, if it comes again; those who think we are in no danger of it, need be under no Concern at this Account, and those who think we are, will make a good Use of it.

SATURDAY, NOVEMBER 8, 1712.

THIS *Review*, by my Annual Custom, is sacred to the Memory of the Glorious King WILLIAM, it being the first after his Birth-Day,[15] and Dedicated to his Name; a Name, Immortal, as much from the Immortal Infamy of the *English* Name, as the Glory of his own: A Name! that Reproaches Men of Conscience with want of Honour; Men of Honour with want of Gratitude, and Men of Gratitude with want of Sense.

To see *Tories* and *Jacobites*, to see *High-Flyers* and Persecutors, to see Mad-Men and Tyrants forget, or despise, or Reproach his Memory, is nothing but what the Nature of the Thing implies, the Usage and Custom of the Party practices, and the Principles of the Men lead them to.

But to hear Men call themselves honest Men, boast of Revolution-Principles, talk of keeping out the Pretender, and own their Privileges secur'd to them, by the great Undertaking of the Prince of *Orange*, and yet find them forget and slight the great Hand that procur'd it; this is so Unnatural, so inconsistent, that I know nothing that resembles it, but the same People's forgetting, *with the Instrument that wrought the Revolution*, the God whose Providence directed it.

Nor can I forget to acknowledge here, that GOD and King *William*, in proportion to the degree of Influence they had in the Revolution, have their proportion'd Share in the Ingratitude; and the Sin of the Ingrateful, is also proportion'd after the same manner, *viz. To the one*, inconceivably, as the Author and first Mover of the Revolution, who gave motion to the Minds of Men at that Time, and made *Vox Populi* be so Unanimous at that Day, that, *even to the Conviction of Enemies*, it appear'd to be *Vox Dei*; and to the other, in its degree, as the Instrument in the Hand of Heaven, to whom, nevertheless, our Obligation was inexpressibly great, and such as could never be wip'd out, but with a brand of the highest Ingratitude, I mean that one Man is capable of to another.

Indeed, as King *William* could not expect, but that they, who forgot the Debt of Praises and Obedience which they ow'd to their Maker, for the Advantages of the Revolution, should forget the Debt to himself, who was but the Instrument in the Hand of Heaven, to Execute his Decrees in it; so neither can we expect, but that they, who forgot their Gratitude to King *William*, should add Sin to Sin, and forget the Original and the Agent both together.

If it seems strange to you, that I Reproach both Parties with Ingratitude, let me ask both Parties, whether the Memory of the Revolution remains equally upon your Minds, as before? The luke-warm Croud stand wavering between the *Revolution* and the *Pretender*, ready to unravel the first, and cry Hosannah to the last, on the first Popular Occasion; the abjuring Ignorant Justice of Peace, tells you, he would never have Abjur'd him, if he had thought he had been King *James*'s Son; then reflects on King *William*, for saying he was a Bastard, and promising to prove it, but omitting that proof; tho' King *William* neither said the first, or declin'd the last, but the other run away, declin'd the Enquiry, and render'd it impracticable.[16]

How have his best Actions been unravell'd, and cover'd with Dirt and Reflection even by another Party? How was the *Partisan Treaty*,[17] *the best Peace that ever was made for this Nation*, been bandy'd about by prejudic'd *Tories*, ignorant *Whigs*, and the Mountebank States-Men of our Modern Parties, till the Reproaches laid upon the Treaty, have reach'd the Person that made it? How has the care he took of the *Dissenters*, by passing a Legal Toleration, been Insulted by their own Friends, in giving their Liberties up in the Occasional Bill?[18]

How have we rejected his Measures, both in War and in Peace, till Heaven hath chastis'd us for both, by letting us gain Victory without Success, carry on the War without Advantage, and make Peace without Agreement?

Would King *William* have joyn'd with the Men of this Generation? Would he have hung back from a Treaty, till the Treaty had hung back from him? Would he have attacked

Landrecy before *Maubeuge,* refus'd *Dunkirk* as a Pledge, and broke off a Treaty for want of *an Answer in Writing?* [19]

· · ·

From this let me conclude, *call it Prophetick or what you please,* the time is coming when you shall have more occasion to remember and value the Merit of King *William,* and the Blessing of the Revolution, than ever you had in your Lives.

Every Day his Memory revives; your dark Circumstances call him to your Minds; those that formerly Revil'd him, now call him the Immortal *William:* It would make any Man smile, and at the same time pity you, to see how you begin to see who it was ye Insulted, and who slighted, and how Heaven is bringing you by the want of him, to remember, you had such a Prince: When another does for you what he did, it is to be hoped, either you will use him better, or he may use you worse.

SATURDAY, JANUARY 31. 1713.

IT is a Remark of my own, but, perhaps, too well to be justified by the Experience of most who shall read this Paper, that tho' the Trade of the Nation, by the Confession of all Men of Sense, was *never* more decayed, Money *never* scarcer, the Number of Bankrupts *never* greater, the Cries of the Poor *never* louder, and the rate of Provisions, for some Years past, one with another, *never* higher; yet the Pride, the Luxury, the Expensive Way of Living, the costly Furniture and Ostentation, both in Equipage, Cloaths, Feeding and Wearing, were never greater in this Nation.

If any of the Temper, which I know some, (*viz.*) *so Cavil at every thing,* disputes the Fact, I could descend to Particulars in most undeniable Instances: But let the Rich Coaches, and the Extravagance of costly House-Furniture, even in this City, and among the middling Tradesmen of it, speak for what I have advanc'd.

I will allow, *and I'll speak of it fuller in its place,* that the usual Habits of our People, even of both Sexes are altered

from former Times, *and that to great Advantage;* the Ladies
never Dress'd so Modest, nor the Gentlemen so Grave and
Becoming as they do now; I am no Cynick, nor am I finding
Faults for the Pleasure of the Complaint; I remember when
there was reckoned 70000 Ribband-Weavers in *Spittle-fields*,
&c. And I believe there are not now, half so many Hundred in
England; I remember the naked Shoulders and Breasts, the
Monstruous Towers of Hair, the Heads three Story high, *and
the like*, of the Women: The Pantaloons, the Shoulder-Knots,
and the Shoulder-Belts, of the Gentlemen.—Both Sexes have
tired themselves of those Follies, and I acquit the Habits of
the Age of any part of the *Antick* in the Excess I speak of:
But I cannot acquit them of the Excess, in the Richness and
Costleyness of Cloaths, tho', I acknowledge, that is not the
Thing I am now complaining of, in particular.

I remember an Accident, which gave me a Scetch of this
very Thing, and which I could not avoid taking Notice of:
Sometime since, being upon Business, *very late*, in the City,
it was my Lot to come along the Street, just as a sudden and
terrible Fire broke out in a Citizens House, *in none of the
Wealthiest part of the Town neither;* I forebear the Place, for
the sake of the Particulars.—I could contribute little to the
helping the Good People in their Distress; nor was I very well
qualified to Carry Water, or Work an Engin; besides, the
Street was presently full of People for that Work: But, I
plac'd my self in a convenient Corner, near the Fire, to look
on, and, indeed, the Consternation of the Poor People was
not fruitless of Remarks.

And First, I was, I confess, surpriz'd to hear the Skreeks and
Lamentations of the Poor Ladies, as well in the Houses on
either side, as opposite to the House that was on Fire; after
the first Fright was express'd with a great deal of Noise, terrible Gestures and Distortions, I observ'd all hands at Work, to
Remove: The Chamber-Maids were hurried down Stairs,
Betty, Betty, says a Lady, aloud you may be sure, *have you
got the Plate?* Yes, Madam, says *Betty: Here take the Cabinet,*

says Madam, *Run to my Mothers: there's all my Jewels, have a Care of them BETTY:* Away runs *Betty:* This, I think, was about the Degree of a Fish-monger's Lady:—At a House that was in great Danger, they were, like Sea-Men in a Storm, to lighten the Ship, throwing their Goods out at Window; and, *Indeed, I think, they had as good have let them be burnt:* Here I saw, out of *a Shopkeeper's* House, Velvet Hangings, Embroidered Chairs, Damask Curtains, Plumes of Feathers; and, in short, Furniture equal to what, formerly, suffis'd the greatest of our Nobility; thrown into a Street flowing a Foot Deep with Water and Mud, trodden Under-Foot by the Crowd, and then carried off Piece-Meal as well as they could: It was not the Fright the People were in, or the Error of their destroying their Goods in that Hurry, that was so much matter of Observation to me, as to see the Furniture that came out of such Houses, far better than any Removed at the late Fire, at the *French* Ambassadors.

In the House which I stood nearest too, which was opposite to the Fire, and which was in great Danger too, the Wind blowing the Flame, which was very Furious, directly into the Windows; The Woman, or Mistress, or Lady, call her as you will, had several small Children; her Maids, or Nurses, or whatever they were, made great Diligence to bring the Poor Children half naked, and asleep, Down-Stairs in their Arms; and wrapping them up carefully, run out of the House with them; One of these Maids coming again, as if to fetch Another, meets her Mistress, whose Concern, it seems, lay another way, with a Great Bundle, the Mistress screams out to her, *MARY, MARY, Take care of my Cloaths; Carry them away; I'll go fetch the Rest:* The Maid, more concern'd for the Children, than the Mother, *Cries out louder* than her Mistress, *Lord, Madam, Where's Master* Tommy? *The Child will be burnt in the Bed:* Throws down the Cloaths, and runs up Stairs: The Mistress, whose fine Cloaths lay nearer her Heart, than her Child, Cries out, *Oh! There's all my Cloaths;* Snatches up the Great Bundle, and runs out of the House half naked,

with it, and leaves the Wretch to go fetch her Child; who, Poor
Lamb, was almost suffocated with the Smoke and Heat.

The Mother was back again in an Instant, with two or three
Porters, and some Friend's Servants which she had got to help
her; and, away they run up Stairs with her, and came down
as quickly, loaden with Baskets, and Bundles of Rich Goods,
and about half an Hour after, when the Good Lady had dis-
charged her Passions, of those Things that lay nearest her
Heart, and was come a little to her Memory, I saw her in
Dreadful Fury, Raving and Skreaming, and tearing her Hair
for her Child; Her Child, Oh, her Child! for the House had
taken Fire on the Top, and there was no bearing to be in the
Rooms; and she remembered the Wench had cryed out, that
the Child was in its Bed; but never saw the Maid who had
fetch'd the Poor Child down, at the Hazard of her own Life,
and had carried it away,[20] and came not back for some time;
at last, Word was brought her that the Child was safe.

This Scene eased me of the Wonder I had been in, to see our
Citizens, who go all Day with Blue Frocks, and Blue-Aprons,
Dirty Hands, and foul Linnen, have their Chambers hung with
Velvet, and their Wives with Jewels: How should it be otherwise, when the Ladies love their Cloaths and Furniture so
much better than their Children, and no doubt, as much in
proportion, better than their Husbands Prosperity?

This costlyness in Furniture, as the Foundation of many
fatal Disasters to trading People, I shall have much reason to
speak to hereafter:—And, in the mean time, not so much as to
point at particular Families and Persons, I refer it to those
Gentlemen who have so often Occasion to Sit upon Commissions, in the Case of Bankrupts. How often have they seized the
Houses, and sold the Furniture of our City trading People;
which has been as good as, and perhaps better than, in former
Times has serv'd our Princes; where the Bankrupt's Estate, has
not divided to his Creditors, half a Crown in the Pound.

I think the Age was never so madly bent upon these Extremes as they are now, when Trade is at the lowest Ebb

imaginable, and this, to me, is a very ill Sign, for when Trade suffers all imaginable Hardships and Convulsions, is under a General Decay, and the Scarcity of Money is the general Grievance of the Nation, to have the Humour of the Town run so excessively upon Extravagance, in Equipage, Furniture, and costly Living, I say, it is a Plague upon Trade, and Portends the Reducing it to yet greater Extremities than ever.

AN
APPEAL
TO
Honour and *Justice*,

Tho' it be of
His Worst ENEMIES.

By *DANIEL DE FOE*.

BEING
A True Account of his Conduct in Publick Affairs.

JEREM. xviii. 18.

Come and let us smite him with the Tongue, *and let us not give heed to any of his Words.*

LONDON:

Printed for J. BAKER, at the *Black Boy* in *Pater-Noster-Row.* 1715.

AN
APPEAL
TO
HONOUR AND
JUSTICE,
Tho' it be of
HIS WORST ENEMIES.

By DANIEL DE FOE.

BEING
A True Account of his Conduct
in Publick Affairs.

JEREM. xviii. 18.
Come and let us smite him with the Tongue, *and let
us not give heed to any of his Words.*

LONDON:

Printed for J. BAKER, at the Black Boy *in*
Pater-Noster-Row. *1715.*

160

In this important autobiographical statement, published 24 February 1715, and actually carrying Defoe's name as author, Defoe seeks to consolidate his position with the government upon the change of ministry that followed the accession of George I. The "CONCLUSION by the Publisher," for example, was probably written by Defoe himself.

I Hope the Time is come at last, when the Voice of moderate Principles may be heard; hitherto the Noise has been so great, and the Prejudices and Passions of Men so strong, that it had been but in vain to offer at any Argument, or for any Man to talk of giving a Reason for his Actions: And this alone has been the Cause why, when other Men, who, I think, have less to say in their own Defence, are appealing to the Publick, and struggling to defend themselves, I alone have been silent under the infinite Clamours and Reproaches, causeless Curses, unusual Threatnings, and the most unjust and injurious Treatment in the World.

I hear much of Peoples calling out to punish the Guilty; but very few are concern'd to clear the Innocent. I hope some will be inclin'd to Judge impartially, and have yet reserv'd so much of the Christian, as to believe, and at least to hope, that a rational Creature cannot abandon himself so as to act without some Reason, and are willing not only to have me defend my self, but to be able to answer for me where they hear me causlesly insulted by others, and therefore are willing to have such just Arguments put into their Mouths as the Cause will bear.

As for those who are preposses'd, and according to the modern Justice of Parties are resolv'd to be so, *Let them go,* I am not arguing with them, *but against them;* they act so contrary to Justice, to Reason, to Religion, so contrary to the

Rules of Christians and of good Manners, that they are not to
be argued with, but to be expos'd, or entirely neglected. I have
a Receipt against all the Uneasiness which it may be supposed
to give me, and that is, to contemn Slander, and think it not
worth the least Concern; neither should I think it worth while
to give any Answer to it if it were not on some other Accounts,
of which I shall speak as I go on.

If any Man ask me, why I am in such hast to publish this
Matter at this time? Among many other good Reasons which
I could give, these are some:

1. I think I have long enough been made *Fabula Vulgi*,[1] and
born the Weight of general Slander; and I should be wanting
to Truth, to my Family, and to my Self, if I did not give a fair
and true State of my Conduct for impartial Men to judge of,
when I am no more in being to answer for my self.

2. By the Hints of Mortality, and by the Infirmities of a Life
of Sorrow and Fatigue, I have Reason to think that I am not a
great way off from, if not very near to the great Ocean of
Eternity, and the time may not be long e're I embark on the
last Voyage: Wherefore, I think, I should *even Accounts* with
this World before I go, that no Actions (Slanders) may lie
against my Heirs, Executors, Administrators, and Assigns, to
disturb them in the peaceable Possession of their Father's
(Character) Inheritance.

3. I fear, *God grant I have not a second Sight in it,* that this
lucid Interval of Temper and Moderation which shines, *tho'
dimly too* upon us at this time, will be but of short Continuance, and that some Men, who know not how to use the
Advantage God has put into their Hands with Moderation, will
push, in spight of the best Prince in the World, at such extrava-
gant Things, and act with such an intemperate Forwardness,
as will revive the Heats and Animosities which wise and good
Men were in hopes should be allay'd by the happy Accession
of the King to the Throne.

It is and ever was my Opinion, that Moderation is the only
Vertue by which the Peace and Tranquillity of this Nation

can be preserv'd, even the King himself, *I believe his Majesty will allow me that Freedom*, can only be happy in the Enjoyment of the Crown by a moderate Administration, if his Majesty should be oblig'd, contrary to his known Disposition, to joyn with intemperate Councils; if it does not lessen his Security, I am perswaded it will lessen his Satisfaction. It cannot be pleasant or agreeable, and, *I think*, it cannot be safe to any just Prince to Rule over a divided People, split into incens'd and exasperated Parties: Tho' a skilful Mariner may have Courage to master a Tempest, and goes fearless thro' a Storm, yet he can never be said to delight in the Danger; a fresh fair Gale, and a quiet Sea, is the Pleasure of his Voyage, and we have a Saying worth Notice to them that are otherwise minded, *Qui amat periculum periibat in illo.*[2]

To attain at the happy Calm, which, as I say, is the Safety of *Britain*, is the Question which should now move us all; and he would Merit to be call'd the Nation's Physician that could prescribe the Specifick for it. I think I may be allow'd to say, a *Conquest of Parties* will never do it; *a Ballance of Parties MAY*. Some are for *the former;* they talk high of Punishments, letting Blood, revenging the Treatment that have met with, and the like:[3] If they, *not knowing what Spirit they are of,* think this the Course to be taken, let them try their Hands, I shall give them for lost, and look for their Downfall *from that time;* for the Ruin of all such Tempers slumbereth not.

It is many Years that I have profess'd my self an Enemy to all Precipitations in publick Administrations; and often I have attempted to shew, that hot Councils have ever been distructive to those who have made use of them: Indeed they have not always been a Disadvantage to the Nation, as in King *James* II's Reign, where, as I have often said in Print, his Precipitation was the Safety of us all; and if he had proceeded temperately and politickly, we had been undone, *Faelix quem faciunt.*[4]

But these things have been spoken when your Ferment has been too high for any thing to be heard; whether you will hear it now or not, *I know not,* and therefore it was that I said, *I fear* the present Cessation of Party-Arms will not hold long.

These are some of the Reasons why I think this is the proper Juncture for me to give some Account of my self, and of my past Conduct to the World; and that I may do this as effectually as I can, being perhaps never more to speak from the Press, I shall, as concisely as I can, give an Abridgment of my own History during the few unhappy Years I have employ'd my self, or been employ'd in Publick in the World.

Misfortunes in Business having unhing'd me from Matters of Trade, it was about the Year 1694,[5] when I was invited by some Merchants, with whom I had corresponded abroad, and some also at home, to settle at *Cadiz* in *Spain,* and that with Offers of very good Commissions; but Providence, which had other Work for me to do, placed a secret Aversion in my Mind to quitting *England* upon any account, and made me refuse the best Offers of that kind, to be concern'd with some eminent Persons at home, in proposing *Ways* and *Means* to the Government for raising Money to supply the Occasions of the War then newly begun. Some time after this, I was, without the least Application of mine, and being then seventy Miles from *London,* sent for to be Accomptant to the Commissioners of the Glass Duty, in which Service I continued to the Determination of their Commission.[6]

During this time, there came out a vile abhor'd Pamphlet, in very ill Verse, written by one Mr. *Tutchin,* and call'd, THE FOREIGNERS: In which the Author, *who he was I then knew not,* fell personally upon the King himself, and then upon the *Dutch* Nation; and after having reproach'd his Majesty with Crimes, that his worst Enemy could not think of without Horror, he sums up all in the odious Name of FOREIGNER.

This fill'd me with a kind of Rage against the Book, and gave birth to a Trifle which I never could hope should have met with so general an Acceptation as it did, I mean, *The True-Born-Englishman.* How this Poem was the Occasion of my being known to his Majesty;[7] how I was afterwards receiv'd by him; how Employ'd; and how, above my Capacity of deserving, Rewarded, is no Part of the present Case, and is only mention'd here as I take all Occasions to do for the expressing the Honour I ever preserv'd for the Immortal and Glorious Memory of that Greatest and Best of Princes, and who it was my Honour and Advantage to call Master as well as Sovereign, whose Goodness to me I never forgot, neither can forget; and whose Memory I never patiently heard abused, nor ever can do so; and who had he liv'd, would never have suffered me to be treated as I have been in the World.

But Heaven for our Sins remov'd him in Judgment. How far the Treatment he met with, from the Nation he came to save, and whose Deliverance he finished, was admitted by Heaven to be a Means of his Death, I desire to forget for their sakes who are guilty; and if this calls any of it to mind, it is mention'd to move them to treat him better who is now with like Principles of Goodness and Clemency appointed by God, and the Constitution, to be their Sovereign; least he that protects righteous Princes, avenges the Injuries they receive from an ungrateful People, by giving them up to the Confusions their Madness leads them to.

And in their just acclamations at the happy accession of His present Majesty to the Throne, I cannot but advise them to look back, and call to mind who it was that first Guided them to the Family of *Hanover,* and to pass by all the Popish Branches of *Orleans* and *Savoy,* recognizing the just authority of Parliament, in the undoubted Right of Limiting the Succession, and Establishing that Glorious Maxim of our Settlement, (*viz.*) That *it is inconsistent with the Constitution of this Protestant Kingdom to be Govern'd by a Popish Prince.* I say let them call to mind who it was that guided their Thoughts first to the Protestant Race of our own Kings in the House of *Hanover,* and that it is to King *William,* next to Heaven it self, to whom we owe the Enjoying a Protestant King at this time.[8] I need not go back to the particulars of his Majesty's

Conduct in that Affair, his Journey in Person to the Country of *Hanover,* and the Court of *Zell;* his particular management of the Affair afterwards at home, perfecting the Design, by naming the Illustrious Family to the Nation, and bringing about a Parliamentary Settlement to effect it, entailing thereby the Crown in so effectual a manner as we see has been sufficient to prevent the worst Designs of our *Jacobite* People in behalf of the Pretender; a Settlement, together with the subsequent Acts which followed it, and the Union with *Scotland* which made it unalterable, that gave a compleat Satisfaction to those who knew and understood it, and removed those terrible apprehensions of the Pretender (which some entertain'd) from the minds of others who were yet as zealous against him as it was possible for any to be: Upon this Settlement, as *I shall shew presently.* I grounded my Opinion, *which I often express'd,* (*viz.*) that I did not see it possible the Jacobites could ever set up their Idol here; and I think my Opinion abundantly justify'd in the Consequences, of which by and by.

This Digression, as a debt to the Glorious Memory of King *William,* I could not in Justice omit, and as the Reign of his present Majesty is esteem'd Happy, and look'd upon as a Blessing from Heaven by us, it will most necessarily lead us to bless the Memory of King *William* to whom we owe so much of it; How easily could his Majesty have led us to other Branches, whose Relation to the Crown might have had large pretences? What Prince but would have submitted to have Educated a Successor of their Race in the Protestant Religion for the sake of such a Crown——? But the King, who had our Happiness in View, and saw as far into it as any humane sight could Penetrate, who knew we were not to be Govern'd by unexperienc'd Youths; that the Protestant Religion was not to be Establish'd by Political Converts; and that Princes under *French* Influence, or Instructed in *French* Politicks, were not proper Instruments to preserve the Liberties of *Britain,* fixt his Eyes upon the Family who now possesses the Crown, as not only having an undoubted Relation to it by Blood, but as being first and principally Zealous and Powerful assertors of the Protestant Religion and Interest against Popery; And *Secondly,* stored with a visible Succession of worthy and promising Branches, who appear'd equal to the Weight of Government, quallified to fill a Throne, and guide a Nation which, without Reflection, are not famed to be the most easy to Rule in the World.

Whether the Consequence has been a Credit to King *William's* Judgement I need not say, I am not Writing Panegyricks here, but doing justice to the Memory of the King my Master, who I have had the Honour very often to hear express himself with great satisfaction, in having brought the Settlement of the Succession to so good an Issue; and to repeat his Majesty's own Words, *That he knew no Prince in* Europe *so fit to be King of* England, *as the Elector of* Hanover. I am persuaded, without any Flattery, that if it should not every way answer the Expectations his Majesty had of it, the fault will be our own: God Grant the King may have more Comfort of his Crown than we suffer'd King *William* to have.

The King being Dead, and the Queen Proclaim'd, the Hot Men of that Side, as Hot Men of all Sides do, Thinking the Game in their own Hands, and all other People under their Feet, began to run out into those mad Extreams, and precipitate themselves into such Measures, as according to the Fate of all intemperate Councils, ended in their own Confusions, and threw them at last out of the Saddle.

The Queen, who, tho' willing to favour the High Church Party, did not thereby design the Ruin of those who she did not Employ, was soon alarm'd at their wild Conduct, and turn'd them out, adhering to the moderate Councils of those who better understood, or more faithfully pursued her Majesty's and their Countries Interest.[9]

In this Turn fell Sir. *Edw. Seymour's* Party,[10] for so the High Men were then call'd; and to this Turn, we owe the Converson of several other Great Men, who became *Whigs* upon that Occasion, which it is known they were not before; which Conversion afterwards beg at that unkind Distinction of Old Whig, and Modern Whig,[11] which some of the former were with very little Justice pleased to run up afterwards to an Extreme very pernicious to both.

But I am gone too far in this Part. I return to my own Story. In the Interval of these Things, and during the Heat of the first Fury of High-flying, I fell a Sacrifice for writing against the Rage and Madness of that High Party, and in the Service of the Dissenters: What Justice I met with, and above all what Mercy, is too well known to need a Repetition.

This Introduction is made that it may bring me to what has been the Foundation of all my further Concern in publick Affairs, and will produce a sufficient Reason for my adhering to those whose Obligations upon me were too strong to be resisted, even when many things were done by them which I could not approve; and for this Reason it is that I think it is necessary to distinguish how far I did, or did not adhere to, or joyn in or with the Persons or Conduct of the late Government: And those who are willing to judge with Impartiality and Charity, will see reason to use me the more tenderly in their Thoughts, when they weigh the Particulars.

I will make no Reflections upon the Treatment I met with from the People I suffer'd for, or how I was abandon'd even in my Sufferings, at the same time that they acknowledg'd the Service it had been to their Cause; but I must mention it to let you know, that while I lay friendless and distress'd in the Prison of *Newgate*, my Family ruin'd, and my self, without Hope of Deliverance, a Message was brought me from a Person of Honour, who, till that time, I had never had the least Acquaintance with, or Knowledge of, other than by Fame, or by Sight, as we know Men of Quality by seeing them on publick Occasions. I gave no present Answer to the Person who brought it, having not duly weighed the Import of the Message; the Message was by Word of Mouth thus: *Pray ask that Gentleman, what I can do for him?* But in return to this kind and generous Message, I immediately took my Pen and

Ink, and writ the Story of the blind Man in the Gospel, who follow'd our Saviour, and to whom our Blessed Lord put the Question, *What wilt thou that I should do unto thee?* Who, as if he had made it strange that such a Question should be ask'd, or as if he had said, *Lord, dost thou see that I am blind, and yet ask me what thou shalt do for me?* My Answer is plain in my Misery, *Lord, that I may receive my Sight.*[12]

I needed not to make the Application; and from this time, altho' I lay four Months in Prison after this, and heard no more of it, yet from this time, as I learn'd afterwards, this noble Person made it his Business to have my Case represented to Her Majesty, and Methods taken for my Deliverance.

I mention this Part, because I am no more to forget the Obligation upon me to the Queen, than to my first Benefactor.

When Her Majesty came to have the Truth of the Case laid before Her, I soon felt the Effects of her Royal Goodness and Compassion. And first, Her Majesty declar'd, That She left all that Matter to a certain Person,[13] and did not think he would have used me in such a Manner. Perhaps these Words may seem imaginary to some, and the speaking them to be of no Value, and so they would have been if they had not been follow'd with farther and more convincing Proofs of what they imported, which were these, That Her Majesty was pleased particularly to enquire into my Circumstances and Family, and by my Lord Treasurer *Godolphin,* to send a considerable Supply to my Wife and Family, and to send me to the Prison Money to pay my Fine, and the Expences of my Discharge. Whether this be a just Foundation, let my Enemies judge.

Here is the Foundation on which I built my first Sense of Duty to her Majesty's Person, and the indelible Bond of Gratitude to my first Benefactor.

Gratitude and Fidelity are inseparable from an honest Man. But to be thus oblig'd by a Stranger, by a Man of Quality and Honour, and after that by the Sovereign, under whose Administration I was suffering, let any one put himself in my stead, and examine upon what Principles I could ever act against either such a Queen, or such a Benefactor; and what must my own Heart reproach me with, what blushes must have cover'd my Face when I had look'd in, and call'd myself ungrateful to him that sav'd me thus from distress? *Or* Her that fetch'd me out of the Dungeon, and gave my Family Relief? Let any Man, who knows what Principles are, what Engagements of Honour and Gratitude are, make this Case his own, and say what I could have done less or more than I have done.

I must go on a little with the Detail of the Obligation, and then I shall descend to relate what I have done, and what I have not done in the Case.

Being deliver'd from the Distress I was in, Her Majesty, who was not satisfy'd to do me Good by a single Act of her Bounty, had the Goodness to think of taking me into her Service, and I had the Honour to be employ'd in several honourable, tho' secret Services, by the Interposition of my first Benefactor, who then appear'd as a Member in the publick Administration.

I had the Happiness to discharge my self in all these Trusts, so much to the Satisfaction of those who employ'd me, tho' often times with Difficulty and Danger, that my Lord Treasurer *Godolphin,* whose Memory I have always honour'd, was pleas'd to continue his Favour to me, and to do me all good Offices with Her Majesty, even after an unhappy Breach had separated him from my first Benefactor: The Particulars of which may not be improper to relate; and as it is not an Injustice to any, so I hope it will not be offensive.

When upon that fatal Breach, the Secretary of State was dismiss'd from the Service,[14] I look'd upon my self as lost, it being a general Rule in such Cases, when a great Officer falls, that all who came in by his Interest fall with him. And resolving never to abandon the Fortunes of the Man to whom I ow'd so much of my own, I quitted the usual Applications which I had made to my Lord Treasurer.

But my generous Benefactor, when he understood it, frankly told me, That I should by no means do so; for, said he, in the

most engaging terms, My Lord Treasurer will employ you in
nothing but what is for the publick Service, and agreeable to
your own Sentiments of Things: And besides, it is the Queen
you are serving, who has been very good to you. Pray apply
your self as you used to do; I shall not take it ill from you in
the least.

Upon this I went to wait on my Lord Treasurer, who receiv'd me with great Freedom, and told me smiling, *He had
not seen me a long while.* I told his Lordship very frankly
the Occasion, That the unhappy Breach that had fallen out,
had made me doubtful whether I should be acceptable to
his Lordship. That I knew it was usual, when great Persons
fall, that all who were in their Interest fell with them. That
his Lordship knew the Obligations I was under, and that I
could not but fear my Interest in his Lordship was lessen'd
on that Account. *Not at all Mr.* De Foe, reply'd his Lordship;
I always think a Man honest, till I find to the contrary.

Upon this I attended his Lordship as usual, and being
resolved to remove all possible Ground of Suspicion that I
kept any secret Correspondence, I never visited, or wrote to,
or any way corresponded with my principal Benefactor for
above three Years;[15] which he so well knew the Reason of,
and so well approv'd that punctual Behaviour in me, that he
never took it ill from me at all.

In Consequence of this Reception, my Lord *Godolphin*
had the Goodness not only to introduce me for the second
time to her Majesty,[16] and to the Honour of kissing her Hand,
but obtain'd for me the Continuance of an Appointment which
her Majesty had been pleas'd to make me in Consideration
of a former special Service I had done,[17] and in which I had
run as much risque of my Life, as a Grenadier upon the
Counterscarp; and which Appointment however was first
obtain'd for me at the Intercession of my said first Benefactor,
and is all owing to that Intercession, and Her Majesty's Bounty.
Upon this second Introduction Her Majesty was pleased to
tell me with a Goodness peculiar to Her self, That she had

such Satisfaction in my former Services, that she had appointed me for another Affair, which was something Nice, and that my Lord Treasurer should tell me the rest; and so I withdrew.

The next Day his Lordship having commanded me to attend, told me, That he must send me to *Scotland*;[18] and gave me but three Days to prepare my self. Accordingly I went to *Scotland*, where neither my Business, nor the manner of my discharging it is material to this Tract, nor will it be ever any part of my Character that I reveal what should be concealed; and yet my Errand was such as was far from being unfit for a Sovereign to direct, or an honest Man to perform; and the Service I did on that Occasion, as it is not unknown to the greatest Man now in the Nation under the King and the Prince, so I dare say, his Grace was never displeased with the Part I had in it, and I hope will not forget it.

These things I mention upon this Account, and no other, (*viz.*) to state the Obligation I have been in all along to Her Majesty personally, and to my first Benefactor principally, by which, *I say I THINK,* I was at least obliged not to act against them even in those things which I might not approve. Whether I have acted with them farther than I ought, shall be spoken to by it self.

Having said thus much of the Obligations lay'd on me, and the Persons by whom, I have this only to add, That I think no Man will say a Subject could be under greater Bonds to his Prince, or a private Person to a Minister of State; and I shall ever preserve this Principle, that an honest Man cannot be ungrateful to his Benefactor.

But let no Man run away now with the Notion, that I am now intending to plead the Obligation that was upon me from her Majesty, or from any other Person, to justify my doing any thing that is not otherwise to be justify'd in it self.

Nothing would be more injurious than such a Construction; and therefore I capitulate for so much Justice as to explain my self by this Declaration (*viz.*) That I only speak of these Obligations as binding me to a negative Conduct not to fly in the Face of, or concern my self in Disputes with those to whom I was under such Obligations, altho' I might not in my Judgment joyn in many things that were done. No Obligation could excuse me in calling Evil Good, or Good Evil; but I am of the Opinion, that I might justly think my self oblig'd to defend what I thought was to be defended, and to be silent in any thing which I might think was not.

If this is a Crime, I must plead guilty, and give in the History of my Obligation above-mention'd as an Extenuation, at least, if not a Justification of my Conduct; suppose a Man's Father was guilty of several things unlawful and unjustifiable, a Man may heartily detest the unjustifiable thing, and yet it ought not to be expected that he should expose his Father. I think the Case on my side exactly the same. Nor can the Duty to a Parent be more strongly obliging than the Obligation laid on me: But I must allow the Case on the other side not the same.

And this brings me to the Affirmative, and to enquire what the Matters of Fact are, what I have done, or have not done, on Account of these Obligations which I have been under.

It is a general Suggestion, and is affirm'd with such Assurance, that they tell me it is in vain to contradict it; That I have been employ'd by the Earl of O[xfor]d, late Lord Treasurer, in the late Disputes about Publick Affairs, to write for him, or to put it into their own Particulars, have written by his Direction, taken the Materials from him, been dictated to, or instructed by him, or by other Persons from him, by his Order, and the like; and that I have receiv'd a Pension, or Sallery, or Payment from his Lordship for such Services as these.

If I could put it into Words that would more fully express the Meaning of these People, I profess I would do it.

One would think it was impossible; but that since these things have been so confidently affirm'd, some Evidence might be produc'd, some Facts might appear, some one Body or other might be found that could speak of certain Knowledge:

To say things that have been carry'd too closely to be discover'd, *is saying nothing;* for then they must own, *that it is not discover'd:* And how then can they affirm it, as they do, with such an Assurance, as nothing ought to be affirm'd by honest Men, unless they were able to prove it?

To speak then to the Fact: Were the Reproach upon *me only* in this Particular, I should not mention it; I should not think it a Reproach to be directed by a Man to whom the Queen had at that time entrusted the Administration of the Government. But as it is a Reproach upon his Lordship, Justice requires that I do Right in this Case. The Thing is true or false, I would recommend it to those who would be call'd honest Men, to consider but one Thing, (*viz.*) What if it should not be true? Can they justify the Injury done to that Person, or to any Person concern'd? If it cannot be prov'd, if no Vestiges appear to ground it upon, how can they charge Men upon Rumours and Reports, and joyn to run Men's Characters down by the Stream of Clamour.

Sed quo rapit impetus undae.[19]

In Answer to the Charge, I bear Witness to Posterity, that every Part of it is false and forg'd; and I do solemnly protest, in the *Fear* and *Presence* of him that shall Judge us all, both the Slanderers, and the Slandered, that I have not receiv'd any Instructions, Directions, Orders, *or let them call it what they will of that kind,* for the Writing any Part of what I have written, or any Materials for the putting together, for the Forming any Book or Pamphlet whatsoever from the said Earl of O[xfor]d, late Lord Treasurer, or from any Person, by his Order, or Direction, since the Time that the late Earl of G[odolph]in was Lord Treasurer: Neither did I ever shew, or cause to be shew'd to his Lordship, for his Approbation, Correction, Alteration, or for any other Cause, any Book, Paper, or Pamphlet, which I have Written and Publish'd before the same was Printed, work'd off at the Press, and Publish'd.

If any Man living can detect me of the least Prevarication

in this, or in any Part of it, I desire him to do it by all means; and I challenge all the World to do it—*And if they cannot,* then I appeal, *as in my Title,* to the Honour and Justice of my worst Enemies, to know upon what Foundation of Truth or Conscience they can affirm these things, and for what it is that I bear these Reproaches.

In all my Writing, I ever capitulated for my Liberty to speak according to my own Judgment of Things; I ever had that Liberty allow'd me, nor was I ever imposed upon to write this way or that against my Judgment by any Person whatsoever.

I come now historically to the Point of Time when my Lord *Godolphin* was dismiss'd from his Employment,[20] and the late unhappy Division broke out at Court; I waited on my Lord the Day he was displac'd, and humbly ask'd his Lordship's Direction, what Course I should take? His Lordship's Answer was, *That he had the same good Will to assist me, but not the same Power; That I was the Queen's Servant, and that all he had done for me, was by Her Majesty's special and particular Direction; and that whoever should succeed him, it was not material to me, he supposed I should be employ'd in nothing relating to the present Differences: My Business was to wait till I saw things settled, and then apply my self to the Ministers of State, to receive Her Majesty's Commands from them.*

It occur'd to me immediately, as a Principle for my Conduct, that it was not material to me what Ministers Her Majesty was pleas'd to employ, my Duty was to go along with every Ministry, so far as they did not break in upon the Constitution, and the Laws and Liberties of my Country; my Part being only the Duty of a Subject, (*viz.*) to submit to all lawful Commands, and to enter into no Service which was not justifiable by the Laws: To all which I have exactly oblig'd my self.

By this I was providentially cast back upon my Original Benefactor, who, according to his wonted Goodness, was pleased to lay my Case before Her Majesty, and thereby I preserv'd my Interest in Her Majesty's Favour; but without any Engagement of Service.

As for Consideration, Pension, Gratification, or Reward, I declare to all the World I have had none; except only that old Appointment which Her Majesty was pleased to make me in the Days of the Ministry of my Lord *Godolphin:* Of which I have spoken already, and which was for Services done in a foreign Country some Years before. Neither have I been employ'd or directed, or order'd, by my Lord T[reasure]r aforesaid, to do, or not to do, any thing in the Affairs of the unhappy Differences which have so long perplex'd us, and for which I have suffer'd so many, and such unjust Reproaches.

I come next into the Matters of Fact, and what it is I have done, or not done; which may justify the Treatment I have met with. And first, for the Negative Part, what I have not done.

The first Thing in the unhappy Breaches which have fallen out, is the heaping up Scandal upon the Persons and Conduct of Men of Honour on one Side, as well as on the other; those unworthy Methods of falling upon one another by personal Calumny and Reproach. This I have often in print complain'd of as an unchristian, ungenerous, and unjustifiable Practice. Not a Word can be found in all I have written reflecting on the Persons, or Conduct of any of the former Ministry, I serv'd Her Majesty under their Administration, they acted honourably and justly in every Transaction in which I had the Honour to be concern'd with them; and I never publish'd, or said any thing dishonourable of any of them in my Life: Nor can the worst Enemy I have produce any such thing against me. I always regretted the Change, and look'd upon it as a great Disaster to the Nation in general, I am sure it was so to me in particular; and the Divisions and Feuds among Parties, which follow'd that Change, were doubtless a Disaster to us all.

The next Thing which follow'd the Change was THE

PEACE: No Man can say that ever I once said in my Life, that I approv'd of the Peace.[21] I wrote a publick Paper at that time, and there it Remains upon Record against me, I printed it openly, and that so plainly, as others durst not do; That I did not like the Peace, neither that which was made, nor that which was before a making; That I thought the Protestant Interest was not taken care of in either; That the Peace I was for, was such as should neither have given the *Spanish* Monarchy to the House of *Bourbon,* or the House of *Austria;* but that this Bone of Contention should have been broken to Pieces, that it should not have been dangerous to *Europe* on any Account, and that the Protestant Powers, (*viz.*) *Britain,* and the *States,*[22] should have so strengthen'd and fortify'd their Interest by their sharing the Commerce and Strength of *Spain,* as should have made them no more afraid either of *France,* or the *Emperor:* So that the Protestant Interest should have been superior to all the Powers of *Europe,* and been in no more Danger of exorbitant Power, whether *French* or *Austrian.* This was the Peace I always argued for, pursuant to the Design of King *William* in the Treaty of Partition, and pursuant to that Article of the Grand Alliance, which was directed by the same glorious Hand at the Beginning of this last War (*viz.*) That all we should conquer in the *Spanish-West-Indies* should be our own.

This was with a true Design that *England* and *Holland* should have turn'd their Naval Power, which were eminently superiour to those of *France,* to the Conquest of the *Spanish-West-Indies,* by which the Channel of Trade, and Return of Bullion, which now enriches the Enemies of both, had been ours; and as the Wealth, so the Strength of the World had been in Protestant Hands. *Spain,* whoever had it, must then have been dependant upon us; the House of *Bourbon* would have found it so poor without us, as to be scarce worth fighting for; and the People so averse to them for want of their Commerce, as not to make it ever likely *France* could keep it.

This was the Foundation I ever acted upon with relation to

the Peace. It is true, that when it was made, and could not be otherwise, I thought our Business was to make the best of it, and rather to enquire what Improvements were to be made of it, than to be continually exclaiming at those who made it; and where the Objection lies against this Part I cannot yet see.

While I spoke of things in this manner, I bore infinite Reproaches from clamouring Pens of being in the *French* Interest, being hir'd and brib'd to defend a bad Peace, and the like; and most of this was upon a Supposition of my Writing, or being the Author of Abundance of Pamphlets which came out every Day, and which I had no hand in. And indeed, as I shall observe again by and by, this was one of the greatest Pieces of Injustice that could be done me, and which I labour still under without any redress; that whenever any Piece comes out which is not liked, I am immediately charg'd with being the Author, and very often the first Knowledge I have had of a Books being publish'd, has been from seeing my self abused for being the Author of it, in some other Pamphlet publish'd in Answer to it.

Finding my self treated in this manner, I declin'd writing at all; and for a great Part of a Year never set Pen to Paper, except in the publick Paper call'd the *Review*. After this I was long absent in the *North* of *England*,[23] and observing the insolence of the *Jacobite* Party, and how they insinuated fine things into the Heads of the Common People of the Right and Claim of the *Pretender*, and of the great Things he would do for us if he was to come in; of his being to turn a Protestant, of his being resolved to maintain our Liberties, support our Funds, give Liberty to Dissenters, and the like; and finding that the People began to be deluded, and that the *Jacobites* gain'd ground among them by these Insinuations, I thought it the best Service I could do the Protestant Interest, and the best way to open the Peoples Eyes to the Advantages of the Protestant Succession, if I took some Course effectually to alarm the People with what they really ought to expect if the

Pretender should come to be King. And this made me set Pen to Paper again.

And this brings me to the affirmative Part, or to what really I HAVE DONE; and in this I am sorry to say, I have one of the foulest, most unjust, and unchristian Clamours to complain of, that any Man has suffer'd, I believe, since the Days of the Tyranny of King *James* the Second. The Fact is thus.

In order to detect the Influence of *Jacobite* Emissaries, as above, the first thing I wrote was a small Tract, call'd, *A Seasonable Caution*.[24]

A Book sincerely written to open the Eyes of the poor ignorant Country People, and to warn them against the subtle Insinuations of the Emissaries of the *Pretender;* and that it might be effectual to that Purpose, I prevail'd with several of my Friends to give them away among the poor People all over *England,* especially in the *North;* and several thousands were actually given away, the Price being reduced so low, that the bare Expence of Paper and Press was only preserv'd, that every one might be convinc'd, that nothing of Gain was design'd, but a sincere Endeavour to do a publick Good, and assist to keep the People entirely in the Interest of the Protestant Succession.

Next to this, and with the same Design, I wrote Two Pamphlets, one entituled, *What if the* Pretender *should come?* The other, *Reasons against the Succession of the House of* Hanover.[25] Nothing can be more plain, than that the Titles of these Books were Amusements, in order to put the Books into the Hands of those People who the *Jacobites* had deluded, and to bring the Books to be read by them.

Previous to what I shall farther say of these Books, I must observe, that all these Books met with so general a Reception and Approbation among those who were most sincere for the Protestant Succession, that they sent them all over the Kingdom, and recommended them to the Peoples reading as excellent and useful Pieces, insomuch, that about Seven Editions of them were Printed, and they were Reprinted in other Places; and I do protest, had his present Majesty, then Elector of *Hanover,* given me a thousand Pounds to have written for the Interest of his Succession, and to expose and render the Interest of the *Pretender* odious and ridiculous, I could have done nothing more effectual to those Purposes than these Books were.

And that I may make my worst Enemies, to whom this is a fair Appeal, Judges of this, I must take leave by and by to repeat some of the Expressions in those Books which were direct, and need no Explication, and which, I think, no Man that was in the Interest of the *Pretender,* nay which no Man but one who was entirely in the Interest of the *Hanover* Succession, could write.

Nothing can be severer in the Fate of a Man than to act so between two Parties, that both Sides should be provok'd against him. It is certain, the *Jacobites* curs'd those Tracts and the Author; and when they came to read them, *being deluded by the Titles according to the Design,* they threw them by with the greatest Indignation imaginable: Had the *Pretender* ever come to the Throne, I could have expected nothing but Death, and all the Ignominy and Reproach that the most inveterate Enemy, of his Person and Claim could be suppos'd to suffer.

On the other hand, I leave it to any considering Man to Judge, what a Surprize it must be to me to meet with all the publick Clamour that Informers could invent, as being Guilty of writing against the *Hanover* Succession, and as having written several Pamphlets *in Favour of the* Pretender.

No Man in this Nation ever had a more riveted Aversion to the *Pretender,* and to all the Family he pretended to come of, *than I:* A Man that had been in Arms under the Duke of *Monmouth,*[26] against the Cruelty and Arbitrary Government of his pretended Father; That for twenty Years had, to my utmost, opposed him, (King *James*) and his Party after his Abdication; That had serv'd King *WILLIAM* to his Satisfaction, and the Friends of the Revolution after his Death, at all Hazards, and upon all Occasions; That had suffer'd and been ruin'd under the Administration of *Highflyers* and *Jacobites,* of whom some are, *at this Day, COUNTERFEIT Whigs;*[27] It could not be! the Nature of the Thing could by no means allow it, it must be monstrous; and that the Wonder may cease, I shall take leave to quote some of the Expressions out of these Books, of which the worst Enemy I have in the World is left to Judge, whether they are in Favour of the *Pretender,* or no; but of this in its Place.

For these Books I was prosecuted, taken into Custody, and oblig'd to give Eight hundred Pound Bail.[28]

I do not in the least object here against, or design to reflect upon the Proceedings of the Judges which were subsequent to this; I acknowledg'd *then,* and *now* acknowledge *again,* that, upon the Information given, there was a sufficient Ground for all they did, and my unhappy entring upon my own Vindication in Print, while the Case was before their Lordships in a Judicial Way, was an Error which I neither understood, and which I did not foresee; and therefore, altho' I had great Reason to reflect upon the Informers, yet I was wrong in making that Defence in the Manner and Time I then made it, and which, when I found, I made no scruple afterward to Petition the Judges, and acknowledge, that they had just Ground to resent it: Upon which Petition and Acknowledgement, their Lordships were pleas'd, with particular Marks of Goodness, to release me, and not take the Advantage of an Error of Ignorance, as if it had been consider'd and premeditated.

But against the *INFORMERS,* I think, I have great Reason to complain; and against the Injustice of those Writers, who, in many Pamphlets, charged me with writing for the *Pretender;* and the Government, with pardoning an Author who wrote for the *Pretender;* and indeed the Justice of those Men can be in nothing more clearly stated, that in this Case of mine; where the Charge, in their Printed Papers and Publick Discourse was brought, not that they themselves believ'd me Guilty of the Crime, but because it was necessary to blacken the Man; That a general Reproach might serve for an Answer to whatever he should say that was not for their Turn: So that it was the Person, not the Crime they fell upon, and they may justly be said to persecute for the sake of Persecution, *as will thus appear.*

This Matter making some Noise, People began to enquire into it, and to ask what *De Foe* was prosecuted for, seeing the Books were manifestly written against the *Pretender,* and for the Interest of the House of *Hanover?* And my Friends expostulated freely with some of the Men who appear'd in it, who answer'd, *with more Truth than Honesty,* That they knew this Book had nothing in it, and that it was meant another way; but that *De Foe* had disoblig'd them in other things, and they were resolv'd to take the Advantage they had both to punish and expose him. They were no inconsiderable People who said this; and had the Case come to a Tryal, I had provided good Evidence to prove the Words.

This is the Christianity and Justice by which I have been treated; and this Injustice is the thing that I complain of.

Now as this was a Plot of a few Men to see if they could brand me in the World for a *Jacobite,* and perswade rash and ignorant People that I was turn'd about for the *Pretender, I think they might as easily have prov'd me to be a Mahometan;* therefore, I say, this obliges me to state that Matter as it really stands, that impartial Men may Judge whether those Books were written for, or against the *Pretender;* and this cannot be better done, than by the Account of what follow'd after the first Information, which in few Words is thus:

Upon the several Days appointed, I appear'd at the *Queen's Bench-Bar* to discharge my Bail; and at last had an Indictment for High Crimes and Misdemeanours exhibited against me by Her Majesty's Attorney-General, which, as I was inform'd, contain'd two hundred Sheets of Paper.

What was the Substance of the Indictment I shall not mention here, neither could I enter upon it, having never seen the Particulars: But I was told, that I should be brought to Tryal the very next Term.

I was not ignorant that in such Cases it is easy to make any Book a Libel, and that the Jury must have found the Matter of Fact in the Indictment, (*viz.*) That I had written such Books, and then what might have follow'd I knew not: Wherefore I thought it was my only way to cast my self on the Clemency of her Majesty, whose Goodness I had had so much Experience of many ways; representing in my Petition, that I was far from the least Intention to favour the Interest of the *Pretender,* but that the Books were written with a sincere Design to promote the Interest of the House of *Hanover;* and humbly laid before her Majesty, as I do now before the rest of the World, the Books themselves to plead in my behalf; representing farther, that I was maliciously inform'd against by those who were willing to put a Construction upon the Expressions different from my true Meaning, and therefore, flying to her Majesty's Goodness and Clemency, I entreated her Gracious PARDON.

It was not only the native Disposition of her Majesty to Acts of Clemency and Goodness, that obtain'd me this Pardon; but, as I was inform'd, her Majesty was pleas'd to express it in the Council, *She saw nothing but private Pique in the first Prosecution;* and therefore, I think, I cannot give a better and clearer Vindication of my self, than what is contain'd in the Preamble to the Pardon which her Majesty was pleas'd to grant me, and I must be allow'd to say, to those who are still willing to object, that, I think, what satisfy'd her Majesty might be sufficient to satisfy them; and I can assure them, that this Pardon was not granted without her Majesty's being specially and particularly acquainted with the things alledg'd in the Petition, the Books also being look'd in to find the Expressions quoted in the Petition. The Preamble to the Patent for a Pardon, as far as relates to the Matters of Fact, runs thus: *WHereas, in the Term of the* Holy Trinity *last past, our*

Attorney General did exhibit an Information, in our Court of Queens Bench *at* Westminster, *against* DANIEL DE FOE, *late of* London, *Gent. for Writing, Printing, and Publishing, and causing to be Written, Printed, and Published, THREE LIBELS, the one entituled,* Reasons against the Succession of the House of *Hanover;* with an Enquiry, how far the Abdication of King *James,* supposing it to be legal, ought to affect the Person of the *Pretender. One other entituled,* And what if the *Pretender* should Come? Or some Considerations of the Advantages and real Consequences of the *Pretender's* possessing the Crown of *Great Britain. And one other entituled,* An Answer to a Question that nobody thinks of (*viz.*) What if the Queen should Die?

And whereas the said Daniel De Foe *hath, by his humble Petition, represented to us, that he, with a sincere Design to propagate the Interest of the* Hanover Succession, *and to animate the People against the Designs of the* Pretender, *whom he always looked on as an Enemy to our Sacred Person and Government,* did publish *the said Pamphlets: In all which Books, altho' the Titles seem'd to look as if written in Favour of the* Pretender, *and several Expressions, as in all ironical Writing it must be, may be wrested against the true Design of the Whole, and turn'd to a Meaning quite different from the Intention of the Author, yet the Petitioner humbly assures us, in the solemnest Manner, that his true and only Design in all the said Books was, by an ironical Discourse of recommending the* Pretender, *in the strongest and most forcible Manner to expose his Designs, and the ruinous Consequences of his succeeding therein; which, as the Petitioner humbly represents, will appear to our Satisfaction by the Books themselves, where the following Expressions are very plain,* (viz.) *That the PRETENDER is recommended* as a Person proper to amass the *English* Liberties into his own Soveraignty, supply them with the Privileges of wearing WOODEN SHOES; easing them of the trouble of chusing Parliaments; and the Nobility and Gentry of the Hazard and Expence of Winter Journeys, by governing them in that more righteous Method of his ABSOLUTE WILL, and enforcing the Laws by a Glorious STANDING ARMY; paying all the Nations Debts at once by stopping the Funds, and shutting up the *Exchequer;* easing and quieting their Differences in Religion, by bringing them to the UNION OF POPERY, or leaving them at Liberty to have no Religion at all: *That these were some of the very Expressions in the said Books which the Petitioner sincerely design'd to expose, and oppose as far as in him lies the* Interest *of the* Pretender, *and with no other Intention:* NEVERTHE-LESS, *the Petitioner, to his great Surprize, has been misrepresented, and his said Books misconstrued, as if written in Favour of the* Pretender, *and the Petitioner is now under Prosecution for the same; which Prosecution, if farther carried on, will be the utter Ruin of the Petitioner and his Family: Wherefore the Petitioner humbly assuring us of the Innocence of his Design, as aforesaid, flies to our Clemency, and most humbly prays our most Gracious and Free Pardon. WE taking the Premisses, and the Circumstances aforesaid into our Royal Consideration, are graciously pleas'd,* &c.

Let any indifferent Man Judge whether I was not treated with particular Malice in this Matter, who was, notwithstanding this, reproach'd in the daily Publick Prints with having written treasonable Books, in behalf of the *Pretender;* nay, and in some of those Books, as before, the Queen her self, was reproach'd, *with having granted her Pardon to an Author who writ for the* Pretender.

I think I might with much more Justice say, I was *the first Man* that ever was oblig'd to seek a Pardon for writing for the *Hanover* Succession; and *the first Man* that these People ever sought to Ruin for writing against the *Pretender:* For if ever a Book was sincerely design'd to farther and propogate the Affection and Zeal of the Nation against the *Pretender,* nay, and was made use of, and that with success too, for that purpose, THESE BOOKS *were so;* and I ask no more Favour of the World to determine the Opinion of honest Men for or against me than what is drawn constructively from these Books. Let one Word, either written or spoken by me, either publish'd, or not publish'd, be produced, that was in the least disrespectful of the Protestant Succession, or to any Branch of the Family of *Hanover*, or that can be judg'd to be favourable to the Interest or Person of the *Pretender*, and I will be willing to wave her Majesty's Pardon, and render my self to Publick Justice, to be punish'd for it as I should well deserve.

I freely and openly Challenge the worst of my Enemies to charge me with any Discourse, Conversation, or Behaviour in my whole Life, which had the least Word in it injurious to the Protestant Succession, unbecoming or disrespectful to any of the Persons of the Royal Family of *Hanover*, or the least favourable Word of the Person, the Designs, or Friends of the *Pretender*.

If they can do it, let them stand forth and speak, no doubt but they may be heard; and I, for my part, will relinquish all Pleas, Pardons, and Defences, and cast my self into the Hands of Justice.

Nay, to go farther, I defy them to prove, that I ever kept Company, or had any Society, Friendship, or Conversation with any *Jacobite;* so averse have I been to the Interest, and to the People, that I have studiously avoided their Company upon all Occasions.

As nothing in the World has been more my Aversion than the Society of *Jacobites*, so nothing can be a greater Misfortune to me than to be accus'd, and publickly reproach'd with what is, of all things in the World, most abhorr'd by me, and which has made it the more afflicting is that this Charge arises from those very things, which I did, with the sincerest Design, to manifest the contrary.

But such is my present Fate, and I am to submit to it, which I do with Meekness and Calmness, as to a Judgment from Heaven, and am practising that Duty which I have studied long ago, of *Forgiving my Enemies, and praying for them that despitefully use me.*

Having given this brief History of the Pardon, &c. I hope the Impartial part of the World will Grant me, That being thus Graciously Deliver'd a second Time from the Cruelty of my Implacable Enemies, and the Ruin of a Cruel and unjust Persecution, and that by the meer Clemency and Goodness of the Queen, my Obligation to her Majesty's Goodness, was far from being made less than it was before.

I have now run through the History of my Obligation to her Majesty, and to the Person of my Benefactor aforesaid. I shall state every thing that follow'd this with all the Clearness I can, and leave my self lyable to as little Cavil as I may; for I see my self assaulted by a sort of People who will do me no justice. I hear a Great Noise made of Punishing those that are GUILTY, but as I said before not one Word of Clearing those that are INNOCENT; and I must say in this Part, they Treat me not only as I were no Christian, but as if they themselves were not Christians. They will neither prove the Charge, nor hear the Defence, which is the unjustest thing in the World.

I foresee what will be alledged to the Clause of my Obligation, &c. to Great Persons: And I resolve to give my Adversaries all the Advantage they can desire; by acknowledging beforehand, That *no Obligation to the QUEEN, or to any Benefactor, can justify any Man's acting against the Interest of his Country, against his Principles, his Conscience, and his former Profession.*

I think this will Anticipate all that can be said upon that Head, and it will then remain to state the Fact as I am, or am not Chargeable with it; which I shall do as clearly as possible in few words.

It is none of my Work to enter into the Conduct of the Queen or of the Ministry in this Case, the Question is not what *they have done,* but what *I have done?* And tho' I am very far from thinking of them as some other People think, yet for the sake of the present Argument, I am to give them all up, and Suppose, *tho' not Granting,* that all which is suggested of them by the worst Temper, the most censorious Writer, the most scandalous Pamphlet or Lampoon should be True, and I'll go through some of the Particulars, as I meet with them in Publick.

1st, That they made a Scandalous Peace, unjustly Broke the Allyance, Betray'd the Confederates, and Sold us all to the *French*.

God forbid it should be all Truth, in the manner that we see it in Print; But that, I say, is none of my Business. —— *But what hand had I in all this?* I never wrote one word for the Peace *before it was made*, or to Justify it after *it was made*, let them produce it if they can; Nay, in a *Review* upon that Subject, while it was making I Printed it in plainer Words than other Men durst Speak it at that Time, That *I did not like the Peace*, nor did I like any Peace that was a making, since that of the PARTITION, and that the Protestant Interest was not taken Care of either in that or the Treaty of *Gertrudinburgh* before it.[29]

It is true, that I did say, That since the Peace was made, and we could not help it, that it was our Business and our Duty to make the best of it, to make the utmost Advantage of it by Commerce, Navigation, and all kind of Improvement that we could, and this I SAY STILL; and I must think it is more our Duty to do so, than the Exclamations against the thing it self which it is not in our power to Retrieve. This is all that the worst Enemy I have can Charge me with: *After the Peace was made*, and the *Dutch* and the Emperor stood out, I gave my Opinion of what I foresaw would necessarily be the Consequence of that Difference, (*viz.*) That it would inevitably involve these Nations in a War with one or other of them; *any one* who was Master of Common Sense in the publick Affairs, might see that the standing out of the *Dutch* could have no other Event: For if the Confederates had Conquer'd the *French*, they would certainly have fallen upon us by way of Resentment, and there was no doubt, but the same Councils that led us to make a Peace, would Oblige us to maintain it, by preventing too great Impressions upon the *French*.

On the other hand, I alledged, that should the *French* prevail against the *Dutch,* unless he stopt at such Limitations of Conquest as the Treaty oblig'd him to do, we must have been under the same necessity to renew the War against *France;* and for this Reason, seeing we had made a Peace, we were oblig'd to bring the rest of the Confederates into it, and to bring the *French* to give them all such Terms as they ought to be satisfied with.

This way of Arguing was either so little Understood, or so much Malign'd, that I suffer'd innumerable Reproaches in Print, for having Written for a War with the *Dutch,* which was neither in the Expression, or ever in my Imagination: But I pass by these Injuries as small and trifling compar'd to others *I* suffer under.

However one thing *I* must say of the Peace, *Let it be Good or Ill in its self,* I cannot but think we have all reason to Rejoyce in behalf of his Present Majesty, That at his accession to the Crown, He found the Nation in Peace; and had the Hands of the King of *France* tied up by a Peace, so as not to be able, without the most infamous breach of Articles, to offer the least Disturbance to his taking a Quiet and Leisurely possession, or so much as to Countenance those that would.

Not but that *I* believe, if the War had been at the height, we should have been able to have preserved the Crown for his present Majesty, its only Rightful Lord: But *I* will not say it should have been so Easy, so Bloodless, so Undisputed as now, and all the Difference must be acknowledged to the Peace, and this is all the Good *I* ever yet said of the Peace.

I come next to the general Clamour of *the Ministry being for the Pretender;* I must speak my Sentiments solemnly and plainly, as I always did in that matter, (*viz.*) That if it was so, *I* did not see it, nor did I ever see Reason to believe it; this *I* am sure of, that if it was so, *I* never took one step in that kind of Service, nor did *I* ever hear one Word spoken by any one of the Ministry that *I* had the Honour to know or Converse with, that favour'd the Pretender: But have had the Honour to hear them all Protest that there was no Design to Oppose the Succession of *Hanover* in the least.

It may be Objected to me, That they might be in the Interest of the Pretender for all that: *It is true they might;* But that is nothing to me, *I* am not Vindicating their Conduct, but my own; as *I* never was Employ'd in any thing that way, so *I* do still protest, *I* do not believe it was ever in their Design, and *I* have many Reasons to confirm my Thoughts in that Case, which are not material to the present Case: But be that as it will, it is enough to me that *I* acted nothing in any such Interest, neither did *I* ever Sin against the Protestant Succession of *Hanover* in Thought, Word, or Deed; and if the Ministry did, *I* did not see it, or so much as suspect them of it.

It was a Disaster to the Ministry, to be driven to the Necessity of taking that Set of Men by the hand, who, no body can deny, were in that Interest:[30] But as the former Ministry answer'd, when they were charg'd with a Design to overthrow the Church, because they favour'd, joyn'd with, and were united to the *Dissenters;* I say they answer'd, *That they made use of the* Dissenters, *but granted them nothing* (WHICH BY THE WAY WAS TOO TRUE:) So these Gentlemen Answer, *That it is true, they made use of* Jacobites, *but did nothing for them.*

But *this by the by.* Necessity is pleaded by both Parties for doing things which neither Side can justify. I wish both Sides would for ever avoid the Necessity of doing Evil; for certainly it is the worst Plea in the World, and generally made use of for the worst Things.

I have often lamented the Disaster which I saw, employing *Jacobites,* was to the late Ministry, and certainly it gave the greatest Handle to the Enemies of the Ministry to fix that universal Reproach upon them of being in the Interest of the *Pretender:* But there was no Medium. The *Whigs* refused to shew them a safe Retreat, or to give them the least Opportunity to take any other Measures but at the Risque of their own Destruction; and they ventur'd upon that Course, in hopes of being able to stand alone at last without help of either the one or the other, in which no doubt they were mistaken.

However, in this Part, as I was always assur'd, and have good Reason still to believe, that her Majesty was steady in the Interest of the House of *Hanover*, and that nothing was ever offer'd to me, or requir'd of me to the Prejudice of that Interest, On what Ground can I be reproach'd with the secret reserv'd Designs of any, if they had such Designs as I still verily believe they had not?

I see there are some Men who would fain perswade the World, that every Man that was in the Interest of the late Ministry, or employ'd by the late Government, or that serv'd the late Queen, was for the *Pretender*.

God forbid this should be true; and I think there needs very little to be said in Answer to it. I can answer for my self, that it is notoriously false; and I think the easy and uninterrupted Accession of his Majesty to the Crown contradicts it: I see no End which such a Suggestion aims at, but to leave an Odium upon all that had any Duty or Regard to her late Majesty.

A Subject is not always Master of his Sovereign's Measures, nor always to examine what Persons or Parties the Prince he serves Employs; so be it that they break not in upon the Constitution; that they govern according to Law, and that he is employ'd in no illegal Act, or have nothing desir'd of him inconsistent with the Liberties and Laws of his Country: If this be not right, then a Servant of the King's is in a worse Case than a Servant of any private Person.

In all these things I have not err'd, neither have I acted or done any thing in the whole Course of my Life, either in the Service of her Majesty, or of her Ministry, that any one can say has the least Deviation from the strictest Regard to the Protestant Succession, and to the Laws and Liberties of my Country.

I never saw an Arbitrary Action offer'd at, a Law dispens'd with, Justice deny'd, or Oppression set up, either by Queen or Ministry, in any Branch of the Administration, wherein I had the least Concern.

If I have sin'd against the *Whigs*, it has been all NEGATIVELY, (*viz.*) that I have not joyn'd in the loud Exclamations against the Queen, and against the Ministry, and against the Measures; and if this be my Crime, my Plea is twofold.

1. I did not really see Cause for carrying their Complaints to that violent Degree.

2. Where I did see what, as before, I lamented and was sorry for, and could not joyn with, or approve, as joyning with *Jacobites*, the *Peace,* &c. My Obligation is my Plea for my silence.

I have all the good Thoughts of the Person, and good Wishes for the Prosperity of my Benefactor; that Charity, and that Gratitude, can inspire me with: I ever believ'd him to have the true Interest of the Protestant Religion, and of his Country in his view; if it should be otherwise, I should be very sorry. And I must repeat it again, that he always left me so entirely to my own Judgment in every thing I did, that he never prescrib'd to me what I should write, or should not write in my Life; neither did he ever concern himself to dictate to, or restrain me in any kind; nor did he see any one Tract that I ever wrote before it was Printed: So that all the Notion of my writing by his Direction, is as much a Slander upon him, as it is possible any thing of that kind can be; and if I have written any thing which is offensive, unjust, or untrue, I must do that Justice as to declare, He has had no hand in it; the Crime is my own.

As the Reproach of his directing me to write, is a Slander UPON THE PERSON I am speaking of; so that of my receiving Pensions and Payments from him for writing, is a Slander UPON ME; and I speak it with the greatest Sincerity, Seriousness, and Solemnity that it is possible for a Christian Man to speak, That except the Appointment I mention'd before, which her Majesty was pleas'd to make me formerly, and which I receiv'd during the time of my Lord *Godolphin's* Ministry, I have not receiv'd of the late Lord Treasurer, or of any one else by his Order, Knowledge, or Direction, one Farthing, or the Value of a Farthing, during his whole Administration; nor has all the Interest I have been suppos'd to have in his Lordship, been able to procure me the Arrears due to me in the time of the other Ministry. SO HELP ME GOD.

I am under no Necessity of making this Declaration. The Services I did, and for which her Majesty was pleas'd to make me a small Allowance, are known to the greatest Men in the present Administration; and some of them were then of the Opinion, and I hope are so still, that I was not unworthy of her Majesty's Favour. The Effect of those Services, however small, are enjoy'd by those Great Persons, and by the whole Nation to this Day; and I had the Honour once to be told, *That they should never be forgotten.* It is a Misfortune, that no Man can avoid, to forfeit for his Deference to the Person and Services of his Queen, to whom he was inexpressibly oblig'd: And if I am fallen under the Displeasure of the PRESENT Government, for any thing I ever did in Obedience to her Majesty in THE PAST, I may say it is my Disaster; but I can never say it is my Fault.

This brings me again to that other Oppression which as I said I suffer under, and which, I think, is of a Kind, that no Man ever suffer'd under so much as my self: And this is to have every Libel, every Pamphlet, be it ever so foolish, so malicious, so unmannerly, or so dangerous, be laid at my Door, and be call'd publickly by my Name. It has been in vain for me to struggle with this Injury; It has been in vain for me to protest, to declare solemnly, nay, if I would have sworn that I had no hand in such a Book, or Paper, never saw it, never read it, and the like, it was the same thing.

My Name has been hackney'd about the Street by the Hawkers, and about the Coffee-Houses by the Politicians, at such a rate, as no Patience could bear. One Man will swear to the Style; another to this or that Expression; another to the Way of Printing; and all so positive, that it is no purpose to oppose it.

I publish'd once, to stop this way of using me, that I would Print nothing but what I set my Name to, and I held it for a Year or Two; but it was all one, I had the same Treatment. I now have resolv'd, for some time, to write nothing at all; and yet I find it the same thing. Two Books lately publish'd being call'd mine, for no other reason that I know of, than that, at the Request of the Printer, I revised two Sheets of them at the Press, and that they seem'd to be written in Favour of a certain Person; which Person also, as I have been assur'd, had no Hand in them, or any Knowledge of them, till they were publish'd in Print.[31]

This is a Flail which I have no Fence against, but to complain of the Injustice of it, and that is but *the shortest Way* to be treated with more Injustice.

There is a mighty Charge against me for being Author and Publisher of a Paper call'd, *The MERCATOR.* I'll state the Fact first, and then speak to the Subject.

It is true, that being desir'd to give my Opinion in the Affair of the Commerce with *France,* I did, as I often had done in Print many Years before, declare, That it was my Opinion we ought to have an open Trade with *France,* because I did believe we might have the Advantage by such a Trade; and of this Opinion I am still. What Part I had in the *Mercator,* is well known; and would Men Answer with Argument, and not with personal Abuses, I would, at any time, defend every Part of the *Mercator* which was of my doing. But to say the *Mercator* was mine, is false; I neither was the Author of it, had the Property of it, the Printing of it, or the Profit of it. I had never any Payment or Reward for writing any Part of it; Nor had I the Power to put what I would into it:[32] Yet the whole Clamour fell upon me, because they knew not who else to load with it. And when they came to Answer, the Method was, instead of Argument, to threaten, and reflect upon me;

reproach me with private Circumstances and Misfortunes, and give Language which no Christian ought to give, and which no Gentleman ought to take.

I thought any *Englishman* had the Liberty to speak his Opinion in such things; for this had nothing to do with the Publick. The Press was open to me as well as to others; and how, or when I lost my *English* Liberty of speaking my Mind, I know not; neither how my speaking my Opinion without Fee or Reward could authorize them to call me Villain, Rascal, Traytor, and such opprobious Names.

It was ever my Opinion, and is so still, that were our Wooll kept from *France*, and our Manufacturers spread in *France* upon reasonable Duties, all the Improvement which the *French* have made in Woolen Manufactures would decay, and in the End be little Worth, and consequently the Hurt they could do us by them, would be of little Moment.

It was my Opinion, and is so still, that the Ninth Article of the Treaty of *Commerce*[33] was calculated for the Advantage of our Trade, let who will make it, *that is nothing to me:* My Reasons are, because it TYED up the *French* to open the Door to our Manufactures at a certain Duty of Importation THERE, and left the Parliament of *Britain* at Liberty to shut theirs out by as high Duties as they pleas'd HERE, there being no Limitation upon us as to Duties on *French* Goods; *but that other Nations should pay the same.*

While the *French* were thus bound, and the *British* free, I always thought we must be in a Condition to Trade to Advantage, or it must be our own Fault: This was my Opinion, and IS SO STILL, and I would venture to maintain it against any Man upon a publick Stage, before a Jury of fifty Merchants, and venture my Life upon the Cause, if I were assured of fair Play in the Dispute. But that it was my Opinion, That we might carry on a Trade with *France* to our great Advantage, and that we ought for that reason to Trade with them, appears in the Third, Fourth, Fifth, and Sixth Volume of the *Reviews*, above Nine Year before the *Mercator* was thought of;[34] it was not thought Criminal to say so then, how it comes to be Villainous to say so now God knows, I can give no account of it; I am still of the same Opinion, and shall never be brought to say otherwise, unless I see the state of Trade so altered, as to alter my Opinion; and if ever I do, I will be able to give good Reasons for it.

The Answer to these things, whether mine or no, was all pointed at me, and the Arguments were generally in the Terms of Villain, Rascal, Miscreant, Lyer, Bankrupt, Fellow, Hireling, Turn-coat, &c. what the Arguments were better'd by these Methods, that I leave to others to Judge of. Also most of those things in the *Mercator*, for which I had such Usage, were such as I was not the Author of.

I do grant, had all the Books which have been called by my Name been written by me, I must of Necessity have exasperated every Side, and perhaps have deserved it; but I have the greatest Injustice imaginable in this Treatment, as I have in the perverting the Design of what really I have written. To sum up therefore my Complaint in few Words:

I was from my first entring into the Knowledge of publick Matters, and have ever been to this Day, a sincere Lover of the Constitution of my Country; zealous for Liberty, and the Protestant Interest; but a constant Follower of moderate Principles, a vigorous Opposer of hot Measures in all Parties: I never once changed my Opinion, my Principles, or my Party; and let what will be said of changing Sides, this I maintain, That I never once deviated from the Revolution Principles, nor from the Doctrine of Liberty and Property, on which it was founded.

I own I could never be convinc'd of the great *Danger* of the PRETENDER, in the Time of the late Ministry: Nor can I be now convinc'd of the great *Danger* of the CHURCH under this Ministry. I believe the Cries of one was politically made use of then to serve other Designs; and I plainly see the like Use made of the other now. I spoke my Mind freely then, and I have done the like now, in a small Tract to that purpose not

yet made publick; and which, if I live to publish, I will publickly own,[35] as I purpose to do, every thing I write, that my
Friends may know when I am abused, and they impos'd on.

It has been the Disaster of all Parties in this Nation to be
very HOT in their Turn, and as often as they have been SO,
I have differed with them all, and ever must and shall do so.
I'll repeat some of the Occasions on the *Whigs* Side, because
from that Quarter the Accusation of my turning about comes.

The first Time I had the Misfortune to differ with my
Friends, was about the Year 1683, when the *Turks* were besieg-
ing *Vienna,* and the *Whigs* in *England,* generally speaking,
were for the *Turks* taking it; which I having read the History
of the Cruelty and perfidious Dealings of the *Turks* in their
Wars, and how they had rooted out the Name of the Christian
Religion in above Threescore and Ten Kingdoms, could by no
means agree with: And tho' then but a young Man, and a
younger Author, I opposed it, and wrote against it; which
was taken very unkindly indeed.

The next Time I differed with my Friends was when King
James was wheedling the *Dissenters* to take off the Penal
Laws and Test, which I could by no means come into. And
as *in the first* I used to say, I had rather the Popish House of
Austria should ruin the Protestants in *Hungaria,* than the Infi-
del House of *Ottoman* should ruin both Protestant and Papist,
by over-running *Germany;* So in the other, I told the *Dissenters*
I had rather the Church of *England* should pull our Cloaths
off by Fines and Forfeitures, than the Papists should fall both
upon the *Church,* and the *Dissenters,* and pull our Skins off
by Fire and Fagot.

The next Difference I had with good Men, was about the
scandalous Practice of *Occasional Conformity,*[36] in which I
had the Misfortune to make many honest Men angry, rather
because I had the better of the Argument, than because they
disliked what I said.

And now I have lived to see the *Dissenters* themselves very
quiet, if not very well pleased with an Act of Parliament to

prevent it.[37] Their Friends indeed laid it on; they would be Friends indeed if they would talk of taking it off again.

Again, I had a Breach with honest Men for their Male-treating King *William;* of which I say nothing: Because, I think, they are now opening their Eyes, and making what amends they can to his Memory.

The fifth Difference I had with them, was about the *Treaty of Partition,*[38] in which many honest Men were mistaken, and in which I told them plainly then, That they would at last End the War upon *worse Terms;* and so it is my Opinion they would have done, tho' the Treaty of *Gertrudenburgh* had taken Place.

The sixth Time I differed with them, was when the *Old Whigs* fell upon the *Modern Whigs;* and when the Duke of *Marlborough* and my Lord *Godolphin* were used by the *Observator* in a Manner worse, *I must confess for the Time it lasted,* than ever they were used since; nay, tho' it were by *Able* and the *Examiner:*[39] But the Success failed. In this Dispute my Lord *Godolphin* did me the Honour to tell me, *I had served him* and *his Grace also,* both *faithfully* and *successfully.* But his Lordship is Dead, and I have now no Testimony of it but what is to be found in the *Observator,* where I am plentifully abused for being an Enemy to my Country, by acting in the Interest of my Lord *Godolphin,* and the Duke of *Marlborough: What Weather-Cock can Turn with such Tempers as these!*

I am now in *the seventh* Breach with them; and my Crime now is, That I will not believe and say the same things of the *Queen,* and the late *Treasurer,* which I could not believe before of my Lord *Godolphin,* and the Duke of *Marlborough,* and which in Truth I cannot believe, and therefore could not say it of either of them; and which, if I had believed, yet I ought not to have been the Man that should have said it, for the Reasons aforesaid.

In such Turns of Tempers and Times a Man must be tenfold *a Vicar of* Bray,[40] or it is impossible but he must one Time or other be out with every Body. This is my present Condition, and for this I am reviled with having abandon'd my Principles, turn'd *Jacobite,* and what not: God Judge between me and these Men. Would they come to any Particulars with me, what real Guilt I may have I would freely acknowledge; and if they would produce any Evidence, of the Bribes, the Pensions, and the Rewards I have taken, I would declare honestly, whether they were true or no. If they would give a List of the Books which they charge me with, and the Reasons why they lay them at my Door, I would acknowledge any Mistake, own what I have done, and let them know what I have not done. But these Men neither shew Mercy, or leave place for Repentance, in which they act not only unlike their Maker, but contrary to his express Commands.

It is true, good Men have been used thus in former times; and all the Comfort I have is, that these Men have not the last Judgment in their Hands, if they had, dreadful would be the Case of those who oppose them. But that Day will shew many Men and Things also in a different State from what they may now appear in; some that now appear clear and fair, will then be seen to be black and foul; and some that are now thought black and foul, will then be approved and accepted; and thither I chearfully appeal, concluding this Part in the Words of the Prophet, *I heard the Defaming of many; Fear on every side; Report,* say they, *and we will Report it; All my Familiars watch'd for my halting, saying, Peradventure he will be enticed, and we shall prevail against him, and we shall take our Revenge on him,* Jerem. 20.10.

Mr. *Pool's Annotations* has the following Remarks on these Lines, which, I think, are so much to that Part of my Case which is to follow, that I could not omit them. His Words are these.

"The Prophet," *says he,* "here rendreth a Reason why he thought of giving over his Work as a Prophet; his Ears were continually filled with the Obloquies and Reproaches of such as reproached him; and besides, he was afraid on all Hands, there were so many Traps laid for him, so many Devises devised against him. They did not only take Advantage against him, but sought Advantages, and invited others to raise Stories of him. Not only Strangers, but those that he might have expected the greatest Kindness from; those that pretended most courteously, they watch," *says he,* "for opportunities to do me Mischief, and lay in wait for my Halting, desiring nothing more than that I might be enticed to speak, or do something which they might find Matter of a colourable Accusation, that so they might satisfie their Malice upon me. This hath always been the Genius of wicked Men; *Job* and *David,* both made Complaints much like this." These are Mr. *Pool's* Words.[41]

And this leads me to several Particulars, in which my Case may, without any Arrogance, be likened to that of the Sacred Prophet; except only the vast Disparity of the Persons.

No sooner was the Queen Dead, and the King as Right required, proclaim'd, but the Rage of Men encreased upon me to that Degree, that the Threats and Insults I receiv'd were such as I am not able to express: If I offered to say a word in favour of the present Settlement, it was called fawning and turning around again; on the other hand, tho' I have meddled neither one way or other, nor written one Book since the Queen's Death, yet a great many things are call'd by my Name, and I bear every Day the Reproaches which all the Answerers of those Books cast as well upon the Subject as the Authors. I have not seen or spoken to my Lord of *Oxford* but once since the King's Landing, nor receiv'd the least Message, Order, or Writing from his Lordship, or any other way Corresponded with him, yet he bears the Reproach of my Writing in his Defence, and I the Rage of Men for doing it.[42] I cannot say it is no Affliction to me to be thus used, tho' my being entirely clear of the Facts, is a true support to me.

I am unconcerned at the Rage and Clamour of *Party-men;* but I can not be unconcern'd to hear Men, who I think are good Men and good Christians, prepossess'd and mistaken about me: However I cannot doubt but some time or other It will please God to open such Mens Eyes. A constant, steady adhering to *Personal Vertue,* and to *Publick Peace,* which, I thank God, I can appeal to him, has always been my Practice; will AT LAST restore me to the Opinion of Sober and Impartial Men, and that is all I desire: What it will do with those who are resolutely Partial and Unjust I cannot say, neither is that much my Concern. But I cannot forbear giving one Example of the hard Treatment I receive, which has happened, even while I am Writing this Tract: I have six Children, I have Educated them as well as my Circumstances will permit, and so as I hope shall recomme[n]d them to better Usage than their Father meets with in the World. I am not indebted One Shilling in the World for any part of their Education, or for any thing else belonging to bringing them up; yet the Author of the *Flying-Post* Published lately,[43] That I never pay'd for the Education of any of my Children. If an[y] man in *Britain* has a Shilling to demand of me for any part of their Education, or any thing belong[ing] to them, let them come for it.

But these Men care not what Injurious Things they Write, nor what they Say, whether Truth or Not, if it may but raise a Reproach on me, tho' it were to be my Ruine. I may well Appeal to the Honour and Justice of my worst Enemies in such Cases as this.

Conscia Mens Recti fama Mendacia Ridet.[44]

CONCLUSION by the Publisher.

WHile this was at the Press, and the Copy thus far finish'd, the Author was seiz'd with a violent Fit of an Apoplexy, whereby he was disabl'd finishing what he design'd in his farther Defence, and continuing now for above Six Weeks in a Weak and Languishing Condition, neither able to go on, or likely to recover, at least in any short time, his Friends thought it not fit to delay the Publication of this any longer; if he re-

covers, he may be able to finish what he began; if not, it is the Opinion of most that know him, that the Treatment which he here complains of, and some others that he would have spoken of, have been the apparent Cause of his Disaster.

APPLEBEE'S ORIGINAL Weekly Journal

With fresh Advices, Foreign and Domestick

SATURDAY, *November* 19, 1720.

Mr. Applebee,

Oxford, Nov. 15, 1720.

I Obferve, with a particular Satisfaction, that the Annual Feaft of the Gentlemen Natives of the City and Univerfity of OXFORD, is ftill continued in *London,* and that Tickets are given out already for their Meeting this Year: It is, I fay, a particular Satisfaction to us here, and will be fo, no doubt, to all the Lovers of Charity and Beneficence, to fee a Society of this Nature thus kept up, and applying themfelves to Hofpital and Charitable Defigns, when all the Meetings and Societies of other Counties and Cities, formerly fet up in *London,* are funk and loft. This is an unanfwerable Teftimony to the good Difpofition of the Gentlemen concern'd in your Society, and to the Principles of Honour and Liberality, Charity and good Works, which appear among them; and we hope, without Arrogance, fomething may be claim'd from it, in behalf of the good Education and Inftruction which they receiv'd here; and which is fo much the natural Confequence of their being bred up in this Place, a City and Univerfity, which has for fo many Ages been a Fountain of Inftruction and good Principles to all its Inhabitants; as well as of Knowledge and Wifdom to the learned Part of the World; which flock hither for Education.

I cannot but make a Remark to you on this Occafion, which I believe you will acknowledge to be juft; *namely,* That from this very Thing may be feen fomething of the Reafon and Caufe of the fhort Period of other Societies of this Nature: How comes it to pafs, that the numerous Meetings and Societies of People, fet up in *London* by your Example, are fo generally funk and come to nothing? That they who made fuch vaft Appearances for a few Years, talk'd fo loud of their great Collections, their juft Applications of what was gather'd, their Charity, their Bounty to the Poor, and other good Actions, Things really good, had they continued as they began: (in fhort, they talk'd too much, and did too little) I fay, How comes it to

pafs that we hear no more of them? That their great Cavalcades thro' the City of *London* are forgot, their Colours and Streamers laid afide, the poor Orphans pretended to be taken into their Care, neglected, difafted, fetting up the Trades they were put out to, and fo left in a worfe Cafe than they were found? How comes it to pafs, that not a Society but yours, and that of the Sons of the Clergy, *in whom, we hope, we may alfo claim fome Share, as an Honour to our City and Univerfity;* I fay, How comes it to pafs that none but thefe two Societies remain? Pofterity will join with us in faying, T'was becaufe your early Defign was laid on the folid Foundation of Vertue and Charity; others on the loofe and weak Surface of Pomp and Oftentation, to fay nothing of the Luxury and Excefs conftantly atte ding their Affemblies; Things equally unfound in Principle, and confequently deftructive of themfelves; Things tending naturally to make the Sober and Religious Part of Mankind decline them, and to bring their whole Defign to an early Diffolution.

Vanity and Vice are born of Vapour, are the Mufhrooms of a Day, and dye of themfelves: But Vertue and juft Principles are the Daughters of Time, derive from the Fountain of Life, and have a native Tendency to Durations; nay, fo truly immortal are they, that befides the Eternity of their Reward with good Men, *whofe Works follow them,* they live in the Memory of juft Men, thro' all the Ages of Time, and are preferv'd to be fpoken of, both for Reverence and Example.

I fend you this fhort Memorial, that you may make it publick, for the Honour of our Country-Men, and for their Encouragement in fo good a Work; and as we know you are, yourfelf, a Native of this City, of OXFORD, we doubt not your doing us, and the Society, fo much Juftice. Our City Honours their Benevolence; we fee the Children of our Poor Annually provided for by them, and put out to handfome Employments: and, we doubt not, many of thofe perifhing Orphans may, by an honeft Induftry, build up Fortunes on the Foundation of this Charity, which fhall enable them to be Supports, in Time to come, to the Society which they derive from, and to be Benefactors to others, in Return for the Bounty they now receive. Thus the Gentlemen are laying up
an

APPLEBEE'S
ORIGINAL
WEEKLY JOURNAL

With fresh Advices, Foreign and Domestick

Between 16 July 1720 and 27 August 1726 Defoe contributed introductory essays on a wide variety of topics, foreign news, and criminal biographies to *Applebee's Original Weekly Journal*.

SATURDAY, MAY 20, 1721.

We have very dismal Accounts from France of the Ravages which the Plague makes in Provence, and particularly at the City of Thoulon:[1] But they tell one Story which indeed strikes every Body with Horror that reads it; and this relates to the terrible Famine which rages in Thoulon, where the Want of Bread, and indeed of all Provisions, is such, that the People are made desperate and distracted. 'Tis said that they have devour'd entirely all the Corn, or Flesh, that was in the City, and have eaten the most loathsome and nauteous Things, such as Dogs, Cats, Rats, Mice, Leather, Starch, Soap, and, in a Word, that they are ready to prey even upon one another. They add, that in Troops they break into the Houses which are shut up, and robb the richer Inhabitants of what they had laid up for their Provisions: But that which is most hor-

rible of all is, that on the 9th a Rabble of the People, Men,
Women, and Children, to the Number of 1700, made desperate
by their Diseases, and quite raging by their Hunger, sally'd
out into the Fields by force, and wandering about to seek
Food, came up to the Lines, which are guarded by several
Regiments of regular Troops, they demanded Bread; the Soldiers told them they had none but the Ammunition-Bread, that
was allowed them for their daily Subsistence, but feeling their
Distress, they threw them what they had, which the poor
Creatures devour'd like revenous Beasts: They then desir'd
they might pass into the plain Country, to get Bread, that they
might not be starved; but the Soldiers told them they could
not let them do so, it being contrary to their Orders; but the
poor desperate Wretches told them they must, and would go,
for they could but dye, and accordingly attempted the Lines in
Sixteen or seventeen Places: At the same Time the Soldiers
kept them back as long as they could with Blows, and with
the Muzzles of their Pieces, but were at length obliged to fire
at them, by which almost 178 were killed, and, as they say,
137 wounded: Among the first were three and thirty Women
and Children, and four and fifty among the latter; so that most
of them were driven back into the City, where they must
inevitably perish. They add, that notwithstanding this, several
hundreds of them got over the Lines, and spread themselves
every way over the Fields; but 'tis thought that most of those
that are got over will fall into the Soldiers Hands, and be
killed in cold Blood, or will be starv'd in the Mountains. The
same Letters say, that the Government having had an Account
of this dreadful Story, has order'd that the Guards should be
doubled in the said Lines, but that a sufficient Quantity of
Corn and Cattle, and Salt, should be furnish'd by the Intend-
ants of Dauphine, and be deliver'd weekly to the Officers commanding in the Lines, to be deliver'd by them to the Magistrates of Thoulon, for the supply of the City; and that the City
shall be liable to be tax'd for the Value of the said Provisions,
after they are restor'd to their former State of Health. The

Numbers that dye every Day in the City are diversely reported; some say about two hundred, others that there dies above three hundred a Day, but that as many perish for Want of Food, that is, are starved to Death, as dye of the Plague; so that the Misery of that Place is not to be express'd, and is infinitely worse than it was at Marseilles.

SATURDAY, *SEPTEMBER* 16, 1721.

To the Author of the Original Journal.

Sir,

I Cannot but observe in many of our Papers, a very affecting melancholy Account of the spreading of the Plague in our neighbouring Country of France, and a heavy Judgment it is no doubt, and the Consternation of the People must be very great.

But I must also take Notice to you, that had that Distemper happen'd among us, as it did among them, it must certainly have spread a great deal faster than it has among them; and if its contagious Nature be, as they say it is, so much more virulent and furious than former Contagions have been, it must, by this Time, have destroy'd infinite Numbers of People here more than it has there; and if it be true, that in the Cities of Marseilles, Thoulon, and Arles, especially the two latter, nine Parts of ten of the People have died, what Havock must it have made among us!

The Methods used in France with the Towns and Places infected, has been to surround them with Lines, and guard them with Troops, so that they should not stir out to mix with the rest of the Country, and spread the Contagion; and that Method has been so severe, and been executed so rigorously, that many very cruel barbarous Things have been done, when Despair or Famine has driven the distress'd People to break out beyond the Lines prescrib'd: In short, the Government has declared a sort of defensive War against all the infected Towns and Places, prohibited the People, on Pain of Death, to stir out, or to offer to pass those Lines; and though, notwithstanding all their Precaution, the Plague has broke Bounds, and is discover'd in Places remote and distant from the Places first infected; as in the Country of Rovergue, the Gevaudan, and Parts adjacent; yet, without doubt, had not that severe Method been taken, Paris it self had, by this Time, been as Thoulon, and perhaps no Part of France had been wholly free.

The Methods therefore which they have taken, have been certainly just and prudent, with Respect to the Rest of the Country; but suffering not the sound to come away from the sick, must most certainly be infinitely the worse for those Towns which have been visited, and where had the People had liberty to have gone away, one half of that Number could not have died.

But now to bring this Case home to ourselves, methinks we might, without alarming and distracting our People here, I say, we might talk of using some proper Measures for our Conduct in England, where such Measures as are practic'd in France cannot be taken.

It is true, we have these Things call'd Priviledges and Liberties, which will not allow the Government to proceed with the People as they do in France: For Example: If a Town should be infected, we cannot surround it with Lines, and shoot the Innocent despairing People, that attempt to break out; we cannot imprison the People, and oblige the sound to stay and die among the sick: No Officer dare command his Soldiers to fire at a Man that offers to come out of any infected Town, no, tho' he had the Plague upon him; if he did, that Officer commanding would be try'd, and being convicted, would be condemn'd to die for willful Murther; and if the Widow of the Person so kill'd lodg'd any Appeal, that Officer must die, the King himself could not pardon him.

What then must we do? and what Remedy must we prepare for our Preservation, and to prevent the Confusions which threaten us in case of an Infection? I am not entering too far into such an Enquiry, because People will take more Alarm from such Things than is intended; but certainly it cannot be our Prudence entirely to neglect such a Thing, till it comes to the very Door, the Consequence of which will be, that then we shall be all in Confusion and Distraction.

The French tell us, that at Paris the King has order'd that all Beggars and Vagabonds, and People who are not settled Inhabitants, and cannot give a very good Account of their Business there, shall depart the City; and they have order'd twenty thousand Beds to be prepar'd in the Great Hospital, call'd *La Charity*, and others; which, in case of Infection, are to be as Pest-Houses, and it is a very good Thing without doubt: But nothing of 'his can be done here; Beggars and Vagabonds may indeed be pass'd away; but as for those Poor who have, as we call it, legal Settlements, be they from what County or Town soever, they cannot be compell'd to stir. These happy, unhappy Obstructions, call'd Privileges and Liberties, stand in the way of all this.

It is doubtless, the Wisdom of the People to disperse as much as possible, and separate themselves into the several Countries of England where they have any possible Resort, and to perswade them to do this, as soon as they have any just Cause to apprehend the Distemper will appear here, would be the best piece of Service any Man could do them; and were it effectually done by all such Families whose immediate Business, or want of Friends to retreat to did not hinder them, and that such as are oblig'd to stay would send away their Wives and Children, and Servants, into such Retreats; I say, this by thinning the City of Inhabitants, would go a great way to prevent the Encrease, as well as the spreading the Distemper.

But I have yet other Methods to propose for regulating and disposing of the People; so as that if the Distemper should come, it should find no considerable Numbers together, and consequently would much sooner be stopp'd than it may otherwise be; for certainly nothing can stop the Progress of such a terrible Destroyer, Providence concurring, like separating effectually the vast Concourse of People which live here in so little room, throng'd together as they do (so that their very Breath would infect one another) and giving them a clear Air to breath in.

It will be objected, that the Poor cannot remove, being not able to subsist for want of Work and Wages, which they depend upon, and would starve without it. I shall state a Method to make this easy also, if the Mischief appears nearer our view: In the mean Time, 'tis but Prudence to conclude before-hand upon what must be done, when the Time and Occasion comes upon us, to avoid the Confusions which necessarily attend such Cases, when they find us undetermin'd: *The Prudent Man foreseeth the Evil, and hideth himself; but the Simple pass on and are punish'd.* Prov. 27. 12.

Yours, *Prudential.*

SATURDAY, *OCTOBER* 7, 1721.

To the Author of the Original Journal
Sir,

I Observe other Papers are very particular in their Accounts of the Plague, with which our neighbouring Countries are visited, but that you say little of it, which I suggest may be either, first, that you do not give entire Credit to whatever they say, or that, secondly, you are loth to alarm us too much at home.

As to the first, I do believe, as I suppose you do, that we have not true Accounts from Abroad, nor can I blame the French for concealing their own Disasters; I know we did so in England when the same kind of Judgment was upon us; many Reasons are to be given why we should allow them the same Latitude; they are a trading Nation as well as we, and it is already very heavy upon them that their Commerce is shut up on several Sides; nor are they without Reason to apprehend it would be quickly shut up on every Side, if the Distemper should spread much further, or that it should be known how far it has been spread already: It is therefore their Prudence to conceal, as much as in them lyes, their Misery from all the rest of the World; and, upon this Foundation, I doubt not but that the Southern Parts of France are much more afflicted than they suffer us to know. The Infection of Avignon is a Proof of this, where the Pope's Legate, tho' surrounded by the French, concealed the Towns being Infected for above a Month.

I have heard, and have a great deal of Reason to believe what I have heard of that Kind, that in the City of London, when visited with the Plague, many Thousands perished more than an Account could be taken of, and that many Thousands of those that were known, and of whom they might have given an Account, were not put into the Bills, least the People of other Parts of the Kingdom should have been frighted from bringing Provisions for the rest. Thousands likewise died in the Fields and Ditches adjacent to the City, whose Bones lye there still, and have been frequently dug up on several Occasions, who were never bury'd at all, otherwise than by the People of the next Hamlet or Village, throwing Earth upon them as they lay. I doubt not the World never will have a true Account of the Numbers of People that dye at this Time Abroad; neither shall we know how far the Distemper spreads, if they can help it, till perhaps it may come so near us as to discover itself, in a manner not to be conceal'd.

But I come to the second Reason, which I give why you are perhaps backward to speak in the Case, (*viz.*) That you are loth to alarm our People too much; 'tis a Charitable and a Christian Reason I confess, in the main part of it; but I cannot say that it is a good Reason why we should not let the People know the true State of their Condition, and what it is they ought to do, or to expect; nay, on the contrary, it may be injurious to many Families, in not giving them timely Notice to take needful Measures for their own Safety, and that of their Families; and this will certainly encrease the Hurry and Fright that such People will be in, if it should once come upon them.

It may pass for a doubtful Question among some People, whether it would be best, that the People of this City should know the Plague will visit them, if it is to come; or that they should not know it before it should come; and many I know pretend to be of the Opinion they should not know it.

I know my Reasons why I am not of that opinion, and I know them to be good Reasons, but the Town will not hear them at this Time. I remember what our Saviour says of the Day of Judgment, that the People will buy and sell, marry, and be given in Marriage, even to the last Gasp; and I doubt I may say the same of the City of London, they will Drink, Swear, Blaspheme, deny Christ that Divinity which they will after tremble at; they will Trade, Cheat, Stock-Job, set up Bubbles, act lewd Plays, keep Whores, robb on the Highway, and, in a Word, go on as they do now, not only until the Judgment comes upon them, but even till they, as we may justly call it, bring it upon themselves; and are these the Men that should not be allarm'd? You may, with as much Justice, say, when an House is on Fire, you should not allarm the Family, or wake them out of their Sleep, for fear of frighting and terrifying them: Such a Family would say afterwards you were very unjust to them to let them lye till they were in Danger of being burnt in their Beds; and so will the People here say, if they should be surpriz'd with this Calamity, that it was very unkind not to inform them of their Danger, that they might have Time to provide for themselves and Families, but to let them be led on in Ignorance till the Evil was upon them.

I am, Sir,

Your Humble Servant,

H. R.

SATURDAY, *NOVEMBER* **18, 1721.**

Mr. Applebee,

I Have spent some Hours lately pouring over those ridiculous Legends, call'd Bills of Mortallity, or Weekly and Yearly Bills; that is to say, an Account Weekly publish'd of the Diseases and Casualties, and Burials, and Christenings in the several Parishes within the Circuit, which we formerly call'd the Lines of Communication, and which we now call within the Bills of Mortality.

These Bills of Mortallity have been publish'd, and an (exact) Account taken (so they would have us believe it) of the Numbers bury'd within the said Communication ever since the Year 1603, or thereabouts, which was the Year when the first Plague happen'd in England in the last Century.

It is our great Misfortune, that all the Calculations of Numbers of Inhabitants of Increase and Decrease of People of the Magnitude of the City, and the Proportions it bears to other Parts of the Kingdom, and to other Kingdoms, and other Cities, and to other Parts of the World; I say, it is our great Misfortune that all these Calculations are taken from the Numbers of People that dye, or rather the Numbers of People bury'd in the City of London, and Lines of Communication, as above, with Calculations; were they to be depended upon, would be very valuable Things; but being taken from wrong Foundations, are themselves all wrong also. The Reasons is this: If a Patient sends for a Physician, and gives him a wrong Account o[f] his Constitution, or of his Condition, he will give him wrong Physick: If a Client give his Council a wrong State of his Case, he will give him wrong Advice: Thus if these Bills of Mortallity, and Accounts of Deaths and Burials, are wrong, so will be all the Calculations that are made from them.

Now I am afraid that not only now, but even from the beginning, these Parish Clerks, to whom that Matter is committed, have been such a Gang, I had almost said such a

Drunken Gang of AMEN MEN, that they never made it any of their Care to be exact in that Affair, notwithstanding it has been, and is still many ways a thing of the greatest Consequence of any thing of that kind that can happen in the World; and not to enter into a long detail of the usefulness of the thing, and the Necessity there is that it should be exact, nor into a particular Discourse of the neglect to say no worse of it of that important Matter, and how much a thing of Course it is made among the People whose Business it is, I crave leave to observe.

First, it is for want of this that we have no exact Account to this Day of the Numbers of People who have died in any former Time of Infection; nor are we likely, I doubt, which is much the Reason of writing this, to have a true Account of what may happen in the like Case for the future.

I shall, at a little Leisure, show the scandalous Deficiency of these Mortallity Men in the Time of the late Infection in 1665, and in the several Times of Infection before that, but for the present let me only tell you in general, that this Affair calls for an immediate Inspection, that, if possible, we might bring it to be depended upon.

I am perswaded, were there Encouragement given for it, the greatest Fraud, chiefly by way of Omission, would be found in this Case; Why else is it almost a constant Observation, that the Bills decrease one Week, and increase another? That several Parishes are every Year exactly, and the same, or with very little Alterations the same? That the Diseases are all, as it were on a sudden chang'd; and that the greatest Numbers are transferr'd from the Article of the Consumption to that of the Convulsion, which could never be from the positive change of the Distemper; but certainly from the ignorance of the Searchers, and the slight Inquiries they make after the Fact, and till this is Detected, and Search'd into, I expect nothing can be depended upon from our Bills of Mortality.

That several of the Clarks of the small City Parishes carry in their Accounts once a Fortnight, instead of once a Week, that some of them happen, and that when they come to be Examin'd, their Yearly Accounts do not agree with their Weekly, that the Diseases are the same kind of guess Work; that the Searchers are a sort of old Women, Ignorant, Negligent; that many times the Clarks, who are not above half a Degree better old Women than the Searchers, often supply the Searchers Office, and put the Dead down of what comes next in their Heads: And in short, 'tis not one time in many, that in some Parishes any Searchers come near a dead Body; often not near the House, and as often ask what the Person died of; get Money, and perhaps Drink, and go about their Business.

How this was in the Time of the late Plague; and how it will be, if another should happen, I shall take the liberty to tell you more at large hereafter.[2]

Your Servant,
Tom Beadle.

SATURDAY, JANUARY 26, 1723.

To the Author of the Original Journal.
SIR,

I HAVE been often thinking to write a line or two to you about the desperate Temper of our wicked People, *I mean those they call convict Felons* in returning from Transportation, as we see they do daily, at the Peril of their Lives.[3]

How they find ways and means at *Virginia,* and the Places they are carried to, to avoid the Servitude they are Sentenc'd to, and to get Passage back to *England,* is a thing well worth consideration; and I may speak of it by it self; but that is not the present business, no doubt Measures might be taken by the Governments Direction to prevent it, and to make it impossible, so that the poor wretched Creatures should not have it in their Power, to bring themselves to the Gallows as they do every Day, but of that I say hereafter, it is not our present Work.

But what Infatuation is it that possesses the People I am

speaking of, that they should at all hazards, nay, almost at a certainty of Death and Shame, push back *as they do* from their Transportation, to a place where, they are as it were, almost sure to be taken, as they are sure to Dye when they are taken.

It can not be the meer Dread and Terror of the Place and Labour they are doom'd to do at *Virginia*, for tho' it be what may be call'd Labour, yet I affirm, it is the best and easiest of its kind, that any Country in the World confines their Criminals to undergo.

It is not like the *Spaniards* sending them to the Mines to work a hundred Fathom deep, in the Bowels of the Mountain *Potoss*,[4] and dig up the Silver they are sure never to enjoy an Ounce of; they do not labour with Chains and Clogs upon them, as among the marble Quarries in *Italy;* and in the *Appenin* Mountains of *Genoa;* they do not tug at the Oar, chain'd down to the Bench they sit on, as in the Gallies of *France* and *Spain;* they do not hunt *Sables* as in *Siberia*, with the Extrmiety of Cold and Hunger, in the Latitude of 72 Degrees North.

In a Word, their Labour is not harder, or their Usage worse than many hired Servants in *England* o[n] Yearly Wages; and tis evident even before their Eyes, the Negro Servants even in the same Plantation, and under the same Masters, are in worse Circumstances (infinitely worse) than they; as they are not only us'd worse, but are without Redemption, without Hope, without any end of their Misery, for them or their Posterity.

But here their time being out, which generally is no more than seven or fourteen Years, they are sure of being Free, and not only so, but have an opportunity of Planting for themselves, and that with such Encouragement, that nothing but a stated Aversion to an honest Life, or to a diligent Application to Business, can prevent their accepting it with the utmost Thankfulness; nor are they without innumerable Instances on the Spot, which way soever they turn, of good substantial Families, rais'd from the same beginnings; namely, where

Offenders like themselves, made sensible of the Danger of Death which they had escap'd, and of the benefit of an industrious Life, which was before them, have applyed themselves to the planting of Land, and by their own Labour and Application, with the Assistance of the Country Bounty, have by little and little, rais'd themselves to good Circumstances, and in the end, by a continu'd addition, have prosper'd and grown Rich.

It is certain, that every Servant thus finishing the Time of his Servitude, has an Opportunity put into his Hands (as it may be call'd) to set up for himself: He may have Land assign'd him by the Country, and he may have Credit for Cloaths, Tools and Necessaries for his Support, till what he can prepare and plant may be brought to perfection, and then he pays by the Crop, and gains Credit till the next Crop; so that they cannot say they have no Stock to set up with, no Tools to work with, no Cloaths, and the like.

This is a fair Offer of Heaven to such Creatures to begin, not only a new Condition of Life, but even a new Life itself; and, which is very particulair, here they are sure never to be upbraided with either the Crimes or Misfortunes of their former Life: To be reform'd, is so much real Credit to them, and so valued by all about them in that Place, that it is equal, if not superior, even to not having been guilty at all.

Upon their being thus reform'd, and applying themselves with Honesty and Industry to a due Course of Business, they are as sure of rising in the World, as they are sure of Misery and Death in the contrary.

Who then in their Wits would decline wearing out with Patience the Life of Servitude, which is in it self but short, with so certain a Prospect of Safety and Success; who would choose to come back a thousand Leagues, to seek in the stead of it certain Death, Infamy, and the Gallows: and yet we see every Day Examples of these Creatures, who suffer Death for flying from their own Felicity, and who choose to die with

Shame, rather than to live happy and easy, at the small Expense of five or six or seven Years Servitude.

Nor is it less wonderful to observe the Infatuation these Creatures are under, they are not content to venture back and to come over before their time, which is punishable with Death, but they come in to the very Places from whence they went, and fall into the same Channel of Crime, as that for which they were sent away, if it was a House-breaker, he becomes a House-breaker, if a Pick-pocket, a Pick-pocket, and that in the very same Walks, and among the same Gang of Rogues as before, as if they resolv'd to come to the same Jayl they went out of, whereas would they but change the Place of Action, were the Felon transported from *England* to go back to *Ireland,* or the Felon transported from the City to begin his Practice in the Country, and the Country Felon in the City, and the like; there might be some Room to escape, but harden'd to a Degree, and secured their certain State, they come even to the very Spot they were at before, nay, some of them have had the Impudence to come to the very Door of the Prison, and some have been taken not far from it. This is such an Infatuation, as indeed I can give no Account of, and only take notice of it as a Mark of Astonishment. I shall say more of it hereafter.

Yours, *&c.*

SATURDAY, *SEPTEMBER* 19, 1724.

The Recorder, as well as his Deputy, being at the Bath, the Execution of John Sheppard will not be so expeditious as expected. He hath confess'd, that on Tuesday the 8th Instant, two Days before he was taken, he came from Finchly into Bishopsgate-street, and drank at several Publick Houses; and in the Evening came into Smithfield, went thro' Christ's Hospital, and pick'd two People's Pockets in the Cloysters, and from thence pass'd under Newgate, down the Old-Bailey, and into Fleet-street; where taking Notice of Mr. Martin's, a Watch-maker's Shop, against St. Bride's Church, and only a little Boy to look after it, he meditated to robb the same, and per-fected his Villanious Design in the Manner following, viz. He first fix'd a Nail-Piercer into the Post of the Door, next fasten'd the Knocker thereto with a Packthread, and then cut out a Pane of Glass, and took three Silver Watches out of the Shop Window; the Boy seeing him take the Watches, but could not get out to pursue him, by reason of his subtle Contrivance; one whereof he pawn'd for a Guinea and an half, and the two others were taken upon him at Hinchly. He denies that his Fellow-Traveller Page[5] was privy to this Robbery; but, if we are rightly instructed, Mr. Page was accompanying him all that Night, and was aiding and assisting in this Fact; and, just before it was executed, came into the Shop, and ask'd the Boy some trifling Questions, the better to observe the Inside, &c. This, with some other Circumstances, will as we are told, be prov'd against Page: if so, in all probability he may accom-pany his Friend Sheppard in his Cart and Two.

And on Saturday Night the Rev. Mr. Wagstaff,[6] being at-tending John Sheppard, the notorious Malefactor, in the Con-demn'd Hold, in order to prepare him for his approaching Dissolution, discover'd a small File concealed in his Bible, which is suppos'd to have been convey'd to him by his Brother, who is a Prisoner on the Common Side Felons over his Head, in Order for Transportation, and between whom there is a sort of Communication thro' a little Hole.

And on Wednesday Morning the Keeper going into the Con-demn'd-Hold to Sheppard, found two Files, a Chisel, and a Hammer, hid in the Bottom of a matted Chair, with which he had begun to file his Irons, who when he perceiv'd his last Effort to escape thus discovered and frustrated, his wicked and obdurate Heart began to relent, and he shed abundance of Tears; he was carried up to an Apartment called the Castle, in the Body of the Gaol, a Place of equal, if not superior Strength to the Condemn'd-Hold; and there Chain'd to the Floor.

SATURDAY, *OCTOBER* 24, 1724.

The following was communicated to us as a true Copy
of a Letter sent by Sheppard to his Mother.

My dear loving Mother,

THIS with my Duty to you, hoping these Lines will find you
in good Health, as I am at this present Writing; and this is to
let you know, that in my Attempt, by the Assistance of God,
the Fortune that I had in making my Escape from the Castle
of Newgate, save my Life; and I hope that by the Grace of
God I shall keep myself from any more of such heinous Crimes,
and from the Hands of mine Enemies. And dear Mother, cast
yourself not down, but be of good Heart; for I hope to be as
much Comfort to you as ever I was Dishonour. I would feign
let you know where I am, but dare not for fear of Miscarriage.
So no more at present, but I rest

Your Loving, Dutiful,

Misfortune Son,

JOHN SHEPPARD.

SATURDAY, *OCTOBER* 31, 1724.

The following LETTER was brought on *Saturday* last, after a
Eleven o' Clock to Mr. Applebee's House in *Black-Fryers*, by
a Person like an Ostler; and is well known to be the Handwriting of JOHN SHEPPARD. The Original whereof is now
to be seen at Mr. Applebee's.

Mr. Applebee,

THIS with my kind Love to you, and pray give my kind
Love to Mr. *Wagstaff;* hoping these Lines will find you in good
Health, as I am at present; but I must own you are the Looser
for want of my Dying-Speech; but to make up your loss, if you
think this Sheet worth you while, pray make the best of it.
Though they do say I am taking among the Smugglers, and

put in *Dover Castle*, yet I hope I am among Smugglers still. So no more, but your humble Servant,

JOHN SHEPPARD.

And I desire you would be the Post-Man to my last Lodging. So farewell now, I quit the *English* Shore.

NEWGATE Farewell.

    Mr. Austin,[7]

YOU was pleased to pass your Jokes upon me, and did say you should not be Angry with me, had I took my leave of you; but now pray keep your Jokes to your self, let them laugh that wins: For now it is a equal Chance, you to take me, or I to get away; but I own my self Guilty of that Ill-Manners, but excuse me, for my Departure being private and necessary, spoil'd the Ceremony of bidding adue. But I wish you all well, as I am at present. But pray be not Angry for the loss of your Irons, had you not gave me them, I had not taking them away, but really I had left them behind me, had convenience aserv'd. So pray don't be Angry.

How Austin, and Perry, you did say,
If are the SHEPPARD got away,
That in his Room Hanged you'd be,
Upon that fatal *Tyburn* Tree.

But that rash Way I pray forsake,
Though SHEPPARD is so fortunate:
I would have you with Patience waite,
Tell that again you do him take.

For you are large and heavy Men,
And two the weight what was of him;
And if away to that Tree you take,
Upon my word you'd make it Shake.

So farewel now, my leave I take, and what's amiss done, you write, for my Schoularship is but small.

This from your fortunate Prisoner,
                    JOHN SHEPPARD.

SATURDAY, *NOVEMBER* **7, 1724.**
To the Author of the Original Journal.
Mr. App.

AS the Taking and Re-taking of *John Sheppard*, the House-breaker, is the Subject of all Conversation, pray let me Entertain you with a Paralel *Story*, of a less Criminal Nature; indeed my case will let you see, that all the Art of *breaking Prison* is not contain'd in SHEPPARD's suppos'd Ingenuity.

You must understand then, that I am a young Body, such as in common Speech you call a *young Lady*, and having a good Fortune left me by a distant Relation, I am much in the same Case with *John Sheppard*, for I am Condemn'd, and Confin'd, and Imprison'd, having twice made my Escape, and being unhappily taken the third Time, believe the Sentence will now be executed upon me without Mercy: My Story, in short, is much like that of *John Sheppard*, as follows.

First, I was desperately in Love, that you must know, is call'd a most wicked abominable Thing in our House, worse than *Sheppard's* Crime abundantly: My Father is of an austere ridg'd Disposition, full of invincible Aversions against my being Marry'd; he says, his Daughters are his proper Goods, every one of us, he says, is a *Chattel*. I suppose, if he should die he would have us Apprais'd, and put into the Inventory of his Household Goods. I had Application made to me by a young Gentleman of a good Estate, and in the most honourable Way possible, only indeed, that he made Love to me before he spoke to my Father of it: This my Father took Occasion to Resent, and that to such a Height, that it threw him into Indecencies, and he charg'd him with a Design to rob his House; That is, by the way to rob him of one of his Daughters; but I put an End to that, for I told my Father in so many Words, I was willing to have him. My Father told me, and him too, that *it was all one for that*, that I had no Right to dispose of my self without his Consent, that I was his Property, as much as his Horses, or his Cows; and that if I would stray from the Pastures, I ought to be Pounded, and accordingly, that very Night caus'd the Stair-Head Door to be lock'd at the Top of the Stair-Case, after I was gone to Bed, and setting an OLD MAID, which by the way, is the worst Jaylor in the World, for they have natural Aversion to any Bodies being Married; I say, he set this wither'd Thing as a Centinel over me, made me a close Prisoner up two Pair of Stairs, and sent my Lover, an insulting Message; Namely, that he had secur'd me, and he might take me if he thought he could come at me.

This at first put me into such a Rage, that I could hardly forbear laying violent Hands on my self: However, in a few days I compos'd my self, and from that time apply'd my self wholly to make my Escape; and first I found Means to let my Lover know my Condition, by calling out at the Window to a Neighbour's Maid, who faithfully convey'd the News of my Circumstances to him; and he and I convers'd freely together afterwards through a back Window over an Alley, where we by her help contriv'd all that followed.

This indefatigable Girl making her way over two or three Houses, came round the End of the Alley, and with infinite Hazzard got into the Chamber to me about Midnight, I opening the Garret Door, on the Top of the House; here we decently ty'd the OLD MAID, my Jaylor fast down in the Bed, bringing the Rope about her Neck, so that if she stirr'd or struggl'd she would be hang'd, and Gagg'd her to Boot.

Having done this, we went both out at the Top of the House, and got over the Houses the same way she came in, shutting the Door so after us, that they never imagined we went out that way; but thought I had let my self down by a Rope from the Window, which we left open with a Rope hanging to it on purpose; and thus with most desperate Hazzard I escap'd the first time.

My Lover had been Contriving my Escape all the while another way, but waiting an Answer from me, could not proceed, and heard nothing of my real Escape, till afterwards, when it was too late. When I was at Liberty, the first thing I did, was to give Notice to the Family to go up, and to Relieve my old Jaylor, who I was loth should be strangl'd, as indeed she was in danger of being; and this brought it to my Father's Ears that I was gone.

Mr. *Wild* never made more diligent Search after SHEPPARD, or his Brother BLEUSKIN,[8] than my Father did after me; had I been half as sharp in securing my self, he had never found me at all. But to my no small Surprize, some days after, my Father having by his indefatigable Diligence found me out; comes furiously into the House, where I was, with a Lord Chief Justice Warrant, and seiz'd me, as if I had been a Thief, or a Murtherer, and carried me away almost frighted to Death.

Being thus brought back to my Prison, my Father after a great many outragious Words, and fierce Looks, carry'd me up Stairs to the same Apartment, and to my no small Mortification had Iron Bars made to the Window, where he thought I had Escap'd, and though he did not suspect that little Door that I had really Escap'd, yet he had it nail'd up fast, so that there was no getting out that way neither; and to make the Securing me his own Care, caus'd my Mother, who if possible was more Severe than himself to lye with me every Night.

He endeavour'd by all the threatning Words imaginable to make me Confess, who it was that got into the Room to me, and which way; but I would never Confess any Thing, but deny'd there was any Body there, the OLD MAID affirm'd that she saw her; at last I carry'd it so cunningly, that in short, my Mother concluded it was the Devil, and it began to work upon her old Heart so far, that she was affraid to lye in the Room with me alone, so got the OLD MAID to bring a Bed into my Room, and so they both lay there to Guard me.

In the mean time my trusty Friend the Maid-Servant, who had let me out before, finding how it was, found Means to throw a Letter in at the Top of the Chimney for me, in which she propos'd a way to get the little Door open a second time; and in a Word, I by Signs to her out of the Window, desir'd she would help me to something to open it with by force; accordingly she tyed a strong Claw-Hammer, and a File to a String, and gave me Notice of it by Signal at the Window, and let it down the same Chimney, and so I got it safe without Discovery.

Having gotten this Implement, I filed the Hinges of the little Door, and with the Hammer I wrench'd open the Door gently, and got out in the Day time, when my two Keepers were gone down Stairs; and now I thought I had been safe enough.

But this being in the Day time, some unlucky People of the Neighbours seeing me clambering over the Houses, which gave the allarm, and behold! when I was got down Stairs at the House where the good honest Girl my Assistant had secur'd my Passage, and I was just going out at the Door, behold! I say, there stood my cruel hard hearted Father ready to receive me, and carry me to my old Prison again; and thus far you see I am in a kind of a Case much like JOHN SHEPPARD's, though a Thousand times more disconsolate about it.

My Crime it seems according to my Father is Robbery, which by the Law is punish'd with *Death,* and my Sentence is, that I shall live to be an OLD MAID, than *which you know* to be hang'd in ones Youth is much more Bearable. Now as some of my Neighbours (I hear) pitty SHEPPARD, and say, 'tis pitty he should die, but that he should be let go for his Ingenuity. Then why should not I Escape for my Ingenuity too? but I hear my Father is inexorable, so that I know no Remedy, but I must *lead Apes,* unless I can Escape a third Time, which I am resolv'd to try, come of it what will; and if I do get off you shall hear farther.

Yours, &c.

SATURDAY, *NOVEMBER* 21, 1724.

To the Author of the Original Journal.

Mr. App.

I AM a poor unfortunate Creature, as my Story will tell you at large, I was born in *Newgate*, the famous *Moll Flanders* was my Aunt,[9] but she met with good Fortune to set her above all her poor Relations, and I am left under infinite Disappointments.

I have been Transported twice, and have both times found Ways and Means not only to come back again, but to avoid being Taken again till Acts of Indemnity, and length of Time gave me leave to appear Abroad.

I have follow'd the Trade of Pilfering, and stealing some Years, and was got to a tollerable State of Life, that I could now have liv'd without it; but the habit has been so become a Nature to me, that I believe I should have walk'd in my sleep to pick Pockets, if I had deny'd my self the liberty of doing it waking, so I have continu'd the Trade a great many Years with uninterrupted Success, and now what strange Thing do you think has befallen me: Would you think it Mr. *App.* that I should have fall in Love after so much good Education as I have been Mistress of?

But so it is, I have been so deeply in Love with your late Friend *John Sheppard,* that I have been quite distracted. His Escaping with such Dexterity as you have heard out of *Newgate* charm'd me, and if I could have found him during the little time of Liberty he enjoy'd, I had certainly had him.

What tho' I am 20 Year older than he, we should have made a suitable Match in all other things: For as he was the most dexterous House-breaker in England; so I pretend to be the cleanest-handed Shoplift, and the nicest Pick-Pocket in *Europe.* I offer Mr. *App.* to go into a Mercer's-Shop, and tell him I come to take such a peice of Silk by slight of Hand, and he shall neither miss the peice, or perceive me to touch it, but shall think he sees the peice of Silk lye upon the Compter all the while.

I never went to *Salters-Lecture,* or St. *Lawrences* Church, and came away without a Gold Watch, or a Tweeser, or some other valuable Prize in my Life. I rarely came empty handed from the *Theatre,* especially, if the Play was any thing Popular: I assure you, *Cato*[10] was worth above a 100 Guineas to me, and yet I reckon the things taken, as we generally sell such things; Namely, at half Value.

The last Opera of *Tamerlane*[11] has done pretty well, and as 'tis likely to take, and to be Acted pretty often this Winter, I won't take a 100 Guineas for my Marketing, especially, if the Quality comes pretty much to it.

Harlequin[12] has been tollerably Beneficial to me; but the Auditories were a little too much *French,* there was not so many Gold Watches there, as on other Occasions; however, don't Complain.

Now the Parliament is met, and the Term in being, I am pretty much at *Westminster;* nor is my Success there so mean, but I may get a fair Livelihood; and all this while Mr. *App.* if you will believe that I not only have [not] been taken, but that I have brought the Art of Picking a Pocket to such Perfection, and have such exquisite Skill at it, that I not only have not, but I will not be taken, no never: I say, if you will believe this of me, you must believe also, that I am an extraordinary Person, and that I have an Art something beyond the D[evi]l.

Perhaps you have never heard of me, nor does the Fame of our Profession ever spread to any extraordinary a Degree, till they come to *Newgate;* but I have been so long forgotten there, that the present Incumbents, not Mr. [Pitt] himself knows any thing of me.[13]

Now had *John Sheppard* and I made a Match, what cleaver Couple should we have made, and what Pockets, what fasten Watches, what Purses of Money could have escaped us by Daylight, and what Bolted Shops, or Barricaded Houses have kept me out by Night? In a Word, Mr. *App.* we would have visited

Lombard-street[14] itself, no Iron Bars could have kept us out, no Iron Chest have withstood us within; but all is over, poor SHEPPARD is gone, and in him the expertest House-breaker in *England* is gone.

And am I not under a vast Disappointment now, when poor dexterous *Jack* is thus snatch'd from us by his evil Fate, after two of the immitable Escapes, and after having twice had his Liberty, but not been able to preserve himself.

Alas poor SHEPPARD! I have lost my Love, and all the hopes I had cherish'd of an universal Plunder are gone so far that I am left under an inexpressible Grief.

> Your Humble Servant,
> *Betty Blewskin*. (Catch me if you can.)

John Sheppard, the famous House-breaker, was on Monday last executed at Tyburn, pursuant to the Rule of Court of the King's-Bench, Westminster. He being an enterprizing Fellow, it was thought necessary to put Handcuffs on him in carrying him to the Gallows; which could not be done but by main Force, he struggling against it with all his Might; and being search'd before he was put in the Cart, they found conceal'd about him a Claspe Knife, with which 'tis thought he designed to cut the Cord wherewith he was ty'd, and then to leap among the Mob, as his last Refuge. The Crowd of Spectators all the Way was prodigiously great. An Undertaker with a Hearse follow'd him to Tyburn, in order as we are told, to bring back the Corpse to be interr'd in St. Sepulcher's Church Yard; but the Populace having a Notion that it was design'd to convey him to the Surgeons, carry'd off the Body upon their Shoulders to an Alehouse in Long-Acre, and the Undertaker and his Men got off with great Difficulty.

SATURDAY, *MAY* 29, 1725.

On *Monday* about the usual Time *Jonathan Wild* was executed at *Tyburn*. Never was there seen so prodigious a Concourse of People before, not even upon the most popular Occasion of that Nature. The famous *Jack Sheppard* had a tolerable Number to attend his *Exit*, but no more to be compared to the present, than a Regiment to an Army; and which is very remarkable, in all that innumerable Crowd there was not one pitying Eye to be seen, nor one compassionate Word to be heard, but on the contrary, where-ever he came, there was nothing but Hollowing and Huzzas as it had been upon a Triumph; nay, so far had he incurr'd the Resentment of the Populace that they pelted him with Stones, &c. in several Places, one of which in *Holbern* broke his Head to that Degree that the Blood ran down plentifully, which Barbarity tho' as unjustifiable as unusual, yet may serve to deterr others from treading in his Steps when they find the Consequence so universally odious. At the Place of Execution the People continu'd very outragious, so that it was impossible either for *Jonathan* or any of the rest to be very compos'd; however he behav'd himself better than could be well expected, considering the perpetual Insults, Peltings, &c. that he suffer'd. All the Indulgence he receiv'd was his not having his Hands ty'd all the Way; and at the Place of Execution, he was admitted to sit in the Cart till the Minister came, the others having been ty'd up a considerable Time. When he was turn'd off, there was an Universal Shout among the Spectators. As the Cart drew away, his Arms being loose, he happen'd to catch hold of the Coiner, but was immediately parted from him. His body was carry'd off in a Coach and four to the Sign of the *Adam and Eve* near *Pancreas* Church, in order to be interr'd in the Church-yard there, where one of his former w[i]ve[s] lies buried, which was done on *Tuesday* Night last. About two of the Clock in the Morning he had taken a Dose of Liquid *Laudanum*,[15] in order to have dispatch'd himself, but swallowing too much, it proved too strong for his Stomach and came up again, however it seem'd to have a stupifying Effect upon him; So desirous he was to avoid the Execution of one Sentence, tho' with the utmost Hazard of suffering another unspeakable more dreadful. At the same Time and Place were executed *Robert Harpham* for High Treason, in counterfeiting the current Coin of the Kingdom, *William Sterry* and *Robert Samford* for the Highway.

THE
HISTORY
Of the remarkable LIFE of
JOHN SHEPPARD,
CONTAINING
A particular Account of his many
ROBBERIES and ESCAPES,
Viz.

His robbing the Shop of Mr. *Bains* in White-Horse-Yard of 24 Yards of Fustian. Of his breaking and entering the House of the said Mr. *Bains*, and stealing in Goods and Money to the Value of 20 l. Of his robbing the House of Mr. *Charles* in *May Fair* of Money, Rings, Plate, &c. to the Value of 30 l. Of his robbing the House of Mrs *Cook* in *Clare-Market*, along with his pretended Wife, and his Brother, to the Value of between 50 and 60 l. Of his breaking the Shop of Mr. *Philips* in *Drury-Lane*, with the same Persons, and stealing Goods of small Value. Of his entering the House of Mr. *Carter*, a Mathematical Instrument Maker in *Wytch-street*, along with *Anthony Lamb* and *Charles Grace*, and robbing of Mr. *Barton*, a Master Taylor who lodged therein, of Goods and Bonds to the Value of near 300 l. Of his breaking and entering the House of Mr. *Kneebone*, a Woollen-Draper, near the *New Church* in the *Strand*, in Company of *Joseph Blake* alias *Blewskin* and *William Field*, and stealing Goods to the Value of near 50 l. Of his robbing of Mr. *Pargiter* on the Highway near the Turnpike, on the Road to *Hampstead*, along with the said *Blewskin*. Of his robbing a Lady's Woman in her Mistress's Coach on the same Road. Of his robbing also a Stage Coach, with the said *Blewskin*, on the *Hampstead* Road. Likewise of his breaking the Shop of Mr. *Martin* in *Fleet-street*, and stealing 3 silver Watches of 15 l. Value. ALSO

A particular Account of his rescuing his pretended Wife from St. *Giles's* Round-House. Of the wonderful Escape himself made from the said Round-House. Of the miraculous Escape he and his said pretended Wife made together from *New-Prison*, on the 25th of *May* last. Of his surprizing Escape from the Condemn'd Hold of *Newgate* on the 31st of *August* : Together with the true manner of his being retaken ; and of his Behaviour in *Newgate*, till the most astonishing and never to be forgotten Escape he made from thence, in the Night of the 15th of October. The Whole taken from the most authentick Accounts, as the Informations of divers Justices of the Peace, the several Shop-keepers above-mention'd, the principal Officers of *Newgate* and *New Prison*, and from the Confession of *Sheppard* made to the Rev. Mr. *Wagstaff*, who officiated for the Ordinary of *Newgate*.

LONDON : Printed and Sold by JOHN APPLEBEE in *Black-Fryers*, Printed, at the *Golden-Ball* near *Chancery-Lane* in *Fleet-street*, and the Booksellers of *London* and *Westminster*. (Price One Shilling.)

THE
HISTORY
Of the remarkable Life of
JOHN SHEPPARD,
CONTAINING
A particular Account of his many
ROBBERIES and ESCAPES,

VIZ.

His robbing the Shop of Mr. *Bains* in White-Horse-Yard of 24 Yards of Fustian. Of his breaking and entering the House of the said Mr. *Bains*, and stealing in Goods and Money to the Value of 20 l. Of his robbing the House of Mr. *Charles* in *May Fair* of Money, Rings, Plate, &c. to the Value of 30 l. Of his robbing the House of Mrs. *Cook* in *Clare-Market*, along with his pretended Wife, and his Brother, to the Value of between 50 and 60 l. Of his breaking the Shop of Mr. *Philips* in *Drury-Lane*, with the same Persons, and stealing Goods of small Value. Of his entering the House of Mr. *Carter*, a Mathematical Instrument Maker in *Wytch-street*, along with *Anthony Lamb* and *Charles Grace*, and robbing of Mr. *Barton*, a Master Taylor who lodged therein, of Goods and Bonds to the Value of near 300 l. Of his breaking and entering the House of Mr. *Kneebone*, a Woollen-Draper, near the *New Church* in the *Strand*, in Company of *Joseph Blake* alias *Blewskin* and *William Field*, and stealing Goods to the Value of near 50 l. Of his robbing of Mr. Pargiter on the Highway near the Turnpike, on the Road to *Hampstead*, along with the said *Blewskin*, Of his robbing a Lady's Woman in her Mistress's Coach on the same Road. Of his robbing also a Stage Coach, with the said *Blewskin*, on the *Hampstead* Road. Likewise of his breaking the Shop of Mr. *Martin* in *Fleet-street*, and stealing 3 silver Watches of 15 l Value.

ALSO

A particular Account of his rescuing his pretended Wife from St.
Giles's Round-House. Of the wonderful Escape himself made from
the said Round-House. Of the miraculous Escape he and his said
pretended Wife made together from *New-Prison,* on the 25th of
May last. Of his surprizing Escape from the Condemn'd Hold of
Newgate on the 31st of August: Together with the true manner
of his being retaken; and of his Behaviour in *Newgate,* till the
most astonishing and never to be forgotten Escape he made from
thence, in the Night of the 15th of October. The Whole taken from
the most authentick Accounts, as the Informations of divers Justices
of the Peace, the several Shop-keepers above-mention'd, the principal Officers of *Newgate* and *New Prison,* and from the Confession
of *Sheppard* made to the Rev. Mr. *Wagstaff,* who officiated for the
Ordinary of Newgate.[1]

LONDON:

Printed and Sold by John Applebee in Black-Fryers,
J. Isted, at the Golden-Ball *near* Chancery-Lane *in*
Fleet street, *and the* Booksellers *of* London *and*
Westminster. (*Price One Shilling.*)

On Saturday, 17 October 1724, *Applebee's Original Weekly
Journal* advertised that the *History* would be published "On
Monday next." A *Narrative Of All The Robberies, Escapes,
&c. Of John Sheppard,* published on 15 August 1724, is also
attributed to Defoe. Both pamphlets were immensely popular.

TO THE
CITIZENS
OF
LONDON AND *WESTMINSTER*

Gentlemen,

Experience has confirm'd you in that everlasting Maxim, that there is no other way to protect the Innocent, *but by Punishing the* Guilty.

Crimes ever were, and ever must be unavoidably frequent in such populous Cities as yours are, being the necessary Consequences, either of the Wants, *or the* Depravity, *of the lowest part of the* humane Species.

At this time the most flagrant Offenses, as Burning of Dwellings; Bur[g]laries, and Highway Robberies *abound; and* Frauds *common* Felonies, *and* Forgeries *are practic'd without Number; thus not only your* Properties, *but even your very* Lives *are every way struck at.*

The Legislative Power *has not been wanting in providing necessary and wholesome Laws against these* Evils, *the executive part whereof (according to your great Privileges) is lodged in your own Hands: And the Administration hath at all times applyed proper Remedies and Regulations to the* Defects *which have happen'd in the* Magistracy *more immediately under their Jurisdiction.*

Through the just and salutary Severities of the Magistrates, *publick excessive* Gaming *has been in a manner Surpress'd; and some late* Examples *of divine Vengeance have overtaken certain of the most notorious lewd* Prostitutes *of the* Town, *which together with the laudable endeavours of the great and worthy Societies,[2] has given no small check to that enormous and spreading* Vice.

But here's a Criminal *bids Defiance to your Laws, and Justice who declar'd and has manifested that the Bars are not made that can either keep him Out, or keep him In, and accordingly hath a second time fled from the very* BOSOM OF DEATH.

His History *will astonish! and is not compos'd of Fiction, Fable, or Stories plac'd at* York, Rome, *or* Jamaica, *but* Facts *done at your Doors,* Facts *unheard of, altogether new, Incredible, and yet Uncontestable.*

He is gone once more upon his wicked Range in the World. Restless Vengeance is pursuing, and Gentlemen *'tis to be hop'd that she will be assisted by your Endeavours to bring to Justice this notorious Offender.*

THIS *John Sheppard,* a Youth both in Age and Person, tho' an old Man in Sin; was Born in the Parish of *Stepney* near *London,* in the Year 1702, a Son, Grandson, and great Grandson of a *Carpenter:* His Father died when he was so very Young that he could not recollect that ever he saw him. Thus the burthen of his Maintenance, together with his Brother's and Sister's, lay upon the Shoulders of the Widow Mother, who soon procured an Admittance of her Son *John* into the *Work-House* in *Bishopsgate-street,* where he continued for the space of a Year and half, and in that time received an Education sufficient to qualifie him for the Trade his Mother desgin'd him, *viz. a Carpenter:* Accordingly she was recommended to Mr. *Wood* in *Witch-Street* near *Drury-Lane,* as a Master capable of entertaining and instructing her Son: They agreed and Bound he was for the space of seven Years; the Lad proved an early profficient, had a ready and ingenious Hand, and soon became Master of his Business, and gave entire Satisfaction to his Masters Customers, and had the Character of a very sober and orderly Boy. But alas unhappy Youth! before he had compleated six Years of his Apprenticeship, he commenced a fatal Acquaintance with one *Elizabeth Lyon,* otherwise call'd, *Edgworth Bess,* from a Town of that Name in *Middlesex* where she was Born, the reputed Wife of a Foot Soldier, and who lived a wicked and debauch'd Life; and our young *Carpenter* became Enamour'd of her, and they must Cohabit together as Man and Wife.

Now was laid the Foundation of his Ruin; *Sheppard* grows weary of the Yoke of Servitude, and began to dispute with his Master; telling him that his way of Jobbing from House to House, was not sufficient to furnish him with a due Experience in his Trade; and that if he would not se[t] out to undertake some Buildings, he would step into the World for better Information. Mr. *Wood* a mild, sober, honest Man, indulg'd him; and Mrs. *Wood* with Tears, exhorted him against the Company of this lewd Prostitute: But her Man prompted and harden'd by his HARLOT, D[am]n'd *her Blood,* and threw a Stick at his Mistress, and beat her to the Ground. And being with his Master at Work at Mr. *Britt's* the *Sun* Ale-house near *Islington,* upon a very trivial Occasion fell upon his Master, and beat and bruised him in a most barbarous and shameful Manner. Such a sudden and deplorable Change was there in the Behaviour of this promising young Man. Next ensued a neglect of Duty, both to God and his Master, lying out of Nights, perpetual Jarrings, and Animosities; these and such like, were the Consequences of his intimacy with this she *Lyon;* who by the sequel will appear to have been a main load-stone in attracting of him up to this Eminence of Guilt.[3]

Mr. *Wood* having Reason to suspect, that *Sheppard* had robb'd a Neighbour, began to be in great Fear and Terror for himself. And when his Man came not Home in due season at Nights bar'd him out; but he made a mere jest of the Locks and Bolts, and enter'd in, and out at Pleasure; and when Mr. *Wood* and his Wife have had all the Reason in the World to believe him Lock'd out, they have found him very quiet in his Bed the next Morning, such was the power of his early Magick.

Edgworth Bess having stol'n a Gold Ring from a Gentleman, whom she had pick'd up in the Streets, was sent to St. *Giles's* Round-house;[4] *Sheppard* went immediately to his Consort, and after a short Discourse with Mr. *Brown* the Beadle, and his

Wife, who had the Care of the Place, he fell upon the poor old Couple, took the Keys from them, and let his Lady out at the Door in spight of all the Out-cryes, and Opposition they were capable of making.

About *July* 1723, He was by his Master sent to perform a Repair, at the House of Mr. *Bains,* a Peice-Broker in *White-Horse Yard;* he from thence stole a Roll of Fustain, containing 24 Yards, which was afterwards found in his Trunk. This is supposed to be the first Robbery he ever committed, and it was not long e're he Repeated another upon this same Mr. *Bains,* by breaking into his House in the Night-time, and taking out of the *Till* seven Pounds in Money, and Goods to the value of fourteen Pounds more. How he enter'd this House, was a Secret till his being last committed to *Newgate,* when he confess'd that he took up the Iron Bars at the Cellar Window, and after he had done his Business, he nailed them down again, so that Mr. *Bains* never believed his House had been broke; and an innocent Woman a Lodger in the House lay all the while under the weight of a suspicion of committing the Robbery.

Sheppard and his Master had now parted, ten Months before the expiration of his Apprenticeship, a woeful parting to the former; he was gone from a good and careful Patronage, and lay expos'd to, and comply'd with the Temptations of the most wicked Wretches this Town could afford as *Joseph Blake,* alias *Blewskins, William Field, Doleing, James Sykes,* alias *Hell* and *Fury,* which last was the first that betray'd, and put him into the Hands of Justice, as will presently appear.

Having deserted his Masters Service, he took Shelter in the House of Mr. *Charles* in *May-Fair,* near *Piccadilly,* and his Land-lord having a Necessity for some Repairs in his House, engag'd one Mr. *Panton* a *Carpenter* to Undertake them, and *Sheppard* to assist him as a Journeyman; but on the 23d of *October,* 1723, e're the Work was compleat, *Sheppard* took Occasion to rob the People of the Effects following, *viz.* seven Pound ten Shillings in Specie, five large silver Spoons, six plain Forks ditto, four Tea-Spoons, six plain Gold Rings, and a

Cypher Ring; four Suits of Wearing Apparel, besides Linnen, to a considerable value. This Fact he confess'd to the Reverend Mr. *Wagstaff* before his Escape from the Condemn'd Hold of *Newgate*.

Sheppard had a Brother, nam'd *Thomas*, a *Carpenter* by Profession, tho' a notorious *Thief* and *House-breaker* by Practice. This *Thomas* being committed to *Newgate* for breaking the House of Mrs. *Mary Cook* a *Linnen-Draper*, in *Clare-street*, *Clare-Market*, on the 5th of *February* last, and stealing Goods to the value of between 50, and 60 *l*. he impeach'd his Brother *John Sheppard*, and *Edgworth Bess* as being concerned with him in the Fact; and these three were also Charg'd with being concern'd together, in breaking the House of Mr. *William Phillips* in *Drury-Lane*, and stealing divers Goods, the Property of Mrs. *Kendrick* a Lodger in the House, on the 14th of the said *February*: All possible endeavours were us'd by Mrs. *Cook*, and Mr. *Phillips*, to get *John Sheppard* and *Edgworth Bess* Apprehended, but to no purpose, till the following Accident.

Sheppard was now upon his wicked Range in *London*, committing Robberies every where at Discretion; but one Day meeting with his Acquaintance, *James Sykes*, alias *Hell* and *Fury*, sometimes a Chair-man, and at others a Running Footman. This *Sykes* invited him to one *Redgate's*, a Victualling-house near the *Seven Dials*, to play at *Skettles*, *Sheppard* comply'd, and *Sykes* secretly sent for Mr. *Price* a Constable in St. *Giles*'s *Parish*, and Charg'd him with his Friend *Sheppard* for the Robbing of Mrs. *Cook*, &c. *Sheppard* was carried before Justice *Parry*, who order'd him to St. *Giles*'s Round-house till the next Morning for farther Examination: He was Confin'd in the Upper part of the Place, being two Stories from the Ground, but e're two Hours came about, by only the help of a Razor, and the Stretcher of a Chair, he broke open the Top of the Round house, and tying together a Sheet and Blanket, by them descended into the Churchyard and Escap'd, leaving the Parish to Repair the Damage, and repent of the Affront put upon his Skill and Capacity.

On the 19th of *May* last in the Evening, *Sheppard* with another Robber named *Benson*, were passing thro' *Leicester-fields*, where a Gentleman stood accusing a Woman with an attempt to steal his Watch, a Mobb was gathered about the Disputants, and *Sheppard's* Companion being a *Master*, got in amongst them and pick'd the Gentleman's Pocket in good earnest of the Watch; the Scene was surprizingly chang'd, from an imaginary Robbery to a real one; and in a moment ensued an Out-cry of *stop Thief*, *Sheppard* and *Benson* took to their Heels, and *Sheppard* was seiz'd by a Serjeant of the Guard at *Leicester* House, crying out *stop Thief* with much earnestness. He was convey'd to St. *Ann's Round House* in *Soho*, and kept secure till the next Morning, when *Edgworth Bess* came to visit him, who was seiz'd also; they were carried before Justice *Walters*, when the People in *Drury-Lane* and *Clare-Market appeared*, and charged them with the Robberies aforemention'd: But *Sheppard* pretending to Impeach certain of his Accomplices, the Justice committed them to *New-Prison*, with intent to have them removed to *Newgate*, unless there came from them some useful Discoveries. *Sheppard* was now a second time in the hands of Justice, but how long he intended to keep in them, the Reader will soon be able to judge.

He and his MATE were now in a strong and well guarded Prison, himself loaded with a pair of double *Links* and *Basils*[5] of about fourteen pounds weight, and confined together in the safest Appartment call'd *Newgate Ward; Sheppard* conscious of his Crimes, and knowing the *Information* he had made to be but a blind Amusement that would avail him nothing; he began to Meditate an Escape. They had been thus detained for about four Days, and their Friends having the Liberty of seeing them, furnish'd him with Implements proper for his Design, accordingly Mr. *Sheppard* goes to work, and on the 25th of *May* being *Whitson Monday* at about two of the Clock in the

Morning, he had compleated a practicable breach, and sawed of his Fetters; having with unheard of Diligence and Dexterity, cut off an Iron Bar from the Window, and taken out a Muntin, or Bar of the most solid Oak of about nine Inches in thickness, by boring it thro' in many Places, a work of great Skill and Labour; they had still five and twenty Foot to descend from the Ground; *Sheppard* fasten'd a Sheet and Blanket to the Bars, and causes Madam to take off her Gown and Petticoat, and sent her out first, and she being more Corpulent than himself, it was with great Pain and Difficulty that he got her through the Interval, and observing his Directions, she was instantly down, and more frighted than hurt; the *Phylosopher* follow'd, and lighted with Ease and Pleasure; But where are they Escap'd to? Why out of one Prison into another. The Reader is to understand, that the *New Prison* and *Clerkenwell Bride-well* lye Contiguous to one another, and they are got into the Yard of the latter, and have a Wall of twenty-two Foot high to Scale, before their Liberty is perfected; *Sheppard* far from being unprepared to surmount this Difficulty, has his Gimblets[6] and Peircers ready, and makes a Scaleing-Ladder. The Keepers and Prisoners of both Places are asleep in their Beds; he Mounts his *Bagage,* and in less than ten Minutes carries both her and himself over this Wall, and compleats an entire Escape. Altho' his Escape from the Condemn'd Hold of *Newgate,* has made a far greater Noise in the World, than that from his Prison hath. It has been allow'd by all the Jayl-Keepers in *London,* that one so Miraculous was never perform'd before in *England;* the broken Chains and Bars are kept at *New Prison* to Testifie, and preserve the Memory of this extraordinary Event and Villain.

Sheppard not warn'd by this Admonition, returns like a *Dog to his Vomit,* and comes Secretly into his Master *Wood's* Neighborhood in *Witch-street,* and concerts Measures with one *Anthony Lamb,* an Apprentice to Mr. *Carter* a Mathematical Instrument-maker, for Robbing of Mr. *Barton* a Master Taylor; a Man of Worth and Reputation, who Lodg'd in Mr. *Carter's*

House. *Charles Grace,* a graceless Cooper was let into the Secret, and consented, and resolved to Act his Part. The 16th of *June* last was appointed, *Lamb* accordingly lets *Grace* and *Sheppard* into the House at Mid-Night; and they all go up to Mr. *Barton's* Appartment well arm'd with Pistols, and enter'd his Rooms, without being disturb'd. *Grace* was Posted at Mr. *Barton's* Bedside with a loaded Pistol, and positive Orders to shoot him through the Head, if in case he awak'd. *Sheppard* being engag'd in opening the Trunks and Boxes, the mean while. It luckily happen'd for Mr. *Barton,* that he slept Sounder than usual that Night, as having come from a Merry-making with some Friends; tho' poor Man little Dreaming in what dreadful Circumstances. They carried off in Notes, and Bonds, Guineas, Cloaths, Made and Unmade, to the value of between two and three Hundred Pounds; besides a Padesuoy⁷ Suit of Cloaths, worth about eighteen or twenty Pounds more; which having been made for a Corpulent Gentleman, *Sheppard* had them reduc'd, and fitted for his own Size and Wear, as designing to Appear and make a Figure among the *Beau Monde*. *Grace* and *Sheppard,* having disposed of the Goods at an Alehouse in *Lewkenors Lane* (a Rendezvous of Robbers and Ruffians) took their Flight, and *Grace* has not been since heard of. *Lamb* was apprehended, and carried before Justice *Newton,* and made an ample Confession; and there being nothing but that against him at his Tryal, and withal, a favourable Prosecution, he came off with a Sentence of Transportation only. He as well as *Sheppard* has since confirm'd all the above particulars, and with this Addition, *viz*. That it was Debated among them to have Murder'd all the People in the House, save one Person.

About the latter End of the same Month, *June,* Mr. *Kneebone,* a Woollen-Draper near the New Church in the *Strand,* receiv'd a Caution from the Father of *Anthony Lamb,* who intimated to Mr. *Kneebone* that his House was intended to be broke open and robb'd that very Night. Mr. *Kneebone* prepar'd for the Event, ordering his Servants to sit up, and gave Directions to the Watchman in the Street to observe his House: At about two in the Morning *Sheppard* and his Gang were about the Door, a Maid-Servant went to listen, and heard one of the Wretches, say, *Da[m]n him, if they could not enter that Night, they would another, and would have 300 l. of his,* (meaning) Mr. *Kneebone's* Money. They went off, and nothing more was heard of them till *Sunday* the 12th Day of *July* following, when *Joseph Blake,* alias *Blewskins, John Sheppard,* and *William Field* (as himself Swears) came about 12 o'Clock at Night, and cut two large Oaken-Bars over the Cellar-Window, at the back part of the House in *Little-Drury-Lane,* and so entered; Mr. *Kneebone,* and his Family being at Rest, they proceeded to open a Door at the Foot of the Cellar-Stairs, with three Bolts, and a large Padlock upon it, and then came up into the Shop and wrench'd off the Hasp, and Padlock that went over the Press, and arriv'd at their desir'd Booty; they continu'd in the House for three Hours, and carry'd off with them One Hundred and eight Yards of Broad Woollen Cloth, five Yards of blue Bays,[8] a light Tye-Wig, and Beaver-Hat, two Silver Spoons, an Handkerchief, and a Penknife. In all to the value of near fifty Pounds.

The *Sunday* following, being the 19th of *July, Sheppard* and *Blewskins* were out upon the *Hampstead* Road, and there stopt a Coach with a Ladies Woman in it, from whom they took but Half-a-Crown; all the Money then about her; the Footman behind the Coach came down, and exerted himself; but *Sheppard* sent him in hast up to his Post again, by threat of his Pistol.

The next Night being the 20th of *July,* about Nine, they Robb'd Mr. *Pargiter,* a Chandler of *Hamstead,* near his Halfway-House; *Sheppard* after his being taken at *Finchley* was particularly examin'd about this Robbery. The Reverend Mr. *Wagstaff* having receiv'd a Letter from an unknown Hand, with two Questions, to be propos'd to *Sheppard, viz.* Whether he did Rob *John Pargiter,* on *Monday* the 20th of *July,* about Nine at Night, between the *Turnpike* and *Hamstead;* How much Money he took from him? Whither *Pargiter* was Drunk, or not, and if he had Rings or Watch about him, when robb'd? which, Request was comply'd with, and *Sheppard* affirm'd, that Mr. *Pargiter* was very much in Liquor, having a great Coat on; neither Rings on his Fingers or Watch, and only three Shillings in his Pocket, which they took from him, and that *Blewskins* knock[ed] him down twice with the Butt-end of his Pistol to make sure Work, (tho' Excess of drink had done that before) but *Sheppard* did in kindness raise him up as often.

That next Night, *July* 21, they stopt a Stage-Coach, and took from a Passenger in it, Twenty-two Shillings, and were so expeditious in the Matter, that *not two Words were made about the Bargain.*

Now Mr. *Sheppard's* long and wicked Course seemingly draws towards a Period, Mr. *Kneebone* having apply'd to *Jonathan Wild,* and set forth Advertisements in the Papers, complaining of his Robbery. On *Tuesday* the 22d of *July* at Night *Edgworth Bess* was taken in a Brandy-shop, near *Temple-Bar* by *Jonathan Wild;* she being much terrify'd, discover'd where *Sheppard* was: A Warrant was accordingly issued by Justice *Blackerby,* and the next Day he was Apprehended, at the House of *Blewskin's* Mother, in *Rose-Mary-Lane,* by one *Quilt,* a Domestick of Mr. *Wild's,* though not without great opposition, for he clapt a loaded Pistol to *Quilt's* Breast, and attempted to shoot him, but the Pistol miss'd fire; he was brought back to *New Prison,* confin'd in the Dungeon; and the next Day carried before Justice *Blackerby.* Upon his Examination he Confess'd the three Robberies on the Highway aforemention'd, as also the Robbing of Mr. *Bains,* Mr. *Barton,* and Mr. *Kneebone,* he was committed to *Newgate,* and at the Sessions of *Oyer* and *Terminer,*[9] and Goal delivery, holden at the *Old-Baily,* on the 12th, 13th and 14th of *August,* he was try'd upon three several Indictments, *viz.* First for breaking the House of *William Philips.*

John Sheppard, of the Parish of St. *Martin* in *the Fields,* was indicted for breaking the House of *William Philips*, and stealing divers Goods, the 14th of February last. But there not being sufficient Evidence against the Prisoner, he was acquitted.

He was also indicted a Second Time, of St. *Clement Danes*, for breaking the House of *Mary Cook*, the 5th of *February* last, and stealing divers Goods: But the Evidence against the Prisoner being defficient as to this Indictment also, he was acquitted.

He was also indicted the Third Time, of St. *Mary Savoy*, for breaking the House of *William Kneebone*, in the Night-Time, and stealing 108 Yards of Woollen Cloth, the 12th of *July* last. The Prosecutor depos'd, That the Prisoner had some Time since been his Servant, and when he went to Bed, the Time mention'd in the Indictment, about 11 a-Clock at Night, he saw all the Doors and Windows fast; but was call'd up about four in the Morning, and found his House broke open, the Bars of a Cellar-Window having been cut, and the Bolts of the Door that comes up Stairs drawn, and the Padlock wrench'd off, and the Shutter in the Shop broken, and his Goods gone; whereupon suspecting the Prisoner, he having committed ill Actions thereabouts before, he acquainted *Jonathan Wild* with it, and he procur'd him to be apprehended. That he went to the Prisoner in *New Prison*, and asking how he could be so ungrateful to rob him, after he had shown him so much Kindness? The Prisoner own'd he had been ungrateful in doing so, informing him of several Circumstances as to the Manner of committing the Fact, but said he had been drawn into it by ill Company. *Jonathan Wild*, depos'd, The Prosecutor came to him, and desir'd him to enquire after his Goods that had been stolen, telling him he suspected the Prisoner to have been concern'd in the Robbery, he having before committed some Robberies in the Neighbourhood. That inquiring after him, and having heard of him before, he was inform'd that he was an Acquaintance of *Joseph Blake*, alias *Blewskins*, and *William Field*: Whereupon he sent for *William Field*, who

came to him; upon which he told him, if he would make an
ingenuous Confession, he believ'd he could prevail with the
Court to make him an Evidence. That he did make a Discovery
of the Prisoner, upon which he was apprehended, and also of
others since convicted, and gave an Account of some Parcels
of the Cloth, which were found accordingly. *William Field*
depos'd, That the Prisoner told him, and *Joseph Blake*, that
he knew a *Ken* where they might get something of Worth. That
they went to take a View of the Prosecutor's House, but dis-
prov'd of the Attempt, as not thinking it easy to be perform'd:
But the Prisoner perswaded them that it might easily be done,
he knowing the House, he having liv'd with the Prosecutor.
That thereupon he cut the Cellar Bar, went into the Cellar,
got into the Shop, and brought out three Parcels of Cloth,
which they carried away. The Prisoner had also confest the
Fact when he was apprehended, and before the Justice. The
Fact being plainly prov'd, the Jury found him guilty of the
Indictment.

Sentence of Death was pronounc'd upon him accordingly.
Several other Prosecutions might have been brought against
him, but this was thought sufficient to rid the World of so
Capital an Offender: He beg'd earnestly for Transportation,
to the most extream Foot of his Majesty's Dominions; and
pleaded Youth, and Ignorance as the Motive which had pre-
cipitated him into the Guilt; but the Court deaf to his Im-
portunities, as knowing him, and his repeated Crimes to be
equally flagrant, gave him no satisfactory Answer: He return'd
to his dismal Abode the Condemn'd Hold, where were Nine
more unhappy Wretches in as dreadful Circumstances as himself. The Court being at *Windsor,* the Malefactors had a longer
Respite than is usual; during that Recess, *James Harman,*
Lumley, Davis and *Sheppard* agreed upon an Escape, con-
certed Measures, and provided Instruments to make it effectual; but put off the Execution of their Design, on Account
the two Gentlemen having their hopes of Life daily renewed
by the favourable Answers they receiv'd from some consider-

able Persons; but those vanishing the day before their Execution, and finding their Sentence irreversible, they two dropt their hopes, together with the Design, they form'd for an Escape, and so in earnest prepar'd to meet Death on the Morrow, (which they accordingly did.) 'Twas on this Day Mr. *Davis* gave *Sheppard* the Watch Springs, Files, Saws, &c. to Effect his own Release; and knowing that a Warrant was Hourly expected for his Execution with Two others, on the *Friday* following; he thought it high time to look about him, for he had waited his Tryal, saw his Conviction, and heard his Sentence with some patience; but finding himself irrespitably decreed for Death, he could sit passive no longer, and on the very Day of the Execution of the former; whilst they were having their Fetters taken off, in order for going to the Tree, that Day he began to saw; *Saturday* made a progress; but *Sunday* omitted, by Reason of the Concourse in the *Lodge:* *Edgworth Bess* having been set at Liberty, had frequent Access to him, with others of his Acquaintance. On *Monday* the Death *Warrant* came from *Windsor,* appointing that he, together with *Joseph Ward,* and *Anthony Upton* should be Executed on the *Friday* following, being the 4th of *September.* The Keepers acquainted him therewith, and desir'd him to make good use of that short time. He thank'd them, said *he would follow their Advice,* and *prepare. Edgworth Bess,* and another Woman had been with him at the Door of the Condemn'd Hold best part of the Afternoon, between five and six he desir'd the other Prisoners, except *Stephen Fowles* to remain above, while he offer'd something in private to his Friends at the Door; they comply'd, and in this interval he got the Spike asunder, which made way for the Skeleton to pass with his Heels foremost, by the Assistance of Fowles, whom he most ungenerously betray'd to the Keepers after his being retaken, and the fellow was as severely punish'd for it.

Having now got clear of his Prison, he took Coach disguis'd in a Night Gown at the corner of the *Old Baily,* along with a Man who waited for him in the Street (and is suppos'd to be

Page the Butcher) ordering the Coachman to drive to *Black-Fryers Stairs*, where his prostitute gave him the Meeting, and they three took Boat, and went a Shoar at the *Horse-Ferry* at *Westminster*, and at the *White-Hart* they went in, Drank, and stay'd sometime; thence they adjourn'd to a Place in *Holbourn*, where by the help of a Saw he quitted the Chains he had brought with him from *Newgate;* and then like a Freeman took his Ramble through the City and came to *Spittle-Fields*, and there lay with *Edgworth Bess*.

It may be easy to imagine what an alarm his Escape gave to the Keepers of *Newgate*, three of their People being at the farther End of the *Lodge*, engag'd in a Discourse concerning his wonderful Escape from *New-Prison*, and what Caution ought to be us'd, lest he should give them the slip, at that very Instant as he perfected it.

On *Tuesday* he sent for *William Page* an Apprentice to a Butcher in *Clare-Market*, who came to him, and being Penny-less, he desir'd *Page* to give him what Assistance he could to make his way, and being a Neighbour and Acquaintance, he comply'd with it; but e're he would do any thing, he consulted a near Relation, who as he said, encourag'd him in it; nay, put him upon it, so meeting with this Success in his Application to his Friend, and probable an Assistance in the Pocket, he came to *Sheppard* having bought him a new blue *Butchers* Frock, and another for himself, and so both took their Rout to *Warnden* in *Northamptonshire*, where they came to a Relation of *Page's*, who receiv'd and Entertain'd them kindly, the People lying from their own Bed to Accommodate them. *Sheppard* pretending to be a *Butcher's* Son in *Clare-Market*, who was going farther in the Country to his Friends, and that *Page* was so kind as to Accompany him; but they as well as their Friend became tir'd of one another; the *Butchers* having but one Shilling left, and the People poor, and Consequently unable to Subsist two such Fellows, after a stay of three or four Days, they return'd, and came for *London*, and reach'd the City on *Tuesday* the 8th of *September*, calling by the way at *Black-*

Mary's-Hole, and Drinking with several of their Acquaintance, and then come into *Bishopsgate street,* to one *Cooley's* a *Brandyshop;* where a *Cobler* being at Work in his Stall, stept out and Swore *there was* Sheppard, *Sheppard* hearing him, departed immediately. In the Evening they came into *Fleet*-street, at about Eight of the Clock, and observing Mr. *Martin's* a Watchmakers Shop to be open, and a little Boy only to look after it: *Page* goes in and asks the Lad whether Mr. *Taylor* a *Watchmaker* lodg'd in the House? being answer'd in the Nega-tive, he came away, and Reports the Disposition of the Place: *Sheppard* now makes Tryal of his old Master-peice; fixeth a Nail Peircer into the Door post, fastens the Knocker thereto with Packthread, breaks the Glass, and takes out three *Silver Watches* of 15 *l.* value, the Boy seeing him take them, but could not get out to pursue him, by reason of his Contrivance.[10] One of the Watches he Pledg'd for a Guinea and Half. The same Night they came into *Witch-street, Sheppard* going into his *Masters* Yard, and calling for his Fellow 'Prentice, his Mistress heard, knew his Voice, and was dreadfully frightened; he next went to the *Cock* and *Pye Ale-House* in *Drury Lane,* sent for a *Barber* his Acquaintance, drank Brandy and eat Oysters in the view of several People. *Page* waiting all the while at the Door, the whole Neighbourhood being alarm'd, yet none durst attempt him, for fear of Pistols, &c. He had vow'd Revenge upon a poor Man as kept a Dairy-Cellar, at the End of *White-Horse-Yard,* who having seen him at *Isling-ton* after his Escape, and engag'd not to speak of it, broke his Promise; wherefore *Sheppard* went to his Residence took the Door off the Hinges and threw it down amongst all the Mans Pans, Pipkins, and caus'd a Deluge of Cream and Milk all over the Cellar.

This Night he had a narrow Escape, one Mr. *Ireton* a Sheriffs Officer seeing him and *Page* pass thro' *Drury-Lane,* at about Ten o'Clock pursu'd 'em, and laid hold of *Page* instead of *Sheppard,* who got off, thus *Ireton* missing the main Man, and thinking *Page* of no Consequence, let him go after him.

Edgworth Bess had been apprehended by *Jonathan Wild*, and by Sir *Francis Forbes* one of the Aldermen of *London*, committed to the *Poultry-Compter*, for being aiding and assisting to *Sheppard* in his Escape; the Keepers and others terrify'd and purg'd her as much as was possible to discover where he was, but had it been in her Inclination, it was not in her Power to do so, as it manifestly appear'd soon after.

The People about the *Strand*, *Witch-street* and *Drury-Lane*, whom he had Robb'd, and who had prosecuted him were under great Apprensions and Terror, and in particular Mr. *Kneebone*, on whom he vow'd a bloody Revenge; because he refus'd to sign a Petition in his behalf to the *Recorder* of *London*. This Gentleman was forc'd to keep arm'd People up in his House every Night till he was Re-taken, and had the same fortify'd in the strongest manner. Several other Shopkeepers in this Neighbourhood were also put to great expence and Trouble to Guard themselves against this dreadful Villian.

The Keepers of *Newgate*, whom the rash World loaded with Infamy, stigmatiz'd and branded with the Title of Persons guilty of Bribery; for Connivance at his Escape, they and what Posse in their Power, either for Love or Money did Contribute their utmost to undeceive a wrong notion'd People. Their Vigilance was remarkably indefatigable, sparing neither Money nor Time, Night or Day to bring him back to his deserv'd Justice. After many Intelligences, which they endeavour'd for, and receiv'd, they had one which prov'd very Successful. Having learnt for a certainty that their Haunts was about *Finchly Common*, and being very well assur'd of the very House where they lay; on *Thursday* the 10th of *September*, a posse of Men, both of Spirit and Conduct, furnish'd with Arms proper for their Design, went for *Finchley*, some in a Coach and Four, and others on Horseback. They dispers'd themselves upon the *Common* aforesaid, in order to make their View, where they had not been long e're they came in Sight of SHEPPARD in Company of WILLIAM PAGE, habited like two *Butchers* in new blue Frocks, with white Aprons tuck'd round their Wastes.

Upon *Sheppard's* seeing *Langley* a Turnkey at *Newgate,* he
says to his Companion *Page, I see a Stag;* upon which their
Courage dropt; knowing that now their dealing way of Business
was almost at an end; however to make their Flight as secure
as they could, they thought it adviseable to take to a Foot-path,
to cut off the pursuit of the *Newgate* Cavalry; but this did not
prove most successful, *Langley* came up with *Page* (who was
hindermost) and Dismounting with Pistol in Hand, commands
Page to throw up his Hands, which he trembling did, begging
for Life, desiring him to *Fisk* him, *viz.* (search him,) which
he accordingly did, and found a broad Knife and File; having
thus disarm'd him, he takes the *Chubb* along with him in quest
of the slippery *Ele, Sheppard;* who had taken Shelter in an old
Stable, belonging to a Farm-House; the pursuit was close, the
House invested, and a Girl seeing his Feet as he stood up hid,
discover'd him. *Austin* a Turnkey first attach'd his Person,
Langley seconded him, *Ireton* an Officer help'd to Enclose,
and happy was the hindermost who aided in this great Enter-
prise. He being shock'd with the utmost Fear, told them he
submitted, and desir'd they would let him live as long as he
could, which they did, and us'd him mildly; upon searching
him they found a broad Knife with two of the Watches as he
had taken out of Mr. *Martin's* Shop, one under each Armpit;
and now having gain'd their Point, and made themselves Masters of what they had often endeavoured for, they came with
their *Lost Sheep* to a little House on the *Common* that sold
Liquors, with this Inscription on the Sign, *I have brought my
Hogs to a fair Market;* which our two unfortunate *Butchers*
under their then unhappy Circumstances, had too sad Reason
to apply to themselves. *Sheppard* had by this time recover'd
his Surprize, grew calm and easy, and desir'd them to give him
Brandy, they did, and were all good Friends, and Company
together.

They adjourn'd with their Booty to another Place, where
was waiting a Coach and Four to Convey it to Town, with
more Speed and Safety; and Mr. *Sheppard* arriv'd at his old

Mansion, at about two in the Afternoon. At his a-lighting, he made a sudden Spring; He declar'd his Intention was to have slipt under the Coach, and had a Race for it; he was put into the Condemn'd-Hold, and Chain'd down to the Floor with double *Basels* about his Feet, &c. *Page* was carried before Sir *Francis Forbes*, and committed to the same Prison for Accompanying and aiding *Sheppard* in his Escape. The prudence of Mr. *Pitt* caus'd a Separation between him and his Brother the first Night, as a Means to prevent any ensuing Danger, by having two Heads, which (according to our Proverbial Saying) *are better than one.*

The Joy the People of *Newgate* conceiv'd on this Occasion is inexpressible, *Te Deum* was Sung in the *Lodge*, and nothing but Smiles, and Bumpers, were seen there for many Days together. But *Jonathan Wild* unfortunately happen'd to be gone upon a wrong Scent after him to *Sturbridge*, and Lost a Share of the Glory.

His Escape and his being so suddenly Re-taken made such a Noise in the Town, that it was thought all the common People would have gone Mad about him; there being not a *Porter* to be had for Love nor Money, nor getting into an Ale-house, for *Butchers, Shoemakers* and *Barbers*, all engag'd in Controversies, and Wagers, about *Sheppard. Newgate* Night and Day surrounded with the Curious from St. *Giles's* and *Rag-Fair*, and *Tyburn Road* daily lin'd with Women and Children; and the *Gallows* as carefully watch'd by Night, lest he should be hang'd *Incog.* For a Report of that nature, obtain'd much upon the Rabble; In short, it was a Week of the greatest Noise and Idleness among Mechanicks that has been known in *London*, and *Parker* and *Pettis*, two *Lyricks*, subsisted many Days very comfortably upon *Ballads* and *Letters* about Sheppard.[11] The vulgar continu'd under great Doubts and Difficulties, in what would be his Case, and whether the *Old Warrant*, or a *New One* must be made for his Execution, or a New Tryal, &c. were the great Questions as arose, and occasion'd various Reasonings and Speculation, till a News

Paper, call'd the *Daily Journal* [12] set them all to Rights by the
Publication of the Account following, *viz.* '*J. Sheppard* having
been Convicted of Burglary, and Felony, and received Sentence
of Death, and afterwards Escap'd from *Newgate;* and being
since Re-taken; we are assur'd that it must be prov'd in a
Regular, and *Judicial* way, that he is the same Person, who
was so Convicted and made his Escape, before a Warrant can
be obtain'd for his Execution; and that this Affair will be
brought before the Court at the *Old Baily* the next Sessions.'
This was enough; People began to grow calm and easy, and
got *Shav'd,* and their Shoes *finish'd,* and Business returned
into its former Channel, the Town resolving to wait the *Sessions* with Patience.

The Reverend Mr. *Wagstaff,* who officiated in the absence
of the *Ordinary,* renew'd his former Acquaintance with Mr.
Sheppard, and examin'd him in a particular manner concerning
his Escape from the Condemn'd Hold: He sincerely disown'd,
that all, or any, belonging to the Prison were privy thereto;
but related it as it has been describ'd. He declar'd that *Edgworth Bess,* who had hitherto pass'd for his Wife, was not
really so: This was by some thought to be in him Base, and
Ungenerous in that, as she had Contributed towards his Escape, and was in Custody on that Account, it might render
her more liable to Punishment, than if she had been thought
his Wife; but he endeavour'd to acquit himself, by saying, that
she was the sole Author of all his Misfortunes; That she betray'd him to *Jonathan Wild,* at the time he was taken in *Rose-
mary-Lane;* and that when he was contriving his Escape, she
disobey'd his orders, as when being requir'd to attend at the
Door of the Condemn'd-Hold by Nine, or Ten in the Morning
to facilitate his Endeavours, she came not till the Evening,
which he said, was an ungrateful Return for the care he had
taken in setting her at Liberty from *New-Prison;* and thus
Justify'd himself in what he had done, and said he car'd not
what became of her.

He was also Examined about Mr. *Martin's* Watches; and whether *Page* was privy to that Robbery; he carefully guarded himself against uttering any thing that might affect him, peremptorily declar'd him Innocent of that, as well as of being privy to his Escape, and said, that he only out of Kindness, as being an old Companion, was resolv'd to share in his Fortunes after he had Escap'd.

He was again continually meditating a second Escape, as appear'd by his own Hardiness, and the Instruments found upon him, on *Saturday* the 12th, and *Wednesday* the 16th of *September*, the first Time a small File was found conceal'd in his Bible, and the second Time two Files, a Chisel and an Hammer being hid in the Rushes of a Chair; and whenever a Question was mov'd to him, when, or by what Means those Implements came to his Hands; he would passionately fly out, and say, *How can you? you always ask me these, and such like Questions;* and in a particular manner, when he was ask'd, Whether his Companion *Page* was an Accomplice with him, either in the affair of the Watches, or any other? (he reply'd) *That if he knew, he would give no direct Answer,* thinking it to be a Crime in him to detect the Guilty.

It was thought necessary by the Keepers to remove him from the Condemn'd-Hold to a Place, call'd the Castle, in the Body of the Goal, and to Chain him down to two large Iron Staples in the Floor; the Concourse of People of tolerable Fashion to see him was exceeding Great, he was always Chearful and Pleasant to a Degree, as turning almost every thing as was said into a Jest and Banter.

Being one *Sunday* at the Chapel, a Gentleman belong to the *Lord Mayor,* ask'd a Turnkey, Which was *Sheppard,* the Man pointed to him? Says *Sheppard, yes Sir, I am the* Sheppard, *and all the Goalers in the Town are my Flock, and I cannot stir into the Country, but they are all at my Heels* Baughing *after me,* &c.

He told Mr. *Robins,* the *City Smith, That he had procur'd*

*him a small Job, and that whoever it was that put the Spikes
on the Condemn'd-Hold was an honest Man, for a better peice
of Metal,* says he, *I never wrought upon in my Life.*

He was loth to believe his frequent Robberies were an
Injury to the Publick, for he us'd to say, That *if they were ill
in one Respect, they were as good in another, and that though
he car'd not for Working much himself, yet he was desirous
that others should not stand Idle, more especially those of his
own Trade, who were always Repairing of his Breaches.*

When serious, and that but seldom, he would Reflect on
his past wicked Life. He declar'd to us, that for several Years
of his Apprenticeship he had an utter abhorrence to Women of
the Town, and us'd to pelt them with Dirt when they have
fell in his way; till a *Button-Mould-Maker* his next Neighbour
left off that Business, and set up a Victualling-house in *Lewkenhors-Lane,* where himself and other young Apprentices
resorted on *Sundays,* and at all other Opportunities. At this
House began his Acquaintance with *Edgworth Bess.* His Sentiments were strangely alter'd, and from an Aversion to those
Prostitutes, he had a more favourable Opinion, and even Conversation with them, till he Contracted an ill Distemper, which
as he said, he cur'd himself of by a Medicine of his own preparing.

He inveigh'd bitterly against his Brother *Thomas* for putting
him into the Information, for Mrs. *Cook's* Robberry, and pretended that all the Mischiefs that attended him was owing to
that Matter. He acknowledg'd that he was concern'd in that
Fact, and that his said Brother broke into his Lodgings, and
stole from him all his Share and more of the acquir'd Booty.

He oftentimes averr'd, that *William Field* was no ways concern'd in Mr. *Kneebone's* Robbery; but that being a Brother
of the Quill; *Blewskin* and himself told him the particulars,
and manner of the Facts, and that all he Swore against him
at his Tryal was False, and that he had [no] other Authority
for it, than what came out of their (*Sheppard* and *Blewskin*)
Mouths, who actually committed the Fact.

And moreover, that *Field* being acquainted with their Warehouse (a Stable) near the *Horse-Ferry* at *Westminster*, which *Sheppard* had hir'd, and usually reposited therein the Goods he stole. He came one Night, and broke open the same, and carried off the best part of the Effects taken out of Mr. *Kneebone's* Shop.

Sheppard said he thought this to be one of the greatest Villanies that could be acted, for another to come and Plunder them of Things for which they had so honourably ventur'd their Lives, and wish'd that *Field*, as well as his Brother *Tom* might meet with forgiveness for it.

He declar'd himself frequently against the Practice of *Whidling*, or *Impeaching*, which he said, had made dreadful Havock among the *Thieves*, and much lamented the depravity of the *Brethren* in that Respect; and said that if all were but such *Tight-Cocks* as himself, the *Reputation* of the *British Thievery* might be carried to a far greater height than it had been done for many Ages, and that there would then be but little Necessity for Jaylors and Hangmen.

These and such like were his constant Discourses, when Company went up with the Turnkeys to the *Castle* to see him, and few or none went away without leaving him Money for his Support; in which he abounded, and did therewith some small Charities to the other Prisoners; however, he was abstemious and sparing enough in his Diet.

Among the many Schemes laid by his Friends, for the preserving himself after his Escape, we were told of a most Remarkable one, propos'd by an ingenious Person, who advis'd, that he might be Expeditiously, and Secretly convey'd to the Palace at *Windsor*, and there to prostrate his Person, and his Case at the Feet of a most Gracious Prince, and his Case being so very singular and new, it might in great probability move the Royal Fountain of unbounded Clemency; but he declin'd this Advice, and follow'd the Judgment and Dictates of *Butchers*, which very speedily brought him very near the Door of the *Slaughter-house*.

On the 4th of *September*, the Day as *Joseph Ward*, and *Anthony Upton* were Executed, there was publish'd a whimsical Letter, as from *Sheppard*, to *Jack Ketch*,[13] which afforded Diversion to the Town, and Bread to the Author, which is as following, *Viz.*

SIR,

"I Thank you for the Favour you intended me this Day: I am a Gentleman, and allow you to be the same, and I hope you can forgive Injuries; fond Nature prompted, I obey'd, Oh, propitious Minute! and to show that I am in Charity, I am now drinking your Health, and a *Bon Repo* to poor *Joseph* and *Anthony*. I am gone a few Days for the Air, but design speedily to embark; and this Night I am going upon a Mansion for a Supply; it's a stout Fortification, but what Difficulties can't I encounter, when, dear *Jack*, you find that Bars and Chains are but trifling Obstacles in the way of your Friend and Servant."

From my Residence in　　　　　　　　　John Sheppard.
Terra Australi *incognito*.

"P.S. Pray my Service to Mr. *Ordi*[*nar*]*y* and to Mr. *App*[*le-b*]*ee*.

On *Saturday* the 10th of *October*, *Anthony Lamb*, and *Thomas Sheppard*, with 95 other Felons were carried from *Newgate* on Shipboard, for Transportation to the Plantations; the last begg'd to have an opportunity of taking his final Leave of his Brother *John*; but this was not to be Granted, and the greatest Favour that could be obtain'd, was that on the *Sunday* before they had an Interview at the *Chapel*, but at such a distance, that they neither saluted, or shook Hands, and the Reason given for it, was that no Implements might be convey'd to *Sheppard* to assist him in making an Escape.

This Caution seem'd to be absolutely necessary, for it appear'd soon after that *Sheppard* found Means to release himself from the Staples to which he was Chain'd in the *Castle*, by unlocking a great Padlock with a Nail, which he had pickt up on the Floor, and endeavour'd to pass up the Chimney, but was prevented by the stout Iron Bars fix'd in his way, and wanted nothing but the smallest File to have perfected his Liberty. When the Assistants of the Prison, came as usual with his Victuals, they began to examine his Irons; to their great Surprize they found them loose, and ready to be taken off at Pleasure. Mr. *Pitt* the Head Keeper, and his Deputies were sent for, and *Sheppard* finding this Attempt entirely frustrated, discover'd to them by what means he had got them off; and after they had search'd him, found nothing, and Lock'd and Chain'd him down again: He took up the Nail and unlock'd the Padlock before their Faces; they were struck with the greatest Amazement, as having never heard, or beheld the like before. He was then Hand-Cuff'd, and more effectually Chain'd.

The next Day, the Reverend Mr. *Purney Ordinary* of the Place came from the Country to visit him, and complain'd of the sad Disposition he found him in, as Meditateing on nothing, but Means to Escape, and declining the great Duty incumbent upon him to prepare for his approaching Change. He began to Relent, and said, that since his last Effort had prov'd not Successful, he would entertain no more Thoughts of that Nature, but entirely Dispose, and Resign himself to the Mercy of Almighty God, of whom he hop'd still to find forgiveness of his manifold Offences.

He said, that *Edgworth Bess* and himself kept a little Brandy-shop together in *Lewkenhors-Lane,* and once sav'd about Thirty Pounds; but having such an universal Acquaintance amongst Theives, he had frequent calls to go *Abroad,* and soon quitted that Business, and his Shop.

On *Friday* the 2d, of *October* his old Confederate *Joseph Blake* alias *Blewskin,* was apprehended and taken at a House in St. *Giles*'s Parish by *Jonathan Wild,* and by Justice *Blackerby* committed to *Newgate. William Field* who was at his Liberty, appearing and making Oath, that *Blewskin* together with *John Sheppard* and himself, committed the Burglary and Felony in Mr. *Kneebone's* House, for which *Sheppard* was Condemn'd.

The Sessions commencing at the *Old-Bailey* on *Wednesday* the 14th of *October* following, an Indictment was found against *Blewskin* for the same, and he was brought down from *Newgate* to the *Old-Bailey* to be Arraign'd in order to his Tryal; and being in the Yard within the Gate before the Court: Mr. *Wild* there drinking a glass of Wine with him, he said to Mr. *Wild, You may put in a word for me, as well as for another Person?* To which Mr. *Wild* reply'd, I cannot do it, *You are certainly a dead Man, and will be tuck'd up very speedily*, or words to that effect: Whereupon *Blewskin* on a sudden seiz'd Mr. *Wild* by the Neck, and with a little Clasp Knife he was provided with he cut his Throat in a very dangerous Manner; and had it not been for a *Muslin* Stock twisted in several Plaits round his Neck, he had in all likelyhood succeeded in his barbarous Design before *Ballard* the Turnkey, who was at Hand, could have time to lay hold of him; the Villain triumph'd afterwards in what he had done, Swearing many bloody Oaths, that if he had murder'd him, he should have died with Satisfaction, and that his Intention was to have cut off his Head, and thrown it into the Sessions House-Yard among the Rabble, and Curs'd both his Hand and the Knife for not Executing it Effectually.[14]

Mr. *Wild* instantly had the Assistance of three able Surgeons, *viz.* Mr. *Dobbins*, Mr. *Marten* and Mr. *Coletheart*, who sew'd up the Wound, and order'd him to his Bed, and he has continu'd ever since, but in a doubtful State of Recovery.

The Felons on the Common Side of *Newgate*, also animated by *Sheppard's* Example, the Night before they were to be Shipt for Transportation, had cut several Iron Bars assunder, and some of them had saw'd off their Fetters, the rest Huzzaing, and making Noises, under pretence of being Joyful that they were to be remov'd on the Morrow, to prevent the Workmen being heard; and in two Hours time more, if their Design had not been discover'd, near One Hundred Villians had been let loose into the World, to have committed new Depredations; nothing was wanted here but *Sheppard's* great Judgment, who was by himself in the strong Room, call'd the *Castle*, meditating his own Deliverance, which he prefected in the manner following.

On *Thursday* the 15th of this Instant *October*, at between One and Two in the Afternoon, *William Austin*, an Assistant to the Keepers, a Man reputed to be a very diligent, and faithful Servant, went to *Sheppard* in the strong Room, call'd the *Castle*, with his Necessaries, as was his Custom every Day. There went along with him Captain *Geary*, the Keeper of *New Prison*, Mr. *Gough*, belonging to the *Gate-house* in *Westminster*, and two other Gentlemen, who had the Curiosity to see the Prisoner, Austin very strictly examined his Fetters, and his Hand-Cuffs, and found them very Safe; he eat his Dinner and talk'd with his usual Gayety to the Company: They took leave of him and wish'd him a good Evening. The Court being sitting at the *Old-Bailey*, the Keepers and most of their Servants were attending there with their Prisoners: And *Sheppard* was told that if he wanted any thing more, then was his Time, because they could not come to him till the next Morning: He thank'd them for their Kindness, and desir'd them to be *as early as possible*.

The same Night, soon after 12 of the Clock Mr. *Bird*, who keeps a Turners-shop adjoyning to *Newgate*, was disturb'd by the Watchman, who found his Street Door open, and call'd up the Family, and they concluding the Accident was owing to the Carelessness of some in the House, shut their Doors, and went to Bed again.

The next Morning *Friday*, at about eight Mr. *Austin* went up as usual to wait on *Sheppard*, and having unlock'd and unbolted the double Doors of the Castle, he beheld almost a Cart-load of Bricks and Rubbish about the Room, and his

Prisoner gone: The Man ready to sink, came trembling down again, and was scarce able to Acquaint the People in the Lodge with what had happen'd.

The whole Posse of the Prison ran up, and stood like Men depriv'd of their Senses: Their surprize being over, they were in hopes that he might not have yet entirely made his Escape, and got their Keys to open all the strong Rooms adjacent to the *Castle*, in order to Trace him, when to their farther Amazement, they found the Doors ready open'd to their Hands; and the Strong Locks, Screws and Bolts broken in pieces, and scatter'd about the Jayl. Six great Doors (one whereof having not been open'd for seven Years past) were forc'd, and it appear'd that he had Descended from the Leads of *Newgate* by a Blanket (which he fasten'd to the Wall by an Iron Spike he had taken from the Hatch of the *Chapel*) on the House of Mr. *Bird*, and the Door on the Leads having been left open, it is very reasonable to conclude he past directly to the Street Door down the Stairs; Mr. *Bird* and his Wife hearing an odd sort of a Noise on the Stairs as they lay in their Bed, a short time before the Watchman alarm'd the Family.

Infinite Numbers of Citizens came to *Newgate* to behold *Sheppard's* Workmanship, and Mr. *Pitt* and his Officers very readily Conducted them up Stairs, that the World might be convinc'd there was not the least room to suspect, either a Negligence, or Connivance in the Servants. Every one express'd the greatest Surprize that has been known, and declar'd themselves satisfy'd with the Measures they had taken for the Security of their Prisoner.

One of the Sheriffs came in Person, and went up to the *Castle* to be satisfy'd of the Situation of the Place, &c. Attended by several of the City Officers.

The Court being sat at the *Sessions-House*, the Keepers were sent for and Examin'd, and the Magistrates were in great Consternation, that so horrid a Wretch had escap'd their Justice. It being intended that he should have been brought down to the Court the last Day of the *Sessions*, and order'd for Execution in two or three Days after; if it appear'd that he was the Person Condemn'd for the breaking Mr. *Kneebone's* House, and included in the Warrant for Execution, &c.

Many of the Methods by which this miraculous Escape was effected, remain as yet a Secret; there are some indeed too Evident, the most reasonable Conjecture that has hitherto been made, is, that the first Act was his twisting and breaking assunder by the strength of his Hands a small Iron Chain, which together with a great Horse Padlock, (as went from the heavy Fetters about his Legs to the Staples) confin'd him to the Floor, and with a Nail open'd the Padlock and set himself at Liberty about the Room: A large flat Iron Bar appears to have been taken out of the Chimney, with the Assistance whereof 'tis plain he broke thro' a Wall of many Foot in Thickness, and made his way from the *Castle* into another strong Room Contiguous, the Door of it not having been open'd since several of the *Preston* Prisoners[15] were Confin'd there about seven Years ago: Three Screws are visibly taken off of the Lock, and the Doors as strong as Art could make them, forc'd open. The Locks and Bolts, either wrench'd or Broke, and the Cases and other Irons made for their Security cut assunder: An Iron Spike broke off from the Hatch in the *Chapel*, which he fix'd in the Wall and fasten'd his Blanket to it, to drop on the Leads of Mr. *Bird's* House, his Stockings were found on the Leads of *Newgate;* 'tis question'd whether sixty Pounds will repair the Damage done to the Jayl.

It will perhaps be inquir'd how all this could be perform'd without his being heard by the Prisoners or the Keepers; 'tis well known that the Place of his Confinement is in the upper part of the Prison, none of the other Felons being Kept any where near him; and 'tis suppos'd that if any had heard him at Work, they would rather have facilitated, than frustrated his Endeavours. In the Course of his Breaches he pass'd by a Door on his Left belonging to the *Common-Side* Felons, who have since Curs'd him heartily for his not giving them an opportunity to kiss his Hand, and lending them a favourable lift when his Hand was in; but that was not a Work proper for Mr. *Sheppard* to do in his then Circumstances.

His Fetters are not to be found any where about the Jayl, from whence 'tis concluded he has either thrown them down some Chimney, or carried them off on his Legs, the latter seems to be Impracticable, and would still render his Escaping in such Manner the more astonishing; and the only Answer that is given to the whole, at *Newgate* is, *That the* Devil *came in Person and assisted him.*

He undoubtedly perform'd most of these Wonders in the darkest part of the Night, and without the least Glimpse of a Candle; In a word, he has actually done with his own Hands in a few Hours, what several of the most skilful Artists allow, could not have been acted by a number of Persons furnish'd with proper Implements, and all other Advantages in a full Day.

Never was there any thing better Tim'd, the Keepers and all their Assistants being obliged to a strict Attendance on the Sessions at the *Old-Bailey,* which held for about a Week; and *Blewskin* having confin'd *Jonathan Wild* to his Chamber, a more favourable opportunity could not have been presented for Mr. *Sheppard's* Purposes.

The Jaylors suffer'd much by the Opinion the ignorant Part of the People entertain'd of the Matter, and nothing would satisfie some, but that they not only Conniv'd at, but even assisted him in breaking their own Walls and Fences, and that for this Reason too, *viz.* That he should be at Liberty to instruct and train up others in his Method of House-Breaking; and replenish the Town with a new set of Rogues, to supply the Places of those Transported beyond Sea.

This is indeed a fine way of Judging, the well-known Characters of Mr. *Pitt,* and his Deputies, are sufficient to wipe of such ridiculous Imputations; and 'tis a most lamentable Truth, that they have often-times had in their Charge Villains of the deepest Die; Persons of Quality and great Worth, for whom no

Entreaties, no Sums how large soever have been able to inter-
fere between the doleful Prison, and the fatal Tree.

The Officers have done their Duty, they are but Men, and
have had to deal with a Creature something more than Man,
a *Protoeus,* Supernatural, Words cannot describe him, his Actions and Workmanship which are too visible, best testifie him.

On *Saturday* the 17th, *Joseph Blake,* alias *Blewskin,* came
upon his Tryal at the *Old-Bailey: Field* gave the same Evidence
against him, as he had formerly done against *Sheppard;* and
the Prisoner making but a triffling Defence, the Jury found
him Guilty of Burglary and Felony. The Criminal when the
Verdict was brought in, made his Obeysances to the Court,
and thank'd them for their Kindness.

It will be necessary that we now return to the Behaviour of
Mr. *Sheppard,* some few Days before his last Flight.

Mr. *Figg*[16] the famous Prize Fighter coming to see him, in
NEWGATE, there past some pleasant Raillery between them;
and after Mr. *Figg* was gone, *Sheppard* declared he had a Mind
to send him a formal Challenge to Fight him at all the Weapons
in the strong Room; and that let the Consequence be what it
would, he should call at Mr. *Figg's* House in his way to Execution, and drink a merry Glass with him by way of Recon-
ciliation.

A young Woman an Acquaintance of his Mother, who wash'd
his Linnen and brought him Necessaries, having in an Affray,
got her Eyes beaten Black and Blue; says *Sheppard* to her,
How long hast thou been Married? Replyes the Wench, *I
wonder you can ask me such a Question, when you so well
know the Contrary:* Nay, says *Sheppard* again, Sarah *don't
deny it, for you have gotten your* CERTIFICATE *in your Face.*

Mr. *Ireton* a Bailiff in *Drury-Lane* having pursued Sheppard
after his Escape from the Condemn'd-Hold with uncommon
Diligence; (for the safety of that Neighbourhood which was
the chief Scene of his Villanies) *Sheppard* when Re-taken,
declared, he would be even with him for it, and if ever he

procur'd his Liberty again, *he would give all his Prisoners an* ACT OF GRACE.

A Gentleman in a jocose way ask'd him to come and take a Dinner with him, *Sheppard* reply'd, *he accepted of the Invitation, and perhaps might take an opportunity to wait on him;* and there is great Reason to believe he has been as good as his Word.

He would complain of his Nights, as saying, *It was dark with him from Five in the Evening, till Seven in the Morning;* and being not permitted to have either a Bed or Candle, his Circumstances were dismal; and that he never slept but had some confus'd Doses, he said he consider'd all this with the Temper of a Philosopher.

Neither his sad Circumstances, nor the solemn Exhortations of the several Divines who visited him, were able to divert him from this ludicrous way of Expression; he said, They were all *Ginger-bread Fellows,* and came rather out of Curiosity, than Charity; and to form *Papers* and *Ballads* out of his Behaviour.

A *Welch* Clergyman who came pretty often, requested him in a particular Manner to refrain Drinking; (tho' indeed there was no necessity for that Caution) *Sheppard* says, Doctor, *You set an Example and I'll follow;* this was a smart Satyr and Repartee upon the Parson, some Circumstances consider'd.[17]

When he was visited in the *Castle* by the Reverend Mr. *Wagstaff,* he put on the Face only of a Preparation for his End, as appear'd by his frequent Attempts made upon his Escape, and when he has been press'd to Discover those who put him upon Means of Escaping, and furnish'd him with Implements, he would passionately, and with a Motion of striking, say, *ask me no such Questions, one* File's *worth all the* Bibles *in the World.*

When ask'd if he had not put off all Thoughts of an Escape and Entertain'd none but those of Death, would Answer by way of Question, not directly, whether they thought it possible, or probable for him to Effect his Release, when Manacled in the manner he was. When mov'd to improve the few Minutes that seem'd to remain of his Life; he did indeed listen to, but not regard the Design and Purport of his Admonition, breaking in with something New of his own, either with respect to his former Accomplices, or Actions, and all too with Pleasure and Gayety of Expression.

When in *Chapel,* he would seemingly make his Responses with Devotion; but when (as an Auditor of the Sermon) he would either Laugh, or force Expressions of Contempt either of the Preacher, or of his Discourse.[18]

In fine, he behav'd so, in Word, and Action, (since re-taken) that demonstrated to the World, that his Escape was the utmost Employ of his Thoughts, whatever Face of Penitence he put on when visited by the Curious.

An Account of SHEPPARD'S Adventures of five Hours
immediately after his Escape from *Newgate,*
in a Letter to his Friend.[19]

DEAR FRIEND!

OVER a Bottle of Claret *you'll give me leave to* declare it, *that I've fairly put the* Vowels *upon the good Folks at* Newgate, i.o.u. *When I'm able, I may, or may not discharge my* Fees, *'tis a* Fee-simple, *for a Man in my Condition to acknowledge; and tho' I'm safe out of* Newgate, *I must yet have, or at least, affect, a* New Gate *by Limping, or turning my Toes in by making a right* Hand *of my* Feet. *Not to be long, for I hate* Prolixity *in all Business:* In short, *after* Filing, Defileing, Sawing, *when no Body* Saw. Climbing (*this* Clime in) *it prov'd a good* Turner *of my Affairs, thro' the House of a* Turner. *Being quite past, and safe from* Estreat *on Person or Chattels, and safe in the* Street, *I thought Thanks due to him who cou'd* Deliver *hence; and immediately (for you must know I'm a* Catholick) *to give Thanks for my Deliverance, I step't amongst the* Grey-Fryers *to come and joyn with me, in saying a* Pater-Noster, *or so, at* Amen-Corner. *The* Fryers *being* Fat *began to* Broil, *and soon after* Boild up *into a Passion to be disturb'd at that time of* Night. *But being got* Loose *and having no Time to Lose, I gave them good Words, and so the Business was done. From thence I soon slip'd through* Ludgate, *but was damnably fearful of an* Old Bailey *always lurking thereabout, who might have brought me to the* Fleet *for being too* Nimble, *besides, I was wonderfully apprehensive of receiving some unwelcome Huggings from the* W[arde]n *there; therefore with a step and a stride I soon got over* Fleet-ditch, *and (as in* Justice *I ought) I prais'd the* Bridge *I got over. Being a* Batchelor, *and not being capable to manage a* Bridewell *you know. I had no Business near St.* Brides, *so kept the right hand side, designing to* Pop *into the* Alley *as usual; but fearing to go thro' there, and* harp *too much on the same* String, *it gave an* Allay *to my Intention, and on I went to* Shoe-Lane *end but there meeting with a* Bully Hack *of the Town, he wou'd have shov'd me down, which my* Spirit *resenting, tho' a* brawny Dog, *I soon* Coller'd *him, fell* Souse *at him, then with his own* Caine *I strapp'd till he was force to* Buckle *too, and hold his* Tongue, *in so much he durst not say his* Soul *was his own, and was glad to pack of at* Last, *and turn his* Heels *upon me: I was glad he was gone you may be sure, and* dextrously *made a* Hand *of my Feet under the* Leg-Tavern; *but the very Thoughts of* Fetter-Lane *call'd to mind some Passages, which made me avoid the* Passage *at the end of it, (next to the* Coffee House *you know) so I soon whip'd over the way, yet going along two wooden* Logger-heads *at St.* Dunstan's, *made just then a* damn'd Noise *about their* Quarters, *but the sight of me made perfectly* Hush *in a Minute; now fearing to goe by* Chance-a-wry-Lane, *as being upon the* Watch *my self, and not to be de-barr'd at* Temple-Bar; *I stole up* Bell-Yard, *but narrowly escap'd being* Clapper-claw'd *by two Fellows I did not like in the* Alley, *so was forc'd to goe round with a design to*

Sheer-off *into* Sheer Lane, *but the* Trumpet *sounding at that very time, alarm'd me so, I was forc'd to Grope my way back through* Hemlock-Court, *and take my Passage by* Ship-Yard *without the Bar again; but there meeting with one of our trusty Friends,* (*all Ceremonies a-part*) *he told me under the* Rose *I must expect no* Mercy *in* St. Clement's *Parish, for the* Butchers *there on the* Back *on't would* Face *me, and with their* Cleavers *soon bring me down on my* marrow Bones; *you may believe I soon hasten'd thence, but by this time being Fainty and nigh Spent, I put forward, and seeing a* Light *near the* Savoy-Gate, *I was resolv'd not to make* Light *of the Opportunity, but call'd for an hearty Dram of* Luther *and* Calvin, *that is,* Mum *and* Geneva[20] *mix'd; but having Fasted so long before, it soon got into my Noddle, and e'er I had gone twenty steps, it had so intirely* Stranded *my Reason, that by the time I came to* Half-Moon-Street *end, it gave me a* New-Exchange *to my Senses, and made me quite* Lunatick.

However, after a little Rest, I stole down George-Passage *into* Oaf-Alley *in* York-Buildings, *and thence* (*tho' a vile Man*) *into* Villiers-Street, *and so into the* Strand *again, where having gone a little way,* Hefford's-Harp *at the Sign of the* Irish-Harp, *put me a* Jumping *and* Dancing *to that degree, that I could not forbear making a* Somerset *or two before* Northumberland-House. *I thought once of taking the* Windsor Coach *for my self* John Sheppard, *by the Name of* Crook—*but fearing to be* Hook'd *in before my Journey's End, I stept into* Hedge-Lane, *where two Harlots were up in the* Boughs (*it seems*) *Branching out their Respects to one another, through their Windows, and People beginning to gather thereabout, I ran* Pelmel *to* Piccadilly, *where meeting, by meer Chance a* Bakers Cart *going to* Turnham-Green, *I being not* Mealy Mouth'd, *nor the* Man *being* Crusty *I wheel'd out of Town.*

I did call at Hammersmith, *having no occasion directly. I shall stay two or three Days in that Neighbourhood, so, if you Direct a Letter for Mr.* Sligh Bolt, *to be left with Mrs.* Tabitha

Symmington *at* Cheese-wick, *it's Safety will* Bear Water *by any* Boat, *and come Current, with the Tyde to*

Dear Bob

Yours from the Top of *Newgate* to the Bottom

J. SHEPPARD.

P.S. If you see *Blewskin*, tell him I am well, and hope he receiv'd my last—I wou'd write by the *Post* if I durst, but it wou'd be, certainly *Post-pon'd* if I did, and it would be *stranger* too, to trust a Line by a *Stranger*, who might Palm upon us both and never Deliver it to *Hand*.

I send this by a *Waterman*, (I dare trust) who is very Merry upon me, and says he wou'd not be in my *Jacket*.
Saturday Octob. 17, 1724.

We shall conclude with what had been often observ'd by many Persons to *Sheppard; viz.* That it was very Imprudent in him to take Shelter in the City, or the adjacent Parts of it, after his Escape from the Condemn'd Hold; and withal to commit a *Capital Offence*, almost within Sight of *Newgate*, when his Life and all was in such Danger. His Reply was general, *viz.* That it was his Fate: But being ask'd a particular Reason for his not taking a longer Rout than the City, and the Neighbouring parts; pleaded Poverty as his Excuse for Confinement within those Limits; at the same time urging, that had he been Master at that time of five Pounds, *England* should not have been the Place of his Residence, having a good Trade in his Hands to live in any populated Part of the World.

THE
TRUE and GENUINE
ACCOUNT
OF THE
LIFE and ACTIONS
Of the Late
JONATHAN WILD;

Not made up of *Fiction* and *Fable*,
but taken from his Own Mouth, and
collected from PAPERS of his
Own Writing.

LONDON:

Printed and Sold by JOHN APPLEBEE, in *Black-*
Fryers; J. ISTED, at the *Golden Ball* near *Chan-*
cery-Lane in *Fleet-street*; and the Bookfellers of
London and *Westminster*, 1725. (Price Six-Pence.)

THE
TRUE and GENUINE
ACCOUNT
OF THE
LIFE and ACTIONS
Of the Late
JONATHAN WILD;

Not made up of *Fiction* and *Fable*,
  but taken from his Own Mouth, and
  collected from PAPERS of his
  Own Writing.

LONDON:

Printed and Sold by John Applebee, in Black-Fryers; *J. Isted, at the* Golden-Ball *near* Chancery-Lane *in* Fleet-street; *and the Booksellers of* London *and* Westminster, 1725. (*Price Six-Pence.*)

In addition to this account, published by Applebee on 8 June 1725, Defoe may have written *The Life of Jonathan Wild*, published for T. Warner on 29 May 1725.

THE PREFACE.

THE several absur'd and ridiculous Accounts which have been *Publish'd, notwithstanding early and seasonable Caution given, of the Life and Conduct of this famous, or if you please infamous Creature,* Jonathan Wild, *make a short Preface to this Account absolutely necessary.*[1]

IT is something strange, that a Man's Life should be made a kind of a Romance before his Face, and while he was upon the Spot to contradict it; or, that the World should be so fond of a formal Chimney-corner Tale, that they had rather a Story should be made merry than true.

THE Author of this short but exact Account of Mr. Wild *assures the World, that the greatest Part of all that has hitherto appeared of this Kind, has been evidently invented and framed out of the Heads of the scribbling Authors, meerly to get a Penny, without regard to Truth or Fact, or even to Probability, or without making any Conscience of their imposing on the Credulous World.*

NAY, so little Ground has there been for them, that except there was such a Man as Jonathan Wild, *that he was born at* Wolverhampton, *liv'd in the* Old-Bailey, *was call'd a Thief-Catcher, and was Hang'd at* Tyburn, *there is not one Story printed of him that can be call'd Truth, or that is not mingled up with so much Falshood and Fable as to smother and drown that little Truth which is at the bottom of it.*

THE following Tract does not indeed make a Jest of his Story as they do, or present his History, which indeed is a Tragedy of itself, in a stile of Mockery and Redicule, but in a Method agreeable to the Fact. They that had rather have a Faleshood to laugh at, than a true Account of Things to inform them, had best buy the Fiction, and leave the History to those who know how to distinguish Good from Evil.

INTRODUCTION.

THE Undertaker of this Work having easily foreseen that the Story of this eminent Criminal would be acceptable to the World, resolved sometime ago to publish it, but knowing at the same time it would be attempted over and over by our Hackney Grub-street *Writers, upon the old Pick-pocket Principle of Publishing any Thing to get a Penny; they therefore took care not only to furnish themselves with authentick and full vouchers for the Truth of what they have to say, but also to have the Account of him be very Particular, and such as may answer their Title.*

UPON *the Assurance of their being thus provided, not only to give a true, but also a full and compleat Account of him, they took care to give the World an early and timely Notice that such a Work was preparing for the Press,*[2] *in order to prevent Peoples being impos'd upon; and to that purpose they advertis'd this Work in several Publick Prints; and they are satisfy'd that as on one Hand, it has prepared the World to expect this Account, so it will fully answer their Expectation now it appears.*

THEY *have not satisfy'd themselves in their Enquiries, to take Things upon the Credit of Common Fame, which (generally speaking) is a Common Something; nor have they supplyed, by Invention, the Particulars of what wanted such Helps. The Life of this unhappy Wretch is too full of Incidents, and that of an uncommon Nature, to stand in Need of any such Helps; and we are so far from wanting Matter to fill up this Tract, and make the Story out, that on the contrary, we are forc'd to abridge and contract some of the most considerable Passages of his Life, that we may bring it all into as narrow a Compass as we can.*

THE Life *of* Jonathan Wild *is a perfectly new Scene; as his Conduct has been Inimitable, so his Imployment has been singular to him, and is like to be so, for as it began, so it is like to dye with him; no Man among the most daring of the Clan being, we believe, so hardy as to venture to take it up after him.*

EVERY Step *he took was Criminal, and the very Actions which he did with the greatest openness and an avowed profess'd Allowance, merited the Gallows even by the very Letter; but pray Note, when we say* Allowance, [w]e *mean his own Allowance, for no other Power or Person could allow him in it.*

IT *is true, he had an inimitable Boldness in his Behaviour and by detecting some Criminals, he assumed a kind of Power to protect others, only the difference lay here, namely, that he did the first Publicky, and the last Privately; so that in a Word, he served the Publick in the first, and abused the Publick in the second, and was only deceived in this, that he thought his being Useful in the first, would protect him in being Criminal in the last; but here he was, we say Mistaken, and fell into a Snare which all his pretended Merit could not deliver him from.*

TAKE *him as a Man, only he had a kind of brutal Courage which fitted him to be an Instrument in attacking some of the most desperate of the several Gangs of Rogues he had to do with. But as this Courage also serv'd to make him Audacious in the other wicked Things he undertook, he was rather Bold than Couragious, and might be call'd Impudent, but we cannot say he was Brave, as appeared in a more particular manner in his stupid and confus'd Behaviour, during his lying in* Newgate, *and at his Execution, of which in its Place.*

WE *have the Advantage in this Account to come at the particular of his Story from unquestioned Authority, for as he was sensible wrong Accounts would be publish'd of him, he was not backward to give Materials from his own Mouth which no Body can contradict, and others fully conversant with him, having given the same Stories or Accounts of the same Facts, we have the Satisfaction to see them agree fully together, and thereby be assured of the Truth of both; for in such Cases there could be no Combination to deceive us.*

NOT *that it is possible to obtain a full Account of all the particular Villainies of* Jonathan Wild, *during a series of sixteen Years, in which he reign'd in all his Wickedness with such Success, as no Age can produce the like. 'Tis enough if we give you a general View of his Life, or a Scheme of his Practice, illustrated by Examples; which Examples likewise might be farther set forth by more Examples and by Stories full of an infinite Variety, which if collected together, would make up a large Volume in Folio, and yet leave many of them unrelated.*

IT *is true, as we shall take Notice in its Place, that the World does not charge* Jonathan *with being himself actually a Highwayman or Robber; or that when any of the Gangs of* Prancers *(as they are call'd in the* Newgate *Cant) went out upon the Grand Design, he ever went with them, and we are assur'd he did not: He knew the Trade too well, to put his Life into such a Hazard; he knew how common a Bite it was among such People to save their own Lives at the Expence of their Companions; but he was too Cunning for that. And he had likewise a so much better Trade in Hand, by which he was sure to make a Prey both of the Persons Robb'd, and of the Rogues that robb'd them; that he would have been worse than Lunatick, if he had been drawn in to be a Party.*

THE Part he acted in the Fact for which he suffer'd, was more than he ordinarily did, or than we ever find he ventur'd to do before, for here he was both Thief and Thief-Catcher too, which he did not usually venture. But a secret Infatuation was now upon him, and Heaven who had determined his Fate, no doubt left him to Expose himself more in this one Action, than he had done in many Years before, and by this he Fell.

IT is said, that if this had not fix'd him, there were other Facts charg'd which would effectually have done; to that we shall say nothing, because those others have not been try'd. 'Tis enough, Jonathan dy'd not in his own way of Thief-Catching, but by going out of his Road and taking a Share in the Robbery as he did after in the Reward: And here he was taken in his own Snare, for the very Thieves he employ'd, were the Witnesses that Hang'd him. But we say no more of that, till we come to the Story itself. We now proceed to the particular Account of his Life.

JONATHAN WILD the wretched Subject of this History, was born at *Wolverhampton* in *Staffordshire;* and to do Justice to his Original his Parents, tho' mean, had the repute of Honest and Industrious People, his Father being a *Carpenter,* and his Mother sold *Herbs* and *Fruit* in the Market of *Wolverhampton:* They had three Sons, and two Daughters, the two Daughters are yet living and Married to honest Tradesmen in *Wolverhampton,* one to a *Comb-Maker,* and the other a *Buckle-Maker,* and whose Characters we do not hear are any way Blemish'd; but the Sons have all a different Fame.

THE Brothers I say were three in Number, *Jonathan, John* and *Andrew: John* was a publick Officer in the Town where they Liv'd, being the Cryer of *Wolverhampton;* but stepping out of his Employment in the time of the late *Preston* Rebellion, and making himself popular by Heading and appearing among the Rable, for pulling down the Meeting-House at *Wolverhampton;* he was taking up for a Rioter, brought to LONDON, and put into Custody of a Messenger, where he continued sometime, till he was sent down again in Custody to *Stafford,* to be Try'd at the Assizes held there for the County: There he was Convicted, and received'd Sentence to be publickly Whipt, and afterwards to lye in Prison for a certain Time, which Sentence was accordingly Executed: But the same *John* being afterwards at Liberty, the time of his Imprisonment being expir'd, Dyed about four Years ago, as did also his Mother much about the same Time, that is to say, within a Month of One another.

THE younger Brother *Andrew* being by Trade a *Birmingham* Ware-man, or in particular a Buckle-Maker; left his own Country and came up to *London,* what Trade he has driven here we shall not meddle with, the Man being yet alive; and as we are not writing his Story, but that of his elder Brother, so we are not willing to enter into any thing that may be prejudicial to particular Persons on any Account whatever; 'tis enough to say, that we hear he is at this Time a Prisoner in the *Poultry-Compter*[3] for Debt; so that it seems, all the three Brothers have had some Acquaintance with the inside of a Goal, tho' on different Accounts.

Jonathan as I have said, was the eldest Brother, he was born about the year 1683, being at the time of his Execution, about two and forty years of Age, of which something more than thirteen years has been spent in the most exquisite Villanies, of which we shall give some Account in this Work.

HIS Education was suitable to his Fathers Circumstances, being taught in the Free-School of *Wolverhampton,* to Read and Write, and then his Father put him Apprentice to a *Birmingham* Man, or as they call them there, a Hardware Man, and particularly a *Buckle maker.*

AUTHORS are not agreed in the Name of his Master, and as it is not Material, we also let it pass without any Notice, having serv'd his Time out, or as some say but part of it. He got into the Service of one Counsellor *Daniel* of *Staffordshire*, and came up with him to *London* as his Servant, this was about the year 1704. But whether he did not please his Master, or that he took ill Courses so early, we have not enquir'd; but that Counsellor dismissing him, he went home again to *Wolverhampton*, and very honestly work'd for some time at his Trade.

BUT his Thoughts, *as he said*, being above his Trade, tho' at that time he had no Tast of the Life he afterwards led, yet he grew uneasie in the Country, was sick of his Work, and in short, after a few Years came away to *London*, to see if he could get into any Business there.

HERE he found but little Encouragement, and tho' he Work'd at his Trade, yet what he could get at his day Labour, but ill serv'd to maintain him, whose Temper even then, was not much given to Frugality, which with his being not enclin'd to sit very close to his Work neither, made him run out pretty much, till at length it was his Misfortune to be Arrested for Debt, and carried to *Wood-street Compter*.

HERE he suffer'd great hardship, having no Friends to help him out, or Money to maintain him within, so that he was on the Common-side, and far'd as other People in those Circumstances do fare, that is to say, very hard.

HOWEVER, after having lain a long time there, he at length having behaved himself well enough among the Prisoners, got so much Favour with the Keepers, that he got *the Liberty of the Gate*, as they call it.

HIS Business here was chiefly to attend in the Night, in Case any Prisoners were brought in for Disorders in the Street; to wait upon them, and guard them with the Officers to any Justice of the Peace, and so back again if they were Committed; and in this, he Discharg'd himself to Satisfaction, so that he was at length trusted to go of Errands, and the like Liberties to get a Penny.

AMONG the great variety of Night-walking Offenders which came into his Custody, at length there comes in one *Mary Milliner*, who after having been carried before a Justice, might be remanded to the *Compter* for the present; but being a Jade of some Fame, she soon found her way out again, for we do not find she was reckoned to be a Prisoner there at all.

WHETHER it was that she was frequently brought in there in her Night Rambles, and might receive some Favours from him on that Occasion, it being much in his way to favour such as she was, he being a kind of Keeper set over them; or whether they Contracted a Friendship at first sight, or what other Incident brought it about I know not; but Mr. *Wild* not only became acquainted with her, but a more than common Intimacy soon grew between them; insomuch, that she began to teach him a great many New, and to him unknown Ways of getting Money, and brought him into her own Gang, whether of Thieves or Whores, or of both, is not much Material.

BY the Advantage of this new Correspondence Mr. *Wild* soon clear'd himself of his Imprisonment, the Debt for which he was thrust into the *Compter* being but small; and tho' he had a Wife at that time living at *Wolverhamton,* and had a Son by her, which Son is still living, as we shall hear presently. And tho' this new Favourite he had pitch'd upon, had also a Husband then living, a *Waterman* by his Profession; yet they pretended to be Married and liv'd together some time as Man and Wife, and this we are to call his second Wife, for he had six of them in all. This Mrs. *Milliner* as I am inform'd is still living, so that Mr. *Wild* has left several Widows still behind him at his *Exit*, whether they go by his Name or not, that he could not inform us.

DURING his Intimacy with this Mrs. *Milliner,* and by her means he grew Acquainted with some other of the wicked ways of Living, which it seems she practis'd besides that of Whoring: And first it seems she carried him out with her upon the TWANG: This is One of the Cant Words for those who attend upon the Night-walking Ladies in their Progress, and who keep at a distance, that if the Lady they are employ'd by, happens to fall into any Broil, they may come in timely to her Assistance, and making a Noise and a Quarrel, if possible fall a Fighting, and so give her an Opportunity to walk off, which *Jonathan* often practis'd with good Success.

HE improv'd his time during his Acquaintance with this *Mary Milliner* to a very great Degree, for she brought him acquainted with several Gangs, or Societies of the Sharping and Thieving World, in so much, that in a little time he knew all their several Employments, and the several Parts they Acted, their Haunts and their Walks, how they perform'd, and how they manag'd their Effects when they had met with Success: And as he seem'd to set up for a Director to them, under the Government of that Dextrous Lady his first Instructor, so he found ways to make himself as useful to them, as if he had gone Abroad with them, which however he always avoided: Nor, indeed, had he any occasion to run a Hazard himself, he finding himself as much a gainer in the Part he Acted, as if he had shar'd in the Adventure: So that, in a Word, He had the Profit without the Danger; and politically kept himself from the Last, on pretence of his encreasing the First, by his Art in managing for them.

THUS without being a Thief or a Receiver, he brought a Gain to himself, and his Business went on Prosperously.

HOW he and his Lady parted after this, is a Story, which has nothing Extraordinary in it; 'tis enough to say, that *Jonathan* became such a Proficient in his Business, that he stood no longer in need of her Instructions; and as she had a Trade of her own, which he began to be sick of assisting her in, they made no difficulty of seperating, with as little Ceremony as they came together.

THO' I do not find but that they kept a kind of remote Correspondence after they were separated, as to Cohabitation; and the other Trade was carried on with mutual Assistance, as well as to mutual Advantage, for some time. And here it is very Remarkable, That tho' during this Intercourse of Mr. *Wild* among these loose People (as above) many of them dayly fell into the Hand of Justice, and some went off the Stage, the High

Road (as they call it) that is to say, by the Gallows; yet none
of them had any thing to say to *Jonathan,* or to his She Friend,
Mrs. *Milliner:* but these always did their Business so Clean,
with such Subtilty, and so much to the Advantage of the Criminals, that it was of no Use to them to charge him or her with
any Thing.

IN this dextrous way of Managing, it came frequently in his
way, where any Thing of Value was Stolen, to make it worth
more Money, both to himself and to the Thief that had Stolen
it, by his private Ways; which at the same time the Criminal
knew nothing of. The Case was thus.

IT is not to be doubted, that when a Robery was committed,
the Thieves sometimes run as much Hazard in securing what
they had got, as they did in the getting of it, and often times
much more; nay, they were very often discovered and detected
in their Attempts, to turn what they had got into Money; or
to sell and dispose of it, when they had escaped the Danger
of the Fact it self, and come off Clean.

THERE was a Time indeed, when there were Brokers and
Receivers, whose Business it was to take every Thing off of
their Hands as soon as they had gotten it; and a young Shop-
lifter or House-breaker had no sooner got a Booty, but he
knew where to go and carry it in, as to a Warehouse or Reposi-
tory; where he was sure to have Money for it, and that something near the Value of it too; and this was a great Encouragement to the Light-finger'd Gang: So that when it was a Misfortune of a Family or Person to lose any Goods, they were
effectually lost, and seldom or never were they heard of any
more.

BUT there being an Act in the Reign of the late King *William,* making it Felony to buy or receive any Stolen Goods,
knowing them to be Stolen;[4] and one or two bold People having suffered on that very Account; the Receiving Trade was
spoil'd all at once. And when the poor Adventurer had, at the
hazard of his Neck, gotten any Purchase, he must run all that
Hazard over again to turn it into Money.

IT is true, after some time, the Temptation being strong, and the Profits great, there were Persons frequently found again that did help the Adventurers and took of their Goods; but then the Thief got so small a Share, that the Encouragement was very small; and had it continued so, the Thieving Trade might (for ought I know) have been in danger of being lost: For the Receivers running so extreme a Hazard, they got all the Profit; and the poor Lifter or House-breaker was glad to part with Things of the greatest Value for a Trifle.

BUT *Jonathan* and his Director, soon found out a Way to encourage the Trade again, and to make it worth while as they call'd it, and the first Method was this: When a Purchase was made, *Jonathan* enquir'd first where it was gotten, what House had been robb'd, or, who had lost the Goods; and having learn'd that, his next Business was to have the Goods deposited in proper Places, alway[s] avoiding the receiving them himself, or bringing himself into any Jeopardy as to the Law.

THEN he found out proper Instruments to employ to go to the Persons, who had been robb'd, and tell them, that if they could describe what they had lost, they believ'd they could help them to them again, for that there was a parcel of stolen Goods stopt by an honest Broker, to whom they were offered to be sold, and if their Goods were among them they might have them again for a small matter of Expence.

THE People who had been robb'd, it may be suppos'd were always willing enough to hear of their Goods again, and very thankful to the Discoverer, and so readily gave an Account of the Things they had lost, with such proper Descriptions of them as were needful; The next Day they should be told; there was such or such Part of their Goods stopt among other Goods, which it was supposed were stolen from other People, and so upon Assurance given on both Sides to make no Enquiry into the particular Circumstances of stopping the Goods, and a Consideration to the Person who went between, for helping the Loser to his Goods again, the Things were restor'd, and the Person receiv'd abundance of Thanks and Acknowledgements

for their Honesty and Kindness, and this part always fell to
Jonathan, or his Mistress *Milliner,* or perhaps both, who always
pretended they got nothing for their Pains but the Satisfaction
of having help'd the People to recover their own again, which
was taken by a Company of Rogues; professing their Sorrow
that they had not had the good Luck at the same time to detect
the Rogues that took them, and bring them to the Punishment
they deserv'd.

ON the other hand, they acted as safe a Part with the Thief
also, for rating and reproving the Rogue for his Villany, they
would pretend to bring them to an honest Restoring the Goods
again, taking a reasonable Consideration for their Honesty, and
so bring them to lodge them in such Place as should be directed; and sometimes, as I have been told, he has officiously
caused the Thief, or Thieves, to be taken with the Goods upon
them, when he has not been able to bring them to comply, and
so had made himself both Thief and Chapman, as the Proverb
says; getting a Reward for the Discovery, and bringing the
poor Wretch to the Gallows too, and this only because he could
not make his Market of him to his Mind; but I must be so just
to *Jonathan* too, as to say he did not acknowledge this, so
that this Part was not had from his own Mouth, yet perhaps
it may not be less true, nor do I think it would be very hard
to prove the Fact.

AS to the other Part, he was never backward to own that it
was his early Practice, and boasted of it as doing a piece of
Service which none but himself could manage, and that he
thereby assisted honest People in the recovery of their own;
how far he acted honestly in the doing it, supposing he had no
hand in the Robbery itself, I leave to the Casuists to determine;
no Question, in their *Newgate* Divinity, they might think it a
mighty honest way of getting Money, for as to the Encouragement it was to the Robbery itself, while the Thief knew before
hand how to come off of the Guilt and get Money in his Pocket,
that they gave their Thoughts no trouble about.

THIS Trade I found by his own Discourse he carry'd on a

great while, and had he gone no farther, I question whether it
had been in any Man's Power to have hurt him to the last; nay,
or that even the Laws would have reach'd his Life, notwithstanding the late Act which seem'd to be calculated on purpose
to put a stop to his Trade:[5] But he knew no Bounds to his Gain,
and therefore knew no Restraint of Laws, or at least considered
of none, till he involved himself in a mass of Crimes, out of
which it was impossible he should recover.

BUT to return to the first Part of this unjust Commerce,
which, whatever Gloss he might put upon it, was no other than
an encouraging Rogues to rob and plunder, and then demand-
ing Money for them to bring back what they had stolen, out
of which he secur'd always a Share for himself. This Practice
of giving People notice of their Goods after they were robb'd
becoming pretty Publick, and especially several People recovering their lost Goods upon the easie Conditions of giving a
Gratuity to the Discoverer, being known, it introduced another weak foolish Practice as a Consequence, namely, that
after this, when any Person was robb'd, they always publish'd
the Particulars of their lost Goods, with the Promise of a Reward to those who should discover them: It [is] reasonable
indeed to suppose that this might occasion a Discovery one
way or other, either by the Thieves betraying one another, or
else by directing the Buyers of Goods, who were honestly
inclin'd, to stop such Goods if they came to be offer'd, and
hence it was a usual Practice in such Advertisements to add,
that if such Goods were offered to be sold or pawn'd, they were
desir'd to stop both the Goods and the Persons, and give notice
so and so, as directed.

BUT this was every Way an ineffectual Method, and indeed
the latter part was particularly so, for, indeed it was neither
more or less than giving a Caution to the Thief, not to venture
to offer any thing he had gotten to Sale, for he should be sure
to be stopt as well as the Goods and indeed it was strange,
that the People who publish'd such Advertisements should not
foresee the making such a Publication would be an effectual

shutting the Door against the Discovery they design'd it for, and was therefore nothing but a throwing good Money after bad.

ON the other hand, neither was the Advertizing or Publishing their Loss any real Service, or of any use to the Loser, for that the only Person who could assist in the Recovery of the Goods, was quite out of the Question, having no need of the Information, but coming by his Intelligence another Way, *viz.* from the Thief himself; and that if there had been no such Information, I mean by publick Print, he would, as usual, have been sure to have sent an Account to the Loser, and have come to a Treaty with him another Way; for the Thief giving an Account to Mr. *Jonathan Wild* where the Robbery was committed, and whose Goods they were, the cunning Artist always made Application [t]o the Loser first; and if it was asked, how they come to know who the Goods were taken from? it was always answer'd, That it was meerly Providential; being, by meer Accident, at a Tavern, or at a Friend's House in the Neighbourhood, they heard that such a Gentleman had his House broken open, and such and such Goods Stolen, and the like.

THIS was so plausible a Story, and carryed so much an appearance of Truth with it, that it left Room for no Enquiry. But on the other hand, if the People, to whom the Discovery was made, were too Inquisitive, the Party sent, presently seem'd to take it Ill, and reply'd, Sir, I come to serve you, If you think to make any Discovery by me, of the Thieves that robb'd you, I must tell you, that you are Mistaken: I converse with no such Cattle; I can give a very good Account of my self to you, or any Body else: I only come to tell you that some Goods being offer'd to Sale by a suspected Hand, the Person to whom they were offer'd, had the Honesty to stop them, and the Goodness to give you some Notice of it, that you may see whether your Goods are among them or not; if this is not enough to oblige you, I have done. If you have any thing to say to me, or think to talk to me about the Thief or Thieves that robb'd you, I have no more to say to you, but to let you know, my Name is so and so; and I live in such a Place, if you have any thing to say to me, I am to be found, Sir, at any Time. And thus they take their leave in a Huff. And this never fails to bring the Enquirer to a better Temper; and either immediately, or soon after, to treat them with more Civility.

AND indeed the offer itself appears so Good, and the appearance so above Board, that not a Magistrate, or Justice of Peace, could find the least Flaw in it: Only enquire where the Goods are which are stopt, in which Case, a Place and Person is named, and Goods produced when any one is sent to view them; but then the Party so Caviling at that offer, is sure to find none of his own Goods among them: And so being lost as it were in a Wood, he is perfectly amused, and has not one Word to say; for he neither sees his own Goods, nor knows that the other Goods are stolen, much less by whom or from who: And thus by his being too Curious, or rather Impertinent, he loses his Goods entirely, and has no second Offer made him.

IT must be confess'd, *Jonathan* play'd a sure Game in all this; and therefore it is not to be wonder'd at that he went on for so many Years without any Disaster: Nay, he acquir'd a strange, and, indeed, unusual Reputation, for a mighty honest Man, till his Success hardened him to put on a Face of publick Service in it; and for that Purpose, to profess an open and bare Correspondence among the Gangs of Thieves; by which his House became an Office of Intelligence for Enquiries of that Kind; as if all Stolen Goods had been deposited with him, in order to be restor'd.

BUT even this good Character of his, as it did not last long, so neither did it come all at once; and some tell us (how true it is, I will not affirm) that he was oblig'd to give up every now and then one or two of his Clients to the Gallows, to support his rising Reputation: In which cases, he never fail'd to proclaim his own Credit in bringing Offenders to Justice, and in delivering his Country from such dangerous People.

SOME have gone so far as to tell us the very Particulars

which recommended any of the Gangs to him for a Sacrifice, and to divide them into Classes: For Example, (1.) such as having committed the Secret of a Fact to him, yet would not submit their Purchase to his Disposal; or (2.) would not accept reasonable Terms of Composition for restoring the Goods; or (3.) used any threatning Speeches against their Comrades: These he would immediately cause to be apprehended, he knowing both their Haunts, and where the Goods were deposited; and in such Cases, none so vigilant in the Discovery, or so eager in apprehending the Thief: And, generally speaking, he had his ways and means to bring in others of the Gang, to come in and Confess, that they might Impeach the Person so intended to be given up to Justice.

THIS, I say some have affirmed was his Practise, and assured me of the Truth of it; and that in these Cases, they add, That he managed with such Dexterity, that he always obtain'd publick Applause, as a mighty forward Man to detect the Villanies of those People, and bring Offenders to Justice.

HOW many he murthered in that manner, for as his End was only making a Sacrifice to his own Interest and Fame, I can call it no other: I say, how many they were, I cannot learn;[6] but if it has been a Practice of so many Years standing, and so frequent in that Time, it cannot be doubted but the Number has been very considerable; nor does it a little contribute to the belief of the Thing, that the fraternity of Thieves in general were of late so exasperated against him; for tho' the Method was in it self wicked in him, yet it certainly brought a great many Criminals to just Condemnation, who would otherwise have liv'd to do much more Mischief than they did.

AND this occasion'd him doubtless to push on with the more Heat and Fury against those who stood in his way, and where he could exert his Power without fear of being Touch'd himself, as particularly against the late *J. Sheppard*, *Blueskin*, and others, in the taking, re-taking, and prosecuting of whom, he was very Officious; while at the same time those audacious Criminals exclaim'd against him, as a Man who had [been] the first great Encourager of their Villanies, or at least had been instrumental to draw them into the very Practice it self; in Revenge for which, the said *Blueskin* bid fair for giving *Jonathan* his *quietus* in the very Face of Justice. But his fate was to dye with more Infamy than he would have gone off with, if he had been sent off at that Time.

BUT to return to the History it self, what ever was at the bottom of his Designs, 'tis evident, he had two very clear Pretences for what he did; and on these two Pretences, it was that he s[u]pported the Credit of all his monstrous doings, and which indeed no Man but himself could have shown his Face in; 1. The Publick Good, in taking and apprehending the most open and notorious Criminals; and, 2. The procuring and restoring the Goods again to the right Owners, which had been stolen from them either by Fraud or Violence.

IT was allowed, that neither of these could be done effectually, as *Jonathan* did them, but by an avowed Intimacy and Acquaintance among the Gangs and Societies of Thieves of every sort; and it was very hard to Imagine, that such an Intimacy could be maintain'd without being really a Party to their Management, and without a criminal Correspondence with them in the very Facts: And *Jonathan* was often told so, as well by those who believed him really guilty of such a criminal Correspondence, as those that did not.

BUT be that as it will, *Jonathan* himself always deny'd it, and insisted not only on his Innocence, but on his Merit: And that as he was indeed acquainted with the wicked ways made use of by all the several Classes of Thieves, and by consequence with many of them Personally, he only made use of that Acquaintance, to perswade and prevail upon them, when good Rewards were offer'd for it, to restore the Goods to the People who had lost them, placing himself so only in the middle, between the Loser and the Robber; as to capitulate for the latter, that if the Goods were return'd, the Loser would keep Promise, and give a Reward without Enquiry into the Particulars, or Persons, which would otherways put an end to all Restorings or Returnings of Stolen Goods for ever after.

THIS part he insisted on as not only very Honest but very Serviceable; always insisting that whatever he took on either side, was no otherwise than as a Sollicitor takes his Fee, on Consideration from both Parties, for honestly putting an end to a Law-suit, and bringing the contending Parties to a friendly Accommodation; and had he gone no farther, I cannot say but he might be in the Right: But he acted in a more difficult Station, as placing himself in the middle, between the Law and the Offender, in a manner, commuting the Felony, and making a kind of Composition where the Fact was Punishable; which Punishment no Man had Power to anticipate, but the Hand above, which had Power also to remit the Penalty; namely, the supreame Magistrate.

IT must be allow'd to *Jonathan*'s Fame, That as he steer'd among Rocks and dangerous Shoals, so he was a bold Pilot; he ventur'd in, and always got out in a manner equally surprising; no Man ever did the like before him, and I dare say, no Man will attempt to do the like after him: Two Things indeed favour'd him; (1.) The willingness the Government always shows to have Criminals Detected, and brought to Justice. And, (2.) The Willingness of the People who had been Robb'd, and lost Things of considerable Value, to get their Goods again.

I. THE willingness of the Government to bring Rogues to their Reward, as well to Punish the Persons, as to discourage the Crime; all just Governments discover a Disposition to bring Offenders to Justice: And on this Account, they not only receive and accept of Informations of the worst of Crimes, from the worst of Criminals, and take Knowledge of the Offence from the Offenders themselves, but encourage such Criminals to come in and confess the Offence, and Discover their Accomplices, Promising as well Pardon for the Crimes, as a Reward for the Discovery, even to those who are Guilty. Now this willingness of the Government to detect Thieves, seem'd to be a kind of Authority, for *Jonathan* in his vigorus persuit of those who he thought fit to have Punished; tho' 'tis true, it was no Authority to him to draw poor Fellows first into the Crime, that he might afterwards obtain a Reward from the Government for Detecting and Apprehending them, and there indeed is the nice turn of *Jonathan*'s Case, and which indeed has turn'd him off of the Stage at long run, as we shall see in its Place.

HE continued in the prosperous part of his Business about ten Year, without being so publickly taken notice of, or making himself so famous as he has been lately; and in this time it was not doubted but he got a large stock of Money, as well as of Credit; and had he contented himself with the same Cautious Way of Acting, which his first Instructor introduc'd him by, he might have grown Rich, and been safe too; but as he was of a pushing, enterprizing Nature, he could content himself with nothing but every thing he could get, nor could he act moderately in any part of his Conduct.

IN this time of his Prosperity, he Married a third Wife, (his two former, *if they were Wives*, being still living) her Name was *Elizabeth Man*, who tho' she was a Woman of the Town, was yet a very sensible and agreeable Person; and her short History is this: He lov'd her above all the other Women he had taken for Wives, and liv'd publickly with her, which he did not with any of the rest; he had no Children by her, but she was as he himself Confess'd, a true Penitent for all her former Life, and made him an excellent Wife, she expiated her former bad Life by a formal full Confession and Pennance, having on that Occasion been perswaded to turn *Roman Catholick*, and having receiv'd Absolution from her Confessor, liv'd a very sober Life for some Years, after which she Died, and was buried at St. *Pancrass in the Fields;* and *Jonathan* retain'd such an impression of the Sanctity and goodness of this Wife, that he never forgot it as long as he liv'd; and order'd himself to be Buried close to her when he Died, which his Friends took care to see perform'd, about Two of the Clock in the Morning.

HE had two Wives as they are call'd, besides this; and after her Death, who I understand, he did not live with, or not long at a Time, (*viz.*)

Sarah Parrin, alias *Gregstone,* who I understand is yet Living.

Judith Nun by whom he had a Daughter, who is now about ten Years of Age, and the Mother also still Living.

BESIDES those five, he Married his Sixth and last Wife about seven Year ago, and with whom he liv'd to the Time of his Execution; her maiden Name was *Mary Brown,* but when he took her to Wife, her Name was *Mary Dean,* being the Widow or Relict of *Skull Dean,* a Man of the Trade who was executed for House-breaking, that is to say, for Burglary, about the Year 1716, or 1717: Some have tax'd *Jonathan* with being Instrumental to the Execution of this *Dean,* her said first Husband, that he might have the Liberty to make Court to his Wife, but he deny'd it possitively, and [I] see no room for such a Reproach. I shall not reflect on his Memory, without good Evidence.

THE said *Skull Dean,* Mrs. *Wild's* first Husband, was a very dextrous Fellow in his Calling, and particularly expert in breaking into Houses: After he was condemn'd, he got out of the Prison, on pretence of going to the Necessary-house, and being gotten quite clear for a little while, he made his way as far as *Guiltspur-street,* towards *Smithfield,* but being pursued by the Keepers, and having his Fetters on, he could not go long undiscovered, so they over-took him, and carryed him back to Prison.

THIS Mrs. *Dean* is his present apparent Relict, she has had the mortification to have had two Husbands, and both Hang'd; and was so affected with the Disaster of this last, that as *Jonathan* himself declar'd a few Days before his Execution, she had twice attempted to destroy herself, after she had the Account of his receiving Sentence of Death.

HE had no Children by this *Sixth* Venture; but we are assur'd, she has been an extraordinary Wife to him on many Accounts, and particularly in the way of his Business, in which she could not be perfectly unacquainted, having had so extraordinary a Husband before; tho' we do not find that *Jonathan* himself wanted any Assistance, being by this Time perfect Master of his Trade.

IN the Time of this Wife, or on the Marrying her, he removed from his former Lodging, (a House in the *Little Old Baily*, where his said Wife had liv'd before) and took a House in the *Great Old Baily*, and there he liv'd to the last; and in no mean Figure neither, for his Wife made a very good Appearance; and as to *Jonathan*, he carryed on a very flourishing Business, as the Town well knows.

HE was now Master of his Trade, Poor and Rich flock'd to him: If any Thing was Lost, (whether by Negligence in the Owner, or Vigilance and Dexterity in the Thief) away we went to *Jonathan Wild*. Nay, Advertisements were Publish'd, directing the Finder of almost every Thing, to bring it to *Jonathan Wild*, who was eminently impower'd to take it, and give the Reward.

HOW Infatuate were the People of this Nation all this while? Did they consider, that at the very time that they treated this Person with such a Confidence, as if he had been appointed to the Trade? He had, perhaps, the very Goods in his keeping, waiting the Advertisement for the Reward; and that, perhaps, they had been Stolen with that very Intention?

IT was not a little Difficult to give his Eminence his true Title; he was, indeed, call'd a Thief-Catcher, and on some extraordinary Occasions, he was so, as in the Case of *Sheppard, Blueskin,* and others: But this was no Explanation of his Business at all, for his Profits came in another way, not in catching the Thief, but more properly, in Catching (that is, Biting) the Persons robb'd: As for the Thief, it was not his Business to catch him, as long as he would be subjected to his Rules; that is to say, as often as he had committed any Robbery, to bring it to him, to be restor'd to the Owner.

IF the Correspondence he kept was large, If the Number of his Instruments was very great, his dexterity in Managing them, was indeed wonderful: And how cleverly he keept himself out of the reach of the Act for receiving Stolen Goods, mentioned above, is hardly to be Imagin'd; and yet we find he was never charg'd Home 'till now; notwithstanding so many Fellons who he exasperated to the last Degree, and made Desperate, by falling upon them to their Destruction.

IT is true, the young Generation of Thieves, who as we may say liv'd under him, were always kept low and poor, and could not subsist but by the Bounty of their Governour; and when they had a Booty of any Bulk or Value, they knew not what to do with it, but to deposite it, and get some Money for the present Use, and then have a little more upon its being disposed the right way.

FOR the managing this Part, he had his particular Servants to take and receive, so that *Jonathan* receiv'd nothing, deliver'd nothing, nor could any thing be fasten'd on him to his hurt, I mean for receiving stolen Goods, and yet as things stood, almost all the stolen Goods were brought to him, and put into his Hands.

HE openly kept his Compting House, or Office, like a Man of Business, and had his Books to enter every thing in with the utmost Exactness and Regularity: When you first came to him to give him an Account of any thing Lost, it was hinted to you, That you must first deposite a Crown, this was his Retaining Fee; Then you were ask'd some needful Questions, that is to say needful, not for his Information, but for your Amusement; as where you liv'd, where the Goods were Lost, whether out of your House, or out of your Pocket, or whether on the Highway, and the like; and your Answers to them all were Minuted down, as if in order to make a proper Search and Inquiry; whereas perhaps the very Thing you came to enquire after, was in the very Room where you were, or not far off: After all this Grimace was at an end, you were desir'd to call again, or send in a day or two, and then you should know whether he was able to do you any Service or no, and so you were dismiss'd.

292 SELECTED POETRY AND PROSE OF DANIEL DEFOE

AT your second coming, you had some Encouragement given you, that you would be serv'd, but perhaps the Terms were a little rais'd upon you, and you were told the Rogue that had it was Impudent, that he insisted it was worth so much, and he could sell it when he would for double the Money you offer'd; and that if you would not give him such a Sum, he would not treat with you; however, says *Jonathan,* if I can but come to the Speech of him, I'll make him be more reasonable.

THE next time he tells you, that all he can bring the Rogue to is, that ———— Guineas being paid to the *Porter* who shall bring the Goods, and a Promise upon Honour that nothing shall be said to him, but just take and give; the gold Watch, or the Snuff-Box, or whatever it is, shall be brought to you by such a time exactly; and thus upon mutual Assurances the Bargain is made for restoring the Goods.

BUT then it remains to be ask'd, what Mr. *Wild* expects for his Pains in managing this nice Part, who answers with an air of Greatness, he leaves it to you; that he gets nothing but what is to be given the *Porter,* that he is satisfyed in being able to serve Gentlemen in such a Manner, so that it is in your Breast to do what you think is handsome by Mr. *Wild,* who has taken a great deal of Pains in it to do you a Service.

IT must be confess'd that in all this, if there was no more than is mention'd, such a Part might be Acted on all Sides without any Guilt fasten'd any where but on the Thief: For Example, a House is Robb'd, or a Lady has lost her Gold Watch: *Jonathan* by his Intelligence among the Gang, finds out who has done it; that is to say, he is told 'tis such a one; 'tis no matter how he hears it, he is not bound to the Discovery upon a hear-say; nor is he oblig'd to prosecute a Felony committed on he does not know who, by he knows not who, that's none of his Business.

HOWEVER, having a kind of Knowledge of the Person, he sends to him, to let him know, that if he is his own Friend, he will carry, that is, send the Watch, or the Cane, or the Snuff-

box, so, and so, to such a Place; and that if he does so, and
the *Porter* receives ten Guineas, or more, or less, whatever it
is that is offer'd, all will be well; if not, he adds a Threatning,
that he will be prosecuted with the utmost Severity.

UPON this, the Thief sends the Goods, has the Money, and
never sees *Jonathan*, nor any Person else: What can *Jonathan*
be charg'd with, in such an Affair as this? I must confess I do
not see it; no, nor if the Thief sends him a present of four or
five Guineas out of the Money, provided as he said it is without
any Conditions made before-hand, or being present, at the
Time 'tis done.

NOR, on the other hand, does the treating for delivering
the Goods, as above, with a second or third Person give any
Room to fix any Thing on *Jonathan:* So that, in short, he treats
both with the Thief and with the Person robb'd, with the
utmost safety and security. Indeed I do not see why he might
not have carryed on such a Commerce a[s] this, with the
greatest Ease, I do not say Honesty, in the World, if he had
gone no farther; for he took none of your Money for restoring
your Goods neither did he restore you any Goods; you gave
him Money indeed for his Trouble in enquiring out the Thief,
and for using his Interest by awing or perswading to get your
stolen Goods sent you back, telling you what you must give
to the *Porter* that brings them, if you please, for he does not
oblige you to give it.

BUT the Danger lay on the other side of the Question,
namely, not being contented with what the Person robb'd,
gave upon the Foot of a grateful Acknowledgement, for Trouble; but imprudently taking the Goods of the Thief, sending
the *Porter* himself, taking the Money, and then capitulating
with the Thief, for such a Part of the Reward; and then this
Thief coming in against him as a Witness. This was the very
Case in the Fact upon which *Jonathan* miscarried.

SO that in a Word, *Jonathan*'s Avarice hang'd him. It is true,
in the Case he was try'd for, it was Apparent that he set the
Robbery, as they express it; that is, he directed the Persons

to the Place, nay, went with them to show them the Shop, described the Woman and the Business; and after all, receiv'd the Goods, and gave them the Money for returning them, reserving it in his own Power to take what more he pleas'd for himself; and at last all this being testifyed by the Thieves themselves.

IT is not to be doubted, but *Jonathan,* to carry on this Commerce to such a Highth as he really had rais'd it, had a perfect Understanding with all the profess'd Thieves in the Town; at least the young Beginners, for these are a Class generally more out of his Power than others, and who are not so easily to be governed as the others are; and yet he finds ways to Influence them too in the way of their Practice. But the rest, I say, he had in his Reach[,] manag'd them as he thought fit; nay, he generally knew, or perhaps appointed them the Quarter they should walk in; so that when ever any Person came to enquire for his Goods lost, he could make a tollerable Guess at the Thief, by the quarter part of the Town you liv'd in, or where you were when you lost it.

I Remember I had occasion, in a Case of this Kind, to wait upon Mr. *Jonathan* with a Crown in my Hand, as above, and having made a Deposite, I was ask'd, as above, where the Thing was lost? At first he smil'd, and turning to one, I suppose of his Instruments, who can this be? says he, why all our People are gone down to *Sturbridge* Fair;[7] the other answer'd, after some pause, I think I saw *Lynx,* in the Street, Yesterday: Did you, says he, then 'tis that Dog, I warrant you. Well, Sir, says he, I believe we can find out your Man; you shall know more of it, if you let me see you again a *Monday,* this was on the *Friday:* When the *Monday* came, truly I was told, they could not see the young Rogue, and they believ'd he was gone after the rest to the Fair, it being about the beginning of *September.*

AFTER the Fair, I came again and again, but was put off from time to time, and could not at last be serv'd in the Case, it being only a Silver-hilted Sword, which the Thief it seems had found means to turn into Money, and then there was no coming at it; the Time also having been laps'd by his Honour, having been gone to the Fair.

ANOTHER Person applying in another and more material Affair, was treated with Respect by Mr. *Wild,* and a Pot of Tea brought out in Form: (N.B. The Crown being first deposited as usual) The Case related to a Gold Watch, with Trinkits and some Diamonds about either the Watch, and the Lady offer'd very considerably, for the restoring it, as I remember, 30 *l.* but no Advertisements had been publish'd. Mr. *Wild,* after the usual Enquiries of when it was lost? and where? And being told it was at St. *Ann's* Church, *Westminster,* pauses a while, and calls up a Servant, and asks aloud, where was M[o]ll K[in]g last *Sunday?* About *Westminster,* says the Man, but the Bi[tc]h would not tell where. Was she Crank? says Mr. *Wild.* I don't know, says the Fellow. However, turning to the Lady, says he, Madam, I fancy I shall be able to serve you, and perhaps for less Money than your Ladyship speaks off, If it be M[o]ll K[in]g, that Woman, I have in my Thoughts, as I believe 'tis, for she is a dextrous Jade at the Work, I'll have her safe before Morning. The Lady full of Compassion returns, O Sir! don't take her up; I assure you I won't prosecute, I'll rather lose my Watch, than have any poor Wretch Hang'd for it.

Why? Madam, says Mr. *Wild,* We can't talk with her, but by Threatning: We must not make a Bargain with her, that would be to compound a Felony. If I can perswade her to come and bring your Watch, and ask your Pardon, will that satisfy you. Nay, says the Lady, I don't know whether that would be safe, neither: If she will send it me, I had rather; and I'll forgive her, without asking Pardon. Well, Madam, will you take it, and give the *Porter* that brings it 20 Guineas, if you please, but not to oblige you to it. Whatever you say, Mr. *Wild,* says the Lady.

Well, Madam, says Mr. *Wild,* if I may have the Honour to see your Ladyship again.

Lady. Will it not do if I send any Body?

Wild. Why, truly, no Madam: People that deal in these Things, do not care for Witnesses.

Lady. Well, well, that's true: I'll come my self. What Day would you have me come?

Wild. On *Thursday*, Madam.

Lady. Well, Mr. *Wild*, what must I do? What will satisfy you for your Trouble?

Wild. It is time enough, Madam, to speak of that when I am sure I can do you any Service. These Creatures are very loose, and I can't tell you how it may be.

Well, Mr. *Wild*, I'll come furnish'd to pay my Respects to you.

Wild. Madam, Your most obedient Servant.

[*Waits on her to her Coach.*]

Accordingly, *Thursday* coming, the Lady appears. Mr. *Wild*, in his Callimancoe[8] Night-gown, (*the same he was hang'd in*) receives her; and with a pleasant Look, tells her, he is very glad, to be able to say, that he believes he shall serve her. That it was the same Woman he suspected, and that the Jade had already pawn'd the Watch for some Money, but that it was but a little, and he was glad she had.

Lady. Why? Mr. *Wild*.

Wild. Because, Madam, if she had kept it all this while, it would have been ten to one but she had Broke something about it, or done it some Mischief.

Lady. That's true, indeed. Pray what has she Pawn'd it for?

Wild. Not much, Madam, she has got but seven Guineas upon it yet.

Lady. Well, Mr. *Wild*, what must be done?

Wild. Why, Madam, If the People, that have it, bring it safe and sound to your Ladyship, will you give me your Honour that you will ask no Questions, or stop the Person that comes with it?

Lady. I promise you, on my Word, I will not.

Wild. The Man that brings it may be a poor Innocent Fellow, that knows nothing of it.

Lady. Well, well, he shall have no Harm or Interruption from me.

Wild. Then I believe your Ladyship may hear something of it to Night.

Lady. And what must I give him?

Wild. I don't yet know, Madam, but I'll bring them as low as I can. Not above 20 Guineas, to be sure, Madam.

Lady. That is very kind, indeed. Well, Mr. *Wild*, then I'll make it up to you. [*So the Lady Pulls out her Purse in order to give him some Money.*] [9]

Wild. No, Madam, not a Farthing. Besides you have not got your Watch yet: Pray stay till you see whether the Jade will Perform; tho' I think, indeed, I am pretty sure of her.

Lady. Well, I'll take your Word, Mr. *Wild*. [*Offers him Money again.*]

Wild. By no Means, Madam; let me see if I can serve you.

Lady. Well, Mr. *Wild*, if it must be so, I must come again then.

Wild. It may be not. Will your Ladyship be pleas'd to stay about half an Hour.

Lady. Ay, with all my Heart.

In about half an Hour, *Jonathan* having been call'd hastily out, comes in again immediately. Madam, says he, if your Ladyship pleases to go into your Coach, and drive gently up . . . . . *Street*, perhaps a Messenger may desire to speak with you as you go along.

Very well, Mr. *Wild*, I understand you.

Upon the Lady's going along . . . . . *Street*, a *Ticket-Porter*, with his Hat in his Hand, shows himself by the Coach-side, and the Lady taking the Hint, stops her Coach, and lets down the Glass, and speaking to the Fellow, says, Would you speak with me Friend?

The Fellow says not a Word, but delivers into her Hand

the Watch with all the Trinkits and Diamonds perfectly safe; and when she had look'd upon it a little, gives her a Note, wherein was written nothing but thus in Words at length,
        Eighteen Guineas.

THE Lady immediately tells out the Money to the *Porter*, and he was going away: Hold! Honest Friend, says the Lady, there's somewhat for your self; and gives him half a Guinea, and so dismiss'd him.

A Day or two after she makes Mr. *Wild* a Visit, and presents him with 15 Guineas more: But with great Difficulty made him accept of it; telling her it was a great deal to much; that he would not take it by any means, but at last accepts it, with the Ceremony of saying, he would not take it on account of the Watch, but for having been at some Trouble in serving her Ladyship, in which she was pleas'd to Reward him much more than he deserv'd; when at the same time 'twas very likely [he] had part of the 18 Guineas too from *M[o]ll K[in]g*, who he frighted out of the Watch with threatning to have her put into *Newgate* for stealing of it.

THIS may serve for a Sketch of *Practice*, as I call it; and to let the World see in what manner this Secret Service was carryed on; how the Thieving Trade was managed, how the People were gull'd out of their Money, and how a Crew of Hell-born Rogues and Whores, which is much the same, have been bred up to the Trade by their grand Patron and Master of Art, *Jonathan Wild*. It would be endless to give a particular of the many Tricks and Cheats of this Kind that he has manag'd, during a continued Life of Wickedness, for about 16 Years, among which it would be very Instructing, to give an account of the numbers of poor wretched Creatures, like himself; who he having first led them on in the Road of Crime for several Years, as long as they would be subservient to him, and put all their Purchase into his Hands, abandon'd as soon as they offer'd to set up for themselves, and leaving them to the mercy of the Government, made himself the Instrument of their Destruction, and then pleaded the Merit of it to the Publick. But these require a long History, rather than a Pamphlet, and therefore I wholly omit them.

IT is time now to enter into a particular Account of the conclusion of this Life of Crime, it has been a kind of Comedy, or a Farce rather all a long, but it prov'd a Tragedy at last; and *Jonathan* being brought to Justice, has summ'd up his Account here in a most ignominious End, satisfyed how in a manner not uncommon only, but such as History can not give one Instance of the like, except lately, that of a Murther at St. *Edmunds-Bury* in *Suffolk*.

THE Sum of the matter is this, *Jonathan* had long been so Notorious, and his Practice tho' not within the Compass of the Law, was yet in its Nature so Criminal in itself, and *above all*, was so dangerous in its Example, that the Publick began to be justly Alarm'd at it, and to consider of proper Measures for putting a stop to it, which purpose an Act of Parliament, (the only Remedy for growing Evils of this kind) was pass'd the last Session to make it Felony, to take or receive any Reward for the restoring of any stolen Goods, knowing them to be Stolen: The Clause in the said Act is as follows.

"AND whereas there are several Persons who have secret Acquaintance with Felons, and who make it their Business to help Persons to their stol'n Goods, and by that means gain Money from them, which is divided between them and the Felons, whereby they greatly encourage such Offenders: Be it Enacted by the Authority aforesaid, That where ever any Person taketh Money or Reward, directly or indirectly, under pretence or upon Account of helping any Person or Persons to any stol'n Goods or Chattels, every such Person so taking Money or Reward as aforesaid (unless such Person do apprehend, or cause to be apprehended, such Felon who stole the same, and cause such Felon to be brought to his Tryal for the same, and give Evidence against him) shall be Guilty of Felony, and suffer the Pains and Penalties of Felony, according to the Nature of the Felony committed in stealing such Goods and Chattels, in the Manner and with such Circumstances as the same were stol'n."

THIS Act was so directly aim'd at *Jonathan's* general Practice, that he could not be Ignorant enough not to see it; but least he should, a certain Honourable Person, too just to favour him, and yet too human not to warn him of his Danger that he might avoid it; gave him Notice that this very Act was made against his unlawful Practice, and therefore in time warn'd him, in few, but significant Words, to take heed to himself and avoid the Consequences by leaving off the Trade of Thief-Catching, as it is unjustly call'd, that is, of compounding for the return of stol'n Goods.

BUT good Advice to *Jonathan Wild,* was like talking *Gospel* to a kettle Drum, bidding a Dragoon not Plunder, or talking of Compassion to a *Hussar;* he that was hardened above the Baseness of all cautionary Fear, scorn'd the Advice, and went on in his wicked Trade; not warily and wisely as he had formerly done, but in short, with more Impudence and shameless Boldness than ever, for as if he despis'd Laws, and the Governours, and the provok'd Justice of the Nation: He now not only took Rewards for returning Goods stolen, but even directed the Stealing of them, and making himself a Party to the very Robberies themselves; acted a Part of the Thief, and the Receiver also; and this in so many Cases, that we are told if the Indictment had fail'd for which he was justly Condemn'd, there were several others ready to have been brought on, and the Witnesses ready to have been produc'd for Proof of the Facts.

BUT one Felony being fully prov'd was sufficient; and upon a full Hearing he was Convicted in so evident a Manner, that he really had nothing to say in his own Behalf, not being able to deny the Fact; his Council would have pleaded, that the Offence was not within the late Statute upon which he was Indicted; but the Court answer'd them fully, and over ruled

the Plea; so that being fully proved by several Witnesses, he
receiv'd Sentence of Death the 15th of *May* last.

THE Circumstances of this Fact seem to be so agreeable
to the whole tenor of *Jonathan*'s former Practice, and so like
other Parts of his Life, that we can not but observe the Paralel,
and conclude the particular Accounts of other parts of his
Life to be true likewise.

IT has been said of him, that if ever he was mov'd to promote any Man, or to help any Man to Business, which he often
pretended to do in Compassion to their Poverty, that still he
did it always in his own way, that is to say, endeavour'd to
make Thieves of them, to bring them to be Hang'd, to keep
them from Misery, and to make *Newgate* Birds of them, to
keep them out of the *Compters;* this he practis'd principally
upon young Creatures, and little destitute Children, such as
seem'd to be left to wander about in Want and Beggery; and
many a poor Boy he has pick'd up in the Street pretending
Charity, and a willingness to do them good, which when it
has come to the Issue, has been no more or less than to breed
them up to Thieving, and ripen them for the *Devil.*

BUT which is still worse than all the rest, I have several
Stories by me at this Time, which I have particular Reasons
to believe are true, of Children thus strolling about the Streets
in Misery and Poverty, whom he has taken in on pretence of
providing for them, and employing them; and all has ended
in this (*viz.*) making Rogues of them.[10] *Horrid Wickedness!*
his Charity has been to breed them up to be Thieves, and
still more Horrid! several of these his own *forster Children,*
he has himself caused afterwards to be apprehended and
Hang'd for the very Crimes which he first taught them how to
Commit.

I AM not indeed to make a jest of these things, there is
something shocking and dismal in the very Relation, and
therefore it is, that this Account of the Life of *Jonathan Wild,*
which in its Nature, is all a Tragedy, is not related with an air

of Banter and Ridicule as Others are; 'tis hoped it will not be the less acceptable to Men of Sense; it is a solemn and terrible thing to look back on a Life of such harden'd, abominable Practices; to see it carried on in defiance, either of God or Devil; and that with such Success too, passing for so many Years unpunish'd; and tho' there are some things in the long Series of his wicked Life, which may relish with the Levity of a drol-way of Writing; yet to see a Man turn'd into an incarnate Devil, his Life a Scene of intimitable Crimes; his very Society a Hell, and equally devouring both to Soul and Body; he that can read it without some Horror, must have very little of what we call Christianity about him.

TO see him take up an unthinking Youth in the Street cover'd with Dirt and Rags, and willing on any Terms to get out of his Misery; to see this superlative Wretch pretend Charity to the Child, and tell him he will provide for him, and thereby engage the Lad to him, as to a Gentleman that intends to do him good; and then instead of providing for him, lead him by the Hand to Hell-gates, and after that, like a true Devil, thrust him in! First to tempt, and then accuse, which is the very nature of the Devil; first to make poor desolate vagabond Boys, Thieves, and then betray them to the Gallows! Who can think of such a thing without a just Abhorrence, who can think it to be any less than the worst sort of Murther; such was the Life, and such the Practice of this wretched Man, and in these very last Scenes of his Life, he grew so audacious, that it seem'd as if he was really ripening up a pace for his own Destruction.

IT is said of him in the Case of that harden'd Felow *Blueskin,* that he should say, *Jonathan* first made him a Thief, and then abandoning him, left him to carry it on by himself; and it being necessary to his (*Jonathan's*) Fame to have always some Chase in his view, to build his own Merit upon, with the Government; he kept a Watch upon him, that he might at last bring him to the Gallows, for which the said *Blueskin* was very near giving him a pass into another World, by that desperate Attempt to cut his Throat in the face of a Court of

Justice; which *Jonathan* tho' surpriz'd at then, as had leisure since to wish, had been effectually done at that time, and said so publickly in the *Press-Yard*, two days before his Tryal.[11]

BUT to come then to the particular Fact for which he Suffer'd, the Story as it was related upon Oath at his Tryal, and the several Circumstances belonging to it stands thus,

Katherine Stetham deposed: That on the 22d, of *January*, between Three and Four in the Afternoon a Man and Woman came into her Shop, under Pretence of buying some Lace: They were *said she* so very difficult, that I had none below that would please them; and so, leaving my Daughter in the Shop, I stept up Stairs, and brought down another Box. We could not agree about the Price, and so they went away together; and in about half an Hour after I miss'd a Tin Box of Lace, that I valu'd at 50 *l.* The same Night, and the next, I went to *Jonathan Wilde*'s House; but not meeting with him, I advertised the Lace that I had lost, with a Reward of 15 Guineas, and no Questions ask'd. But hearing nothing of it, I went to *Jonathan*'s House again, and then met with him: He desir'd me to give him a Description of the Persons that I suspected, which I did as near as I could; and then he told me that he'd make Enquiry, and bade me call again in two or three days. I did so; and then he said, that he had heard something of my Lace, and expected to know more of the Matter in a little time. I came to him again on that day that he was apprehended, (I think 'twas the 15th of *February*.) I told him, that tho' I had advertised but 15 Guineas Reward, yet I'd give 20 or 25 rather than not have my Goods. *Don't be in such a Hurry,* says he, *I don't know but I may help you to it for less; and if I can, I will. The Persons that have it, are gone out of Town, I shall set them to quarrelling about it, and then I shall get it the cheaper.* On the 10th of *March*, he sent me word, that if I would come to him in *Newgate*, and bring 10 Guineas in my Pocket, he could help me to the Lace. I went: He desired me to call a *Porter;* but I not knowing where to find one, he sent a Person who brought one that appeared to be a *Ticket-Porter*. The Prisoner gave me a Letter, which he said was sent him as a Direction where to go for the Lace; but I could not read, and so I deliver'd it to the *Porter*. Then he desired me to give the *Porter* the 10 Guineas, or else (he said) the Persons that had the Lace would not deliver it. I gave the *Porter* the Money; he went away, and in a little time return'd, and brought me a Box that was seal'd up, but not the same that was lost. I open'd it, and found all my Lace but one Piece. *Now, Mr.* Wilde, (says I) *What must you have for your Trouble? Not a Farthing,* (says he) *not a Farthing for me. I don't do these things for wordly Interest, but only for the Good of poor People that have met with Misfortunes. As for the Piece of Lace that is missing, I hope to get it for you e'er be long; and I don't know but that I may help you not only to your Money again, but to the Thief too; and if I can, much good may't do you. And as you're a good Woman and a Widow, and a Christian, I desire nothing of you but your Prayers, and for them I shall be thankful. I have a great many Enemies, and God knows what may be the Consequence of this Imprisonment.*

THIS is a black Story indeed, and it was very remarkable, that the Fact was really committed, that is to say, the Felony was contracted, or that Part which the late Act in particular reach'd (*viz.*) the delivering the Goods, and taking the Money for discovering them; all this Part was acted I say after his being committed to *Newgate*.

IT was likewise very remarkable, that there was another Case much of the same Nature, which lay ready to have been brought to a Hearing if this had not intervened, namely; of a Pocket-Book stolen from Mr. *Tidman,* a *Corn Chandler,* in *Gilt-spur street,* near *Newgate,* in which was a Bank Bill for 116 *l.* in which the Witnesses were two Persons who had pleaded to their Pardons.

WE come now to his Behaviour after his Condemnation, and at the Place of Execution, at which last Place he indeed scarce said a Word to God or Man, being either doz'd with the liquid *Laudanum* which he had taken, or demented and confus'd by the horror of what was before him, and the reflection of what was within him.

NOR even before he took the Dose of *Laudanum* was he in any suitable manner sensible of his Condition, or concern'd about it, very little sign appear'd of his having the least Hope concerning his future State; but as he liv'd harden'd, he seem'd to die stupid.

HE declin'd coming to the Chapel, either to the Sermon or Prayers, pleading his lameness by the Gout, but chiefly the Crowds and Disorders of the People discomposing or disordering him. In the condemn'd Hold, or Place where Malefactors are kept after their Sentence, they had Prayers as usual, and he seem'd to join with them in a kind of Form, but little or nothing of the Penitence of a Criminal, in view of Death, appear'd upon him.

HIS principal Enquiries seem'd to be about what kind of State was to be expected after Death, and how the invisible World was to be describ'd; but nothing of the most certain Judgment which is there to be expected, righteous and terrible, according to the Deeds done in the Body, or of a Saviour to whom we have recourse, as the Slayer in the old Law had to the City of Refuge, to save him from the avenger of Blood.

AS his Time shorten'd he seem'd more and more confus'd, and then began to entertain Discourses of the Lawfulness of dismissing ourselves out of the present Misery, after the Example of the antient *Romans,* which as he said was then esteem'd as an act of Bravery and Gallantry, and recorded to their Honour.

THIS kind of Discourse was indeed sufficient to have caused the Keepers to have had an Eye to him, so as to prevent any Violence he might offer to himself, and they did watch him as narrowly as they could; however he so far deceived them, as that the Day before his Execution he found means to have a small Bottle with liquid *Laudanum* convey'd to him unseen, of which he took so large a Quantity, that it was soon perceiv'd by the Change it made upon him, for he was so drousie that he could not hold up his Head, or keep open his Eyes, at the time of reading the Prayers.

UPON this two of his Fellow Prisoners endeavour'd to rouse him (not suspecting that he had taken enough to hurt him) and taking him by the Hands, they perswaded him to stand up, and walk a little about the Room, which he could not do without help because of his Gout.

THIS walking, tho' it did a little waken him, had several other Operations at the same time; for first it chang'd his Countenance, turning it to be exceeding pale, then it put him into a violent Sweat, which made them apprehend he would faint, upon which they offered to give him something to keep up his Spirits, but he refus'd it, telling them he was very sick; soon after which he vomited very violently, and this in all probability prolong'd his Life for the Execution; for by their stirring him, and making him vomit, he brought up the greatest Part of the *Laudanum* which he had taken, before it had been long enough in his Stomach to mix with the animal Spirits or Blood, which of it had done but one Hour more, he would certainly have taken his last sleep in the Prison.

BUT Nature having thus discharg'd itself of the load, he reviv'd again, and tho' still doz'd and insensible of what he said or did, yet he was able to walk about, speak, and act sufficiently for the Part that remain'd to him, namely, for the last scene of his Life at the Gallows.

ACCORDINGLY On *Monday* the 24th of *May,* he was convey'd in a Cart to *Tyburn,* and tho' it was apparent he was still under the Operation of the *Laudanum,* and that which was left in his Stomach had so far seiz'd upon his Spirits as to make him almost stupid, yet it began to go off, and Nature getting the Mastery of it, he began to be more sensible of what he was going about; but the Scene was then short, and he had little to do but to stand up in the Cart, and, the needful Apparatus being made, be turn'd off with the rest, which was done about 3 a-Clock in the Afternoon.

THE Rudeness of the Mob to him, both at his first going into the Cart, and all the way from thence to the Place of Execution, is not to be express'd, and shews how notorious his Life had been, and what Impression his known Villanies had made on the Minds of the People; for, contrary to the general Behaviour of the Street in such Cases, instead of compassionate Expressions, and a general Cast of Pity, which ordinarily fits on the Countenances of the People, when they see the miserable Objects of Justice go to their Execution; here was nothing to be heard but Cursings and Execrations; abhorring the Crimes and the very Name of the Man, throwing Stones and Dirt at him all the way, and even at the Place of Execution; the other Malefactors being all ready to be turn'd off, but the Hangman giving him leave to take his own Time, and he continuing setting down in the Cart, the Mob impatient, and fearing a Reprieve, tho' they had no occasion for it, call'd furiously upon the Hangman to dispatch him, and at last threatened to tear him to pieces, if he did not tye him up immediately.

IN short there was a kind of an universal Rage against him, which nothing but his Death could satisfie or put an end to, and if a Reprieve had come, it would have, twas thought, been difficult for the Officers to have brought him back again without his receiving some Mischief, if not his Deaths Wound from the Rabble.

SO detestable had he made himself by his notorious Crimes, and to such a height were his wicked Practices come.

THUS ended the Tragedy, and thus was a Life of horrid and inimitable Wickedness finish'd at the Gallows, the very same Place where, according to some, above 120 miserable Creatures had been hang'd, whose Blood in great measure may be said to lye at his Door, either in their being first brought into the thieving Trade, or led on in it by his Encouragement and Assistance; and many of them at last betray'd and brought to Justice by his Means; upon which worst sort of Murther he valued himself, and would have had it prais'd for Merit, even with the Government itself.

Augusta Triumphans:

OR, THE
W A Y
TO MAKE
L O N D O N
The most flourishing
CITY in the Universe.

FIRST,

By establishing an University where Gentlemen may have Academical Education under the Eye of their Friends.

II. To prevent much Murder, &c. by an Hospital for Foundlings.

III. By suppressing pretended Mad-Houses, where many of the fair Sex are unjustly confin'd, while their Husbands keep Mistresses, &c. and many Widows are lock'd up for the Sake of their Jointure.

IV. To save our Youth from Destruction, by clearing the Streets of impudent Strumpets, Suppressing Gaming-Tables, and Sunday Debauches.

V. To avoid the expensive Importation of Foreign Musicians, by forming an Academy of our own.

VI. To save our lower Class of People from utter Ruin, and render them useful, by preventing the immoderate Use of Geneva: With a frank Explosion of many other common Abuses, and incontestable Rules for Amendment.

CONCLUDING WITH
An effectual Method to prevent STREET ROBBERIES;

AND
A LETTER to Coll. *ROBINSON*, on account of the ORPHAN's TAX.

LONDON:
Printed for *J. Roberts* in *Warwick-Lane*, and Sold by *E. Nutt* at the *Royal-Exchange*, *A. Dodd* without *Temple-Bar*, *N. Blandford* at *Charing-Cross*, and *J. Stagg* in *Westminster-Hall*. 1728.   [Price One Shilling.]

AUGUSTA TRIUMPHANS:

Or the
WAY

To Make
LONDON

The most flourishing
CITY in the UNIVERSE.
FIRST,

By establishing an University where Gentlemen may have Academical Education under the Eye of their Friends.

II. To prevent much Murder, &c. by an Hospital for Foundlings.

III. By suppressing pretended Mad-Houses, where many of the fair Sex are unjustly confin'd, while their Husbands keep Mistresses, &c. and many Widows are lock'd up for the Sake of their Jointure.

IV. To save our Youth from Destruction, by clearing the Streets of impudent Strumpets, Suppressing Gaming-Tables, and Sunday Debauches.

V. To avoid the expensive Importation of Foreign Musicians, by forming an Academy of our own.

VI. To save our lower Class of People from utter Ruin, and render them useful, by preventing the immoderate Use of Geneva: With a frank Explosion of many other common Abuses, and incontestable Rules for Amendment.

CONCLUDING WITH
An effectual Method to prevent STREET ROBBERIES;
AND

A LETTER to Coll. ROBINSON, on account of the ORPHAN'S TAX.

LONDON:

Printed for J. Roberts *in* Warwick-Lane, *and Sold by* E. Nutt *at the* Royal-Exchange, A. Dodd *without* Temple-Bar, N. Blandford *at* Charing-Cross, *and* J. Stagg *in* Westminster-Hall. *1728.*
[*Price One Shilling.*]

Projecting all his life, Defoe published AUGUSTA TRI-UMPHANS on 16 March 1728. The selections are taken from pages 3–8, 16–23, and 58 of the first edition.

A Man who has the Publick Good in View, ought not in the least to be alarm'd at the tribute of Ridicule which Scoffers constantly pay to projecting Heads: It is the Business of a Writer, who means well, to go directly forward, without regard to Criticism, but to offer his Thoughts as they occur; and if in twenty Schemes, he hits but on one to the Purpose, he ought to be excused failing in the Nineteen for the Twentieth Sake. 'Tis a kind of good Action to mean well, and the Intention ought to palliate the Failure; but the *English*, of all People in the World, show least Mercy to Schemists, for they treat them in the vilest manner; whereas other Nations give them fair Play for their Lives, which is the reason why we are esteem'd so bad at Invention.

I have but a short Time to live, nor would I waste my remaining Thread of Life in Vain, but having often lamented sundry Publick Abuses, and many Schemes having occur'd to my Fancy, which to me carried an Air of Benefit; I was resolv'd to commit them to Paper before my Departure, and leave, at least, a Testimony of my good Will to my Fellow Creatures.

But of all my Reflections, none was more constantly my Companion than a deep Sorrow for the present decay of Learning among us, and the manifest Corruption of Education; we have been a brave and learned People, and are insensibly dwindling into an Effeminate, Superficial Race: Our young Gentlemen are sent to the Universities 'tis true, but not under Restraint or Correction as formerly; not to study, but to drink; not for Furniture for the Head, but a Feather for the Cap, merely to say they have been at *Oxford* or *Cambridge,* as if the Air of those Places inspir'd Knowledge without Application. 'Tis true, we ought to have those Places in Reverence for the many learned Men they have sent us; but why must we go so far for Knowledge? why should a young Gentleman be sent raw from the Nursery to live on his own Hands; to be liable to a thousand Temptations, and run the Risque of being snapt up by sharping Jilts, with which both Universities abound, who make our Youth of Fortune their Prey, and have brought Misery into too many good Families? Not only the Hazard of their Healths from Debauches of both Kinds, but the waste of their precious Time renders the sending them so for off very hazardous. Why should such a Metropolis as *London* be without an University? [1] Would it not save considerably the Expence we are at in sending our young Gentlemen so far from *London?* Would it not add to the Lustre of our State, and cultivate Politeness among us? What Benefits may we not in time expect from so glorious a Design? Will not *London* become the Scene of Science? And what reason have we but to hope we may vye with any Neighbouring Nations? Not that I would have *Oxford* or *Cambridge* neglected, for the Good they have done: Besides, there are too many fine Endowments to be sunk, we may have Universities at those Places, and at *London* too, without Prejudice. Knowledge will never hurt us, and whoever lives to see an University here, will find it give quite another turn to the Genius and Spirit of our Youth in general.

How many Gentlemen pass their Lives in a shameful Indolence, who might employ themselves to the purpose, were such a Design set on foot? Learning would flourish, Art revive, and not only those who study'd would benefit by it; but the Blessing would be convey'd to others by Conversation.

And in order to this so laudable design, small Expence is required: The sole Charge being the hire of a convenient Hall or House, which if they please, they may call a College. But I see no necessity the Pupils have to lye or diet there; that may be done more reasonably and conveniently at home, under the Eye of their Friends: Their only necessary Business at College being to attend their Tutors at stated Hours, and (Bed and Board excepted) to conform themselves to College Laws, and perform the same Exercises as if they were actually at *Oxford* or *Cambridge*.

Let the best of Tutors be provided, and Professors in all Faculties encourag'd, this will do a double good, not only to the Instructed, but to the Instructors. What a fine Provision may here be made for Numbers of ingenious Gentlemen, now unpreferr'd? And to what a heighth may even a small Beginning grow in time?

As *London* is so extensive, so its University may be compos'd of many Colleges, quarter'd at convenient Distances; for Example, one at *Westminster*, one at St. *James's*, one near *Ormond Street;* (that part of the Town abounding in Gentry) one in the Centre of the Inns of Court; another near the *Royal-Exchange;* and more if Occasion and Encouragement permit.

The same Offices and Regulations may be constituted, Cooks, Butlers, Bed-makers, *&c.* excepted, as at other Universities. As for Endowment, there is no need, the whole may be done by Subscription; and that an easy one; considering nothing but Instructions are paid for.

In a Word, an Academical Education is so much wanted in *London,* that every Body of Ability and Figure, will readily come into it; and I dare engage the Place need but be chosen, and Tutors approved of, to compleat the Design at once.

It may be objected that there is a kind of University at *Gresham-College,*[2] where Professors in all Sciences are maintained and obliged to read Lectures every Day, or at least as often as demanded. The Design is most laudable, but it smells too much of the *Sine Cure;*[3] they only read in Term-Time, and then their Lectures are so hurried over, the Audience is little the better. They cannot be turn'd out; 'tis a good Settlement for Life, and they are very easy in their Studies when once fix'd. Whereas were the Professorship, during good Behaviour, there would be a Study to maintain their Posts, and their Pupils would reap the Benefit.

Upon second Thought, I think Colleges for University Education might be formed at *Westminster, Eaton,* the *Charter-House,* St. *Pauls, Merchant-Taylors,* and other publick Schools, where Youth might begin and end their Studies; but this may be farther consider'd of.

I had almost forgot the most material Point, which is, that his Majesty's Sanction must first be obtain'd, and the University propos'd have Power to confer Degrees, *&c.* and other Academical Priviledges.

As I am quick to conceive, I am eager to have done, unwilling to overwork a Subject; I had rather leave part to the Conception of the Readers, than to tire them or my Self with protracting a Theme; as if like a Chancery Man, or a Hackney Author, I wrote by the Sheet for hire . . . .

OMISSIONS

IN my Scheme for an University in *London,* I proposed only a Hall or publick Room; on Recollection I find it should be a large House or Inn, in the Nature of a College, with store of

convenient Rooms for Gentlemen, not only to study separately,
but wherein to lodge their Books, for 'twould be most inconvenient to lug them backwards and forwards: They may indeed Breakfast, Sup, and Sleep at Home, but 'twill be highly
necessary they should dine in Commons, or at least near the
College; not that I would have Cooks, Butlers, Caterers, Man-
ciples, and the whole Train of College Cannibals retain'd; but
for fear they should stay too long at Home, or be hindred
from returning to Study in due time, some proper Place or
Person might be pitch'd upon to keep an Ordinary at a prefix'd
Price and Hour, and for the Students only.

My Reasons are these:

First, a young Gentleman may live too far from College.

Second, the College Hours for Dinner, may not agree with
those of the Family.

Third, Company may drop in and detain him.

These being, I think, the only material Objections could be
offered, I hope I have amply provided against them, and ren-
dered my Project more perfect and unexceptionable.

A *Proposal to prevent the expensive Importation of* Foreign Musicians, *&c. by forming an Academy of our own.*

IT will no doubt be asked, what have I to do with Musick?
to which I answer, I have been a Lover of the Science from
my Infancy, and in my younger Days was accounted no despi-
cable Performer on the Viol and Lute, then much in Vogue. I
esteem it the most innocent Amusement in Life; it gently
relaxes, after too great a hurry of Spirits, and composes the
Mind into a Sedateness, prone to every thing that's generous
and good; and when the more necessary parts of Education
are finish'd, 'tis a most genteel and commendable Accomplish-
ment; it saves a great deal of Drinking and Debauchery in our
Sex, and helps the Ladies off with many an idle Hour, which
sometimes might probably be worse employ'd otherwise.

Our Quality, Gentry, and better sort of Traders must have

Diversions; and if those that are commendable be denied, they will take to worse: Now what can be more commendable than Musick, one of the seven liberal Sciences, and no mean Branch of the Mathematicks?

Were it for no other Reason I should esteem it, because it was the favourite Diversion of his late Majesty,[4] of glorious Memory; who was as wise a Prince as ever fill'd the *British* Throne. Nor is it less esteem'd by their present Majesties, whose Souls are form'd for Harmony, and who have not disdain'd to make it a part in the Education of their sacred Race.

Our Nobility and Gentry have shown their Love to the Science, by supporting at such prodigious Expence, the *Italian Opera*[5] improperly call'd an Academy; but they have at the same time shown no small Partiality in discouraging any thing *English*, and over-loading the Town with such heaps of Foreign *Musicians*.

An Academy, rightly understood, is a Place for the Propagation of Science, by training up Persons thereto from younger to riper Years, under the Instruction and Inspection of proper Artists: How then can the *Italian Opera* properly be call'd an Academy, when none are admitted but such as are, at least are thought, or ought to be, adepts in Musick? If that be an Academy, so are the Theatres of *Drury-Lane,* and *Lincolns-Inn-Fields:* Nay, *Punch's Opera*[6] may pass for a lower kind of Academy. Would it not be a glorious thing to have an *Opera* of our own, in our own most noble Tongue, in which the Composer, Singers, and Orchestra, should be of our own Growth? Not that we ought to disclaim all Obligations to *Italy,* the Mother of Musick, the Nurse of *Corelli, Handel, Bononcini,* and *Geminiani;*[7] but then we ought not to be so stupidly partial, to imagine our Selves too Brutal a part of Mankind, to make any Progress in the Science: By the same reason that we love it, we may excel in it; Love begets Application, and Application Perfection. We have already had a *Purcel,*[8] and no doubt, there are now many latent Genius's, who only want proper Instruction, Application, and ENCOURAGEMENT, to become great Ornaments of the Science, and make *England* emulate even *Rome* it self.

What a number of excellent Performers on all Instruments, have sprung up in *England* within these few Years? that this is owing to the *Opera*, I will not deny, and so far the *Opera* is an Academy, as it refines the Taste, and inspires Emulation.

But tho' we are happy in Instrumental Performers, we frequently send to *Italy* for Singers, and that at no small Expence: To remedy which, I humbly propose, that the Governours of *Christ's-Hospital* [9] will show their publick Spirit, by forming an Academy of Musick on their Foundation, after this or the like manner.

That out of their great number of Children, thirty Boys be selected, of good Ears and Propensity to Musick.

That these Boys be divided into three Classes, *viz.* Six for Wind-Instruments, such as the Hautboy, Bassoon, and German-Flute.

That sixteen others be selected for String-Instruments, or at least the most useful, *viz.* the Violin and Bass-Violin.

That the remaining eight be particularly chosen for Voice, and Organ, or Harpsicord. That all in due time, be taught Composition. The Boys thus chosen, three Masters should be elected, each most excellent in his Way; that is to say, one for the Wind-Instrument, another for the String'd, and a third for the Voice and Organ, &c.

Handsome Salaries should be allowed these Masters, to engage their constant Attendance every Day, from eight till twelve in the Morning; and I think a 100 *l. per Annum* for each, would be sufficient, which will be a Trifle to so wealthy a Body. The multiplicity of Holidays should be abridg'd, and only a few kept; there cannot be too few, considering what a hinderance they are to juvenile Studies. It is a vulgar Error that has too long prevail'd all over *England*, to the great Detriment of Learning, and many Boys have been made Blockheads, in Complaisance to Kings and Saints, dead for many Ages past.

The Morning employ'd in Musick, the Boys should go in

the Afternoon, or so many Hours, to the Reading and Writing-School, and in the Evening should practice, at least two Hours before Bed-time, and two before the Master comes in the Morning. This Course held for seven or eight Years, will make them fine Proficients; but that they should not go too raw, or young, out of the Academy, 'tis proper, that at the stated Age of Apprenticeship, they be bound to the Hospital to engage their greater Application, and make them thorough Masters, before they launch out into the World; for one great hinderance to many Performers is, that they begin to teach too soon, and obstruct their Genius.

What will not such a Design produce in a few Years? will they not be able to perform a Consort, Choir, or Opera, or all three among themselves, and over-pay the Charge, as shall hereafter be specify'd?

For Example, we will suppose such a Design to be continued for ten Years, we shall find an Orchestre of forty Hands, and a Choir or Opera of twenty Voices, or admitting that of those twenty, only five prove Capital Singers, 'twill answer the Intent.

For the greater Variety they may, if they think fit, take in two or more of their Girls where they find a promising Genius, but this may be further consider'd of.

Now, when they are enabled to exhibit an Opera, Will they not gain considerably, when their Voices and Hands, cost them only a College Subsistance? And 'tis but reasonable the Profits accruing from Operas, Consorts, or otherwise, should go to the *Hospital* to make good all former and future Expences, and enable them to extend the Design to a greater Length and Grandeur; so that instead of 1500 *l. per Ann.* the price of one *Italian* Singer, we shall for 300 *l.* once in ten Years, have sixty *English* Musicians regularly educated, and enabled to live by their Science.

There ought moreover to be annual Probations, and proper Prizes or Premiums alloted, to excite Emulation in the Youths, and give Life to their Studies.

They have already a Musick-School, as they call it, but the Allowance is too poor for this Design, and the Attendance too small; it must be every Day, or not at all.

This will be an Academy indeed, and in Process of Time, they will have even their Masters among themselves; and what is the Charge, compar'd with the Profits or their Abilities?

One thing I had like to have forgot, which is, that with Permission of the Right Reverend the Lords Spiritual, some Performance in Musick, suitable to the Solemnity of the Day, be exhibited every Sunday after Divine Service: Sacred Poesy and Rhetorick, may be likewise introduc'd to make it an Entertainment suitable to a Christian and Polite Audience; and indeed, we seem to want some such commendable Employment for the better Sort: For we see the publick Walks and Taverns crowded, and rather than be idle, they will go to *Newport-Market*.[10]

That such an Entertainment would be much preferable to Drinking, Gaming, or profane Discourse, none can deny, and till it is proved to be prejudicial, I shall always imagine it necessary. The Hall at the *Hospital*, will contain few less than seven hundred People, conveniently seated, which at so small a Price as one Shilling *per* Head, will amount to 35 l. per Week; and if the Performance deserve it, as no doubt it will in time, they may make it half a Crown or more, which must considerably encrease the Income of the *Hospital*.

When they are able to make an Opera, the Profits will be yet more considerable, nor will they reap much less from what the Youths bring in during their Apprenticeship, when employ'd at Consorts, Theatres, or other publick Entertainments. . . .

NOTES

AN ESSAY UPON PROJECTS

[1] See *Genesis*, 4:21–22.

[2] Sir Edward Ford (1605–1670) built many waterworks in London. By 1685 one could buy either Dr. Denis Papin's new water engine or "a Fire Engine with one Pair of Handles" designed by Sir S. Morland for "Twenty three pound." Prince Rupert's (1619–1682) interest in armaments led to the development of stronger gunpowder, a new method of boring cannon, and the discovery of "prince's-metal," a mixture of copper and zinc. John Wilkins, Bishop of Chester (1614–1672), a founder and the first secretary of the Royal Society, wrote the semiscientific *Discovery of a World* in the Moone (1638), referred to in *The Consolidator*, and *Mathematical Magick* (1648).

[3] Sir William Phipps (1651–1695), who became governor of Massachusetts in 1691, gained his knighthood by recovering a great treasure from a sunken plate ship in 1687. Charles Mordaunt, third Earl of Peterborough (1658–1735), joined Sir John Narbrough (1640–1688) late in 1687 to salvage treasure near Cape Samana.

[4] William Dockwra or Dockwray (d. 1716), a London merchant, established a penny postal system in London in 1683, which earned him a pension of £ 500 from Parliament in 1690. Defoe announced to Robert Harley in 1711 that he, too, had ideas about the postal system (*Letters*, 312).

[5] William Penn (1644–1718), the founder of Pennsylvania, tried to help Defoe obtain his release from prison in 1703. Anthony Cooper, first Earl of Shaftesbury (1621–1683), held royal patents to Carolina and served as President of the Council of Trade and Plantation from 1672–1676, but he is best remembered as the villainous Achitophel in John Dryden's *Absalom and Achitophel* (1681). Daniel Coxe, MD (1640?–1730), held patents for lands which became Georgia, Florida, and Louisiana, and served as governor of East and West Jersey in 1697.

6 By 1709 the Old and New East India Companies, which represented England in Asia, had become the United East India Company; the Africa Company of 1662–1672 had become the Royal African Company; and the Hudson's Bay Company was still searching for the northwest passage.

7 The unhappy debtor who could not pay his creditors could try to obtain a grant of immunity from arrest, flee to sanctuary in such places as the Mint and Blackfriars, or face imprisonment in a principal debtors' prison such as the Fleet or in one of the "Compters" such as Southwark. By 1716 as many as 60,000 debtors were said to be imprisoned in England and Wales.

8 The mountains will labor and a funny little mouse will be born. Horace. *Epistles,* II, iii.

9 One who cleaned cesspools.

10 The hospital of St. Mary of Bethlehem, founded as a priory, was incorporated as a royal foundation for the reception of lunatics in 1547.

11 Charles Montagu, Earl of Halifax (1661–1715), proposed a Lottery Act late in 1692 to raise a million pounds for William III's war expenses by offering both prizes and annuities on lives.

12 Parliament wrestled with bankruptcy bills from 1693–1697. Defoe, who paid his creditors most of the £17,000 involved in his bankruptcy in 1692, sought relief from creditors in 1706 under a new Act for Preventing Frauds Committed by Bankrupts.

13 Legally competent to manage his own affairs.

14 From day to day.

15 A judgment authorizing a sheriff to seize a debtor's goods to pay his bills.

16 Mary Astell (1668–1731), author of *A Serious Proposal to the Ladies for the Advancement of their True and Great Interest* (1694).

THE TRUE-BORN ENGLISHMAN

1 Defoe quotes incorrectly William the Conqueror's proclamation of 1070 ordering his subjects throughout his kingdom to worship one God and to keep the one, true, Christian faith. He further ordained that there be peace and mutual security between Englishmen and Normans.

2 Abraham Cowley's (1618–1667) "Pindarique Odes" appeared in his *Poems* (1656).

3 The Treaty of Ryswick (1697), which ended the Nine Years War against France, provided only a brief respite before the beginning of the War of the Spanish Succession in 1702.

4 Robert Spencer, Earl of Sunderland (1640–1702), resigned the office of Lord Chamberlain in December 1697.

5 In the *Anatomy of Melancholy* (1651), Robert Burton wrote, "For where God hath a temple, the divel will have a chappel."

6 Pagan or heathen altars. Used by John Milton in *Paradise Lost* (I, 765).

7 Charles Davenant (1656–1714), who published *A Discourse upon Grants and Resumptions* in 1700, wrote political and economic tracts throughout the rein of Queen Anne.

8 William Sherlock (1641–1707) argued that the Church of England should recognize William III and Mary on the grounds that they represented the *de facto* government in his *Case of Allegiance due to Sovereign Powers* (1691) and in *Their Present Majesties Government . . . Settled* (1691).

9 Royalists who died for their support of Charles I.

10 The "Bastard Dukes" of Charles II were Southampton, Grafton, and Northumberland, sons of Barbara Villiers; Richmond, son of Louise de Keroualle; St. Albans, son of Nell Gwynn; and Monmouth, son of Lucy Walter, executed in 1685 after his abortive rebellion.

11 Frederick Herman Schomberg (1615–1690), created Earl of Brentford and Duke of Schomberg in 1689; William Bentinck (1648–1709), created Earl of Portland in 1689.

12 The boys of Christ's Hospital, founded in 1552 as a foundling hospital and school for fatherless children and children of the poor, wore blue coats.

13 Aristippus (435–356? B.C.), the "founder" of the Cyrenaic school of philosophy, which taught that immediate pleasure was the greatest good. Canary was a sweet wine like madeira.

14 The feast day of the patron saint of musicians, 22 November, was the occasion for a series of distinguished poems and musical settings by such men as John Dryden, George Frederick Handel, and Henry Purcell.

15 John Asgill (1659–1738), expelled from the Irish House of Com-

mons in 1703 for his eccentric view that no Christian need die, published *Several assertions proved* (1696).

[16] John Tutchin (1661?–1707), author of *A Pindarick Ode in Praise of Folly and Knavery* (1696), attacked William III in *The Foreigners* (1700). Editor of *The Observator* (1702–1707), he was convicted of libeling the government in 1704.

[17] Both Tutchin and Defoe used the biblical framework of *II Samuel,* 13–18, best employed by John Dryden in *Absalom and Achitophel* (1681).

[18] Sunderland would have been a *sot* or *fool* to have served William III after having been a favorite in the court of James II.

[19] The basic principles.

[20] William III and his wife Mary (1662–1694), the daughter of James II, were proclaimed joint rulers by the Declaration of Right (1689).

[21] William III routed the forces of James II at the Battle of the Boyne in July 1690.

[22] Schomberg's victory at Villa Viciosa helped establish the independence of Portugal in 1665.

[23] Sidney, first Earl of Godolphin (1645–1712), resigned office as Commissioner of the Treasury in 1696 after Sir John Fenwick had implicated him in a plot to assassinate William III. Godolphin became Lord Treasurer in 1702 and remained a power in Queen Anne's government until leaving office in August 1710. Defoe worked as agent and pamphleteer both for Godolphin and for Robert Harley.

[24] The French captured the Smyrna fleet of English and Dutch merchantmen off Lagos in 1693; General Talmash was fatally injured in an attack against the French at Camaret Bay near Brest in 1694.

[25] Sir Charles Duncombe (d. 1711) rose from an ungrateful apprentice goldsmith to Edward Backwell to become Sheriff of London in 1699 and Lord Mayor in 1708. In 1700 he donated a clock and dial to St. Magnus Church.

[26] Mob.

[27] Duncombe was acquitted on a legal technicality before the King's Bench in 1699 after having been expelled from Parliament for falsely endorsing Exchequer Bills raised upon the land tax in 1698.

²⁸ The keeper of the rolls; the principal justice of the peace or sheriff.

²⁹ In 1698 William III instructed magistrates to punish persons guilty of dissolute, immoral, or disorderly practices.

³⁰ Sir Jeffrey Jeffreys served with Duncombe as Sheriff (1699–1700).

THE MOCK MOURNERS

¹ Although Queene Anne's accession on 8 March 1702 was orderly, her government had cause to insure the loyalty and orderliness of her subjects: Louis XIV had recognized the son of James II, James Francis Edward (1688–1766), as James III of England only the previous September and war with France over the Spanish throne was imminent.

² James Francis Edward Stuart, known as the Old Pretender.

³ As is the House of Commons; see the *Consolidator*, pp. 137 ff.

⁴ Charles Talbot, twelfth Earl and only Duke of Shrewsbury (1660–1718), was one of the seven lords who invited William III to come to England in 1688. Aubrey de Vere, twentieth Earl of Oxford (1626–1703), served with William III at the Battle of the Boyne. Charles Montagu, Earl of Halifax, who also signed the letter of invitation to William III, was responsible for the establishment of the Bank of England.

⁵ Although William III prevented the French from pressing on to Brussels and Liege at Landen in 1693, he lost the battle because of the superior numbers of the French. At Poitiers in 1356 Edward, the Black Prince, defeated the French and captured King John of France.

⁶ James Butler, second Duke of Ormonde (1665–1745), who had commanded the English forces at Cadiz and Vigo Bay, succeeded the Duke of Marlborough as commander of the British forces in 1711. Algernon Capel, second Earl of Essex (1670–1710), "first gentleman of the bedchamber" to William III, married the eldest daughter of William's close friend, the Earl of Portland.

⁷ During 1692–1693 Frederick William, Duke of Württemberg, who had been with William III at the Battle of the Boyne, was taken prisoner by Marshal de Lorges, and Charles, second Duke

of Schomberg, was fatally injured during the French victory at Marsaglia.

8 After Arthur Herbert, Earl of Torrington (1647–1716), had lost an important naval battle at Beachy Head off the Sussex coast in 1690, an unsuccessful attempt was made to try him by impeachment before the House of Lords. Naval historians have vindicated his strategies.

9 After his victory at Namur in 1695, William III was popularly compared with David as the saviour of Israel.

10 Elizabeth I (1533–1603) ascended the throne in 1558.

11 When the horse which William III was riding through Richmond Park in February 1702 stumbled and fell, William broke his collar bone. Although seeming to be making a good recovery from the fall, he died from fever on 8 March.

THE SHORTEST-WAY WITH THE DISSENTERS

1 Roger L'Estrange (1616–1704) published his *Fables of Aesop* in 1692. At least four other translations of the fables appeared between 1660 and 1700.

2 The Toleration Act of 1689 recognized Protestant nonconformity by declaring that penal statutes against Protestant Dissenters not be enforced. Although it ended the concept of a single state church of which all Englishmen were members, it did not guarantee genuine religious freedom in England.

3 In 1689 six bishops and some four hundred clergymen refused to take oaths of allegiance to William III and Mary because James II was still alive. Those who refused the oaths came to be known as *non-jurors*.

4 Charles II had suspended the penal laws against nonconformists in 1672. In 1683 an attempt, known as the Rye House Plot, was made to seize and murder the king and his brother James on their way from Newmarket.

5 Despite arrests and persecutions after the failure of Monmouth's rebellion in 1685, there were Declarations of Indulgence in 1687 and 1688.

6 William III abolished episcopacy in Scotland in 1689.

7 Tutchin's Whig journal began in April 1702. See note 16 to *The True-Born Englishman*.

[8] Anon., *A late letter, giving a full account of the Sufferings of the Episcopal Clergy in Scotland* (1691).

[9] Defoe worked industriously to promote the Union between England and Scotland, finally accomplished in 1707.

[10] When Louis XIV revoked the Edict of Nantes in 1685, thousands of Protestants sought refuge outside of France.

[11] The War of the Spanish Succession, an attempt to keep the Spanish throne from going to the French, was not resolved until the Peace of Utrecht (1713).

[12] In December 1695 the House of Commons accepted Montagu's plan for the recoinage of English silver money.

[13] Archibald Campbell, ninth Earl of Argyle, and Monmouth were executed; Shaftesbury died in exile in Holland.

[14] Do not lose the thing you know to be suitable for yourself; Opportunity has locks before, but is bald behind. Cato. *Distichs*.

[15] *Song of Solomon*, 8:8. Defoe substitutes *your* for *our*.

[16] In 1401 Parliament passed an act entitled *De Heretico Comburendo*, aimed against the Lollards, which allowed a diocesan bishop to pronounce a sentence of heresy and require a sheriff to burn the offender without royal consent.

[17] Cato, not Scipio Nascio, urged that Carthage be destroyed.

[18] Defoe exaggerates; *Exodus*, 32:28 gives 3,000.

[19] One could hold public office by taking communion in the Anglican Church only occasionally. This "Occasional Conformity" was a source of great religious and political controversy.

[20] The Rev. John How (1630–1705), a leading Dissenting clergyman, had replied to Defoe's *An Enquiry Into The Occasional Conformity Of Dissenters, In Cases Of Preferment* (1698).

[21] The Toleration Act of 1689 did not require nonconformists to subscribe to Articles 34 (on tradition), 35 (on homiles), and 36 (on bishops) of the Anglican Church.

THE CONSOLIDATOR

[1] The narrator, having visited China, has been discussing the works of Mira-cho-cho-lasmo, the "Lunarian Naturalist."

[2] Nicholas Malebranche (1638–1715), French metaphysician, author of *De la Recherche de la vérité* (1674); John Locke (1632–1704), English philosopher, author of the *Essay Concerning Hu-*

man Understanding (1700); Thomas Hobbes (1588–1679), author of the *Leviathan* (1651); Robert Boyle (1627–1691), natural philosopher and chemist; John Norris (1657–1711), disciple of Malebranche, author of *A Collection of Miscellanies* (1687) and *An Essay towards the Theory of the Ideal or Intelligible World* (1701–1704); John Asgill (See note 15 to *The True-Born Englishman*); William Coward (1657–1725), author of a pamphlet denying the existence of a separate soul (1702); Jonathan Swift (1667–1745), whose *Tale of a Tub* had been published anonymously in 1704.

3 John Wilkins (See note 2 to *An Essay Upon Projects*); Domingo Gonzales, the narrator of Francis Godwin's (1562–1633) *Man in the Moone* (1638).

4 Music and dance by characters from the *commedia dell' arte* such as Harlequin formed a frequent source of entertainment on the London stage. A "Trumpet Song" was presented at Drury Lane on 23 June 1705 in English and Italian; a new "Italian Trumpet Song" was presented there on 18 August.

5 Incorporated in 1662, the Royal Society included men of letters like John Dryden as well as scientists like Robert Boyle and mathematicians like Isaac Newton.

6 The 1640 edition of John Wilkins's *Discovery of a World in the Moone* had earlier suggested a "flying chariot."

7 At this time the House of Commons had 513 members; the Union with Scotland (1707) increased the membership to 558.

8 Robert Harley, later first Earl of Oxford and Earl Mortimer (1661–1724), became Speaker of the House of Commons in February 1701 and served until 1705. During the reign of Queen Anne he was appointed Secretary of State for the Northern Department (1704), a Commissioner for the Union with Scotland (1706), Chancellor of the Exchequer (1710), and Lord High Treasurer (1711). Imprisoned in 1715 for suspected conspiracy with the Pretender, he was tried and acquitted in 1717. Defoe considered Harley his great patron.

9 Charles I dissolved Parliament in 1629; he was executed in 1649.

10 Charles II was welcomed back to England by his first Parliament in 1660, but fought with four others over money: 1661–1679, March–July 1679, October 1679, and March 1681.

[11] Roman Catholics.

[12] The chamber of the House of Commons after 1547.

[13] Because it would not allow Roman Catholic officers in the army, Parliament was dissolved by James II in 1685. His arbitrary and unsuccessful attempts to rule alone brought about the "Glorious Revolution" of 1688–1689.

[14] When many Anglican clergymen refused to read James II's second Declaration of Indulgence to their congregations in 1688, James tried unsuccessfully to imprison seven Anglican bishops who had spoken out against it.

[15] James II fled to France on 23 December 1688. The French are allegorized later as the "Gallunarians," Roman Catholics like the Spanish or "Ebronians."

[16] When James first tried to escape from England on 11 December 1688, he was robbed and turned back.

[17] The Triennial Bill, passed in 1694, required Parliamentary elections every three years.

[18] Those who remained loyal to James II were called Jacobites.

[19] In 1704 by a vote of 251–134 the House of Commons defeated an Occasional Conformity Bill that would have imposed fines on Occasional Conformists and prevented them from holding office.

[20] Edward Hyde, Earl of Clarendon (1609–1674), wrote *The History of the Rebellion and Civil Wars in England,* published in three volumes between 1702–1704.

[21] Extremist High-Churchmen, later called "Solunarians."

[22] One calls to mind not only Jonathan Swift's floating island in *Gulliver's Travels,* but Dick Tracy's space coupe.

REVIEW

[1] With Volume VI, Defoe began an Edinburgh edition, largely a reprint of the London edition, which continued through Volume VII, no. 35.

[2] The Union of Scotland and England (1707).

[3] See note 12 to *An Essay Upon Projects.*

[4] Out of his own mouth.

[5] He did not continue his discussion on Thursday, but returned to the topic on Saturday.

6 Property and lands held by inheritance.

7 The Escape Warrant Act (1702) permitted sheriffs to retake an escaped prisoner, particularly a debtor, and commit him to custody until his debts were paid. Such a warrant was used to arrest Defoe in March 1713.

8 During the first twenty-five years of the eighteenth century, England lived in constant fear of the plague. Its revival in northern and central Europe, documented quite accurately by Defoe, led to many acts to prevent its importation into England.

9 *The Highland Visions, Or The Scots New Prophecy: Declaring in Twelve Visions what Strange Things shall come to pass in the Year 1712* (1712).

10 Hypochondria.

11 Perhaps Sir William Petty (1623–1687), who explored plague sociology after 1667 with great gusto.

12 England and Europe, especially Vienna, suffered a terrible visitation of plague in 1542–1543.

13 Watson Nicholson, in *The Historical Sources oŢ Defoe's Journal of the Plague Year* (Boston, 1919), documents Defoe's use of historical materials in his writings about the plague. London kept weekly bills of mortality, showing the number who died in a parish and the cause of death, as early as 1593.

14 The curious causes of death suggest the relatively primitive state of medicine. The King's Evil was scrofula; Chrisoms were infants who died within a month of birth.

15 William III was born on 4 November 1650.

16 A rumor had circulated widely that an infant had been smuggled into Queen Mary of Modena's bed in a warming pan in a plot to give James II an heir to the English throne in 1688.

17 Two Partition Treaties (1698 and 1700) were attempts to defeat the French claims to the Spanish throne.

18 The bill against Occasional Conformity passed by Parliament in 1711 was repealed in 1719.

19 Defoe discusses the complicated negotiations leading to the Treaty of Utrecht and the end of the War of the Spanish Succession.

20 Although the *Review* prints "carried it sons, as away," the meaning here is clear. The scene brings to mind Moll Flanders's robbery of a "bundle of plate" at a fire.

AN APPEAL TO HONOUR AND JUSTICE

[1] A public joke.

[2] He that loves danger shall perish in it. *Ecclesiasticus,* 3:27.

[3] Not only had the Tories been almost totally excluded from the first ministry of George I, but Harley was soon to be imprisoned.

[4] Happy is he whom the perils of others puts on his guard. *Cyllenus. Tibullus* (1493).

[5] Defoe's bankruptcy in 1692 was probably caused by his underwriting marine insurance during wartime.

[6] Defoe dedicated *An Essay Upon Projects* to one of the eminent persons, Sir Dalby Thomas. Defoe served until the repeal of the duty in 1699.

[7] Defoe states here that he met William III after the publication of *The True-Born Englishman,* but John Robert Moore suggests that the two may have met as early as 1689 (*Defoe,* 70).

[8] By the Act of Settlement (1701), the English throne was to go to The Electress Sophia of Hanover and to her descendants. Her son, George I, succeeded Queen Anne on 1 August 1714.

[9] Defoe defends the policies of his patron, Robert Harley, as he describes the seesaw political struggles between Whigs and Tories during the reign of Queen Anne (1702–1714).

[10] Edward Seymour (1633–1708) was dismissed from the office of Comptroller of the Household in April 1704 through the influence of Harley and Godolphin.

[11] In essence, the opposition and the ministry; see the *Review* (14 September 1712).

[12] Harley secured Defoe's release from prison in November 1703 and employed him as a pamphleteer and secret agent.

[13] Daniel Finch, Earl of Nottingham (1647–1730), served under William III and Queen Anne. Although a staunch Tory, he joined the Whigs in 1711 in order to get a bill against Occasional Conformity passed. Not only Defoe, but Swift and Harley disliked "Dismal" Nottingham.

[14] Harley resigned as Secretary of State on 10 February 1708 and was succeeded by Godolphin, who continued to use Defoe's services.

[15] He did on 20 February 1708 and on July 1710, at which time a

regular correspondence began again with Harley's return to power (*Letters*, 251, 270 ff.).

[16] Defoe met Queen Anne in August 1704 and in March 1708.

[17] During 1706–1707 Defoe worked in Scotland to promote the Union. He propagandized through the *Review* and pamphlets, acted as source of intelligence for Harley, and in 1709 wrote *The History Of The Union Of Great Britain*.

[18] Defoe arrived in Edinburgh in April 1708 to electioneer and gather information for Godolphin.

[19] So, when the waves had nine times pounded the steep sides of the vessel, a tenth, rising yet higher, came crashing to the attack, and did not abandon its onslaught on the weary ship until it descended, as if inside its captured walls. Ovid. *Metamorphoses*, XI, 530.

[20] Harley returned to power on 8 August 1710.

[21] Defoe wrote about the Treaty of Utrecht in the *Review* (see, for example, 8 December 1711 and 20 May 1712). He also pamphleteered with *Reasons Why This Nation Ought To Put A Speedy End To This Expensive War* (6 October 1711) and, on the other side, *The Felonious Treaty* (6 December 1711).

[22] The Dutch States.

[23] October 1712–February 1713 (*Letters*, 388).

[24] See *A Seasonable Warning And Caution Against the Insinuations Of Papists and Jacobites In Favour of the Pretender* (1712).

[25] Defoe's irony in *Reasons Against The Succession Of the House Of Hanover* (21 February 1713) and *And What If The Pretender Should Come?* (23 March 1713) again brought him into serious trouble.

[26] Defoe had participated in Monmouth's abortive rebellion in the summer of 1685.

[27] Defoe never forgave Nottingham for the ill treatment he received in 1703 following the publication of *The Shortest-Way With the Dissenters*.

[28] On the complaint of three Whig journalists, William Benson, Thomas Burnet, and George Ridpath, Defoe was arrested after publishing *An Answer To A Question That No Body Thinks Of, Viz. But what if the Queen should die?* in April 1713. By May he had been released after apologizing to the court; in November he received a general pardon from the Queen.

29 Peace talks at Geertruidenberg in 1710 broke down because of excessive Allied demands, but paved the way for the Treaty of Utrecht.

30 Defoe outlines Harley's battle to hold power in a coalition government in 1711–1712, but at the same time disassociates himself from the Jacobite movement.

31 If one accepts John Robert Moore's *Checklist*, the paragraph seems patently untrue. Defoe had, for example, supported Harley in the two parts of *The Secret History of the White Staff* (1714).

32 In a letter to Harley (21 May 1714) Defoe admits having control of the *Mercator* (*Letters*, 441).

33 The eighth and ninth articles of the Peace of Utrecht proposed commercial ties between England and France.

34 Really seven years.

35 *Some Considerations On The Danger Of The Church From her own Clergy* (1715).

36 *An Enquiry Into The Occasional Conformity Of Dissenters* (1698).

37 The Occasional Conformity Act passed by Parliament in 1711 prohibited the practice of dissenters qualifying for office by taking communion in the Anglican Church on rare occasions; it was repealed in 1719.

38 Perhaps *The Felonious Treaty* (6 December 1711) *"By the Author of the Review."*

39 Abel Roper (1665–1726) edited *The Post Boy* from 1695 on. Jonathan Swift edited *The Examiner* (1710–1714) in 1710. Defoe discusses the political in-fighting between Whigs and Tories early in 1708.

40 In 1721 Matthew Prior (1664–1721) summed up the Vicar's position: ". . . if we cannot bring the thing to our Conscience, we must e'en Strive as much as we can to bring our Conscience to the thing."

41 Matthew Poole (1624–1679), author of *Annotations upon the Holy Bible* (1685).

42 Defoe wrote to Harley on 28 September 1714; George I had landed on 18 September (*Letters*, 447–8). John Robert Moore's *Checklist* (112–121) suggests that Defoe is lying to avoid implicating himself in further political difficulties, which might be caused by his close association with Harley.

[43] George Ridpath (d. 1726), a Whig journalist, edited *The Flying Post: Or, The Post Master* from 1695–1712 and 1714–1726.

[44] Conscious of innocence, she laughed at fame's untruths; but we of the multitudes are prone to think the worst. Ovid. *Fasti,* IV, 311.

APPLEBEE'S ORIGINAL WEEKLY JOURNAL

[1] As plague threatened England in 1720, Defoe wrote both to satisfy the curiosity of London's growing population and to defend governmental policies designed to prevent the importation of plague. By February 1721 Parliament had passed a three-year quarantine act "for the better preventing the Plague being brought from foreign Ports."

[2] Defoe published *Due Preparations for the Plague* on 8 February 1722 and *A Journal Of The Plague Year* on 17 March 1722.

[3] Defoe also discussed the transportation of convicts to Virginia and Maryland in *The History And Remarkable Life Of the truly Honourable Col. Jacque* (see the New Oxford Edition, edited by S. H. Monk, 1965, pp. 120–121).

[4] In a letter of Harley (23 July 1711), Defoe had urged the colonization of Chile and discussed the city of Potosi in Peru (*Letters,* 345–349). The reference is to the great silver mines of Bolivia.

[5] William Page's adventures with John Sheppard are described on pp. 247 ff.

[6] The Rev. Mr. Wagstaff served as Deputy Ordinary or Chaplain of Newgate Prison for Thomas Purney, Ordinary from 1719–1727. He supplemented his small salary by providing John Applebee with material for the biographies of prominent criminals.

[7] Mr. Austin, a turnkey or assistant to the Keeper of Newgate Prison. Defoe uses the real names of the magistrates, aldermen, and jailers of London throughout his criminal reports.

[8] Jonathan Wild, the great fence and thief-catcher, had pursued Sheppard and Joseph Blake (Blewskin), as the following criminal biographies will show. See, especially, pages 243–244.

[9] *The Fortunes and Misfortunes of the Famous Moll Flanders* had been published on 27 January 1722.

[10] Joseph Addison's (1672–1719) *Cato,* first staged in 1713, had played as recently as 12 November 1724.

[11] After George Frederick Handel's opera, *Tamerlane*, opened at the King's Theater on 31 October 1724, both Drury Lane and Lincoln's Inn Fields played Nicholas Rowe's *Tamerlane* (1701) against it.

[12] On 4 November 1724, for instance, Lincoln's Inn Fields presented John Rich's popular *The Magician; or Harlequin a Director* (1721). *Harlequin Doctor Faustus* played at Drury Lane on 9, 17, and 20 November.

[13] William Pitt, Keeper of the "gaol of Newgate" from 1707–1732.

[14] Lombard Street was the center of great banking and mercantile transactions.

[15] Probably opium in alcohol, as used later by S. T. Coleridge.

THE HISTORY OF . . . JOHN SHEPPARD

[1] The long title served the eighteenth-century reader as a dust jacket or review does us.

[2] According to *A Short Account of the Several Kinds of Societies Set Up of Late Years* (1700), thirty-nine Societies for the Reformation of Manners were operating in and about London and Westminster. Zealous reformers went about discovering brothels, arresting swearers, and having the law upon sabbath-breakers.

[3] The first edition reads "up to the fatal tree," corrected in the *errata*. The original wording indicates that the pamphlet life was being prepared for sale after Sheppard's execution.

[4] Confined seven times himself, Defoe knew London's prisons well: Newgate Gaol, rebuilt in 1672 after the Great Fire; the five night prisons or "Round Houses"; the "Compters," city prisons especially for debtors.

[5] Irons or fetters fastened around the ankles of a prisoner.

[6] Small boring tools.

[7] A corded silk cloth popular in the eighteenth century.

[8] The manufacture of baize came to England in the sixteenth century through French and Dutch immigrants.

[9] Court sessions were held at the Old Bailey about eight times a year. Defoe used such official documents in the biographies as *The Whole Proceedings upon the King's Commission of Oyer and Terminer and Gaol Delivery for the City of London and County of Middlesex.*

[10] On 19 September 1724 *Applebee's Journal* had described the robbery in almost exactly the same language.

[11] *Parker's London News*, published three times a week, began in 1718; Sheppard even inspired *Harlequin Shepard*, performed at Drury Lane on 28 November 1724.

[12] John Applebee had some commercial interest in *The Daily Journal* (1720–1737), but he was not its printer.

[13] Jack Ketch, England's executioner from 1663–1686, gave his name to hangmen from that day on.

[14] The account is repeated, page 302, and in all the newspapers of the time.

[15] Although some 1600 prisoners were taken when the Jacobites were defeated at Preston in November 1715, only about one in twenty was brought to trial and sentenced to seven years indentured service on the West Indian plantations.

[16] James Figg (d. 1734), whose business cards were designed by William Hogarth, established an academy of arms in London where he gave lessons and exhibitions.

[17] Moll Flanders also gives a picture of the drunken cleric.

[18] The transposition of two lines at the top of page 51 of the first edition restores sense to the passage.

[19] The bad puns about locations in London substitute for the account of Sheppard's death which had been intended to close the biography. Sheppard was recaptured on 31 October, tried again on 6 November, and hanged on 16 November.

THE TRUE AND GENUINE ACCOUNT OF . . . JONATHAN WILD

[1] Wild's career, trial, and execution were the subjects of at least six pamphlet lives in 1725, including *The Life and Glorious Actions of the most Heroick and Magnanimous Jonathan Wild* (May 1725).

[2] Applebee advertised the biography, for example, on 5 June 1725.

[3] The Poultry and Wood-Street Compters were prisons for debtors and felons arrested in the city.

[4] As London expanded, problems of law occupied a greater share of the time of the Cabinet Council of England. In 1689 an act was passed "for the discovering and apprehending of high-way-

men"; in 1690 "for apprehending robbers." An act of 1693 not only offered £40 for apprehending a highwayman, but offered a felon his pardon if he could betray and help convict two other felons.

5 Part of the act "For the farther preventing Robberies, Burglaries, and other Felonies, and for the more effectual Transportation of Felons" (1718) is printed, pages 299–300.

6 On 15 May 1725 *Applebee's Journal* had devoted an entire page to a list of thieves taken by Wild. One calls to mind Sheppard's opinion of "Whidling," page 255.

7 Sturbridge Fair, between Newcastle and Cambridge, was said by Defoe to be not only the greatest in the nation but in the world.

8 A brightly colored cotton cloth imported from the East Indies.

9 Defoe's brackets serve as stage directions for this scene.

10 *Col. Jacque* warns of *"the Ruin of so many Thousands of Youths . . . every Year Bred up for the Gallows. . . ."*

11 Recounted in greater detail in the life of Sheppard, page 258.

AUGUSTA TRIUMPHANS

1 The University of London was formed from University and King's College there in 1836. As early as 1647 Samuel Hartlib had recommended that a university be founded in London.

2 Begun in 1597 to rival Oxford and Cambridge, Gresham College became the meeting place for the Royal Society.

3 An office or post that brings profit or advantage without involving much work.

4 George I died in June 1727.

5 Operas on the Italian model had great vogue in England after 1705. When an Academy for Music was founded in 1720, several Italian singers were brought to England at salaries unparalleled in Europe.

6 Puppet shows. George Powell ran Punch's Opera at St. Martin's Lane Theater in 1710–1711, and then opened Punch's Theater.

7 Arcangelo Corelli (1653–1713), Italian violinist and composer who influenced George Frederick Handel (1685–1759), who settled in England in 1712 and wrote operas, oratorios, and orchestral music; his rival, Giovanni Battista Buononcini (1675–1750), came to England in 1720 to be associated with the Acad-

emy for Music and wrote a half dozen operas in the next decade;
Francesco Geminiani (1667–1762), a pupil of Corelli, came to
England in 1714 and gained a great reputation as violinist and
composer.

8 Henry Purcell (1659?–1695), England's greatest native composer.

9 In his *Tour Thro' The Whole Island Of Great Britain,* Defoe ex-
plained that Christ's Hospital had been established for "edu-
cating, nourishing and bringing up the poor Children of the
Citizens, such as, their Parents being dead, or Fathers, at least,
have no way to be supported."

10 One of the fourteen London markets where one could purchase
meat, fish, and herbs.

Rinehart Editions